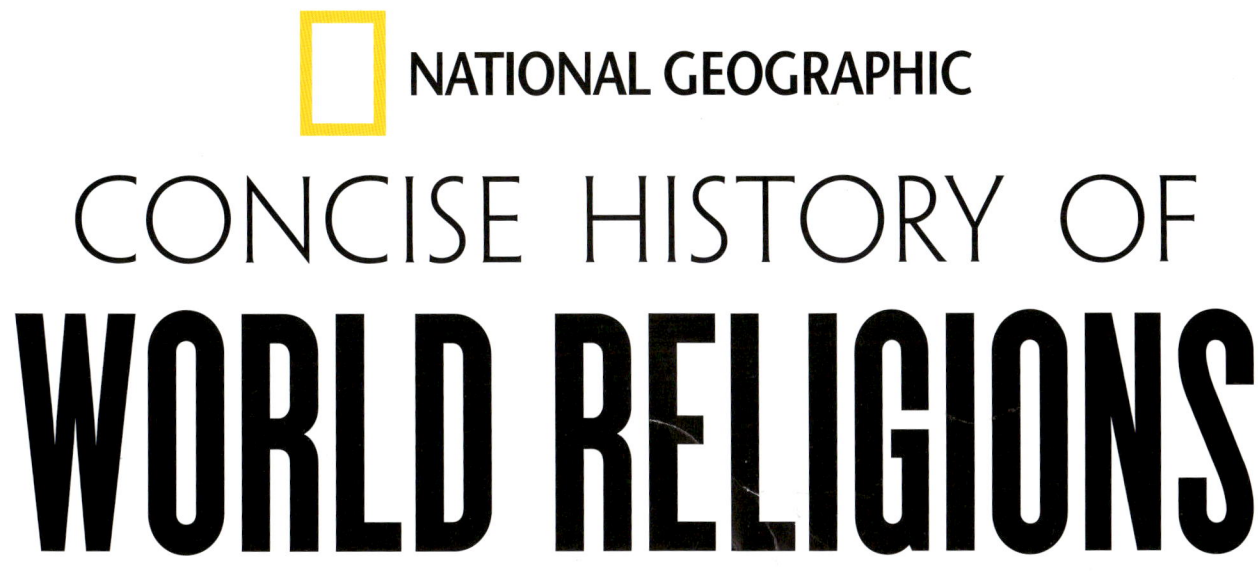

NATIONAL GEOGRAPHIC

CONCISE HISTORY OF
WORLD RELIGIONS

AN ILLUSTRATED TIME LINE

NATIONAL GEOGRAPHIC
CONCISE HISTORY OF
WORLD RELIGIONS

AN ILLUSTRATED TIME LINE

EDITED BY TIM COOKE

National Geographic
WASHINGTON, D.C.

CONTENTS

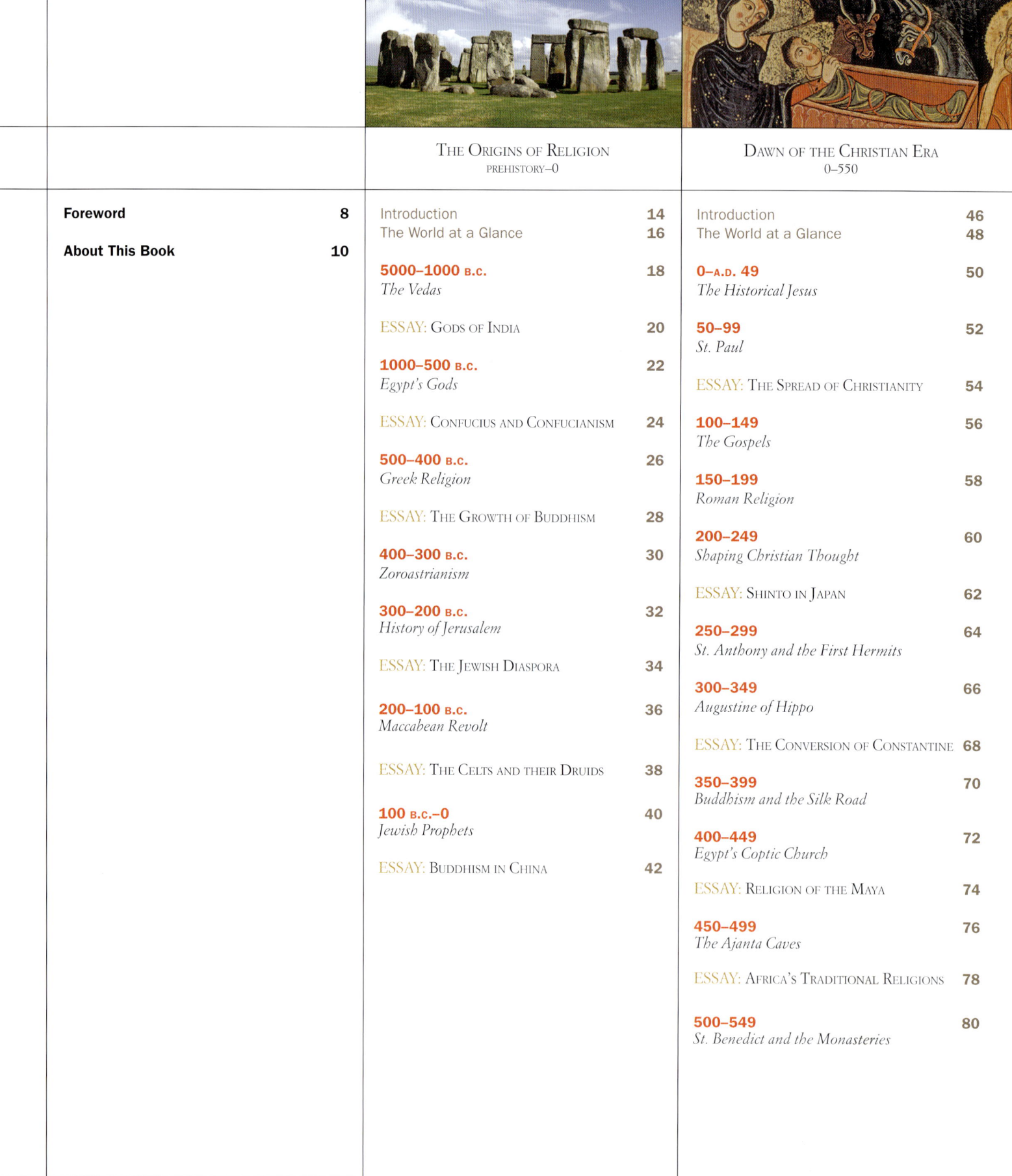

THE ORIGINS OF RELIGION
PREHISTORY–0

DAWN OF THE CHRISTIAN ERA
0–550

A NEW FAITH
550–1000

AGE OF GODS AND KINGS
1000–1350

RENAISSANCE AND REFORMATION
1350–1575

CONTENTS

INDUSTRY, EMPIRE, AND RELIGION
1850–1950

FAITH IN THE MODERN WORLD
1950–2010

FOREWORD

RELIGION LIES AT THE HEART OF THE HUMAN EXPERIENCE. THE GREAT FAITHS—Christianity, Islam, Hinduism, Buddhism, and Judaism—together may account for up to six billion of the world's nearly seven billion people. For all the differences between their beliefs—or between them and followers of Japanese Shinto or animistic faiths in Africa—these adherents seek the same fulfilment from their religious experience: a feeling of connection with the universe, an understanding of their purpose, a moral code, a sense of fellowship, and a sense of the supernatural. As *Concise History of World Religions* shows, such human yearning has inspired many different forms of faith, from the myths of the ancient Egyptians to the storefront churches of San Francisco in the 1960s. The majority of the world's faiths have disppeared; as the timelines reveal, even those that have survived have done so in a constant state of change as the world itself has changed. The

> *This is my simple religion. There is no need for temples; no need for complicated philosophy. Our own brain, our own heart is our temple; the philosophy is kindness.*
>
> HIS HOLINESS THE 14TH DALAI LAMA

universal truths of scripture have undergone review and reinterpretation. Visionary individuals have changed the direction of many churches. Political events have dragged even faiths that profess peace and universal brotherhood into visceral violence and bitterness. Churches have split and formed splinter congregations (some destined to be short-lived, such as the Shakers of 19th-century America, who insisted on celibacy, or the Russian Skoptsy, who reinforced biblical injunctions against lust by practicing male castration). Generations of believers have attempted to revive what they see as purer forms of religious practice from the past. Artists, architects, composers, and writers have been inspired to celebrate their gods. Such is the power of faith that even many of those who reject the idea of the divine adopt their own forms of religious codes, arguing that morality is not the exclusive preserve of the believer.

Concise History of World Religions does not ignore the problems and divisions faith has caused, nor the various secular movements that challenge it. But above all it is a celebration of the enduring power of belief and the fact that the optimism and comfort it offers, although it has on occasion been something to kill for, has far more often been something to live for—the framework that makes sense of everything.

TIME PERIODS AND DATES

Different religions use their own dating systems. In the Islamic calendar, for example, the year 0 equates to 622 in the Western calendar. For convenience, this book uses the familiar terms **B.C.** (before Christ) and **A.D.** (*anno Domini*, a Latin phrase meaning "in the year of the Lord") to refer to all religions. B.C. refers to the same period as B.C.E. (before the Common Era), and A.D. refers to the same time period as C.E. (the Common Era). Cases where an exact date is not known are indicated by the use of ca (*circa*, Latin for "about").

INTRODUCTION

Each chapter opens with an introductory essay that surveys the major trends in religion of the era and how faith interacted with historical events. The example here, which covers the period from 0 to A.D. 550, describes the emergence of Christianity and its impact, exploring how it interacted with other faiths, such as Judaism or the beliefs of the ancient Romans. It describes how Christianity spread and how political circumstances helped to make it stand out among contemporary faiths, along with the intricate process of developing Christian liturgy.

ABOUT THIS BOOK

NATIONAL GEOGRAPHIC CONCISE HISTORY OF WORLD RELIGIONS: *An Illustrated Time Line* chronicles the remarkable story of the human quest for spiritual fulfillment through a versatile design that allows readers to learn in detail about particular periods or regions or to follow themes from prehistory to the modern world. The book traces developments related to all aspects of faith, including not only the world's great organized religions but also smaller belief communities and cults, spiritual and philosophical currents, and nonreligious belief systems. The book is divided into nine chapters covering major historical eras. Each chapter begins with an Introduction, outlining the key developments of that era, followed by The World at a Glance, which provides an overview of the chapter. The bulk of each chapter is a time line that traces the most important events by region and by broad type. The time lines are supplemented by picture essays, sidebars, and text boxes that provide additional detail about particularly important subjects. Throughout the time lines, the symbol 📄 is used to direct the reader to picture essays or sidebars closely related to a particular entry.

Wherever possible, the book provides exact dates for events. However, in some cases it is difficult to say exactly when an event occurred. This is particularly true of the ancient past, when we rely on archaeological evidence or on written records, but it is also true of some occurrences in the modern world. Change in religion is a gradual process rather than a specific event; beliefs and liturgy evolve slowly, so although it may be possible to date the formation of a new church, for example, it is not always clear when its beliefs first began to attract followers. In such cases, the time lines provide approximate dates, acknowledge a number of different possibilities, or occasionally use a degree of necessary simplification in order to place an entry in a particular place in the time line.

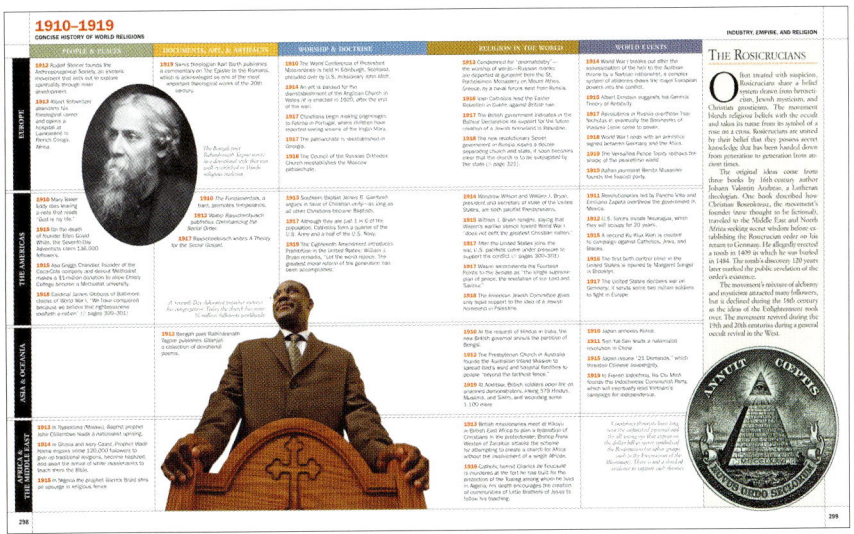

The World at a Glance

The World at a Glance displays the era's most important religious developments chronologically from left to right and regionally from top to bottom. The four regions defined here—**Europe, The Americas** (North and South America), **Asia & Oceania**, and **Africa & the Middle East**—appear in the same order in the time line. This overview allows for quick comparison of developments occurring in different regions at the same time. The sixth vertical column here, for example, reveals that while Spain's Jews were given three months to either convert to Christianity or leave the country, Islamic scholars were studying the Koran in Timbuktu and Buddhists in Japan were rebelling against the social hierarchy.

Time Line

Each time line spread offers a view of religious developments during the period defined in red at top left. (Time spans may vary in length, depending on the length of the era covered in each chapter.) Four vertical columns cover major areas of religion: **People & Places; Documents, Art, & Artifacts; Worship & Doctrine,** and **Religion in the World.** Many events could fit into more than one column, so the arrangement is not always clear-cut. The fifth column, **World Events,** provides a broader historical context. Developments within those areas are listed chronologically within each region. At the right of each spread, sidebars highlight significant developments, and text boxes entitled **Monuments of Faith, Words of Devotion,** and **Faith and Life** give extra information on specific entries.

Picture Essay

Each chapter contains between four and seven picture essays that explore a particularly significant topic. These in-depth articles might focus on the beliefs of a particular people, styles of art and architecture, or specific debates within religion, such as the relationship of faith with science. This example explains how Martin Luther King's faith and his experience as a preacher helped shape the civil rights movement of the 1960s. Many essays and time lines have quotes from prayers, sermons, and religious works that embody something of the nature of faith during the period.

CHAPTER 1

THE ORIGINS OF RELIGION

THE ROOTS OF RELIGION LIE IN HUMANITY'S QUEST TO COMPREHEND THE world and our place within it. How did we get here and what is the purpose of our lives? Is there an agency that controls them? Almost as soon as our ancestors became conscious of being human, they began to attempt to influence events in the world around them through magic. Some 30,000 years ago a prehistoric artist painting animals on the walls of Chauvet Cave in France added a curious figure with the lower half of a human and the upper half of a buffalo. Archaeologists suggest that this "sorcerer" may have played some part in rituals intended to ensure the success of the hunt; they believe that the cave paintings themselves probably had a similar purpose. Clearly, the community that created the Chauvet paintings—the oldest-known cave paintings in the world—believed in the existence of some kind of power that lay beyond the visible and the rational.

Such a belief lies squarely at the base of all modern and ancient faiths. Religion goes beyond magic to propose the existence of deities that have a direct influence on the course of human lives, for better or for worse. Not only that: faith depends on the belief that human intervention can change the behavior of these gods or spirits through propitiation—the act of worship—or through right belief and good conduct. Over time, the rituals of worship have become highly complex. Some involve making the gods happy with offerings and sacrifices; others with hymns and prayers; others by confessing and repenting sins.

The precise nature of the first religions is lost in prehistory. From comparison with later "undeveloped" faiths, however, they likely combined elements of magic with rites of supplication and invocation, possibly involving dancing and music. Such rituals were intended to help worshipers leave the confines of their own existence to come into contact with a more universal, supernatural level of being. Certain individuals who were felt to be particularly adept at communicating with the spirit world began to act as intermediaries between worshipers and their gods. Soon, these

Hindus believe that the god Vishnu has ten avatars, or forms in which he may appear, including a fish, turtle, or boar; in a typical example of the interaction of different religions, one of Vishnu's avatars is Buddha, the founder of Buddhism.

priests became the guardians of ritual and often the arbiters of acceptable and unacceptable behavior. The sites of worship, too, became more regular. Originally such sites were simply points in the landscape associated with the supernatural—a hilltop, say, or a particularly majestic tree—but increasingly buildings were constructed to house artifacts and images sacred to a deity or deities. As their design became more standardized, these temples became the focal points of worship; often they were the largest, most striking structures within a community.

Meanwhile, people began to explain elements of the world that they could not understand by telling stories about the actions of gods and goddesses. These myths mutated as cultures came into contact and their religions evolved, but the stories reflected the environments from which they emerged and came to embody the core values and beliefs of a people. In India, where the oldest of today's religions emerged between 2500 and 1500 B.C., there were many gods. The three major Hindu gods—Brahma, Vishnu, and Shiva—are all embodiments of aspects of the origin of everything: Brahman.

In the Nile Valley, the myths of the ancient Egyptians told of animal-headed deities who controlled various aspects of life but whose equally important role was to preside over the afterlife. For the Greeks, the gods who lived high on Mount Olympus resembled their own aristocratic rulers, who were patrician, flush with power and given to self-indulgence, feuding, deception, and petty jealousies. The Romans inherited gods not only from the Greeks but also from the outer reaches of their empire, including esoteric cults from the east.

Among the cults of the east were the beliefs of the peoples who lived in what would become known as the Holy Land. There, among the Judaeans, prophets preached the special bond that their rulers had made with the almighty: an exalted status as chosen people in return for acknowledgment of the one true God. This monotheistic faith—Judaism—combined belief with politics, a combination that has remained popular. Around the start of the millennium Judaism would produce another religion dedicated to only one God, but this faith appealed also to non-Jews: Christianity.

Meanwhile India had also given birth to another religion that would endure for many centuries; this time one without gods. The teachings of Siddhartha Gautama provided individuals with a set of moral guidelines by which to live and a goal that was not union with a supernatural deity but a state of being beyond happiness or suffering, known as nirvana. The faith later developed the idea of bodhisattvas, semidivine figures who helped believers accomplish their own nirvana.

Like Hinduism, Buddhism incorporated the idea of reincarnation: individuals were reborn as higher or lower beings (even as animals), depending on their conduct during their previous incarnation, until the soul achieved a final escape. In the west, meanwhile, religions took their cue from the religions of Egypt, Greece, and Rome, arguing that death was the start of an afterlife in which the soul would receive either divine rewards in return for a good life or punishment for not following the path of right conduct.

Previous pages *Stonehenge was already ancient when the distinctive standing stones were erected in about 1500 B.C. The precise purpose of the monument is unknown, but its alignment suggests that it may have been used as a astronomical calendar. The need to perform certain rituals on precise days of the year was a major influence on the development of calendars and thus astronomy in the ancient world.*

Massive stone heads of gods and semideities stand near the barren summit of Mount Nemrut in Turkey. The heads belonged to statues—now fallen—commissioned by a first-century-B.C. king to mark the site of his grave: the statues brought together gods from Roman, Persian, and Greek traditions, such as Apollo, Mithras, and Zeus.

THE WORLD AT A GLANCE

CONCISE HISTORY OF WORLD RELIGIONS

	5000 B.C.	2500 B.C.	1000 B.C.	800 B.C.	600 B.C.	
EUROPE	**ca 4300** The first tombs built of huge stones (megaliths) appear in western Europe. **3000** On Malta, people build huge megalithic temples. **ca 2800** Stonehenge in southern England becomes a ritual center.	**ca 2100** The first great stone circle is constructed at Stonehenge. **ca 2000** The Minoans begin to build palaces and temples on Crete. **ca 1500** The circle of trilithons, or stone arches, is erected at Stonehenge.	**ca 900** The Etruscans of southern Italy begin to carve lifelike statues of the dead to place in their tombs. **ca 800** The Celts of northwestern Europe hold rituals at oak trees and springs led by priests named druids; the rituals include human sacrifice.	**776** Greek athletes compete in the first Olympic games at Olympia, in honor of the gods of Mount Olympus. **ca 700** Greek poet Hesiod writes an account of the origins of the gods in *Theogony*.	**ca 530** The Siphians build a treasury to hold their offerings at the Temple of Apollo in Delphi. **509** The Temple of Jupiter, Juno, and Minerva is dedicated in Rome.	
THE AMERICAS	**3372** The first date of the traditional Mayan calendar. **ca 2500** Peoples in the Grand Canyon invoke magic to help their hunting.	**1750** A temple is built in Peru's Rimac Valley. **ca 1300** The Olmec develop religious rituals that include ceremonial ball games and offering blood to the gods.	**ca 900** The Olmec build a ceremonial center at La Venta. **ca 900** The Paracas culture on the Peruvian coast mummify their dead in brightly colored textiles.	**ca 800** Chavín, in Peru, reaches the height of its religious importance; its main U-shaped temple faces east and the rising sun.	**ca 700** The Olmec begin to use hieroglyphs, the oldest known writing in the Americas.	
ASIA & OCEANIA	**ca 2900** According to Chinese tradition, the first divine emperors rule from about this time.	**ca 1700** In China, the kings of the Shang dynasty are buried with sacrificed attendants to serve them in the afterlife. **ca 1500** The first Vedas are composed (hymns to the Hindu gods written in the Aryan language, Sanskrit).	**ca 900** In India the later Vedas are composed; they include the world's oldest sacred book, the *Rig Veda*.	**ca 800** Indians compile the *Upanishads,* a collection of scriptures that forms the basis of Hinduism.	**ca 600** Birth of Lao-Tzu, the Chinese founder of Taoism. **ca 560** Traditional date for the birth of Buddha, Siddartha Gautama. **ca 540** In India, Mahavira begins a life of self-denial, nonviolence, and detachment from the world; his principles form the basis of Jainism.	
AFRICA & THE MIDDLE EAST	**3760** This year marks the start of the Jewish calendar. **ca 2900** Stepped pyramids called ziggurats are built in Sumer, in what is now Iraq. **ca 2650** The Step Pyramid is built for King Djoser in Egypt. **ca 2550** The 480-foot-high Great Pyramid is built at Giza, Egypt, for King Khufu.	**ca 2100** Abraham, the Hebrew patriarch venerated in Judaism, Christianity, and Islam, leads his clan from Ur in Sumer. **ca 1348** Pharaoh Akhenaten replaces Egypt's gods with worship of the sun god, Aten; after his death, his new religion vanishes. **ca 1300** According to the biblical account, Moses receives the Ten Commandments at Mount Sinai, Egypt.	**ca 960** Solomon succeeds David and begins a huge building program in Jerusalem, including the Temple of Solomon. **ca 860** Queen Jezebel of Sidon introduces worship of the god Baal to Israel. **ca 860** The prophets Elijah and Elisha lead a violent campaign against Baal, killing those who worship him.	**ca 800** The Nubians of what is now Sudan adopt Egyptian religious practices, including building pyramids. **ca 620** The Persian aristocrat Zoroaster begins to develop a new religion after visions reveal that there is one supreme god and six lesser deities.	**587** Babylonian ruler Nebuchadrezzar II destroys the Temple of Solomon; it is rebuilt in 520. **587** The Babylonian captivity, remembered as a pivotal event in Jewish history, begins when Nebuchadrezzar II sacks the kingdom of Judah and takes many of its citizens as prisoners. **522** Under Darius I, a form of Zoroastrianism is introduced to the Persian Empire.	

500 B.C.	400 B.C.	300 B.C.	200 B.C.	100 B.C.–0
480 The Athenians practice human sacrifice to win divine favor for the Battle of Salamis against the Persians. **448** In Athens, construction begins on the Parthenon, a temple dedicated to the city's patron goddess, Athena.	**ca 387** In Athens, Plato founds the Academy, where scholars debate philosophy. **373** An earthquake destroys the temple of Apollo at Delphi in Greece. **ca 300** Roman culture becomes increasingly obsessed with militaristic cults.	**ca 280** In Greece the Colossus of Rhodes, a massive bronze statue of the sun god Helios, is constructed at the harbor of Rhodes. **204** Romans begin to worship the Phoenician goddess Cybele to gain additional divine support in their war against Carthage.	**186** Roman authorities suppress the hedonistic cult of Bacchus in Italy.	**42** Emperor Julius Caesar is recognized as a god by the Roman state, beginning a cult of emperor-worship in the empire. **17** The Roman poet Horace writes *Secular Hymn*, praising Augustus' return to fundamental morality.
ca 500 At Monte Albán in southern Mexico the Zapotec establish a hilltop ceremonial center. **ca 500** The Adena people of Indiana build earthen burial mounds.	**ca 300** A massive 34-foot-wide sculpture of a supernatural bird is carved by the Maya at the base of a pyramid in Nakbe, Guatemala.	**ca 300** Construction begins on pyramids and temples in the Mayan capital of Tikal, Guatemala.	**ca 200** In southern Peru the Nazca create the first huge designs in the desert. **ca 200** A new sacred complex of three temples is built at El Mirador.	**ca 100** The Hopewell people build vast burial mounds in Ohio. **ca 100** In northern coastal Peru, the Moche begin building mud-brick pyramid temples.
ca 500 In China, Confucius teaches his students his philosophy of fillial devotion. **ca 485** The likely birthdate of Buddha according to modern scholars. **ca 400** Probable date of the first Buddhist Council, held three months after the death of the Buddha, to decide how his teachings should be preserved.	**ca 400** Buddhism spreads through northern India. **ca 330** Confucianism is spread throughout China by the traveler Mencius. **ca 320** In China the *Taodejing* and the *Zhuangzi* are compiled; they become the core texts of Taoism.	**ca 300** The poet Valmiki begins the compilation of the great Indian epic poem *Ramayana*. **ca 263** The Mauryan emperor Asoka converts to Buddhism. He makes Buddhism the official religion of his empire three years later. **ca 200** The text of the *Bhagavad Gita* is further refined.	**ca 200** Buddhist monks build cave dwellings at Bhaja, India. **189** The first Buddhists arrive in Vietnam. **124** Confucianism is placed at the heart of Chinese society and politics when Emperor Han Wudi uses Confucian works as the basis for a curriculum to train bureaucrats.	**ca 100** Mahayana ("great vehicle") Buddhism emerges in southern India. **17** The *Pali Tripitaka*, a core text in Theravada Buddhism, is written down in Sri Lanka.
ca 500 The Nok culture in northern Nigeria begins making terracotta portrait sculptures for use in ancestor worship. **ca 500** The Torah becomes the basis of Judaism, laying down rules for everyday life and preserving Jewish culture and ritual.	**378** In Egypt the pharaoh Nekhtenebef begins building the first temple on the island of Philae. **ca 332** Many Zoroastrian priests, or magi, are killed by the troops of Alexander the Great as they campaign through Persia; many of the oral doctrines of the faith are lost.	**ca 275** Scholars at Alexandria translate the first five books of the Torah from Hebrew into Greek. **ca 250** The cult of Osiris spreads from Egypt to other regions also under Greek rule. **ca 230** In Egypt a new temple is dedicated to the sun god Horus at Edfu.	**167** The ruler of the Greek Empire, Antiochos IV, outlaws the practice of Judaism even in Jerusalem. His actions spark three years of Jewish revolt, led by Judah Maccabee. **ca 165** The Old Testament Book of Daniel is composed.	**47** Herod becomes the Roman governor of Galilee; later he becomes king of Judea. **4** The probable date of the birth of the historical Jesus.

	PEOPLE & PLACES	DOCUMENTS, ART, & ARTIFACTS	WORSHIP & DOCTRINE
EUROPE	**ca 2800** Stongehenge in southern England becomes a ritual center; at this stage it consists only of circular earthworks. **ca 2100** The first great stone circle is constructed at Stonehenge. **ca 1500** The circle of trilithons, or stone arches, is erected at Stonehenge. *Abraham sacrifices a ram in place of his son Isaac in this late 16th-century Armenian illustration. Abraham was a major figure in three religions: Judaism, Christianity, and Islam.*		**ca 4300** The first tombs built of huge stones ("megaliths") appear in western Europe. **ca 3000** In Scandinavia people bury their dead in passage tombs. **ca 3000** On Malta, people build huge megalithic temples. **ca 2700** Early Minoan civilization develops on Crete; their religion includes the worship of bulls. **ca 1700** Ancestors of the ancient Greeks believe that their gods live on Mount Olympus. **ca 1600** Eleusis in Greece becomes the site of initiations into the cult of Demeter and Persephone—the "Eleusinian Mysteries."
THE AMERICAS	**ca 1750** A temple is built at La Florida, in Peru's Rimac Valley. **ca 1250** The Olmec build their first ceremonial center at San Lorenzo, on Mexico's Gulf coast. **ca 1200** In the valleys of the Peruvian Andes, a new people build the religious center from which they take their name, Chavín.	**ca 1200** The Olmec of Mexico begin to carve colossal stone heads which experts believe had some religious function.	**ca 2500** Peoples in the Grand Canyon invoke magic to help their hunting. **ca 1300** Olmec religious rituals include cutting themselves to offer blood to the gods and a ceremonial ball game: both remain part of Mesoamerican culture for centuries.
ASIA & OCEANIA	**ca 2900** In Chinese tradition, the first divine emperors rule from about this time.	**ca 1500** The first Vedas appear: hymns to the Hindu gods written in the Aryan language, Sanskrit (📄 facing page, pages 20–21).	**ca 1700** In China, the kings of the Shang dynasty are buried with sacrificed retainers to serve them in the afterlife.
AFRICA & THE MIDDLE EAST	**ca 2900** Stepped pyramids called ziggurats are built in Sumer, in what is now Iraq. **ca 2650** The Step Pyramid is built for King Djoser in Egypt. **ca 2550** The 480-foot-high Great Pyramid is built at Giza, Egypt, for King Khufu; for some 4,000 years it is the tallest structure on the planet. **ca 2100** Abraham, the Hebrew patriarch acknowledged by Judaism, Christianity, and Islam, leads his clan from Ur in Sumer. **ca 1504** Amenhotep becomes the first pharaoh to be buried in the Valley of the Kings in Egypt.	*The good God, lord of the two lands, lord of ritual, Djeserkara, son of Ra of his body, beloved of him. Amenhotep, given life, beloved of Amen-Ra.* EGYPTIAN INSCRIPTION, CA 1500 B.C.	**ca 2500** The Egyptians begin to mummify the corpses of the social elite. **ca 2500** The Sumerians bury human sacrifices with their royal dead. **ca 1348** Pharaoh Akhenaten replaces Egypt's gods with worship of the sun god, Aten; after his death, his new religion vanishes. **ca 1300** According to the biblical account, Moses receives the Ten Commandments at Mount Sinai, in Egypt.

RELIGION IN THE WORLD	WORLD EVENTS
	ca 3500 Europeans live as settled farmers from Ukraine to France.
	ca 3000 On Crete, craftsmen begin making tools and weapons from bronze.
	ca 2000 The so-called Palace Culture of the Minoans emerges on Crete.
	ca 1700 A massive volcanic explosion on the island of Thera devastates Minoan civilization.
	ca 1500 The Mycenaeans establish settlements throughout Greece, Anatolia, Crete, and Italy.
	ca 2000 Hunter-gatherers live throughout much of North America.
	ca 2000 In Mesoamerica, farmers form small village settlements.
	ca 2000 In the Andes of Peru, people build ceremonial complexes with temples and pyramids at their heart.
3372 The first date of the traditional Mayan calendar.	
ca 1500 As Aryan immigrants spread throughout India, the Brahmin priesthood rises to the top of a fixed society of "castes" (classes).	**ca 2500** The urban Harappan civilization reaches a highpoint in the Indus Valley in India.
	ca 2200 China's Xia dynasty is founded along the Yellow River.
	ca 1500 Aryan newcomers take control of the Indus Valley.
3760 This year marks the start of the Jewish calendar.	**ca 3300** The Sumerians invent the world's first writing system.
ca 2900 The likely date of the Great Flood, recorded in Sumerian mythology and later in the biblical account of Noah and the ark.	**ca 3200** The first identifiable civilization emerges at Sumer, in modern-day Iraq.
	2660 The beginning of the Third Dynasty marks the start of Egypt's Old Kingdom period.
ca 1300 Moses leads the Hebrews from captivity in Egypt to the "promised land" in Canaan.	**ca 1025** Threatened by the Philistines, the Hebrews unite to form the kingdom of Israel, ruled by Saul.

The Olmec carved stone heads up to 10 feet tall. The helmeted individuals may have been individual leaders, suggesting that Olmec religion may have included an element of ancestor worship.

THE VEDAS

The earliest sacred Hindu writings were based on four texts that originated in the Indus Valley. Begun as oral accounts, they evolved over a period of almost ten centuries between 1400 and 400 B.C. into their present written form. The four texts, which are known collectively as *Vedas* (knowledge), were the foundation of the Vedic religion and today constitute the earliest written texts in the Hindu tradition.

The oldest of the four texts is the *Rig Veda*. It comprises more than 1,000 verses written in Sanskrit, an ancient Indian language, and addressed to the gods of the elements of Earth, ether, fire, water, and air. The text outlines the basics of the polytheistic religion that later evolved into Hinduism.

Two later vedas, the *Yajurveda* and the *Samaveda*, describe the ceremonies and practices of the Vedic religion, as well as the prayers and hymns associated with them. Several variants of these two vedas are common in different regions of India, although all the versions repeat many verses found in the *Rig Veda*. Some Hindu groups still use these texts as the basis of their ceremonies, but the practice is becoming less common.

The youngest of the four texts is a collection of philosophical writings known as the *Upanishads*, which was written between 800 and 500 B.C. They comprise dialogues between a teacher and student and between wise men who examine the meaning of life and try to address questions of human existence and the afterlife.

It is on the *Upanishads* that much of Hinduism is based. The book introduces the central Hindu concepts of *moksa*—the soul's release from the continuous cycle of rebirth—and karma, which is the result of one's behavior. Its principal revelation is that the power of *maya* (illusion) makes the world appear real, but the only true reality is Brahman. According to the *Upanishads*, each person possesses a soul or spirit (*atman*), which cannot be destroyed and which is identical with Brahman.

GODS OF INDIA

WITH APPROXIMATELY ONE BILLION FOLLOWERS, Hinduism is the world's third-largest religion. Most Hindus live in India, but there are significant Hindu communities everywhere from Southeast Asia to the Caribbean. Hinduism encompasses a broad religious tradition that has both monotheistic and polytheistic aspects. Although Hindus worship thousands of gods, the gods are often described as manifestations of a single divine entity.

Hinduism's origins lie in the ancient Vedic religion, which was formed between 2500 and 1500 B.C. The system of beliefs outlined in the later Vedic texts, known as the *Upanishads* (written by the fifth century B.C.), was absorbed into Hinduism. It included the belief that everything in the world was created from a single source, known as Brahman. The concept of Brahman is a highly abstract one that goes beyond the idea of the Christian God. Hindus believe that Brahman is the origin and source of the material world, the afterlife, and all Hindu gods. The three most important Hindu gods, known as the *Trimurti*, are manifestations of different aspects of Brahman. They are Brahma, the creator; Vishnu, the sustainer; and Siva, the destroyer.

Although Brahma is believed by Hindus to be the creator of the human race, he is rarely worshiped and there are few temples devoted to him. In Hindu mythology he is typically depicted as a distant, mysterious figure who rarely gets involved in the affairs of gods or humans. By contrast, Vishnu is often depicted in Hindu myth interacting with and advising humans, either directly or through avatars like Rama and Krishna. In the Hindu epic poem *Mahabharata*, for example, Vishnu (in the form of Krishna) serves as a spiritual guide and teacher to the protagonist, Arjuna. Vishnu's consort, Lakshmi, is worshiped in her own right as the goddess of wealth. Siva, the destroyer, appears in many forms and has many consorts. The cycle of life according to Hindu belief has Brahma creating the world, Vishnu sustaining it, and Siva destroying it in an endless cycle.

Many of the thousands of other Hindu gods are associated with specific qualities, social groups, or places. The elephant-headed god, Ganesha, is believed to bring wisdom and good luck, for example, and the monkey god Hanuman is associated with bravery and loyalty. Many Hindus choose to worship one particular god over all others, a practice known as *Ishtadevata*.

An illustration from the epic poem Mahabharata, showing the hero Arjuna's chariot being guided by the god Krishna, an avatar of Vishnu.

The elephant-headed god Ganesha is one of the most popular Hindu gods.

PEOPLE & PLACES	DOCUMENTS, ART, & ARTIFACTS	WORSHIP & DOCTRINE

EUROPE

ca 725 Possible date of the death of Homer, the ancient Greek poet whose Iliad shows how the Olympian gods inspired the Trojan War.

ca 530 The Siphians build a treasury to hold their offerings at the Temple of Apollo in Delphi, decorated with remarkable stone panels.

509 The Temple of Jupiter, Juno, and Minerva is dedicated in Rome.

The ancient cemetery at Paracas, in Peru, has yielded dozens of mummified bodies wearing colorful textiles and, in this case, gold jewelry.

ca 900 Etruscan craftsmen carve lifelike statues of the dead to place in their tombs.

ca 700 The Greek poet Hesiod writes an account of the origins of the gods in *Theogony*.

ca 600 In France, a Celtic princess is buried with the Vix Krater, a remarkable golden vessel made by craftsmen in Greece.

ca 1000 The Etruscans bury the ashes of their dead in terracotta containers which are sometimes shaped like houses.

ca 800 The Celts of northwest Europe hold rituals at oak trees and springs, led by priests named druids; the rituals include human sacrifice.

ca 800 The worship of Apollo begins at Delphi in Greece.

ca 725 In Greece a cult emerges of worshiping at the tombs of warrior heroes of the Mycenaean age.

THE AMERICAS

ca 900 The Olmec build a ceremonial center at La Venta, based on a large pyramid.

ca 900 Paracas, on the coast of Peru, becomes the site of ceremonial centers.

ca 800 Chavín, in Peru, reaches the height of its religious importance; its main U-shaped temple faces the east and the rising sun.

ca 1000 The Chavín build temples with galleries and statues for rituals.

ca 900 The Paracas culture on the Peruvian coast mummify their dead in brightly colored textiles.

ASIA & OCEANIA

ca 600 Birth of Lao-Tzu, the Chinese founder of Daoism, a philosophy of simple living.

560 Confucius—known in Chinese as Kong Fuzi—is born in northeastern China.

ca 560 Traditional date for the birth of Buddha, Siddartha Gautama; modern authorities date his birth nearly a century later.

ca 540 In India, Mahavira begins a life of self-denial, nonviolence, and detachment from the world; his principles are the basis of Jainism.

ca 900 In India the later Vedas are composed; they include the world's oldest sacred book, a collection of 1,028 hymns called the *Rig Veda* (📄 page 19).

ca 800 Indians compile the *Upanishads*, a collection of scriptures that forms the basis of Hinduism.

ca 900 An Indian ruler named Manu draws up a law code that describes proper moral conduct.

524 According to traditional dating, Siddhartha Gautama has the vision that forms the basis of the Buddhist religion.

AFRICA & THE MIDDLE EAST

ca 960 Solomon succeeds David and begins a huge building program in Jerusalem, including the revered Temple of Solomon.

668 Ashurbanipal comes to the Assyrian throne; possibly history's first literate ruler, he collects a huge library of religious and other works on clay tablets.

587 Babylonian ruler Nebuchadrezzar II destroys the Temple of Solomon; the Jews rebuild it in 520.

587 Ezekiel, the last great prophet of the Old Testament, is said to have prophesied during the Jews' exile in Babylon (📄 page 41)

538 After the return from Babylonian captivity, Jewish scribes begin to use the Aramaic script of the Persians to write Hebrew; it is the basis of the modern Hebrew alphabet.

ca 800 The Nubians of what is now Sudan adopt many Egyptian religious practices, including building pyramids and the worship of the god Amun Re.

ca 620 The Persian aristocrat Zoroaster begins to develop a new religion after visions reveal that there is one supreme god and six lesser deities (📄 page 31).

605 Babylonians abandon the worship of many gods in favor of one supreme deity, Marduk.

522 Under Darius I, a form of Zoroastrianism is introduced to the Persian Empire.

RELIGION IN THE WORLD	WORLD EVENTS

776 Greek athletes compete in the first Olympic games at Olympia, in honor of the gods of Mount Olympus.

ca 900 Etruscan culture spreads through central Italy.

ca 800 The Celts spread west from their heartland in Austria.

ca 800 City-states emerge in Greece, including Athens and Sparta.

753 In Roman tradition, Romulus and Remus found Rome on seven hills near the Tiber river.

616 Rome is ruled by an Etruscan king.

594 In Athens, Solon "the lawgiver" allows free citizens to vote in government; he is credited with introducing democracy.

509 The Romans overthrow their Etruscan rulers and found a republic.

A statue of David, King of Israel. As a young man, David was famed for slaying the giant, Goliath. In his later life he committed adultery with the wife of one of his soldiers, and was punished by God.

ca 1000 The Adena form an agricultural society in the Ohio River Valley.

ca 800 On the Bering Strait, people live by hunting whales, fish, and other marine animals.

ca 700 The Olmec use hieroglyphs, the first writing in the Americas.

ca 700 In Mexico and Guatemala, the Maya begin to organize into numerous states.

ca 1000 Aryan kingdoms emerge in northern India.

ca 1000 China is ruled by the Zhou dynasty.

771 Nomad attacks split China into eastern and western Zhou kingdoms.

ca 700 China enters a period of unrest known as the Spring and Autumn States.

ca 860 The infamous queen Jezebel of Sidon introduces the worship of Baal to Israel.

ca 860 Led by the prophets Elijah and Elisha, Israelites launch a violent campaign against Baal, killing those who worship him.

587 The Babylonian captivity, remembered as a pivotal event in Jewish history, begins when Nebuchadrezzar II sacks the kingdom of Judah and takes many of its citizens as prisoners.

538 Cyrus the Great allows the Jews to return to Israel, but many elect not to do so, marking one start of the Jewish diaspora; those who return home share the territory with other peoples, such as Samaritans.

ca 1000 David becomes king of Israel, uniting Judah and Israel and making Jerusalem his capital.

883 Assyria becomes a major power in Mesopotamia.

813 Phoenicians found Carthage in North Africa.

721 The Assyrians conquer Israel and displace many Hebrews.

625 The Assyrian Empire is destroyed by an alliance of Babylon and Media.

558 Cyrus the Great of Persia begins a campaign of conquest that will win control of Asia Minor and Babylon.

522 Darius I usurps the Persian throne.

Jackal-headed Anubis, here in a tomb painting, was the god of mummification and the afterlife.

EGYPT'S GODS

The great civilization that ruled the Nile Valley for three millennia before the start of the Christian era had many gods. They were local or national, weaker or stronger, male or female. Often their status rose and fell with the particular pharaohs or dynasties with whom they were associated.

All the Egyptian gods were forms of the Creator—sometimes identified with the sun god and sometimes with gods such as Ptah or Amon—but they took on identities of their own. Some had special areas of interest, like Thoth (god of wisdom and writing) and Hathor (goddess of love and death).

Deities took various forms but were usually identified by distinctive head-dresses or sacred symbols. The god Sobek could appear as a crocodile or as a man with the head of a crocodile. The goddess Hathor might be shown as a beautiful woman, as the head of a woman with cow's ears, as a cow, or as a cow-headed woman. The sun god had numerous forms, some of them worshiped as separate gods: The rising sun was Khepri, shown as a scarab-beetle; the noonday sun was Horus, the hawk god; and the setting sun was Atum, shown as a ram-headed man.

To be able under all circumstances to practice five things constitutes perfect virtue: these five things are gravity, generosity of soul, sincerity, earnestness, and kindness.

CONFUCIUS, ANALECTS

CONFUCIUS AND CONFUCIANISM

Incense burns at a Confucian temple in China. Many of the religious and ritual aspects of Confucianism are closely linked to traditional Chinese religious practices, such as ancestor worship.

CONFUCIUS WAS CHINA'S MOST IMPORTANT philosopher and teacher. His social and political philosophy, known as Confucianism, would become the foundation of Chinese life and the basis of Chinese education and government for 2,000 years. The name Confucius is not Chinese but an 18th-century Latinized version of his Chinese name, Kong Fuzi.

Confucianism is not a religion with its own gods. Confucius himself is revered not as a deity or a prophet but as an example of the nobility that can be achieved through study and personal discipline. Confucius believed that all people were capable of leading a good and noble life, regardless of their social background. He believed in the concept of *ren*, or compassion toward others. By putting others before oneself, he argued, society benefited. Confucius believed political leaders were morally bound to set an example for their people to follow. This was at odds with the feudal society to which he belonged, in which his own ruler set a poor example. Confucius believed that a ruler should possess *de* (virtue), so that his subjects willingly showed loyalty to him.

Although written accounts of Confucius's life exist, historians agree that much of the detail cannot be authenticated. It is thought that he was born in Qufu, east China, in 551 B.C. into an impoverished family that had once belonged to the aristocracy. A keen student, Confucius determined by the age of 15 to dedicate himself to learning. He worked as a minor government official while studying a diverse range of subjects. By his 30s, he felt ready to pass his knowledge to others.

During his late 40s and early 50s, Confucius became involved in politics so he could put his teachings into practice. He worked in various positions, eventually becoming the minister of justice for the state of Lu. His political career proved short-lived, however, as his moral uprightness fit poorly with the often chaotic and violent political climate of his time. When he realized that the royal court was not interested in his ideas, Confucius quit to find another feudal state that might want to embrace his moral views. His self-imposed exile lasted about 12 years. During this period, his reputation as a man of moral rectitude and vision spread and a growing band of students joined him.

After his death, Confucius's followers compiled the *Lunyu* (*Analects*). They comprise around 500 comments and conversations with his devotees and others he met. Confucius was vilified during Chairman Mao's Cultural Revolution (1966–1976), but his ideas have become increasingly popular during the first decade of the 21st century as an antidote to China's rapid adoption of capitalism.

A statue of Confucius at a temple in China. Confucius is revered throughout China as an honest man and a wise teacher.

PEOPLE & PLACES	DOCUMENTS, ART, & ARTIFACTS	WORSHIP & DOCTRINE

EUROPE

493 In Rome, the Temple of Ceres, Liber, and Libera becomes a popoular center of worship for ordinary Romans, or plebians.

480 Greek colonists build the vast Temple of Olympian Zeus at Akragas in Sicily.

448 In Athens, the statesman Pericles begins construction of the Parthenon, a temple dedicated to the city's patron goddess, Athena; completed 10 years later, the temple holds a 38-foot-tall statue of the goddess that can be seen by sailors at sea.

ca 451 In Rome, laws called the Twelve Tables try to limit the use of magic.

420 The cult of Asclepios, the healing god, reaches Athens; a sacred snake sent from the god's main sanctuary at Epidauros is looked after by the dramatist Sophocles until the new temple is ready.

Mount Olympus, the tallest mountain in Greece, was believed to be the home of the Greek gods.

THE AMERICAS

ca 500 At Monte Albán in southern Mexico the Zapotec establish a hilltop ceremonial center that will flourish for over a thousand years.

ca 500 On Mexico's Gulf coast, the Olmec abandon and destroy their ceremonial center at La Venta, which is placed by a new site at Tres Zapotes.

ca 500 The Adena, who live in the area of what is now Indiana, Kentucky, and West Virginia, build earthen burial mounds.

ca 500 The Paracas culture of Peru places their mummified dead in sacred locations, such as on mountaintops.

ASIA & OCEANIA

ca 500 In India Mahavira abandons his worldy goods and begins to preach the Jain doctrine of austerity and nonviolence.

ca 500 In China, Confucius—now governor of the city of Chungtu—teaches students his philosophy of filial devotion (📄 pages 24–25).

ca 485 Modern scholarship suggests this is the birthdate of Buddha, born Siddartha Gautama, a prince from the foothills of the Himalaya.

479 Death of Confucius.

ca 500 The *Upanishads*, collections of Hindu sacred texts, are written down in India.

ca 430 The Chinese thinker Mozi founds a school to practice his beliefs, called Mohism: universal love, equality, self-control, and nonviolence.

ca 400 Probable date of the first Buddhist Council, held three months after the death of the Buddha in northern India to reinforce and preserve the dharma, or the teachings of Buddha; other accounts place the death and the council around 500 (📄 pages 28–29).

AFRICA & THE MIDDLE EAST

445 Nehemiah becomes governor of Jerusalem and orders the rebuilding of the city walls following the Babylonian Captivity.

ca 500 In northern Nigeria, the Nok culture emerges; it is noted for its terracotta portrait sculptures, which may have played a role in ancestor worship.

ca 500 Under Darius I, Zoroastrianism becomes a popular religion in Persia, particularly among the social elite.

ca 500 The Torah becomes the basis of Judaism, laying down rules for everyday life and preserving Jewish culture and ritual.

480 The Athenians practice human sacrifice to win divine favor for the Battle of Salamis against the Persians; they are duly victorious, but the Persians sack Athens later in the year.

ca 440 The Athenians mint silver coins showing the patron goddess of their city, Athena, and an owl, symbol of wisdom.

At the heart of El Mirador, which flourished in Guatemala from about 500 B.C., the Maya built three huge platforms topped by temples.

ca 445 In Jerusalem, Nehemiah and Ezra oversee a reconfirmation of the Jews' covenant with God after the Babylonian Captivity, based on following the laws of Moses and supporting the Temple.

410 In Babylon, an astrologer casts the first known horoscope.

480 A small Greek army makes a famous last stand against the massive invasion force of the Persian king, Xerxes I, at the battle of Thermopylae. Xerxes's forces are defeated the following year at the battles of Palatea and Mykale.

457 War breaks out between the powerful Greek city-states of Athens and Sparta.

430 The Greek writer Herodotus, regarded as the first historian in the Western world, completes his nine-book history of the wars between Greece and Persia.

ca 400 Celtic peoples cross the Alps and settle in northern Italy.

ca 500 The Chavín temple culture dominates a region of South America that stretches from the Amazon Basin to the Pacific coast.

ca 400 The Olmec civilization of the Gulf Coast goes into steep decline.

ca 500 Sun Tzu, a Chinese military commander, writes *The Art of War*, a treatise on military strategy and battlefield tactics.

481 The Warring States Period begins in China, lasting until 221 B.C. The Zhou Kingdom breaks into numerous warring feudal states.

ca 500 Arabian merchants from Saba (in present-day Yemen) establish trading settlements on the Red Sea coast of East Africa.

424 King Xerxes II is assassinated; Persia enters a period of weakness and political instability.

ca 404 The Egyptians rebel against their Persian rulers, who have governed the country since 525.

This bust depicts Dionysus, the Greek god of winemaking, farming, and theater.

GREEK RELIGION

The myths of ancient Greece are still familiar to many people. They are widely read and their stories have had a profound influence on Western literature. For the Greeks, however, the gods were far more than literary characters. People lived in fear of offending the gods and goddesses and suffering their anger. Natural processes that were not fully understood were explained as the work of supernatural beings. Volcanic eruptions, earthquakes, and storms were all seen as signs of the gods' displeasure.

The early Greeks compared these deities with their own aristocratic rulers. Zeus, the sky god, was believed to rule from a palace on top of Mount Olympus, among the clouds. There gods and goddesses enjoyed laughter, drink, and feasting—just as human rulers did. Human rulers enjoyed love affairs with women of lower status. So, too, did male gods. Zeus and his handsome son Apollo had many affairs with mortal women. Goddesses had far less freedom in love, again a reflection of real life.

This vision of the gods as divine aristocrats was disputed by some Greek philosophers. Xenophanes. for example, argued that gods were "in no way like mortals, in body or in thought." It was wrong, he claimed, to show gods cheating, stealing, and having love affairs.

THE GROWTH OF BUDDHISM

DESTINED FOR GREATNESS, ACCORDING TO THE SOOTH-sayers, the young prince was kept in isolation from the ills of the world in the palace where he lived with his beautiful wife, the Princess Yasodhara, and their small child. Yet, his curiosity growing, he stole out alone into the city and was shocked by what he saw. He saw signs of suffering and sickness, old age and mortality—and, most moving of all, a holy man who had chosen a life of simplicity.

The young man's name was Siddhartha Gautama, and he lived in the Himalayan foothills of northern India. Leaving his home and family to wander as a beggar, he spent six years in poverty, yet his sacrifices brought no spiritual return. Realizing that to find enlightenment he would have to look inside himself, he sat down beneath a tree, resolved not to move until he had attained spiritual ecstasy. Three nights later Siddhartha stood up and resumed his journey: The bodhisattva (holy man) had become the Buddha.

For over 40 years Buddha wandered through northern India spreading the injunction "Cease to do evil; learn to do good, and purify your heart." Like other Indian thinkers of his time, he believed the dead were reincarnated innumerable times in different human—or even animal—forms, rising or falling in status according to how well they had lived their previous lives. Only when the sacred state of *bodhi* (enlightenment) had been reached could an individual hope to transcend the swirling cycles of death and rebirth known as *samsara*, and find the final peace he himself had attained as the Buddha.

In the third century B.C. the Theravada ("Doctrine of the Elders") and Mahayana ("Greater Vehicle") schools of Buddhism separated. Theravada Buddhism emphasized the search for individual enlightenment outlined by the Buddha in his doctrine of the Eightfold Path: right thinking, right aspiration, right speech, right conduct, right lifestyle, right effort, right mindfulness, and right meditation. Mahayana Buddhism was a more popular faith, encouraging the worship of bodhisattvas—Buddhist saints who had delayed their own attainment of nirvana, or release from suffering, to help others.

Buddhism remained a minority creed until about 259 B.C., when it was taken up by Asoka, India's Mauryan ruler, thus becoming the official religion throughout most of mainland India. Asoka also sent out missionaries to the island of Sri Lanka and overland to Southeast Asia. In time, missionaries would set out from these places in their turn to preach Buddhism in China, Korea, Japan, and Indonesia. The message would prove more enduring in these far-flung lands than in its Indian birthplace.

A Bodhi tree towers over a Buddhist shrine in Myanmar; there are numerous Bodhi trees at Buddhist temples, some of which claim descent from the very tree beneath which Buddha found enlightenment.

PEOPLE & PLACES	DOCUMENTS, ART, & ARTIFACTS	WORSHIP & DOCTRINE

EUROPE

ca 387 In Athens, Plato founds the Academy, where scholars debate philosophy.

373 An earthquake destroys the temple of Apollo at Delphi in Greece.

356 At Persian-ruled Ephesus, a Greek city in Asia Minor, the Temple of Artemis is destroyed by fire but rebuilt.

ca 312 Zeno of Citium arrives to study in Athens, where he will found the philosophy known as stoicism, based on goodness and virtue; it dominates classical thought for centuries.

399 Faced with a domestic crisis, Romans hold the first Lectisternium, a ceremony in which models or busts of gods and goddesses are placed on couches and offered food and drink to make them feel welcome in the city.

323 A cult of the Cabeiri—gods of the earth—begins in Greece.

ca 300 In Greece Euhemerus studies myths and suggests that the Olympian gods were once humans.

THE AMERICAS

ca 400 Chavín de Huantar continues to dominate the culture of northern Peru.

ca 400 Monte Albán is the center of the emergence of Zapotec culture.

ca 300 A huge sculpture of a supernatural bird 16 feet tall and 34 feet wide is carved by the Maya at the base of a pyramid in Nakbe, Guatemala; it is one of the earliest and largest religious monuments. Some archaeologists believe it is evidence of Mayan leaders using religion to help organize and control society.

A ritual executioner brandishes a dagger in his right hand in a mural carved on the Chavín temple at Sechin in Peru. The executioner was a recurrent theme in Chavín art.

ASIA & OCEANIA

ca 330 Confucianism is spread throughout China by the traveler Mencius, who is mocked for his proposal that government should be based upon respect and benevolence.

ca 300 Death of the philosopher Zhuangzi, whose book of the same name forms a classic text of Taoism (📄 pages 100–101).

ca 320 In China the Taodejing and the Zhuangzi are compiled; they become the classic texts of Taoism, arguing that nature provides a model for human life and social organization (📄 pages 100–101).

ca 400 Buddhism spreads through northern India, preached by monks who use everyday languages rather than Sanskrit, the ancient language of Hinduism (📄 pages 28–29).

345 The Second Buddhist Council is held at Vesali to reinforce Buddhist orthodoxy.

308 A council is held at Pataliputra, where Buddhism splits into a number of schools: only Theravada survives today.

AFRICA & THE MIDDLE EAST

ca 332 Many Zoroastrian priests, or magi, are killed by the troops of Alexander the Great as they campaign through Central Asia; many of the oral doctrines of the faith are lost.

These fire altars in Fars, Iran, were used in Zoroastrian ceremonies.

RELIGION IN THE WORLD	WORLD EVENTS
367 The Cumaean sibyl offers the Roman king Tarquinius Superbus nine books of prophecies, the Sibylline books; appalled by the high price, the king declines. The sibyl burns three books and offers the remaining six at the same price. When Tarquinius refuses, the sibyl burns another three books and offers the remaining three, again at the original price. Overcome by doubt, Tarquinius agrees. The books are kept in a temple in Rome and consulted at times of crisis. **303** Booty captured in military campaigns against their neighbors allow the Romans to build the first of 11 major temples constructed in the next 30 years as part of a growing obsession with militaristic cults.	**ca 400** Hippocrates of Cos begins to compile a medical textbook based on observation rather than superstition. **339** The philosopher Socrates is convicted of corrupting the youth of Athens with his teachings, and forced to drink hemlock, a deadly poison. **336** Alexander the Great becomes king of Macedon. He adopts his late father's plan to invade the Persian Empire, and decides to command the army himself.
Men claim that Mao [Qiang] and Lady Li were beautiful, but if fish saw them they would dive to the bottom of the stream; if birds saw them they would fly away, and if deer saw them they would break into a run. Of these four, who knows how to fix the standard of beauty in the world? ZHUANGZI	**ca 350** Cities and states begin to develop among the Maya people of Central America. **ca 300** Pottery, introduced to North America from Mexico, is thought to be in use in the Southwest by this time. **ca 350** Earthen frontier walls are built to protect northern China against raiding nomads. **322** Chandragupta Maurya initiates a Buddhist empire in Magadha in northern India.
378 In Egypt the pharaoh Nekhtenebef begins building the first temple on the island of Philae.	**332** Alexander the Great conquers Egypt and orders the construction of the city of Alexandria on Egypt's Mediterranean coast. **331** Alexander the Great conquers Mesopotamia; within two years he seizes all the lands of the Persian Empire. **323** Alexander the Great dies in Babylon at the age of 32; his generals each seize parts of his kingdom for themselves.

ZOROASTRIANISM

The slaughter of Zoroastrian priests by the troops of Alexander the Great destroyed many of the oral doctrines through which the faith is preserved. As a result, we know far less about how the religion spread or what it taught.

We know equally little about the life of Zoroaster, the founding prophet of the monotheistic religion that emerged in Iran around 3,500 years ago. Some details are mentioned in the Avesta, the holy book of Zoroastrianism.

Zoroaster was born into the religious elite in northeastern Iran. He became a priest in the local polytheistic faith, but grew disillusioned with the rigid and oppressive caste system that it perpetuated. His life changed when he had a vision of Ahura Mazda, the divine creator. Zoroaster learned that all other gods were the creation of Angra Mainyu, Ahura Mazda's demonic adversary, and were not worthy of worship.

It is believed that Zoroaster later traveled to southern Iran, where he gathered many followers. The religion was common throughout Iran by the fifth century B.C.

300–200 B.C.

CONCISE HISTORY OF WORLD RELIGIONS

	PEOPLE & PLACES	DOCUMENTS, ART, & ARTIFACTS	WORSHIP & DOCTRINE
EUROPE	*The person whose mind is always free from attachment, who has subdued the mind and senses, and who is free from desires, attains the supreme perfection of freedom from Karma through renunciation.* BHAGAVAD GITA, CHAPTER 18	**ca 280** In Greece the Colossus of Rhodes, a massive bronze statue of the sun god Helios, is built to stand at the harbor of Rhodes.	**ca 300** In Rome, plebians are allowed to join the priesthood, previously reserved for aristocrats. **293** Worship of the Greek healer god Asclepios begins in Rome when a sanctuary is built there. **204** The worship of the Phoenician goddess Cybele is adopted in Rome to gain divine assistance in the Second Punic War against Carthage.
THE AMERICAS	**ca 300** Construction begins on pyramids and temples in the lowland Mayan capital of Tikal, in present-day Guatemala (📄 pages 74–75).	**ca 250** Carvings in Monte Albán show members of the Zapotec elite committing acts of ritual bloodletting.	
ASIA & OCEANIA	**ca 300** An important Buddhist community is founded at Nagpur in the Deccan in India. **ca 263** The Mauryan emperor Asoka converts to Buddhism. **ca 220** Qin Shihuangdi, the first Chinese emperor, builds himself a vast underground mausoleum and has an army of terracotta warriors buried nearby.	**ca 300** The poet Valmiki begins the compilation of the great Indian epic poem, *Ramayana*. **ca 200** Confucianism inspires the *Classic of Filial Piety* in China, which encourages respect for elders and authorities. **ca 200** The Hindu text *Bhagavad Gita*, or *Song of God*, is further refined.	**ca 250** Buddhism spreads widely through India and into modern-day Sri Lanka with the patronage of the emperor Asoka. **ca 250** A Third Buddhist Council is held at Pataliputra, where Asoka oversees the establishment of the basic tenets of Theravada Buddhism. **ca 220** The monastery at Lo Yang in China becomes a center of Buddhist study and translation.
AFRICA & THE MIDDLE EAST			**ca 275** Scholars in Alexandria translate the first five books of the Old Testament from Hebrew into Greek. **ca 250** The cult of Osiris spreads from Egypt to other regions also under Greek rule. **ca 230** In Egypt a new temple is dedicated to the sun god Horus at Edfu. *The tomb of the first Chinese emperor is guarded by an army of terracotta warriors to accompany him to the afterlife; the face of every warrior is unique.*

RELIGION IN THE WORLD	WORLD EVENTS

264 The First Punic War begins between Rome and Carthage. It ends in 241; Carthage loses its trading colonies in Sicily.

218 The Second Punic War begins. Carthaginian general Hannibal crosses the Alps with a force of 46,000 men and 37 war elephants. His army defeats the Romans at the Battle of Cannae.

201 The Second Punic War ends with the destruction of the Carthaginian Empire. Rome becomes the dominant power in the Mediterranean.

ca 300 The Hohokam culture emerges in Arizona, with a lifestyle based on the cultivation of corn, tobacco, and cotton.

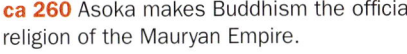

ca 260 Asoka makes Buddhism the official religion of the Mauryan Empire.

247 Asoka sends his son Mahinda as a missionary to Ceylon (Sri Lanka), where he converts King Davanampiyatissa to Buddhism.

ca 221 The Warring States Period ends with a final victory for the Kingdom of Qin and the unification of China under the First Emperor, Shihuangdi.

WORDS OF DEVOTION

Bhagavad Gita

The *Bhagavad Gita* ("*Song of the Lord*") is one of the most important Hindu scriptures. The text is thought to have existed in some form since at least the fourth century B.C., originally as part of the epic poem *Mahabarata* and later as a separate work. Most of the text consists of advice given by Krishna, an avatar of the god Vishnu, to the warrior-prince Arjuna on the eve of a great battle. Krishna discusses the important principles of Hindu philosophy, ethics, and practice before revealing his divine form. The *Bhagavad Gita*'s 700 verses are considered one of the best introductions to Hindu philosophy.

ca 300 Euclid, a Greek mathematician working at the court of Ptolemy I in Alexandria, outlines the fundamental principles of geometry.

ca 250 Ironworking reaches sub-Saharan Africa, probably brought across the desert from southern Mauritania to the Niger Valley.

240 Eratosthenes, a Greek scholar working in the North African colony of Cyrene, calculates the circumference of the Earth.

HISTORY OF JERUSALEM

Jerusalem is a holy city for Christians, Jews, and Muslims. Its long history has seen some of the key events in world religion. For Jews, it is the city founded by King David and the location of Holy Zion, where the Messiah will reveal himself. For Christians it is the site where Jesus was crucified and resurrected. Several early Muslim prophets were connected with Jerusalem and it was from Jerusalem that Muhammad rose to Heaven on the night journey he made to see God.

David, King of Israel, founded the city around 1000 B.C. He began the construction of the Temple of Solomon to hold the Ark of the Covenant, containing the Tablets of the Law and other documents relating to the Israelites' escape from Egypt.

In the sixth century B.C. the city was destroyed by the Babylonians; it has rarely been independent since. When the Romans ruled the city in the first and second centuries A.D., they destroyed the temple and banished the Jews. From the seventh to the 20th centuries, the city was controlled by a succession of Muslim empires. Since 1947, the city has been disputed between Israel and its Muslim neighbors.

The ruins of old Jerusalem can be found at sites throughout the city.

THE JEWISH DIASPORA

This carving, from the Arch of Titus in Rome, shows a group of Roman soldiers carrying the Menorah out of the Temple of Solomon.

SOME HISTORIANS DATE THE start of the Diaspora, or "dispersal," of the Jewish people as far back as 586 B.C., when many Jews were forced into exile in the Babylonian Captivity. After the exile, some Jews did not return to their homeland. The next millennium brought several other forcible dispersals, particularly after unsuccessful uprisings against Roman rule in Judea in the first and second centuries A.D. In addition, many Jews left their homeland voluntarily to seek work in wealthier countries. By A.D. 500 Jewish communities were established in lands from southern Spain to the borders of India.

In the centuries following the Babylonian Captivity, Judaea and Israel fell under the control of a series of foreign powers. First they formed part of the Persian Empire; when that succumbed to Alexander the Great, they came under Greek control. In the second century B.C. Maccabean rebels, taking their name from their leader Judas Maccabeus, were able to establish a semi-independent state; but in 63 B.C. the Hasmonaean dynasty was overthrown by the Roman general Pompey, and the Jews had a fresh imperial master.

The communities of the Diaspora centered on the synagogue (meeting house) and courts of law; Jewish people often lived in a separate quarter of their adopted city. In general they were free to follow their laws and religious practices, although in the Hellenistic period (323–30 B.C.) Jews were encouraged to adopt a Greek lifestyle. The Roman era in Jewish history began with Jerusalem's fall to the Roman general Pompey in 63 B.C. In A.D. 66 its inhabitants launched a revolt against Roman rule that was savagely suppressed; Vespasian and his son Titus, both future Roman emperors, led the Roman forces, which captured Jerusalem after a 139-day siege and largely destroyed it, deporting Jews to Syria and Italy.

A further uprising in A.D. 132, this one led by Simeon bar Kokba, was also put down bloodily. In its wake Judaea was renamed Palestine, and Jerusalem became a Roman city that Jews were forbidden to enter. Thereafter more than 1,800 years would pass before an independent Jewish state would be reestablished in the region.

King Herod and his stepdaughter Salome pictured with the head of John the Baptist. Herod was one of the last Jewish rulers of Jerusalem.

	PEOPLE & PLACES	DOCUMENTS, ART, & ARTIFACTS	WORSHIP & DOCTRINE
EUROPE	**174** The Roman architect Decimus Cossutius is commissioned to complete the Temple of Zeus in Athens, an example of the baroque architecture then fashionable in Greece.		**186** The Roman Senate suppresses the orgiastic cult of Bacchus in Italy.

The Temple of the Jaguar rises above the main plaza in Tikal, Guatemala. Tikal was an important religious center of the Maya of Mexico and Guatemala.

	PEOPLE & PLACES	DOCUMENTS, ART, & ARTIFACTS	WORSHIP & DOCTRINE
THE AMERICAS	**ca 200** In southern Peru the Nazca draw the first huge designs in the desert: the Nazca Lines are drawn for the next 800 years. **ca 200** The Chavín culture in Peru is in decline after its long primacy. **ca 200** A new sacred complex of three temples is built at El Mirador.		
ASIA & OCEANIA	**ca 200** Buddhists build cave dwellings at Bhaja; some 45 are built in the Western Ghats in the following centuries. **ca 100** Construction of the Great Stupa begins at Sanchi in India.	**ca 100** The Sutta Pitaka—a collection of some 10,000 teachings of the Buddha and his companions—is written down in Sri Lanka; it becomes part of the Pali canon.	**ca 185** The coming of the Sunga Empire in India begins a period of probable suppression of Buddhism, although Buddhist sculpture flourishes.
AFRICA & THE MIDDLE EAST	*If we are thrown into the fiery furnace, our God whom we serve is able to save us from it, and he will rescue us from your hand, O king.* BOOK OF DANIEL 3:17	**ca 165** The Old Testament Book of Daniel is composed. **ca 100** The Book of Maccabees, an account of the Maccabean revolt, is written in Hebrew (📄 facing page).	**ca 170** Worship of the Zoroastrian god Mithras begins among the Parthians. **167** The ruler of the Hellenistic Seleucid Empire, Antiochus IV Epiphanes, outlaws the practice of Judaism even in Jerusalem; the Temple of Jerusalem is rededicated to the Greek god Zeus.

MONUMENTS OF FAITH

Mayan Pyramids

Mayan pyramids can be found at sites throughout Central America. These vast structures were once the centerpieces of large planned cities, surrounded by palaces, public buildings, and temple complexes. At their summit there was typically a small temple, where offerings would be left for the gods.

197 Hispania (Spain) becomes part of the Roman Empire.

ca 150 Roman engineers begin constructing buildings with concrete, a technique that allows larger and more durable structures to be built.

102 Uprisings by the Germanic Cimbri and Teutones tribes are ruthlessly put down by the Romans.

MACCABEAN REVOLT

The Maccabee family gave its name to the Jews' fight for independence from the Hellenistic Seleucid dynasty between 168 and 164 B.C. The name loosely means "hammer"; it was bestowed on one of the Jewish leaders.

The revolt was sparked by the efforts of King Antiochus IV (ruled 175–ca 164 B.C.) to unite the extensive Seleucid Empire under a single religion. He and his followers were devotees of the polytheistic Greek religion—the Seleucid dynasty descended from the Greek empire of Alexander the Great—which the Jews dismissed as a form of nature worship.

Antiochus forbade traditional Jewish religious practices such as the observance of the Sabbath, circumcision, and the reading of the Law of Moses. He sent his officers to forcibly convert Jews in the village of Modi'im, home to Mattathias and his sons. Mattathias struck a Jew who was prepared to offer sacrifices to the pagan gods and started a revolt.

Mattathias and his sons fled to the Judaean wilderness from where they organized a guerrilla army to fight Antiochus' men. Following Mattathias' death in 166, he left his oldest son, Judas, in charge of the rebel forces. Despite being severely outnumbered, Judas and his rebels were able to defeat many of Antiochus' captains. Judas was given the nickname "Maccabeus" for his success in hammering the enemy forces and defeating the Seleucid army.

Judas and his men entered Jerusalem to reclaim the temple three years after Antiochus first desecrated it. The Jewish celebrations resulted in the festival of lights or Hanukkah, which is still celebrated today.

A medieval illustration of the Maccabean Revolt.

189 The first Buddhists, refugees from China, arrive in Vietnam.

ca 185 Pushyamitra assassinates the last Mauryan ruler of India, establishing the Hindu Shunga dynasty.

124 Confucianism is placed at the heart of Chinese society and politics when Emperor Han Wudi uses Confucian works as the basis for the curriculum to train bureaucrats.

167 The reforms of Antiochos spark three years of Jewish revolt, led by Judas Maccabee.

164 The Jewish feast of Hanukkah is inaugurated when Judas Maccabee reclaims the Jerusalem Temple for Jewish worship.

ca 112 The Sadducees and Pharisees are opposed groups of Jews in Palestine.

196 Texts celebrating Pharaoh Ptolemy V are carved on the Rosetta Stone in Greek and Egyptian scripts; 2,000 years later they will be the key to deciphering hieroglyphics

146 The city of Carthage is completely destroyed by the forces of Rome.

THE CELTS AND THEIR DRUIDS

THE CELTS WERE A DISPARATE GROUP OF WARRING TRIBES who dominated a vast area across present-day central and northwestern Europe at different times between 600 B.C. and A.D. 50. They are noted for introducing iron-made tools and weapons.

Little is known about Celtic religion, as the Celts left no written record. What we do know comes from accounts written by the Romans, who were enemies of the Celts and likely biased against them. Roman authors, however, acknowledge that religion succeeded in uniting the disparate Celtic groups, giving them both a cohesive belief system and a system of laws by which to live. The Romans highlighted the importance the Celts placed on human sacrifice. One method of sacrifice was to drown the victim in a boggy pool, a ritual some archaeologists believe may have played a part in marking and guarding the boundaries of a settlement. The bodies of dozens of these victims, preserved by the mud, have been discovered in northwestern Europe. Animal sacrifices and well-crafted weapons were also thrown into pools, lakes, and rivers. Because the Celts believed the human head was the site of spiritual power, they cut off the heads of their enemies and their ancestors and displayed them on doorposts or hung them from their belts as a means of harnessing the power of the dead person.

Celts worshiped the sun, the moon, and the stars and believed there were supernatural forces at work across their world. Sacred structures only started to appear in Celtic communities toward the end of their culture and were probably influenced by contact with Roman culture. In England, the Celts started the practice of burying ordinary people in the ground in cemeteries as opposed to the elaborate burial ships of the elite of previous cultures.

The Celts' priests, the druids, administered the religious rites. Although little is known about the druids, it is known that they often performed many different types of religious ceremonies in groves of oak trees and by water, and that they performed both human and animal sacrifice. The druids were educated and powerful members of any Celtic tribe. They combined many roles within their society including that of healer, political advisor, teacher, and arbitrator. They had their own universities and knowledge was passed from one generation to another by an oral tradition. In some situations historians think the druid priests held more authority than the king; on occasion they spoke before the king.

The preserved body of a Celtic bog sacrifice. Human remains such as these, preserved by the conditions in peat bogs, are one of the few pieces of archaeological evidence relating to Celtic religion.

May those who love us, love us.
And those who hate us, may God turn their hearts.

CELTIC PRAYER

PEOPLE & PLACES	DOCUMENTS, ART, & ARTIFACTS	WORSHIP & DOCTRINE

EUROPE

ca 100 Roman architects begin building circular temples in Greek style, starting with the so-called Temple of Vesta in the Forum Boarium in Rome.

46 The forum of Caesar is dedicated in Rome; it is dominated by a huge temple of Venus, who Caesar claims as a divine ancestor.

27 Under Agrippa construction begins on the Parthenon, a temple to Rome's major gods; it is destroyed by fire in A.D. 80.

2 Augustus builds a new forum in Rome as part of a program of public works that includes many temples; the emperor boasts that he found Rome a city of brick and left it a city of marble.

17 The Roman poet Horace writes *Secular Hymn*, praising Augustus' return to fundamental morality.

9 Augustus builds the Altar of the Augustan Peace in Rome to celebrate his military victories: the monument is modeled on the Altar of Pity in Athens.

42 Emperor Julius Caesar is recognized as a god by the Roman state, beginning a cult of emperor-worship in the empire (▤ page 59).

30 A Roman ritual calendar is published, showing strong Etruscan influence.

ca 30 At the end of Rome's civil war, Octavian (Augustus) encourages a return to older forms of Roman religion.

23 The Emperor Augustus is worshiped as a living god.

THE AMERICAS

ca 100 In northern coastal Peru, the Moche begin building mud-brick pyramid temples.

ca 100 The Nazca build Cahuachi, a small ritual center that is probably intended to house pilgrims.

ca 100 Like the Adena before them, the Hopewell build vast burial mounds in the Ohio, Illinois, and Mississippi valleys.

The silver star beneath the altar in Church of the Nativity, Bethlehem, marks the exact spot where it is believed that Jesus was born.

ASIA & OCEANIA

ca 100 The Fourth Buddhist Council at Kashmir compiles the *Mahavibhasa*.

ca 70 The gateways and balustrade are added to the Great Stupa at Sanchi in India.

17 The Pali Tripitaka is written down in Sri Lanka; it is the closest Theravada Buddhism has to holy scripture.

ca 100 A new form of Buddhism emerges: Mahayana ("Great Vehicle") Buddhism offers salvation through the help of bodhisattvas, pious humans who delay the attainment of enlightenment in order to help others.

17 Internal splits cause a division in Sri Lanka's Buddhist monastic community.

AFRICA & THE MIDDLE EAST

47 Herod becomes the Roman governor of Galilee; later he becomes king of Judea.

4 The probable date of the birth of the historical Jesus (▤ page 51).

The cities of the Empire, as well as the citizens and the nations, honor Julius Caesar, the high priest, emperor, and twice consul, the manifest god descended from Ares and Aphrodite, and savior of all human life.

ROMAN INSCRIPTION, EPHESUS

RELIGION IN THE WORLD

76 The Romans send envoys to Greece and Asia Minor to replace the Sybilline Books, destroyed in a fire some years earlier.

18 Augustus introduces the first of a number of reforms aimed at safeguarding marriage and limiting divorce among Rome's notoriously decadent upper classes.

WORLD EVENTS

58 Julius Caesar begins a ten-year campaign to conquer Gaul (France).

55 Julius Caesar introduces the Julian calendar of three 365-day years followed by one of 366 days.

44 Julius Caesar is assassinated on his way to a meeting of the Roman Senate.

31 Caesar's heir Octavian triumphs over his rival Mark Antony in the civil war following Caesar's death.

ca 50 El Mirador in Guatemala develops into the largest lowland Mayan center, covering more than 6 square miles.

The Great Stupa at Sanchi, India, was begun in the third century B.C. and completed around A.D. 70. Stupas were often built to hold relics of the Buddha or of a bodhisattva; monks walk around them as an aid to prayer or meditation.

JEWISH PROPHETS

In Judaism, a prophet (*Nun-Beit-Yud-Alef* in Hebrew) held an important role. He or she was an intermediary between the Jewish people and God, who reinforced the belief that the people of Israel were God's chosen people. The Jewish people believed prophets were chosen by God to deliver his message. The prophets' role was described in the Book of Deuteronomy, in which God says: "I will put my words in his mouth and he will speak to them all that I command him."

The covenant God first made with his chosen people required their obedience to him and his teachings, as contained in the Torah and in oral tradition. God made the covenant with Abraham, who was thus seen as the founder of Judaism and the father of the Jewish people.

Moses was the first prophet to whom God dictated his laws. According to Jewish tradition, Moses was responsible for writing the Torah, the first five books of the Bible which form the basis of Jewish belief: Genesis, Exodus, Leviticus, Numbers, and Deuteronomy.

The Old Testament told how the existence of God was revealed to the Jewish people. They believe the Torah came directly from God and that the texts of the Prophets were the words of God as recounted by chosen people such as Miriam, older sister of Moses and Aaron. Other important prophets include Isaiah, Samuel, Ezekiel, Malachi, and Job. They predicted coming events and passed on instructions from God.

The prophets' special role in society often put them in a difficult position. It was their duty to constantly inform the Jewish people what they should do to fulfill God's wishes, even if it meant reprimanding rulers for breaking God's covenant. Isaiah was said to have been martyred for his faith; Job suffered many afflictions when God withdrew his protection from Satan. But the prophets also offered good news: they reminded people that if they stayed true to God he would fulfill the promises he had made to the Jewish people and they would receive his blessings.

He who controls others may be powerful;

But he who has mastered himself is mightier still.

LAO-TZU

BUDDHISM IN CHINA

TODAY BUDDHISM IS THE MOST IMPORTANT ORGANIZED religion in China. Although it is not native to the country, the practice has been adapted to incorporate the basic tenets of Confucianism and Taoism, such as ancestor worship, creating a religion that is uniquely appropriate to Chinese culture.

Buddhism arrived from India during the Han dynasty (206 B.C.–A.D. 220) when China was still mainly Taoist. The religion gained a foothold in the first century A.D. when the Han emperor Mingdi, who was a follower of both Buddhism and Taoism, sent officials to India to bring back important Buddhist scriptures and translate them.

As Buddhism developed in China, it split into many different strands, the most significant of which were Tiantai, Huayan, Jingtu (Pure Land), and Chan. The Chan school is better known in the West as Zen Buddhism. With the fall of the Han in 220 and the subsequent social upheaval in northern China, Buddhism developed faster in the north than the south as hierarchical structures broke down and the status quo changed. By the time the Tang dynasty (618–907) emerged, Buddhism had supplanted Taoism as the dominant religion and was made a state-supported religion.

Buddhist shrines in China are very different from the domed stupas common in India and Southeast Asia. In the Dunhuang region, on the edge of the Gobi Desert in Western China, for example, Buddhist monks excavated more than 1,000 caves into the cliff face. The caves were used as places for solitary meditation. They were often richly decorated and contained many valuable Buddhist artifacts, including the oldest known printed book, the *Diamond Sutra*. Another example of a Chinese Buddhist shrine is the 233-foot-tall Buddha carved into a hillside in Leshan, Sichuan province, during the Tang dynasty.

The growth of Buddhism in China did not go unopposed. In 845 the Tang emperor Wuzong ordered the destruction of 4,600 Buddhist monasteries and 40,000 temples. He forced around 250,000 Buddhist monks and nuns to give up their monastic lives. Buddhism survived in a reduced form and over centuries rebuilt itself.

This illustration comes from one of the elaborately decorated manuscripts found in the Dunhuang caves.

The Temple of Heaven in Beijing, northeastern China, was built as a combination of the principles of Buddhism with Taoism; Buddhism proved more enduring in China than in its Indian homeland.

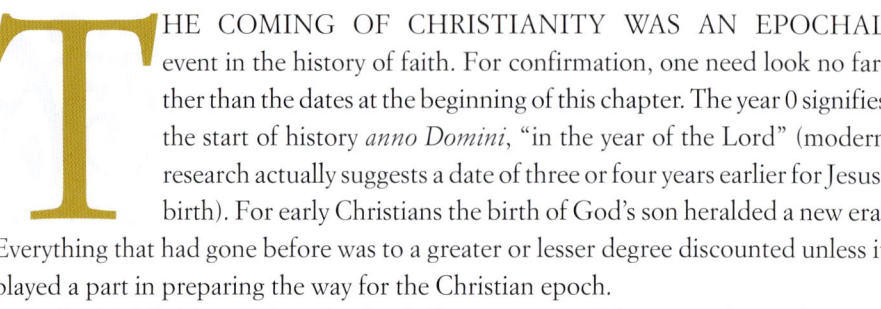

One of the great monuments of early Christianity, the Book of Kells is an illuminated manuscript of the four gospels created in about A.D. 800 by monks, probably in Ireland, which was converted to Christianity by St. Patrick in the fifth century.

T HE COMING OF CHRISTIANITY WAS AN EPOCHAL event in the history of faith. For confirmation, one need look no farther than the dates at the beginning of this chapter. The year 0 signifies the start of history *anno Domini*, "in the year of the Lord" (modern research actually suggests a date of three or four years earlier for Jesus' birth). For early Christians the birth of God's son heralded a new era: Everything that had gone before was to a greater or lesser degree discounted unless it played a part in preparing the way for the Christian epoch.

In the Middle Eastern heartlands of Christianity—still known today as the Holy Land—the teachings of Jesus joined the long tradition of prophets who preached a special bond between the one god, Yaweh, and his chosen people, the Jews. But after Jesus' death Christianity soon grew apart from Judaism and was carried by the Apostles throughout the Roman Empire. The new faith was just one among a number of eastern cults popular among the Romans, but its assertion that there were no gods beyond the Christian God brought persecution from authorities with a vested interest in maintaining the pagan beliefs. That gradually changed, partly through the persistence and faith of early Christians and partly through the conversion of the Emperor Constantine in 313. After Christianity became the official religion of the Roman Empire in 380, it spread rapidly and gained particular popularity in the Italian peninsula, the eastern Mediterranean, and North Africa.

Over the coming centuries, Christianity developed its scripture and liturgy, although not without controversy. As the so-called Church Fathers debated arcane theological disputes, a number of schismatic faiths broke away, to be condemned as heresy and wither or to thrive on their own. In some cases tiny differences in doctrine could mean life or death. Rome and Constantinople became the centers of the church, with slight variations in liturgy that widened as they evolved; the Greek-Egyptian city of Alexandria was another center of theology, home of the Church Father St. Augustine of Hippo.

For some Christians, the finer points of theology were not as important as the determination to live life in a good spirit, spending time in prayer and contemplation and withdrawing from the material world. They formed dedicated religious communities to live as monks and nuns according to God's rules. In the deserts of Egypt Christians lived lives that paralleled Christ's hardships in the Wilderness.

The spiritual life also appealed to people farther to the east, where Buddhist monks in India carved spectacular caves and temples into cliffs for living and meditation. Buddhism knitted together much of East Asia. The faith

had many followers among the urban classes of India's cities, and merchants carried it along trade routes over land and oceans. Monks from India traveled to China to spread the faith, found monasteries, and oversee the translation and transmission of the holy scriptures; meanwhile Chinese pilgrims recorded their travels to India to seek out the great sites associated with the life of the Buddha, which were scattered in the foothills of the Himalaya. Indian rulers were generally content to support all the faiths within their realms, allowing Buddhism to flourish alongside the even-older Hinduism. When that multiculturalism ceased, as it would in the later Middle Ages, Buddhism would largely disappear from its homeland for centuries to the extent that it was virtually forgotten. The monasteries of China, Nepal, and Tibet would be the repositories from which the faith would spread into Southeast Asia.

Farther to the east, the traditional religions of Japan, which consisted of a mixture of ancestor worship and animism, fused into a more formal faith, known as Shinto. As the Japanese came into contact in turn with Buddhist monks and traders, so Shinto and Buddhism merged to create what was essentially a single faith.

In the Americas and Africa, meanwhile, societies had polytheistic or animistic religions that believed in nature spirits and that used myths to explain the creation of humans. The Maya who emerged in what are now southern Mexico, Guatemala, and Belize incorporated deities from other Central American peoples and celebrated their great heroes by playing a sacred ball game that re-enacted the exploits of divine twins from their mythology.

The Mayan city of Tikal was founded in about 300 B.C. and by about A.D. 150 had become the major ceremonial city of the Guatemalan lowlands. The city's pyramid temples and stone acropolises were built over a period of a thousand years.

Previous pages *This 12th-century painting of the Nativity was made by a Catalan artist in Spain. The scene of Jesus' birth in the stable, with attendant animals and sometimes with the kings and shepherds, was a popular subject for Christian artists.*

	0	100	150	200	250
EUROPE	**ca 20** Roman emperor Tiberius attempts to suppress druidism, a nature religion practiced by Celts in Britain. **ca 58** St. Paul sends his Letter to the Corinthians to encourage the Christian community he founded in Corinth, Greece, eight years earlier. **ca 67** The apostle Paul is executed in Rome.	**ca 100** Despite imperial efforts to suppress them, eastern cults such as those of Mithras and Isis become popular in Rome. **126** The rebuilt Pantheon in Rome is completed by the Emperor Hadrian: the temple still stands today. **ca 130** After the death of his favorite and lover Antinonus, Emperor Hadrian has him deified.	**177** As part of a program of persecution under the Emperor Marcus Aurelius, Christians are publicly tortured before being put to death in Lyons, France. **ca 197** The early Christian theologian Tertullian writes his *Apology*, arguing that Christians can be trusted as citizens of the empire.	**ca 200** The bishop of Rome gains his prominent position in the Catholic Church as pope. **236** Author Hippolytus of Rome is martyred during a persecution of Christians: he is said to have been dragged to death by horses, of which he becomes the patron saint.	**250** Fabian, bishop of Rome, is executed during a persecution of Christians launched by the Emperor Decius. **274** Emperor Aurelian reintroduces paganism to Rome, where he builds a temple to Helios, the sun god.
THE AMERICAS	**ca 50** A vast ceremonial city is constructed at Teotihuacan, Mexico. **ca 50** The Nazca create huge line drawings in the desert that are only recognizable from the air.	**ca 100** In eastern North America the mound-building Adena culture slowly disappears.	**ca 150** Tikal becomes the major ceremonial center in the Mayan lowlands.	**ca 200** The Temple of the Feathered Serpent, Quetzalcoatl, is constructed in the ceremonial city of Teotihuacan in Mexico.	**ca 250** The beginning of the Classical period of Maya history on the Yucatán Peninsula is characterized by the worship of divine kings in their own city-states.
ASIA & OCEANIA	**50** The apostle Thomas finds many converts in Gandhara, India, but is killed when he attempts to convert the local ruler. **68** One of China's earliest Buddhist temples, the White Horse Temple, is built outside Luoyang. **ca 78** Emperor Ming dispatches a group of Buddhist monks to northern India to acquire Buddhist scriptures.	**ca 100** Theravada Buddhism has by now become established in southern Burma. **ca 147** The Parthian monk An Shigo arrives in Luoyang, one of China's ancient capitals, and begins translating Buddhist texts from Sanskrit into Chinese, helping establish the faith in China.	**ca 150** The first known inscriptions in Sanskrit, the Hindu holy language, appear in India. **ca 175** In the Han capital Luoyang, extracts from the teachings of Confucius are carved on stone pillars, or stelae, at the Imperial Academy.	**ca 220** Confucianism loses its influence in China after the end of the Han dynasty, which had made it the state ideology. **ca 226** In Persia, Zoroastrian priests called magi begin to compile the Avesta, a written collection of their remaining scriptures.	**ca 273** Zoroastrian high priest Kartir calls for the suppression of Manichaeanism and Buddhism in Iran. **296** Date of the earliest surviving Chinese Buddhist scripture (*Zhu Fo Yao Ji Jing*).
AFRICA & THE MIDDLE EAST	**ca 29** Jesus of Nazareth begins preaching and soon attracts followers with his teachings. **ca 30** The Romans in Palestine execute Jesus of Nazareth, whom they fear is increasing tension between them and their Jewish subjects. **ca 36** The Jewish Pharisee Saul converts to Christianity after a vision on the road to Damascus; as St. Paul of Tarsus, he will become the founder of modern Christianity. **ca 70** The Romans recapture Jerusalem after a Jewish uprising and destroy its temple.	**111** Pliny the Younger, Roman governor of Nithynia in Asia Minor, writes to the Emperor Trajan for advice on how to deal with the growing numbers of Christians. **132** Jewish leader Simeon bar Kochba inspires a four-year revolt against Roman rule in Judea that leads to the expulsion of the Jews from Palestine. **ca 135** In the aftermath of the Jewish Revolt in Judea, scholars known as rabbis become important as they begin gathering and codifying traditional oral law in the Mishnah.	**ca 150** The rise of gnosticism leads early Christians to push for the canonization of the scriptures. **ca 178** Irenaeus becomes bishop of Lyons, a position he holds until about 200; he is a prominent opponent of gnosticism. **ca 185** Led by Irenaeus, the New Testament is canonized; the rule of faith, a new Christian creed, is promulgated.	**203** During a persecution in Carthage, the Roman Christian Perpetua is martyred with her pregnant slave Felicitas: Perpetua's own account of preparing for her martyrdom helps win many converts to Christianity. **248** Anti-Christian rioting breaks out in Alexandria, Egypt.	**256** After an epidemic kills many citizens of Alexandria in Egypt, many survivors convert to Christianity. **268** Bishop Paul of Antioch is deposed for heresy. **286** Anthony of Egypt, a Christian monk, begins 20 years living alone in the desert in an attempt to find spiritual communion with God; he is seen as the founder of Christian monasticism.

300	350	400	450	500–550
310 While visiting a shrine to Apollo, the Roman general Constantine has a vision urging him to adopt Christianity. **312** Constantine defeats the Romans at the Battle of Milvian Bridge and usurps the last pagan emperor, Maxentius. **330** The first Church of St. Peter's is erected in Rome.	**382** Pope Damasus holds a church council and issues a list of the canonical books of the Old and New Testaments. **ca 386** Bishop Ambrose of Milan introduces hymns to church services. **390** Bishop Ambrose of Milan excommunicates the Emperor Theodosius I when he orders the massacre of some 7,000 citizens of Thessalonika after a revolt.	**432** Sent as a missionary from Britain, St. Patrick sets up a diocese at Armagh in Ireland and begins to make converts. **438** Jews are legally forbidden to hold public office in the Roman Empire.	**455** The Persians suppress Christianity in Armenia, which has become a province of the empire, and force Christians to convert to Zoroastrianism. **455** Pope Leo the Great negotiates peace with the Vandals who capture Rome. **496** Clovis, the king of the Franks, is baptized as a Catholic.	**515** The Monks Rule of St. Benedict, which requires monks to take vows of poverty, obedience, and chastity, becomes the rule for monastic life in Europe. **523** Boethius writes *De Consolatione Philosophiae* (*The Consolations of Philosophy*); throughout the Middle Ages it is one of the most widely read books after the Bible.
ca 300 The Hohokam culture which has emerged in southwestern North America builds temple mounds similar to those built in Mexico.		**ca 400** The mound-building Hopewell culture of eastern North America goes into decline.	**455** The Maya found what will become a major city and ritual center at Chichén Itzá on the Yucatán Peninsula in Mexico.	**ca 500** The Maya develop a 260-day sacred calendar for ritual purposes.
ca 300 In Japan a tomb culture flourishes in which the Yamato emperors are buried with clay statues in elaborate sepulchers on keyhole-shaped islands. **ca 320** Political instability and Hun invasions fragment China, allowing Buddhism to become stronger and attract more followers (there are two million Buddhists living in 30,000 monasteries by about 400).	**ca 350** Dunhuang, an oasis on the Silk Road on the edge of the Gobi Desert, becomes an important center of Buddhist scholarship. **372** Buddhism is introduced to the Korean peninsula.	**ca 400** In Chang'an the Indian monk Kumarajiva oversees the translation of Buddhist texts into Chinese at the invitation of Emperor Yao Xing. **ca 400** Under Gupta patronage, Hinduism experiences a revival in India and there is a flowering of classical Sanskrit literature. **ca 425** Buddhism arrives in Sumatra, Indonesia.	**478** The first Shinto shrines appear in Japan. **483** Nestorians flourish in Persia; they even send missionaries to introduce Christianity to China. **485** Five monks from Gandhara, India, are reported to have introduced Buddhism into a country named Fusang, which may be Japan.	**502** Wudi becomes emperor of China; he will convert to Buddhism in 517. **ca 520** Bodhidharma arrives in China to teach Zen Buddhism; in Louyang he spends nine years in meditation. **ca 540** Buddhism begins to wane in India.
325 Emperor Constantine makes Christianity the state faith throughout the Roman Empire. **ca 326** While building the Church of the Holy Sepulcher on the traditional site of Christ's burial in Jerusalem, St. Helena discovers the True Cross on which he was crucified.	**372** King Ezana of Auxum builds the Orthodox Christian Church of St. Mary of Zion, probably the first Christian church in sub-Saharan Africa. **386** Having translated most of the Bible into Latin, St. Jerome enters a monastery in Bethlehem, where he spends his last years. **391** Christianity becomes the official religion of Egypt; many ancient temples are destroyed. In Alexandria, monks and priests incite a mob to destroy the Temple of Serapis.	**415** The philosopher Hypatia of Alexandria is murdered by a mob, possibly on the orders of Cyril, Archbishop of Alexandria, who resents her influence. **420** St. Simeon Stylites withdraws to a platform on top of a pillar in Syria; he stays there for 39 years before his death in 459. **428** Nestorius, bishop of Constantinople, causes a split in the church by emphasizing Christ's human nature over his divine nature; this Nestorian controversy causes deep divisions within the church.	**ca 450** Followers of the Christian monks and nuns who live ascetic lives in Egypt and Syria record some of their words as the *Sayings of the Desert Fathers and Mothers*. **459** The death of St. Simeon Stylites inspires a century of stylites living atop pillars throughout Syria and the Holy Land. **484** The Pope excommunicates Patriarch Acacius of Constantinople, leading to the first schism between the Western and Eastern churches, which lasts until 519.	**ca 500** Jewish tribes settle in Arabia in the regions of Mecca and Yemen. **536** Emperor Justinian orders the closure of the temple of Philae on the Nile, marking the official end of the cult of the ancient Egyptian gods. **537** The biggest Christian church in the world at the time, Hagia Sophia (Holy Wisdom), is built in Constantinople with a dome 100 feet across. **ca 500** The Talmud, a collection of religious texts and laws, is compiled by Jewish scholars.

PEOPLE & PLACES	DOCUMENTS, ART, & ARTIFACTS	WORSHIP & DOCTRINE

EUROPE

ca 40 One of the first Christian churches is built at Corinth, Greece.

ca 20 Roman emperor Tiberius attempts to suppress druidism, a nature religion practiced by Celts in Britain.

In Nubia, south of Egypt, ruling dynasties adopted the ancient Egyptian practice of building pyramids—re-created in this artist's impression—as tombs for their rulers.

THE AMERICAS

ca 0 The religion of the Moche of Peru's northern coast emerges in the area previously dominated by the Chavín culture.

ca 25 Around Lake Titicaca in what is now Bolivia the Tiahuanaco people begin constructing ceremonial centers, which later influence the Inca.

ASIA & OCEANIA

ca 30 The development of Mahayana Buddhism makes the faith more accessible to the majority of people, promoting the contribution of bodhisattvas, enlightened beings who can help others achieve enlightenment.

65 Liu Ying, brother of the Han emperor, sponsors the first-known Buddhist practices in China (pages 42–43).

AFRICA & THE MIDDLE EAST

ca 0 At Naga, Nubians build Egyptian-style temples dedicated to the lion god Apedemek.

6 Death of the biblical King Herod.

ca 15 Birth in what is now Turkey of Apollonius of Tyana, whose reputation as a sage rivals that of Jesus for a time.

19 The temple of Jupiter–Ba'al is built at Palmyra in what is now Syria.

ca 36 The Jewish Pharisee Saul converts to Christianity after a vision on the road to Damascus that leaves him temporarily blinded; as St. Paul of Tarsus, he will be seen as the founder of modern Christianity (page 53).

1 A Jewish sect in Palestine lays out its beliefs, including baptism in water, in a series of scrolls which are now the oldest known documents in Hebrew: the Dead Sea Scrolls.

ca 29 In Palestine the Jewish prophet Jesus of Nazareth begins preaching and attracts followers with his teachings (facing page).

ca 46 St. Paul begins the first of four missionary journeys over the next 16 years, visiting Rome and Jerusalem and founding churches in Syria, Asia Minor, Macedonia, and Greece.

ca 49 In Jerusalem, Jesus' followers decide not to impose Jewish law on non-Jewish Christians.

RELIGION IN THE WORLD	WORLD EVENTS

THE HISTORICAL JESUS

Love is patient, love is kind
and is not jealous;
love does not brag and is
not arrogant, does not act
unbecomingly…
It … does not rejoice in
unrighteousness, but rejoices
with the truth;
bears all things, believes all
things, hopes all things,
endures all things.
Love never fails.

ST. PAUL, LETTER TO THE CORINTHIANS 13: 4–8

ca 0 Roman traders use the seasonal monsoon winds to cross the Indian Ocean and trade with southern India.

ca 0 Greek geographer Strabo publishes a detailed description of the known world.

9 German tribes wipe out three Roman legions at the Battle of Teutoburg Forest, the first significant imperial defeat.

43 Claudius leads the Roman conquest of Britain and establishes London on the Thames River.

ca 0 In what is now southern Ohio and the Illinois and Mississippi River Valleys, the Hopewell culture emerges; it is characterized by large earthwork mounds.

ca 0 The farming "Basketmakers," forerunners of the Anasazi culture, emerge in the American Southwest.

2 A Chinese census records the population of the Han Empire as 57 million.

25 Emperor Wang Mang, who usurped the Han throne 16 years earlier, is assassinated by Chinese princes who establish the Later Han dynasty.

ca 39 Two Vietnamese sisters lead a rebellion against Chinese rule and rule a short-lived independent state before the Chinese take control again.

ca 30 The Romans in Palestine crucify Jesus of Nazareth, whom they fear is increasing tension between them and their Jewish subjects.

ca 30 In northern Ethiopia the kingdom of Axum becomes independent.

39 Jews in Alexandria, Egypt, send an ambassador to the Emperor Caligula in Rome to protest their treatment at the hands of Alexandrine Greeks.

6 Rome annexes Judaea as a province of the empire.

42 Rome annexes Mauritania (parts of modern Morocco and Algeria).

Research in the past 150 years has used historical methods and archaeology to learn about the real Jesus. It echoes earlier efforts such as the Jefferson Bible, which stripped away all supernatural elements to tell the story of Jesus as a man.

Most historians believe that there was indeed a real Jesus, a Jew who lived in Galilee in the early first century A.D. This Jesus emerged as a preacher and leader during a time of great popular discontent, as various peoples of Judaea resented Roman rule. The young man was an impressive speaker, with a gift for telling parables (educational stories). He developed a reputation for working miracles and attracted a group of followers, including a dozen apostles who spread his message. Jesus' provocative

The Resurrection of Christ was one of a watercolor cycle illustrating the events of the Passion painted by the French artist James J. Tissot at the end of the 19th century.

behavior eventually led the Romans to arrest him; he was tried by the governor, Pontius Pilate, and crucified, the Roman punishment for serious crimes.

PEOPLE & PLACES	DOCUMENTS, ART, & ARTIFACTS	WORSHIP & DOCTRINE

EUROPE

ca 67 The apostle St. Paul is executed in Rome.

ca 67 St. Linus becomes bishop of Rome, making him the second pope after St. Peter.

79 Referring to the Roman practice of deifying emperors after their deaths, Vespasian's last words are reported to be, "I think I'm turning into a god."

80 The Pantheon in Rome is destroyed by fire.

88 Clement I becomes pope.

ca 90 Despite having been born a slave, the Stoic philosopher Epicetus becomes a prominent influence among the Roman elite.

ca 58 St. Paul sends his letter to the Corinthians to encourage the Christian community he has founded there.

This giant spider was drawn by the Nazca people in the first century—but as the artists would never have been able to see the finished result, no-one knows how they achieved such accuracy.

ca 50 Paul establishes the Christian church in Corinth, Greece.

ca 85 Jewish authorities expel Christians from Judaism.

ca 87 The Emperor Domitian orders vestal virgins entombed alive for breaking their vows of chastity.

THE AMERICAS

ca 50 In the Valley of Mexico a vast ceremonial city is constructed at Teotihuacan, comprising some 600 pyramids; the Pyramid of the Sun rises 215 feet tall at one end of a broad 2-mile ceremonial avenue.

ca 50 The Nazca people of southern Peru continue to create vast line drawings in the desert that only become recognizable when viewed from a great height.

ASIA & OCEANIA

50 After early success in finding Christian converts in India, the apostle Thomas makes a fatal error when he tries to convert King Gondophernes of Gandhara; the king has the missionary martyred.

68 One of China's earliest Buddhist temples, the White Horse Temple, is built outside Luoyang, the new Han capital.

ca 90 Statues of the Buddha are among the Greek-influenced art created in Gandhara in what is now northwest Pakistan.

ca 78 In Buddhist tradition, Emperor Ming introduces the faith to China after a dream in which he sees a golden man; the emperor sends a delegation to Afghanistan, which returns with Buddhist scriptures, monks, and a statue of the Buddha.

ca 78 According to Mahayana tradition, the fourth Buddhist council takes place in India.

AFRICA & THE MIDDLE EAST

ca 53 St. Paul appears before the Roman proconsul Gallio in Greece to defend his missionary activities against complaints from Jewish elders.

ca 68 The Dead Sea Scrolls are hidden by their creators in Qumran, Jordan; the 600 manuscripts are rediscovered in 1947.

68 Jewish historian Flavius Josephus writes his *History of the Jewish War*, recording the Jews' revolt against the Romans.

ca 70 Early Christians begin compiling accounts of the life and works of Jesus in what will become the first three Gospels: Mark's Gospel is written first (📄 page 57).

ca 50 The teachings of Christ are spread beyond the Jewish world by St. Paul, who writes long letters outlining Christian beliefs, now included in the New Testament (📄 pages 54–55).

RELIGION IN THE WORLD	WORLD EVENTS

64 After a great fire in Rome, the Emperor Nero executes many Christians; his victims likely include Peter, the first bishop of Rome (later known as the popes).

92 The Roman emperor Domitian resumes the violent suppression of Christianity, which threatens the imperial cult.

61 Boudicca, queen of the Iceni, leads a rebellion against Roman rule in Britain.

69 Emperor Nero's suicide begins a year of upheaval as competing generals claim the imperial throne; eventually Vespasian establishes the Flavian dynasty.

79 An eruption of Mount Vesuvius near Naples buries the towns of Pompeii and Herculaneum under layers of ash and lava; rediscovered in 1748, they will give key insights into Roman daily life.

ca 50 El Mirador, at one time the largest city in the Maya lowlands, begins to go into decline.

ca 50 The Hopewell of eastern North America build more ambitious earthwork mounds.

ca 50 Sanskrit, the written language of Hinduism, becomes the standard written script throughout Southeast Asia.

ca 78 The Chinese conquer the Buddhist kingdom of Khotan.

ca 50 The Khusans of Central Asia establish an empire in northwestern India that will last some 300 years.

57 A Japanese mission visits China.

ca 60 Chinese forces reestablish control over Central Asia.

ca 70 Work begins on building China's Grand Canal.

66 Roman troops clash with Jews in Jerusalem, sparking the Great Jewish Revolt.

ca 70 The Romans capture Jerusalem after a 139-day siege and destroy its temple.

73 At Masada in the Judaean Desert, Romans besiege a small group of Jewish rebels in a hilltop fortress; when the attackers finally break into the stronghold, they find its 1,000 men, women, and children dead from mass suicide.

ca 50 The kingdom of Axum dominates Red Sea trade.

ca 60 Hero of Alexander designs an early steam engine.

97 A diplomatic mission from China reaches the head of the Persian Gulf.

This statue of Buddha was carved by a Gandharan craftsman. The Gandharan style of art brought together Greek influences in carving with Buddhist thought from northern India.

A 12th-century French illustration shows Paul struck blind, recovering, and beginning to preach.

ST. PAUL

The apostle Paul, an Orthodox Jew, had once been responsible for persecuting Jesus' followers before he suffered a remarkable conversion. On the road to Damascus, he experienced a vision of the resurrected Jesus that struck him temporarily blind. He became convinced that the central doctrine of faith was the sacrifice of Jesus, bringing him into direct conflict with Judaism and its laws.

After the death of Jesus, Paul undertook four journeys across the Mediterranean world between 46 and 62 to spread the faith. He preached and established Christian churches in Asia Minor before crossing the Aegean Sea and taking his message to Europe. Paul was not popular everywhere he went.

Paul's greatest legacy to the church was his writings, often in the form of letters to communities of believers he had founded. Paul expressed in Greek—a language accessible to many people—the most important parts of Christian belief. He developed the fundamental doctrine of justification through faith alone: that belief in Christ alone could free the believer from sin.

THE SPREAD OF CHRISTIANITY

AFTER THE CRUCIFIXION OF JESUS IN about A.D. 30 his followers in Palestine began to meet in small groups to spread his teachings. They believed that their former teacher was the Messiah, or son of God, who had risen from the dead. They preached the news of his resurrection. In the first decades after Jesus' death the new religion—Christianity—began to spread beyond Palestine. Its first great missionary was Paul of Tarsus, a Roman citizen from a well-to-do Jewish family in Asia Minor. Aided by his ability to speak Greek, Paul traveled throughout the eastern Mediterranean as far as Rome itself to preach the Christian gospel (the word comes from the Old English meaning "good news") to Jews and non-Jews alike.

The Roman authorities distrusted the early Christians because they refused to submit to the official state religion and to make sacrifices to the Roman gods. In A.D. 64 the Emperor Nero blamed Rome's Christians for starting a fire that destroyed much of the city. Many Christians were rounded up and executed in what would be the first of a series of mass persecutions of Christians carried out by the Roman authorities over the next 250 years. As a result, the early Christians lived and worshiped in secret, adopting clandestine emblems such as the sign of a fish to identify their places of worship to each other. These signs can still be seen carved on the walls of the catacombs, their underground cemeteries, in Rome.

Many Roman observers denounced Christians' desire to live by their own rules, apart from the rest of society. Because Christian rituals were secret, they aroused great suspicion. Some anti-Christian propagandists argued that consuming the symbolic flesh and blood of the Eucharist led Christians to commit real cannabalism, or that the injunction to love their brothers and sisters led them to commit incest. The writer Pliny reported the secret oaths of loyalty that Christians took to one another. He was surprised—and possibly somewhat disappointed—to learn that the oath was in fact not sinister at all: "To commit neither theft, robbery, nor adultery, nor to betray a trust, nor to refuse to return a deposit on demand."

The last great persecution of Christians in the Roman Empire took place under the Emperor Diocletian in 303. Shortly afterward Constantine adopted a policy of toleration throughout the empire; he himself converted and became the first Christian emperor. From then on Christianity could be practiced openly, and the faith witnessed a period of rapid growth throughout Italy and the rest of the empire.

The base of this pewter bowl, used in Roman London, features a hidden Christian monogram. The "Chi-Rho" or Christogram symbol is made up of X and P, the first two Greek letters of the name of Christ.

St. Paul—seen here in a sixth-century mosaic from Ravenna, capital of the Byzantine province in Italy—was the most influential of the early Christian apostles.

PEOPLE & PLACES	DOCUMENTS, ART, & ARTIFACTS	WORSHIP & DOCTRINE

EUROPE

126 The rebuilt Pantheon in Rome is completed by the Emperor Hadrian: the temple still stands today.

ca 140 Death of Juvenal, the great Roman writer who satirized the immorality of the empire.

ca 140 In Rome the former slave Hermas begins to write *The Shepherd*, a collection of Christian parables, commandments, and visions which was considered part of holy scripture by early Christians.

ca 100 Despite imperial efforts to suppress them, eastern cults such as those of Mithras and Isis become popular in Rome.

ca 130 After the death of his favorite lover Antinonus, Hadrian deifies the young man, whose worship continues in parts of the empire for well over a hundred years.

THE AMERICAS

The ceremonial city of Teotihuacan—"City of the Gods"—in central Mexico had been deserted for nearly 700 years when the Aztec discovered it. They named its main avenue the Street of the Dead and its major monuments the pyramids of the sun and the moon. Excavations in the Pyramid of the Moon have discovered the remains of extensive animal and human sacrifice during its construction.

ASIA & OCEANIA

ca 147 The Parthian monk An Shigo arrives in Luoyang, one of China's ancient capitals, and begins translating Buddhist texts from Sanskrit into Chinese, helping establish the faith in China.

ca 100 Buddhism arrives in China (📄 pages 42–43).

ca 100 Theravada Buddhism has by now become established in southern Burma.

AFRICA & THE MIDDLE EAST

WORDS OF DEVOTION

The Mishnah

Judaism was traditionally an oral faith until the end of the Jewish republic in A.D. 70, and the Jewish Revolt of the second century, made Jewish teachers (rabbis) realize that the Temple might not always be able to act as a repository of knowledge. That would leave them unable to depend on oral tradition to preserve laws passed down by scholars interpreting the Torah. In the Jewish faith, oral tradition is equally important in terms of scripture as the written texts. Rabbis began to write down their debates and judgments in a collection that became known as the Mishnah. The collection was eventually redacted—edited and organized—by Judah ha-Nasi in about 220.

ca 135 In the aftermath of the Jewish Revolt in Judea, scholars known as rabbis become important as they begin gathering and codifying traditional oral law in the Misnah.

144 Marcion of Sinope is excommunicated for heresy for rejecting the Old Testament.

RELIGION IN THE WORLD	WORLD EVENTS

177 As part of a program of persecution under the Emperor Marcus Aurelius, Christians are publicly tortured before being put to death in Lyons, France.

ca 100 In his history of Rome, the historian Tacitus criticizes the emperors who have followed Augustus.

117 The Roman Empire reaches its greatest extent under the Emperor Trajan.

133 Hadrian's Wall is completed across northern England.

ca 100 In Peru, Moche craftsmen produce ornate pottery vessels and gold jewelry.

ca 100 In eastern North America evidence of the Adena culture slowly disappears.

ca 100 Early Anasazi settle in the Four Corners region of the American Southwest.

In the beginning was the Word, and the Word was with God, and the Word was God.

GOSPEL ACCORDING TO ST. JOHN 1.1

ca 127 The Buddhist convert Kanishka becomes king of the Kushans, who will control the Silk Road of Central Asia; Kanishka's influence helps spread Buddhism west and north from India through Central Asia.

This sixth-century Greek manuscript is a page of the Gospel According to Matthew.

111 Pliny the Younger, Roman governor of Nithynia in Asia Minor, writes to the Emperor Trajan for advice on how to deal with the growing numbers of Christians.

115 Jews in Cyprus, Egypt, Libya, and Mesopotamia begin an unsuccessful revolt against Roman rule.

132 Jewish leader Simeon bar Kochba inspires a four-year revolt against Roman rule in Judea that leads to the expulsion of the Jews from Palestine.

THE GOSPELS

The Gospels is the name given to the four accounts of Jesus' life, death, and resurrection that form the core of the biblical New Testament. They purport to have been written by his disciples, although evidence suggests that at least one was not written down until a considerable time after Christ's death.

The Gospels (from the Old English *godspell*, or "good news") were written in Greek and later translated into Syriac and Latin. They were an important part of spreading the teachings of Christ following Pentecost, when the Holy Spirit entered the disciples.

For Christians, the gospels according to the four evangelists—Matthew, Mark, Luke, and John—are synonymous with the teaching of Jesus himself. They can be seen as versions of the same events that explain how salvation was accomplished through the death and resurrection of Jesus.

Since about 1780, scholars have grouped the first three gospels as the Synoptic Gospels. The stories they recount and the order in which they are told are so similar that it is possible to read the three as parallel texts.

The fourth gospel, John, is different. It includes only certain episodes from Christ's life and ministry. It is more spiritual than the others, and deals with more abstract aspects of Christian doctrine. Because it is less immediate and its theology is more sophisticated than the other gospels, biblical scholars that it may have been written not by John himself but by someone who had learned about Jesus from him.

PEOPLE & PLACES	DOCUMENTS, ART, & ARTIFACTS	WORSHIP & DOCTRINE

EUROPE

ca 197 The early Christian theologian Tertullian converts from paganism and writes his *Apology*, arguing that Christians can be trusted as citizens of the empire.

ca 180 The philosopher-emperor Marcus Aurelius completes his *Meditations*, a compilation of his Stoic philosophy.

ca 190 One of the earliest surviving examples of Christian art—a fresco showing an early mass—is painted in the Catacomb of St. Priscilla in Rome.

ca 155 The Greek philosopher and theologian Justin Martyr reconciles Christian teaching with the philosophy of the ancient Greek, Plato, rejecting Greek mythology.

THE AMERICAS

This 16th-century woodcut shows the ancient Egyptian philosopher Ptolemy with Urania, the Greek muse of astronomy.

ASIA & OCEANIA

178 The Kushan monk Lokaksema settles in Luoyang and begins to translate Mahayana Buddhist texts into Chinese.

ca 150 The Vimalakirti Sutra, one of the canonical scriptures of Buddhism, is composed.

ca 150 The first known inscriptions in Sanskrit, the Hindu holy language, appear in India.

ca 175 In the Han capital Luoyang, extracts from the teachings of Confucius are carved on stone pillars, or stelae, at the Imperial Academy.

AFRICA & THE MIDDLE EAST

ca 156 Montanus begins to prophesy in Asia Minor; he is condemned as a heretic by the Church.

168 Death of Egyptian astronomer and geographer Claudius Ptolemy, whose view that the Earth is at the center of the universe influences later Christian orthodoxy.

ca 178 Irenaeus becomes bishop of Lyons, a position he holds until about 200; he is a prominent opponent of gnosticism (📄 page 61).

ca 150 The rise of gnosticism leads early Christians to push for the canonization of the scriptures.

ca 185 Led by Irenaeus, the New Testament is canonized; the rule of faith, a new Christian creed, is promulgated.

RELIGION IN THE WORLD	WORLD EVENTS

161 The Stoic philosopher Marcus Aurelius becomes emperor of Rome: he is almost constantly at war.

180 A 15-year smallpox epidemic ravages the Roman Empire.

192 The Roman emperor Commodus is strangled to death by an athlete named Narcissus.

197 Roman generals clash after Clodius Albinus is declared emperor by his troops in Britain; he is defeated by Septimius Severus. who reunites the empire.

To put the world right in order, we must first put the nation in order; To put the nation in order, we must first put the family in order; To put the family in order, we must first cultivate our personal life; We must first set our hearts right.

CONFUCIUS

ca 150 Tikal becomes the major ceremonial center in the Mayan lowlands.

166 A mission from Rome reaches China by ship.

184 Chinese peasants known as the Yellow Hats rebel against the Han dynasty, which they denounce as corrupt.

189 General Dong Zhou seizes control of the Han Empire, which has been weakened by the Yellow Hat rebellion.

Ptolemy's view of the universe, which placed Earth at the heart of the solar system, shaped Christian orthodoxy until the late Middle Ages.

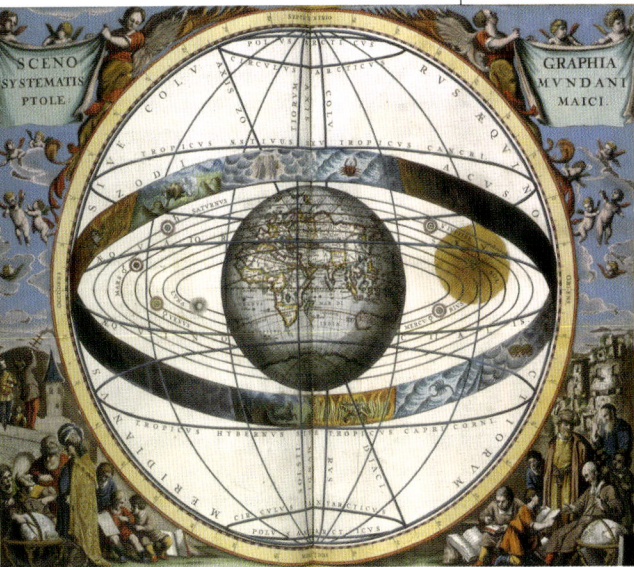

151 The Egyptian geographer Claudius Ptolemy writes a description of the Roman world, from Iceland to what is now Sri Lanka.

197 The Romans sack the Parthian capital Ctesiphon (in modern-day Iraq).

198 Northern Mesopotamia becomes a province of the Roman Empire.

ROMAN RELIGION

The early Romans believed that gods, goddesses, and spirits were everywhere and controlled human actions. Gods and spirits might be friendly if prayers or sacrifices were offered to them. In time, the Romans adopted gods and goddesses from other peoples, particularly the Etruscans and the Greeks. The Romans saw these deities as resembling humans: each had his or her own responsibility.

The king and queen of the Roman deities were Jupiter (the sky god) and Juno (the patron goddess of all women). Somewhat less important were Minerva (wisdom, crafts, and industries), Venus (beauty and love), Mars (war), Vulcan (fire), Vesta (hearth and home), Mercury (merchants), and Janus (the two-headed god of doorways). There were many other lesser gods: every home had its own *lares*, or household spirits. When Rome became an empire, emperors were also considered to be divine; some emperors were worshiped as gods even while they were still alive.

Roman worship took the form of processions, sacrifices, and offerings at an altar. Fine temples were built in towns and cities for the gods considered special by the townspeople. In Rome, the Emperor Hadrian completed a large temple called the Pantheon, which was dedicated to all of the gods. Altars inside the home were used to make sacrifices to the household *lares*.

The Romans were happy to adopt deities from subject peoples of the empire, such as the Egyptian goddess Isis and the Persian god Mithras. But they were also ruthless in suppressing faiths that might threaten the empire's stability. In Jerusalem, they destroyed the Temple during the Jewish Revolt of A.D. 66–70. In northern Europe, they hunted down the druid priests of the Celts. They also persecuted members of the fast-growing Christian religion, who refused to worship the emperor. After the conversion of the Emperor Constantine in 313, Christianity was tolerated in the empire and spread rapidly. It became the official religion in 380.

PEOPLE & PLACES	DOCUMENTS, ART, & ARTIFACTS	WORSHIP & DOCTRINE

EUROPE

ca 212 Caracalla murders his brother and co-emperor Geta saying, "Let him be a god, as long as he is not alive."

218 Elagobalus, a former boy-priest of the cult of Emesa, becomes emperor and introduces the cult to Rome.

236 Author Hippolytus of Rome is martyred during a persecution of Christians; he is said to have been dragged to death by horses, of which he becomes the patron saint.

244 The philosopher Plotinus settles in Rome, where he writes the *Enneads*, a key work of Neoplatonism, a philosophy based on the work of Plato that greatly influenced early Christian thinkers.

202 Hippolytus of Rome, one of the most prolific early Christian commentators, writes *On Christ and Antichrist*; his teachings bring him into conflict with the early popes.

ca 200 The bishop of Rome gains his prominent position in the Catholic Church as pope.

FAITH AND LIFE

Perpetua and Felicitas

The Roman Perpetua, a new mother, and her pregnant slave, Felicitas, were Christians arrested in Carthage, North Africa, and sentenced to die by being torn apart by animals. Perpetua left a moving account of her time in jail, including her sorrow at leaving her baby son, her vision of a ladder to heaven, and her willingness to die. The pair were among the most famous Roman Christian martyrs.

THE AMERICAS

ca 200 In northern Peru the Moche build gigantic platforms of mud bricks to stage religious rituals.

ca 200 The Temple of the Feathered Serpent, Quetzalcoatl, is constructed in the ceremonial city of Teotihuacan in Mexico.

ASIA & OCEANIA

ca 200 The first carvings are made on the Amaravati Stupa in Madras, India.

223 The sutras of Pure Land Buddhism are translated into Chinese.

ca 226 In Persia, Zoroastrian priests called magi begin to compile the Avesta, a written collection of their remaining scriptures.

ca 200 In India, a century-long process begins of codifying Hindu laws.

ca 220 Confucianism loses its influence in China after the end of the Han dynasty, which had made it the state ideology (📄 pages 24–25).

AFRICA & THE MIDDLE EAST

202 Origen escapes a persecution of Christians in Alexandria in which his father is killed; legend has it that his son also wanted to become a martyr but was prevented when his mother hid his clothes so that he could not leave the house. Origen later becomes a leading Church Father.

203 During a persecution in Carthage, the Roman Christian Perpetua is martyred with her pregnant slave Felicitas; Perpetua's own account of preparing for her martyrdom helps win many converts to Christianity.

ca 230 A Christian missionary known as Gregory the Wonderworker makes many converts in Anatolia.

ca 200 The Mishnah, collected oral laws that become part of the Talmud, is compiled.

ca 240 Origen completes his influential translation of the *Hexapla*, which brings together various versions of the Old Testament, including versions in Hebrew and Greek.

ca 240 Mani begins preaching a form of dualism in Mesopotamia; it blends elements of Zoroastrianism, Christianity, and Buddhism (📄 facing page).

RELIGION IN THE WORLD

This elaborate illumination comes from a 14th-century German manuscript copy of Asher ben Jehiel's commentary on the Mishnah, which appeared in about 200.

ca 200 Romans captured by Sassanid Persians begin Christian communities in what is now Iran.

226 Zoroastrianism becomes the state religion of Persia under the first Sassanid king, Ardashir I.

ca 230 A Chinese account describes Japanese society and religion being controlled by a female ruler named Himiko, "sun princess," suggesting that early Japan may have been a matriarchal society.

ca 200 The use of the Mishnah encourages the Neo-Hebrew language, rather than the "classical" Hebrew of the Old Testament.

219 With the establishment of the first Jewish academy at Sura, Babylonia becomes the focus of Jewish life.

248 Anti-Christian rioting breaks out in Alexandria, Egypt.

WORLD EVENTS

212 In an attempt to raise more taxes, the Romans extend citizenship to everyone who lives within the empire.

ca 200 The Moche of northern Peru are at their most influential.

ca 200 The Hohokam of Arizona use irrigation and other techniques to grow crops.

ca 200 Californian coastal communities live off fish and shellfish from the Pacific and become part of an extensive trade network for seashells.

ca 213 On the death of the Emperor Vasudeva, the Kushan Empire is divided into eastern and western parts.

220 When the last Han emperor is deposed, the Chinese empire divides into three separate kingdoms.

225 The Andhra Empire of southern India breaks up after 300 years.

240 Shapur I, son of Ardashir, becomes Sassanid emperor.

224 Ardashir I, from Persia, overthrows the Parthians and founds the Sassanid Empire.

SHAPING CHRISTIAN THOUGHT

The early history of Christianity was influenced by a number of different currents. One was gnosticism, a spiritual approach that emerged in the second century A.D. (its name dates only from the 17th century and derives from the Greek adjective meaning "leading to knowledge").

Gnosticism, attacked by some of the early Christian hierarchy as heresy, stressed an awareness of divine mysteries. It distinguished between the creator of the world—known as Demiurge—and a more transcendent god. Gnostics aimed to return to their spiritual origins through revelation that would open knowledge (*gnosis*) of their divine identity. Humans might get a glimpse of this divine reality, but they are sleepwalking until they are awakened by the revelation of perfect knowledge. In contrast, Christians believe that redemption is only possible through the death and resurrection of Jesus Christ.

Another influence on Christian theology was Manichaeanism, a religion founded by the Parthian prophet Mani in the early third century A.D. in Mesopotamia. The faith thrived until the seventh century; at one point it was practiced as far apart as China and the Roman Empire. The religion disappeared after the 14th century.

Manichaeanism was based on dualism, or the doctrine of opposing principles: light and darkness, good and evil. Light was good and associated with god, while dark was evil and associated with matter. Christianity also proposes a dualistic view of good and evil, but because Christians believe that God is the only creator, they face a dilemma of how to explain the origins of evil.

Manichaeanism mixed religion with science to explain the universe. It advocated reason over faith as a means of redemption. Knowledge—an understanding of the self combined with knowledge of an abstract God—mattered more than faith and dogma.

Bring brightness to our soul.

Encourage us in efforts to live righteously.

Help us live in harmony, with respect and service to others

and anything in the world and Mother Earth.

PRAYER LEFT AT A SHINTO TEMPLE

SHINTO IN JAPAN

ALONG WITH BUDDHISM, SHINTOISM IS JAPAN'S MAJOR religion, although in many ways it is better understood as a set of guidelines for living. Unlike other religions, for example, it has no founder and no scriptures. Its origins date back to the arrival of Buddhism in Japan in A.D. 538, when followers of indigenous nature and fertility religions set about formalizing their belief system to distinguish it from the new faith. *Shinto*, which means "way of the kami," was the name used to distinguish the older beliefs.

At the heart of Shinto are *kami*, sacred spirits that exist in everything, which were originally revered as deities. Later, the *kami* came to be seen as abstract "spirituality" embodied in forms such as the wind, rain, trees, rivers, and mountains. People also become *kami* after they die, so ancestor worship is a significant factor of Shinto. Being able to make offerings to the *kami* at a shrine or temple—or a stream or mountain—is a fundamental part of Japanese life.

The most important *kami* is Amaterasu, the sun goddess, who gives sacred authority to the emperors. According to Japanese tradition, Amaterasu sent her grandson, Ninigi, to drive out chaos and confusion from Japan. Ninigi was the first emperor, from whom the imperial line is descended. The Japanese people revere their emperor as the earthly representative of the heavenly *kami*. As Japan's political power became more centralized, Shinto emerged as a national cult as well as a religion. By the start of the tenth century, Shinto supported around 3,000 shrines for state offerings.

As Buddhism developed in Japan, it was bound increasingly closely with Shinto. By the eighth century, the two were sufficiently merged so that Shinto and Buddhist shrines existed side by side, or within one another's temple precincts.

From the Kamakura period in the 12th century, the close bond between the two religions was formalized with the emergence of syncretic schools. The most important were the Ryobu Shinto and the Sanno Shinto schools. Buddhist Shinto continued to be popular for the next few centuries, until it was stopped during the Meiji Restoration of 1868 and the emergence of state Shinto.

For a thousand years before about 300 B.C. Japan's Neolithic Jomon people molded clay Dogu figures to represent the spirits who were later incorporated into Shintoism. The figures may have been used in healing rituals.

This Shinto high priest was photographed in the 1890s. By then, the government had ordered the separation of Shinto from Buddhism, with the aim of using Shinto to promote Japanese nationalism.

PEOPLE & PLACES	DOCUMENTS, ART, & ARTIFACTS	WORSHIP & DOCTRINE

EUROPE

250 Fabian, bishop of Rome, is executed during a persecution of Christians launched by the Emperor Decius.

270 Death of Plotinus, founder of Neoplatonism.

ca 250 Some of the first depictions of Christian angels are in frescoes in the Catacomb of St. Priscilla in Rome; these early angels do not have wings, probably so that they will not be confused with depictions of winged figures from earlier myths.

ca 250 Christians begin to revere martyrs as saints.

274 The Emperor Aurelian reintroduces paganism to Rome, where he builds a temple to Helios, the sun god.

275 The missionary Denis, said to be the first bishop of Paris, introduces Christianity to Gaul; he later becomes the patron saint of France.

ca 280 The missionary Gregory the Illuminator converts King Tiridates of Armenia to Christianity.

THE AMERICAS

The frescoes that decorate the walls of the synagogue of Dura-Europos in Syria portray narrative scenes from the Hebrew Bible, probably intended to educate an illiterate congregation. The building dates from about A.D. 244, making it one of the earliest synagogues known.

ASIA & OCEANIA

269 An Indian scholar adapts Greek texts to write a manual on astrology—the influence of the movements of heavenly bodies on events on earth.

296 Date of the earliest surviving Chinese Buddhist scripture (*Zhu Fo Yao Ji Jing*).

ca 260 Chinese Buddhists begin making pilgrimages to the sites of Buddha's life in India.

AFRICA & THE MIDDLE EAST

258 Cyprian of Carthage is beheaded by the Romans; he greets his death sentence with the words "Thanks be to God."

268 Bishop Paul of Antioch is deposed for heresy.

276 Mani, founder of Manichaeanism, is executed for heresy by Christians in Persia (📄 page 61).

ca 250 Wall paintings illustrating stories from the Bible are created to decorate the interior of a synagogue at Dura-Europos in present-day Syria.

256 Bishop Cyprian of Carthage organizes a Christian council at Carthage.

286 Anthony of Egypt, a Christian monk, begins 20 years living alone in the desert in an attempt to find spiritual communion with God; he is seen as the founder of Christian monasticism (📄 facing page).

RELIGION IN THE WORLD	WORLD EVENTS

Forsaking the uproars of life
O venerable one,
You completed your life in
quiet, imitating the Baptist.
Therefore, we honor you
with him, O Anthony,
Father of Fathers.

GREEK ORTHODOX HYMN

260 The Roman Emperor Valerian is defeated by the Persians at Edessa in eastern Turkey.

267 The Germanic Goths, from the region of the Black Sea, make one of several incursions into Roman territory, raiding centers in Greece.

285 The Roman Empire is divided into western and eastern halves for administrative purposes.

ca 250 The beginning of the Classic period of Mayan history on the Yucatán Peninsula is characterized by the worship of divine kings ruling over their own city-states (pages 74–75).

ca 250 In southwestern North America the Mogollon use irrigation to grow corn and other crops.

ca 273 Zoroastrian high priest Kartir calls for the suppression of Manichaeanism and Buddhism in Iran.

256 After an epidemic kills many citizens of Alexandria in Egypt, many survivors convert to Christianity.

Spanish artist Diego Velázquez painted St. Anthony visiting his teacher, St. Paul the Hermit, in about 1642.

ST. ANTHONY AND THE FIRST HERMITS

Born in about A.D. 251, Anthony was an Egyptian disciple of Paul of Thebes, who was said to have lived as a hermit in the desert for nearly 100 years. Anthony followed Paul's example, but gained a reputation as the founder of monasticism. He is known as Anthony the Great.

At age 20, Anthony gave away his possessions and withdrew from daily life to live as a hermit. The term described Christians who led solitary and ascetic lives, based on the biblical account of the 40 days and nights Jesus spent wandering in the desert without food. A number of Christians—often known collectively as the Desert Fathers—chose to live such eremitic lives, believing that they would discover true faith in suffering, stoicism, and prayer.

Anthony soon became renowned for the extreme hardships to which he subjected himself. He lived in solitude for decades, first in the Western Desert and later in an abandoned Roman fort on a mountain by the River Nile. According to Athanasius of Alexandria, who wrote *The Life of Saint Anthony*, the saint used prayer to fight off attacks by the devil, including boredom, loneliness, and wild animals. Images of Anthony praying were a staple of Christian art through the Middle Ages and into the Renaissance.

In about 311 Anthony moved to the Eastern Desert with his followers, who were attracted by the renowned asceticism of his lifestyle. There he laid down the first monastic rule, urging his followers to perform manual work. The rule became the basis for the Western monastic tradition.

PEOPLE & PLACES	DOCUMENTS, ART, & ARTIFACTS	WORSHIP & DOCTRINE

EUROPE

304 The actor Genesius is converted to Christianity while appearing before the Emperor Diocletian in a play mocking Christians; he experiences a vision of angels during the performance. When the actor's new faith becomes apparent, he is beheaded on stage on Diocletian's orders.

310 While visiting a shrine to Apollo, the Roman general Constantine has a vision urging him to adopt Christianity (📄 pages 68–69).

326 Acilius Severus becomes the first Christian prefect of Rome.

330 The first Church of St. Peter's is erected in Rome; it is pulled down to make room for a new church in 1506.

315 The Arch of Constantine is built in Rome to mark the emperor's military victories.

ca 300 In Germany, monks play bowls as part of their religious activities.

313 The eastern emperors Constantine and Licinius issue the Edict of Milan, confirming toleration in the empire for Christianity and other religions.

ca 313 Constantine I begins a program of church building in Rome, including the Basilica of St. Peter and St. Paul.

THE AMERICAS

ca 300 The Hohokam culture, which has emerged in southwestern North America, builds temple mounds similar to those built in Mexico.

Emperor Constantine burns books promoting Arianism at the First Council of Nicaea in this medieval drawing from northern Italy.

ASIA & OCEANIA

310 The Buddhist monk Fotudeng arrives in the Chinese city of Chang'an.

344 Birth of the great translator of Buddhist scripture Kumarajiva.

347 Tao-an records the first translation of Buddhist texts into Chinese.

The "kofun" of Emperor Nintoku, said to have ruled between 313 and 399, is the largest tomb in Japan. The imperial tombs are characterized by their keyhole-shaped islands surrounded by moats.

ca 300 In Japan a tomb culture flourishes in which the Yamato emperors are buried with clay statues in elaborate sepulchers on keyhole-shaped islands.

AFRICA & THE MIDDLE EAST

ca 315 Eusebius becomes the bishop of Caesarea in Palestine.

326 Constantine's mother Helena makes a pilgrimage to the Holy Land, building churches to mark significant locations in Jesus' life.

ca 326 While building the Church of the Holy Sepulcher on the traditional site of Christ's burial in Jerusalem, St. Helena discovers the True Cross on which he was crucified.

337 Emperor Constantine is baptized on his deathbed.

347 Donatus of Carthage is sent into exile in Gaul as a punishment for preaching his Donatist heresy.

ca 311 Donatus, archbishop of Casae Nigra and later of Carthage, causes a schism in the African church with his teaching that only people without sin belong in the church.

325 The Council of Nicaea, held in present-day Turkey, condemns Arianism and declares that Christ is "one in essence with the Father."

ca 330 In the Egyptian desert, Macarius of Egypt founds a monastery at Wadi-el-Natrun.

331 Ezana, king of Axum in Ethiopia, is converted to Christianity by the Syrian monk Frumentius.

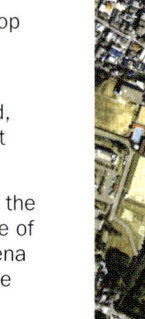

RELIGION IN THE WORLD	WORLD EVENTS
ca 300 The first religious plays are performed.	**306** The Roman army in Britain proclaims Constantine emperor in the west.
ca 303 Armenia becomes the first country in the world to adopt Christianity as an official religion.	**324** The defeat and execution of Licinius, the emperor in the east, leaves Constantine in sole command of the Roman Empire.
303 Roman Emperor Diocletian begins the most intense period of imperial persecution of Christians when he issues four edicts of nontoleration.	
312 Marching under a Christian symbol, Roman general Constantine I defeats the Romans at the Battle of Milvian Bridge and usurps the last pagan emperor, Maxentius.	
	ca 300 A new urban center emerges at Tiahuanaco, on the southern shores of Lake Titicaca in the highlands of what is now the Peru-Bolivia border.
	ca 300 The Maya develop a system of writing, a calendar based on astronomical observation, and a system of mathematics that includes the number 0.
ca 320 Political instability and Hun invasions fragment China, allowing Buddhism to become stronger and attract more followers (two million Buddhists live in 30,000 monasteries by about 400).	**ca 300** The Yamato kings extend their power throughout Honshu in Japan.
	ca 300 China fragments into a mosaic of warring states.
	320 Chandragupta becomes the first emperor of the Hindu Gupta empire of northern India.
	348 The Persians defeat the Romans at Singara, but fail to drive them from Mesopotamia (Iraq).
ca 300 Christian communities are established throughout the Middle East and North Africa.	
325 Emperor Constantine makes Christianity the state faith throughout the Roman Empire.	
330 Constantine I creates a new capital at the ancient Greek city of Byzantium, which he names Constantinople (now Istanbul in modern-day Turkey); he excludes pagan rites from the consecration ceremonies.	

AUGUSTINE OF HIPPO

St. Augustine, Bishop of Hippo (354–430), was the most important early Christian thinker after St. Paul.

Born in present-day Algeria to a pagan father and Catholic mother, Augustine converted to Catholicism after a long struggle with his religious beliefs in 387. Augustine initially joined the Manichaeans, or followers of Mani. He was attracted by the way they used the Bible to support their teachings, as well as by their preoccupation with the question of good versus evil, the story of Adam and Eve, and the idea of original sin. The young man was also preoccupied with such ideas.

After Augustine left Africa in 384, he grew disillusioned with the Manichaeans. In Italy, he came under the influence of Bishop Ambrose of Milan and, after reading a life of St. Anthony the Great, he converted to Catholicism. When he became bishop of Hippo in 396, Augustine devoted his time to refuting Manichaeanism.

Among more than a hundred works—some five million words—Augustine is best known for *Confessions* (397). The book is a personal account of his early life, but many historians read it as a long prayer of penitence and thanksgiving for the grace of God as the saint experienced it in his early life.

THE CONVERSION OF CONSTANTINE

FEW EVENTS IN THE EARLY HISTORY OF CHRISTIANITY WERE as significant as the conversion of Constantine I (ca 280–337), the first Roman emperor to become a Christian. Constantine's conversion marked a key moment in Christianity's rise from a cult to bcome the dominant faith of Western Europe.

Constantine attributed his emperorship to his faith. A successful general and son of the former emperor Constantius, in 312 he led his forces to claim the throne. At the Milvian Bridge over the Tiber River at Rome, legend recounts that Constantine had a vision. In one version, he saw in the sky the image of a cross of light and the words "In hoc signo vinces" ("In this sign, conquer"). In another, Constantine's dream told him to paint the shields of his men with the Christian Chi-Rho symbol. Either way, Constantine took his victory in the battle that followed to be a sign from Christ and converted to Christianity.

In 313 Constantine and Licinius, the emperor in the east (who had married Constantine's daughter), issued the Edict of Milan. It granted tolerance of Christians throughout the empire. Constantine went further, giving land to churches and granting churches special privileges. After Constantine overthrew Licinius to become sole emperor of both western and eastern empires, he moved his capital from Rome to Byzantium (present-day Istanbul); the city was renamed Constantinople in 324. Constantine's refusal to take part in pagan rituals once he was a Christian angered the Romans, many of whom practiced Christianity alongside other beliefs, and he never returned to Rome again.

Under Constantine's patronage, Christianity spread throughout the empire. He commissioned new copies of the Bible for his congregation in Constantinople and built new churches including the Hagia Sophia (originally known as the Church of Holy Wisdom) as well as the first St. Peter's Basilica in Rome.

Constantine's mother, the former concubine Helena, converted to Christianity under his influence. Encouraged by her son, Helena made a pilgrimage to the Holy Land to visit Christian sites and found churches and charitable institutions. In Jerusalem she built churches on the sites of the Nativity and the Crucifixion. Rumors circulated in the city that the remains of Christ's cross had been found during the construction of Constantine's church of the Holy Sepulcher at Golgotha. The legend grew that Helena had personally found the cross. Her devotion led to her becoming a saint.

This fresco from the fourth-century Church of Santi Quattro Coronati in Rome shows St. Helena discovering the three crosses of Calvary on her visit to Jerusalem; the True Cross was revealed when it cured a sick man upon whom it was laid.

350–399

CONCISE HISTORY OF WORLD RELIGIONS

PEOPLE & PLACES	DOCUMENTS, ART, & ARTIFACTS	WORSHIP & DOCTRINE

EUROPE

358 In Rome, the Virgin Mary appears to the emperor and the pope in a dream to inspire the building of a new basilica; a miraculous fall of snow on the Equiline Hill confirms the location and allows the pope to outline the shape of the building, the Basilica di Santa Maria Maggiore.

364 Basil becomes bishop of Caesarea.

374 Ambrose becomes bishop of Milan.

384 The death of the senator Praetextatus illustrates the cosmopolitan nature of religion in Rome; the senator holds priesthoods in six oriental mystical religions and four state religions.

ca 350 The Schola Cantorum is founded in Rome to teach ecclesiastical chanting for church services.

382 Pope Damasus holds a church council and issues a list of the canonical books of the Old and New Testaments.

ca 386 Bishop Ambrose of Milan introduces hymns to church services.

ca 390 The Laws of Theodosius forbid sacrifice in the Roman empire.

THE AMERICAS

A marble relief from about 390 shows the Emperor Theodosius presiding over horse races in the Hippodrome in Constantinople. Theodosius forbade paganism in the Roman Empire in 391.

ASIA & OCEANIA

ca 350 Dunhuang, an oasis on the Silk Road on the edge of the Gobi Desert, becomes an important center of Buddhist scholarship (📖 facing page).

ca 360 An important Buddhist monastery is founded at Nalanda in the Ganges Valley; its reputation attracts many pilgrims and students.

399 The Chinese Buddhist monk Faxian begins a 16-year journey by foot along the Silk Road from China to India and back.

ca 366 The Chinese monk Lo-zun is inspired by a vision to excavate the Caves of a Thousand Buddhas near Dunhuang as a repository for Buddhist statues.

372 Buddhism is introduced to the Korean peninsula.

AFRICA & THE MIDDLE EAST

386 John Chrysostom ("Golden-mouth") begins preaching at Antioch.

386 Having translated most of the Bible into Latin, St. Jerome enters a monastery in Bethlehem, where he spends his last years.

391 Blessed Macarius, an ascetic monk, dies after living for some 60 years in the Egyptian desert.

398 John Chrysostom becomes bishop of Constantinople.

372 King Ezana of Auxum builds the Orthodox Christian church of St. Mary of Zion, probably the first Christian church in sub-Saharan Africa.

374 After the First Council of Constantinople, the see of Constantinople is given "seniority of honor" after the see of Rome.

396 St. Augustine becomes bishop of Hippo (📖 page 67).

RELIGION IN THE WORLD

361 Julian the Apostate becomes sole emperor of Rome and attempts to revive paganism in the empire.

ca 365 The former Roman soldier Martin of Tours founds the first monastery in Gaul to spread Christianity in rural areas.

390 Bishop Ambrose of Milan excommunicates the Emperor Theodosius I after he orders the massacre of some 7,000 citizens of Thessalonika after a revolt.

391 Theodosius officially ends paganism within the Roman Empire.

WORLD EVENTS

ca 372 The nomadic Huns from Central Asia conquer the Ostrogoths of the Black Sea region.

395 The Roman Empire is permanently divided into western and eastern halves after the death of Theodosius.

395 The empire in the west is controlled by Stilicho, a general of barbarian origins who is guardian to the Emperor Honorius.

396 Alaric leads the Visigoths on raids through the Balkans and Greece.

BUDDHISM AND THE SILK ROAD

In its Indian homeland, Buddhism was particularly popular among the merchants of the thriving cities. Such merchants were part of an extensive international trade network, and the Buddhist faith spread with goods along trade routes. Monasteries and shrines were built near the routes or close to trading cities.

The main means of transmission for Buddhism was the network known as the Silk Road, which extended from China across Central Asia to Europe, as well as into South and Southeast Asia. In

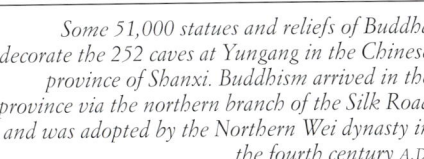

Some 51,000 statues and reliefs of Buddha decorate the 252 caves at Yungang in the Chinese province of Shanxi. Buddhism arrived in the province via the northern branch of the Silk Road and was adopted by the Northern Wei dynasty in the fourth century A.D.

ca 350 Christianity arrives in Ethiopia.

391 Christianity becomes the official religion of Egypt; many ancient temples are destroyed. In Alexandria, monks and priests incite a mob to destroy the Temple of Serapis.

ca 350 After being conquered by Axum, Nubia (modern Sudan) splits into three states: Nobatia, Makkura, and Alwa.

363 The Roman emperor Julian invades Persia but is killed in battle.

ca 370 Huns begin moving westward from the borders of China, clashing with Ostrogoths on the Russian steppes.

378 The forces of Roman Emperor Valens are defeated by an army of Goths and Visigoths at Adrianople, in what is now Turkey.

the third century B.C. Buddhism spread from India to the kingdoms of Central Asia under the patronage of the Mauryan king Ashoka. By the first century A.D. it was established in the Central Asian Kushan Empire. Travelers crossing Kushan territory on their way to China took with them Buddhist beliefs.

The Chinese, meanwhile, were expanding into Asia. It was on the western edges of their empire that they first encountered Buddhism. The eastern end of the Silk Road in what is now Outer Mongolia, for example, was home from the fifth century A.D. to the renowned monastic cave complex of Dunhuang.

PEOPLE & PLACES	DOCUMENTS, ART, & ARTIFACTS	WORSHIP & DOCTRINE

EUROPE

401 Innocent I becomes pope.

432 Sent as a missionary from Britain, Saint Patrick sets up a diocese at Armagh in Ireland and begins to make converts; legend has it that he banishes snakes from the island.

432 Sixtus III becomes pope; he is responsible for building the current basilica of Santa Maria Maggiore in Rome.

440 Leo I becomes pope.

443 Unfairly disgraced following rumors of an affair, Eudocia, wife of the Roman emperor Theodosius II, moves to Jerusalem, where she becomes a benefactor of Christian foundations and a noted poet.

405 St. Jerome completes the first Latin translation of the Bible.

ca 410 After the sack of Rome by the Visigoths, St. Augustine writes his influential work *City of God*.

446 The Mausoleum of Galla Placidia, built in Ravenna for the widow of the Emperor Constantius III, is decorated with outstanding Byzantine mosaics.

Bretheren, let the birth of our Savior Jesus Christ be honored in silence, because the Word of God was conceived in the Holy Virgin by hearing alone. Amen.

CYRUS OF PANOPOLIS, SERMON, 443

THE AMERICAS

ca 400 The mound-building Hopewell culture of eastern North America dissipates and goes into decline.

The Amberd Church on Mount Aragats, Armenia, was built in the 12th century. The Armenian Church had begun to split from the Orthodox Church in the late fourth century.

ASIA & OCEANIA

403 Chinese monk Hui Yuan, later recognized as the first patriarch of the Pure Land School of Buddhism, argues that monks should not have to bow to the emperor.

414 The Chinese Buddhist monk Faxian returns from India with Sanskrit texts that will form the basis of Chinese Buddhism; he also writes a *Treatise on Buddhist Kingdoms*.

ca 400 In Chang'an the Indian monk Kumarajiva oversees the translation of Buddhist texts into Chinese at the invitation of Emperor Yao Xing.

ca 400 The *Bhagavad Gita*, a commentary on Hindu values, reaches its final form after various revisions in previous centuries.

ca 400 Under Gupta patronage, Hinduism experiences a revival in India and there is a flowering of classical Sanskrit literature.

ca 400 Indian traders spread Hinduism to parts of Southeast Asia.

ca 400 There are about 2,000 Buddhist monasteries in southern China.

444 Taoism becomes the state ideology of the Northern Wei kingdom centered on Luoyang in China.

AFRICA & THE MIDDLE EAST

420 St. Simeon Stylites withdraws to a small platform on top of a pillar in Aleppo, Syria, to live a life of contemplation; he remains there for 39 years before his death in 459.

428 Nestorius becomes patriarch of Constantinople.

430 Saint Augustine dies during a Vandal siege of Hippo.

443 Having become dangerously popular in Constantinople, the Roman prefect Cyrus of Panopolis is exiled to Phrygia and appointed bishop of Cotyaeum.

ca 400 The Babylonian Talmud, a commentary on the Mishnah, is compiled under Rev Ashi.

ca 417 Orosius, a student of St. Augustine of Hippo, writes *Against the Pagans*, a Christian history of the world.

ca 425 The Palestinian Talmud is compiled.

416 Saint Augustine calls the Council of Carthage to denounce the heresy of Pelagius, a British monk who argues that it is possible to be without sin without the intercession of Jesus Christ.

428 Nestorius, bishop of Constantinople, causes a split in the church by emphasizing Christ's human nature over his divine nature; this Nestorian controversy causes deep divisions within the church.

431 At the first Council of Ephesus, Turkey, most of the 250 bishops present reject the Nestorian heresy. The Nestorian Church splits from the Orthodox Church.

431 The Council of Ephesus vindicates the title Theotokos ("Godbearer") for Mary.

RELIGION IN THE WORLD

406 At the request of the head of the Armenian Church, the theologian St. Mesrob Mashtots invents the first Armenian alphabet and translates the Bible and liturgy, widening the division between the Armenian and Orthodox churches.

438 Jews are legally forbidden to hold public office in the Roman Empire.

439 The Codex Theodosianus summarizes Roman law.

409 The Sassanian emperor Yazdigird issues an edict allowing Christians to worship in Persia; he later rescinds the order.

414 When Faxian visits Sumatra in Indonesia, he finds no evidence of Buddhism.

ca 425 Buddhism arrives in Sumatra, Indonesia.

431 Persia and India witness the arrival of Nestorian Christians fleeing persecution by the Orthodox Roman emperor Zeno.

415 The philosopher Hypatia of Alexandria is murdered by a mob, possibly on the orders of Cyril, archbishop of Alexandria, who resents her influence.

WORLD EVENTS

406 The Roman province of Gaul (France) is raided by Vandals and other Germanic peoples.

407 Barbarian incursions into the Roman empire are aided when the Rhine River, the imperial frontier, freezes and allows easy crossing.

407 The Roman garrison leaves Britain, which is no longer part of the empire.

410 Visigoths led by Alaric sack Rome.

WORDS OF DEVOTION
Cyrus of Panopolis

Cyrus of Panopolis had been the second-highest official in the Roman Empire, after the Emperor Theodosius himself. When Cyrus grew too popular in Constantinople, however, Theodosius II stripped him of all his positions in 441, accused him of paganism, and exiled him to Phrygia in Anatolia. Cyrus joined the clergy and in 443 Theodosius appointed him bishop of Cotyaeum—possibly because the citizens had murdered their four previous bishops. The first sermon the new bishop delivered (see facing page) is one of the shortest ever recorded. Cyrus survived his congregation but gave up the clergy after the death of Theodosius allowed him to reclaim his former fortune.

EGYPT'S COPTIC CHURCH

Egypt's Christian church takes its name from the Arabic *al-kibt*, meaning "Egyptian." The Copts trace their history to St. Mark, who is said to have founded the church in Alexandria. The Council of Nicaea in 325 gave the bishop of Alexandria authority over a large area. The Coptic hermit St. Anthony of Egypt, meanwhile, organized his followers into the first monastic community in the Christian world. In 541 the churches of Egypt, Syria, Armenia, Nubia, and Ethiopia split from the Eastern Orthodox Church in a doctrinal controversy.

As Egypt came under the rule of successive conquerors, including Persians, Arabs, and Seljuk Turks, the Copts experienced various levels of freedom and persecution. In 1301 the Mamluks finally ordered the closure of all Christian churches in Egypt. Many Copts converted to Islam and the Coptic language virtually disappeared, except in religious writings. By the end of the 15th century the Copts had been reduced to a small minority in Egypt, with communities in neighboring regions such as Ethiopia.

Coptic monks celebrate the Feast of the Epiphany at Lalibela, Ethiopia.

The Temple of the Inscriptions in Palenque, in what is now Mexico, held the tomb of the seventh-century Mayan ruler Pakal. Excavated only in 1952 deep within the temple, the king's sarcophagus was covered by a large stone lid carved with an image of Pakal descending into Xibalba, the Underworld.

RELIGION OF THE MAYA

The Maya, who in about 1000 B.C. spread from the highlands of Guatemala into the lowlands of the Yucatán Peninsula, soon began building monumental temple pyramids and forming city-states. Some elements of Maya culture, such as the sacred ball game or the use of a ritual calendar, were adopted from trading partners like the Olmec and Zapotec. So too was the picture script, or glyphs, which is our main source of information about the warring Mayan city-states.

Warfare was necessary to supply captives to serve as human sacrifices, who were offered to the gods on fixed dates in the calendar or to mark important events, such as royal funerals. Victims had their hearts cut out and put on display. Special temple complexes and pyramids were built to host the ceremonies, which were overseen by a corps of priests.

Mayan kings were intermediaries between the people and their warlike, aggressive gods. The rulers were expected to participate in painful rituals involving bloodletting. Typically, their tongues were pierced with cords barbed with thorns. They offered their blood to sustain the gods, who were thought in their turn to have undergone ritual sacrifices to sustain the human race.

The Maya kept track of their ritual year using a complex and highly accurate calendar based on precise astronomical observations. In later times they produced sacred books written on bark, illustrated with intricate paintings. These works, like their stone carvings, give a glimpse into a violent cosmos of powerful gods. Among other rituals was a sacred ball game, popular also among other Mesoamerican peoples, which involved teams using their hips and knees to try to pass a ball through stone rings set high up on the walls of the court. The game was not simply a test of strength and skill. Carvings around the walls of the Great Ballcourt at Chichén Itzá show members of the winning team sacrificing a defeated opponent by cutting off his head.

Warfare and famine brought about by overcultivation may have brought the end of the Maya. The lowland cities were deserted after A.D. 800. The highland settlements survived longer, but were eventually conquered by Spanish invaders in the 16th century.

In this carved lintel from about 725, the Mayan ruler Shield Jaguar holds a burning torch while his wife, Lady Xoc, makes a blood sacrifice by drawing a rope studded with thorns through her tongue.

PEOPLE & PLACES	DOCUMENTS, ART, & ARTIFACTS	WORSHIP & DOCTRINE

EUROPE

ca 460 Death of Saint Patrick, the "Apostle of Ireland."

469 Sidonius Apollinaris becomes bishop of Clermont in France.

476 The Neoplatonist philosopher Proclus becomes head of the Platonic Academy at Athens.

ca 480 Birth of Boethius in Rome; he will become one of the most influential Christian philosophers of the Middle Ages.

483 Construction begins of the basilica of San Stefano Rotonda in Rome.

ca 495 The *Gelasian Sacramentary*, the second-oldest Catholic liturgical book still existing, is compiled at the request of Pope Gelasius I, providing prayers, chants, and instructions for the celebration of Mass.

ca 450 The Roman Church adopts call-and-response chanting between the priest and the congregation.

491 The Armenian Church secedes from Rome and Byzantium.

499 The Synod of Rome determines procedures for the election of new popes.

THE AMERICAS

ca 450 The Moche of Peru complete an eighth stage of construction on the massive brick-built Pyramid of the Sun on Cerro Blanco near Trujillo.

455 The Maya found what will become a major city and ritual center at Chichén Itzá on the Yucatán Peninsula in Mexico.

The baptism of Clovis, which took place in 496, was painted nearly a thousand years later by the Franco-Flemish artist known as the Master of St. Giles.

ASIA & OCEANIA

457 In Nisibis, Persia, Metropolitan Barsumas founds a Nestorian school.

ca 470 Birth of Bodhidharma, an Indian monk later credited with introducing Zen Buddhism to China.

495 The Indian monk Buddhabhadra becomes the first abbot of the new Shaolin Buddhist temple in Henan, China.

495 Chinese Buddhists begin work carving a cave temple near Luoyang, new capital of the Northern Wei dynasty.

476 Cave temples are carved at Yun-gang in China; their statuary is among the outstanding examples of Buddhist art in China.

478 The first Shinto shrines appear in Japan.

ca 450 Nearly 90 percent of the population of northern China is Buddhist.

483 Nestorians flourish in Persia; they even send missionaries to introduce Christianity to China.

496 Mazdakism, an extreme form of Zoroastrianism preaching social equality, becomes popular in Iran.

AFRICA & THE MIDDLE EAST

459 The death of St. Simeon Stylites inspires a century of stylites living atop pillars throughout Syria and the Holy Land.

489 The Byzantine emperor Zeno builds the Chuch of St. Simeon Stylites around the saint's pillar in Syria.

ca 450 Followers of the Christian monks and nuns who live ascetic lives in Egypt and Syria record some of their words as the *Sayings of the Desert Fathers and Mothers*.

ca 490 The Latin poet Dracontius of Carthage writes his Christian masterpiece *De Laudibsu Dei*.

451 The Council of Chalcedon, the fourth great council of the early church, is held in Asia Minor; it rejects the idea that Jesus had only one nature (the monophysite heresy) and affirms that he was both fully human and fully divine at one and the same time.

451 Christians in Egypt and Syria reject the idea that Christ is one person "in two natures," leading to a split between the "oriental" Orthodox churches and the church in Constantinople.

484 The Pope excommunicates Patriarch Acacius of Constantinople, leading to the first schism between the Western and Eastern churches, which lasts until 519.

RELIGION IN THE WORLD	WORLD EVENTS
455 The Persians suppress Christianity in Armenia, which has become a province of the empire, and force Christians to convert to Zoroastrianism.	**ca 450** Angles and Saxons from northern Germany and Denmark begin to settle in eastern and southern England.
455 Pope Leo the Great negotiates peace with the Vandals who capture Rome.	**455** King Genseric leads a Vandal invasion of Italy from North Africa, capturing Rome.
496 Clovis, the king of the Franks, is baptized as a Catholic.	**476** Odoacer declares himself king of Italy, ending the Roman Empire in the west.
	486 Clovis, king of the Franks, begins to expand his kingdom to the south.
	ca 450 The city of Teotihuacan in central Mexico has a population of some 200,000.
	ca 490 In the plains of North America, people begin hunting using the atlatl, or spear-thrower.
	ca 490 Teotihuacan begins to decline, disrupting trade networks throughout the region.
485 Five monks from Gandhara, India, are reported to introduce Buddhism into a country named Fusang.	**ca 450** The Hephthalites (White Huns) begin a 50-year campaign against the Gupta Empire of India.
498 Kobad, the new ruler of Iran, is forced to abdicate the throne because of his support for the priest Mazdak, who preaches extreme views known as Mazdakism.	**477** A Chinese writer describes for the first time the use of stirrups to control horses.

Whoever strives toward God and really wants to become Christ's follower must follow Him, endeavoring to improve himself and become a new person, not retaining anything within oneself that is peculiar to the ancient person—for it is said: "If anyone is in Christ, he is a new creation."

BLESSED MACARIUS, DESERT FATHER

THE AJANTA CAVES

The sanctuaries and monasteries of Ajanta, cut into a semi-circular cliff in a narrow gorge northeast of modern Mumbai, are the finest examples of Buddhist rock-cut architecture in India. The first monks to use the site hollowed out caves in around the second century B.C., but most of the 30 caves that were eventually carved into the cliff were created and decorated between the fifth and sixth centuries A.D. Experts estimate that each cave would have taken some 30 years to cut and decorate. They range from modest cells where the monks could sleep to highly ornate temples, with elaborately carved columns, massive sculptures of the Buddha, and colorful murals of his life. The artists first outlined the wall paintings with charcoal, then filled in

the background, and finally painted the details. The caves were close to busy trade routes and attracted large numbers of pilgrims. In later centuries they fell into disuse and were overgrown and largely forgotten. They were rediscovered only in 1824 by a party of British Army officers hunting for tigers. Word of the beauty of their decorations soon spread around the world.

*African peoples traditionally wore masks—
this one was carved by the Igbo—during
ritual dances, such as those performed by the
Dogon at funerals to drive out the spirit of a
dead person from his or her former home.*

AFRICA'S TRADITIONAL RELIGIONS

TODAY THE MAJORITY OF AFRICANS ARE CHRISTIANS or Muslims. Christianity and Islam originated near the edge of Africa and spread into North Africa and Ethiopia centuries ago, long before Europeans arrived on the continent, so in those regions they are "traditional" religions. However the term is most often used to refer to the tribal religions followed in Africa before European colonization; today about 13 percent of Africans still follow such religions.

Many traditional religions had one supreme god, who lived in the sky and created the world. Many also belived that there were spirits in trees, rivers, mountains, living creatures, and in parts of a village. These religions had no mosques, churches, or temples. Instead an elder led people as they prayed to the gods and spirits or made gifts to them in special places such as on top of hills or beneath large trees. Gifts included the sacrifice of a family animal, or cooked food and beer. A family's courtyard might contain a tiny house where food could be placed for the spirits. Offerings of food and drink were also commonly made to the spirits of the dead, particularly the recent dead.

The Yoruba of Benin, Togo, and Nigeria had a supreme god, Olorun (or Olodumare), and several hundred deities. These *orishas* were all extensions of Olorun. Some of the *orishas* were as old as the Earth but others were the spirits of real people: Shango, for example, the *orisha* of thunder, was once a king of Oyo.

When the spirits were angry they caused illness or bad luck, so it was important to keep them happy. One form of spirit was the trickster. This might be Eshu, a Yoruba *orisha*, or Legba, who was a god of the Fon. They were mischievous and could easily take offense if they were forgotten in someone's prayers. Trickster animals feature in many traditional myths, in which they outwit stronger or more powerful enemies. In one West African myth—now known around the world—a tortoise trickster challenges a hare to a race; despite being much slower, the tortoise wins.

In traditional African societies, the intermediaries between the worlds of the living and the spirits were shamans. They were consulted about what might cause sickness or ill fortune, so that people could remove whatever wrongdoing had caused the trouble. The shaman might advise them to make an offering to the spirits, for example.

This ornate carving, used to top a wooden staff, portrays Eshu, one of the most widely worshiped of the Yoruba onishas. Eshu protected travelers and also controled whether people had good or bad luck.

PEOPLE & PLACES	DOCUMENTS, ART, & ARTIFACTS	WORSHIP & DOCTRINE

EUROPE

500 The first plans are created for the Vatican Palace, Rome.

511 The convent of St. Césaire is built at Arles, in France.

525 The Roman theologian Dionysius Exiguus compiles a table of the dates of Easter in which he introduces the AD (anno domine) system of dating from Christ's birth, which he dates to the year 0.

529 St. Benedict establishes Monte Cassino Abbey in Italy, establishing the Benedictine monastic order (📄 facing page).

540 Cassiodorus founds the Great Monastery of Vivarium, near Squillace in Italy.

ca 510 Bridget of Kildare, an Irish nun, organizes the copying of Christian manuscripts.

523 Possibly while awaiting his own execution, Roman philosopher Boethius writes *De Consolatione Philosophiae* (*The Consolations of Philosophy*); throughout the Middle Ages it is one of the most widely read books after the Bible.

547 The Church of San Vitale in Ravenna is decorated with outstanding Byzantine mosaics of Justinian and Theodora.

ca 500 Melodus (St. Romanos) composes hymns for Christmas and Easter.

ca 500 The use of incense is introduced to Catholic services.

515 The Monks Rule of St. Benedict, which requires monks to take vows of poverty, obedience, and chastity, becomes the rule for monastic life in Europe.

519 The first schism between the Western and Eastern churches comes to an end.

543 Justinian issues an edict condemning the writings of the early theologian Origen.

THE AMERICAS

ca 500 The Maya develop more than 80 large ceremonial centers in Mexico and Mesoamerica: at different periods Tikal, Uxmal, and Palenque are dominant.

ca 504 In the Mayan city of Copán, a ruler named Waterlily Jaguar begins to expand the Acropolis, the city's ceremonial center.

First recorded in 510, suttee—here in a 19th-century illustration—was a Hindu ceremony in which a widow sacrificed herself on the pyre of her husband. Some Hindus claimed that the practice was sanctioned by the Rig Veda; others found many counter-arguments in scripture.

ASIA & OCEANIA

502 Wudi becomes emperor of China; he will convert to Buddhism in 517.

ca 520 Bodhidharma arrives in China to teach Zen Buddhism; in Luoyang he spends nine years in meditation.

530 The Buddhist monk Bohiruci converts the Taoist T'an-luan, who becomes the first patriarch of the Ching-t'u school of Buddhism.

523 The first known pagoda is built in China at the Songyue Temple in Henan, as a tower modeled on dome-shaped Buddhist stupas in India.

ca 500 Zoroastrianism, based on the ancient teachings of Zoroaster, enjoys a revival in Iran.

517 Wudi bans Taoism in China and forbids animal sacrifices to the gods, which are replaced by the offering of model animals.

ca 540 Buddhism begins to wane in India.

547 A book mentions Christians living in India.

AFRICA & THE MIDDLE EAST

527 The Church of the Nativity in Bethlehem is rebuilt after a fire.

535 A Christian basilica is built at Leptis Magna (in present-day Libya).

537 The biggest Christian church in the world at the time, Hagia Sophia (Holy Wisdom), is built in Constantinople with a dome 100 feet across.

ca 542 Disguised as a beggar, Jacob Baradaeus spends three decades wandering in Palestine, founding Monophysite (Jacobite) churches.

ca 500 Jewish tribes settle in Arabia, in the regions of Mecca and Yemen.

ca 500 Ethiopians adopt Christianity.

ca 500 The Talmud, a collection of religious texts and laws, is compiled by Jewish scholars.

534 The Byzantine theologian Johannes Philoponus Grammaticus refutes the teachings of the Neoplatonists.

536 Emperor Justinian orders the closure of the temple of Philae on the Nile River, marking the official end of the cult of the ancient Egyptian gods.

543 A Christian mission is established in Nubia.

Monks from China's Shaolin Monastery cross a bridge in Beijing. The Buddhist monastery in Henan Province was built in about 500. It became renowned for the martial arts practiced by the monks, known as Shaolin kung fu.

RELIGION IN THE WORLD	WORLD EVENTS

529 In an attempt to counter the survival of pagan beliefs, Justinian closes the 100-year-old School of Philosophy in Athens.

ca 539 The legendary British king Arthur—who has led Christian resistance against the pagan Saxon invaders—is said to have fallen in battle; in some versions of the story, he is wounded and taken to Avalon, where he still waits to help Britain in its hour of greatest need.

500 The Ostrogoth Theodoric becomes ruler of Italy.

511 After the death of Clovis, his Frankish empire is divided among his four sons.

527 The Byzantine emperor Justinian begins to regain former territory of the Roman Empire in the West.

ca 530 Frankish tribes invade Germany and northern France.

---

ca 500 Peoples who worship on temple mounds trade in the Mississippi Valley.

ca 500 The Maya develop a 260-day sacred calendar for ritual purposes.

ca 500 Hunters on the Great Plains of North America are using bows and arrows.

ca 500 The Thule, from the region of the Bering Strait, begin to move into Alaska.

534 A mysterious lull begins at Tikal, a major lowland Mayan center in Guatemala, where few monuments are erected until 593.

---

510 Suttee, the Hindu practice in which a widow dies on her husband's funeral pyre, is first recorded.

528 Buddhism is officially acknowledged in Korea, where Silla is the last of the three kingdoms to adopt it.

ca 500 The Buddhist trading state of Srivijaya emerges in Sumatra, Indonesia.

502 Xiao Yan forces the Qi rulers to submit to his authority and founds China's Liang dynasty.

ca 530 The legendary hero Yasodharman is said to have repelled invading Huns from central India.

547 The Chinese suppress a Vietnamese revolt.

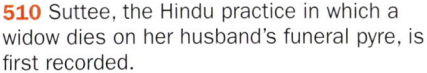

503 War breaks out between the Sassanids of Persia and the Byzantines; neither gain an advantage.

525 After Arabs massacre Christians in the southern Arabian Peninsula, the Christian king Caleb of Axum conquers Yemen.

531 Khusrow I becomes ruler of the Sassanid Empire, which he leads to its greatest height.

533 The Sassanids and Byzantines conclude the "Endless Peace"—in fact, the truce lasts only seven years.

534 The Byzantine general Belisarius conquers the Vandal kingdom in North Africa, which becomes a Byzantine province.

St. Benedict and the Monasteries

Benedict of Nursia (about 480–547) is considered the father of monasticism in the West. Born in Umbria, Italy, he went as a young man to study in Rome. Rejecting the lax morals of the Romans, he devoted himself to prayer and contemplation in a cave for several years. After a brief stay in a monastery he set up and oversaw 12 monastic communities of 12 monks each.

In about 529 Benedict and some followers established a monastery at Monte Cassino, between Rome and Naples. Monte Cassino, a self-sufficient community that balanced a life of prayer with a life of work, became the model for monasteries throughout western Europe.

Benedict wrote a code of conduct to guide monks. These guidelines became known as the Benedictine rule. They required each individual to take a vow of poverty, chastity, and obedience, and laid out guidelines for a life of prayer, manual work, and study.

The Benedictine rule was so influential that in 670 the church made it the standard for all monasteries. It remained so for centuries, providing practical and spiritual guidance, with occasional revisions to reinvigorate monastic life.

FEW FAITHS HAVE BURST ON THE WORLD WITH THE SAME IMPACT AS ISLAM. From the time that the Prophet Muhammad had his first vision of the Angel Gabriel in 610 in Mecca, it took only a few centuries for his small group of followers to spread from the deserts of the Arabian Peninsula to create an empire that covered much of the Middle East, North Africa, and West Asia. This territory—the caliphate—drew together various peoples unified by the Islamic faith and the Arabic language of its followers.

Islam belonged to the same tradition as Judaism and Christianity: all three are monotheistic (they believe in only one god), all three acknowledge Abraham as a patriarchal figure, and Islam recognizes the divinity of Jesus Christ, although it classes him as just one of God's prophets rather than his son. Unlike the other Abrahamic faiths, Islam was allied to a dynamic society with the determination and military expertise to impose itself on its neighbors. While its political influence spread, however, Islam itself split over the succession to the Prophet as leader of the faith. Later that division hardened into a permanent split between Sunnis and Shiites that can occasionally become toxic even today.

The spread of Islam was accompanied by a remarkable flowering of learning and culture. The Abbasid caliphate, established at a capital at Baghdad in what is now Iraq, were leading patrons of scientists and scholars, which it drew from across North Africa and Asia. Islam placed a great emphasis on literacy and education, so that its followers could read the Koran for themselves. The madrasahs and universities of the Muslim world preserved much classical learning when Europe entered its "Dark Ages" after the fall of the Roman Empire in the West in 476.

Previous pages *Sacred to both Jews and Muslims, the Temple Mount in Jerusalem is one of the most revered—and most fiercely disputed—places in the world. The Dome of the Rock is a mosque built to mark the place from where Muhammad ascended on his night journey to Heaven with the Angel Gabriel.*

Muslim pilgrims circle the Kaaba in Mecca, the holiest site in Islam. It is a duty of all Muslims who can afford the journey to make the hajj—a pilgrimage to Mecca—at least once in his or her life.

Christianity in Europe suffered as a consequence of the economic collapse that followed the end of Rome, when pagan peoples were dominant in many parts of the continent. After a few centuries, however, it revived after the coronation of Charlemagne in 800. The Frankish king established a new empire that stretched across much of western Europe and sought consciously to re-create the glory that once was Rome. Monasteries grew in number and in importance, providing centers of education where monks transcribed copies of the gospels. The church hierarchy and dogma were established, with decreasing tolerance for those who diverted from Catholic Orthodoxy.

At the edges of Christendom, however, Catholic missionaries still came up against the pagans of north and eastern Europe. The Vikings of Scandinavia followed their own warlike religion based on a warrior heaven named Valhalla, reserved for those who fell in battle. Their mythology revolved around a constant struggle for the survival of the world against the forces of ice, snow, and rock. Forced to emigrate by the lack of arable land, these farming Northmen fell on the coasts of northwest Europe. The first casualty was the great monastery at Lindisfarne, on Holy Island, in northern Britain, which was raided in 793. Soon the sight of unknown sails on the horizon struck fear into populations throughout coastal Europe. One monk wrote in the margin of his work, "O Lord protect us from the fury of the Northmen."

The strains were growing between the Latin church of Rome and the church based in Constantinople, or Byzantium, which remained preeminent as the headquarters of Greek-speaking Christianity (the ancestor of the Orthodox Church). The characteristics of Greek worship, such as the plentiful use of painted and sculpted icons of holy figures, provided work for outstanding craftsmen whose rich materials—including broad expanses of gold leaf—were paid for by the Byzantines' trade throughout the eastern Mediterranean and into the Muslim empires that dominated the western end of the Silk Road across Asia to China.

In Asia, the arrival of Islam had an inevitable impact on existing faiths. While Islamic dynasties established a series of empires in Persia—significantly they adopted the Shiite form of the faith—the Iranian descendents of the early Zoroastrians moved east ahead of the Muslims and settled among the Hindus of India. Eventually Islam would come to northern India, too, where the Moguls set up a sultanate that ruled over a huge Hindu majority. Although relations between the two faith groups were occasionally tense, the Muslims allowed their subjects to practice their faith freely (albeit sometimes with a higher tax burden than Muslims within the realm).

Around the world, religion was at the very heart of personal experience. Pilgrimage was a duty of all Muslims and was also undertaken by Christians visiting important sites, Buddhists visiting the great shrines of Buddha, and Hindus wishing to bathe in the waters of the Holy Ganges.

Carved into the side of a hill at Ellora in India in the eighth century, the Kailasa Temple is a multistory re-creation of the holy mountain Kailasa, home of the Hindu god Shiva. Ellora is India's richest collection of rock-cut buildings, with more than 30 separate Buddhist, Hindu, and Jain shrines.

THE WORLD AT A GLANCE

CONCISE HISTORY OF WORLD RELIGIONS

	550	600	650	700	750	
EUROPE	**ca 550** Crucifixes first appear as ornaments and decorative items in Europe. **ca 550** Church bells are used for the first time, in France. **590** Gregory I (Gregory the Great) becomes pope. **597** St. Augustine arrives in Britain and founds a Benedictine monastery at Canterbury.	**ca 600** Gregorian chant, a plainsong style of church music, is introduced and named for Pope Gregory. **603** The first church is built on the site of St. Paul's Cathedral in London. **626** The abbey of St. Denis is built in Paris.	**664** In England the Synod of Whitby rejects practices of the Celtic churches of Ireland, Scotland, and Wales and places the English church under the control of the Pope. **ca 690** English missionaries are spreading Christianity in the Netherlands and Scandinavia.	**731** The Venerable Bede, a monk working in a monastery in northern England, completes his *Ecclesiastical History of the English People*. **732** Charles Martel, the effective ruler of the Franks, defeats Muslim forces invading from Spain at the Battle of Tours in central France.	**750** Having escaped Abu al-Abbas' massacre of the Umayyads, Prince abd al Rahman flees to Córdoba in Spain, which becomes the new Umayyad capital. **ca 790** Irish monks sail into the North Atlantic, reaching the Faeroe Islands and Iceland. **793** On their first major raid in Europe, Vikings sack the monastery on Holy Island in northeast England.	
THE AMERICAS	**553** Moon–Jaguar, ruler of the Mayan city of Copán, builds a temple named the Rosalila in honor of the sacred maize plant.	**615** In the Mayan city of Palenque, the ruler Pacal begins to build a lavish temple.	**683** Pacal, lord of Palenque, is buried in a pyramid rediscovered in 1952.	**ca 700** The Caddo build large earthwork mounds in Texas and Oklahoma. **ca 700** Maya at Tikal build a carefully aligned observatory.	**ca 750** The Zapotec ceremonial center at Monte Alban, Mexico, is abandoned.	
ASIA & OCEANIA	**552** Buddhism arrives in Japan from Korea. **557** Luoyang becomes the capital of China and the center of Chinese Buddhism, with more than 1,000 temples and monasteries.	**607** Japanese rulers send envoys to China to obtain copies of Buddhist scriptures. **625** The first shrine to Amaterasu is established at Ise in Japan, which remains one of the foremost Shinto holy places. **645** Buddhism arrives in Tibet.	**ca 650** The Chinese monk Shan-tao begins to popularize Amida or Pure Land Buddhism over more mystical forms of the faith. **651** Arab traders introduce Islam to China.	**ca 700** Zoroastrians fleeing the Islamic advance in Persia settle in western India, where they are known as Parsis. **ca 700** The Buddhist Taktsang monastery is founded in the Himalayan kingdom of Bhutan. **711** Muslim armies conquer Sind in India.	**752** The strength of the Buddhist presence in Japan is confirmed by the erection of a giant statue of Buddha at Nara. **758** Krishnaraja I of the Rashtrakuta dynasty in central India commissions the Kailasa rock-cut Hindu temple at Ellora.	
AFRICA & THE MIDDLE EAST	**553** The Second Council of Constantinople is held to try to reconcile the Eastern and Western Churches: it ends with the excommunication and banishment of Pope Vigilius for refusing to condemn Nestorianism. **ca 570** Birth of the Prophet Muhammad to a merchant family in the city of Mecca.	**610** Muhammad undergoes a spiritual transformation and becomes a prophet. **622** The Hegira, year 0 of the Muslim calendar, is dated from Muhammad's flight from Mecca to Medina. **632** Death of the Prophet Muhammad. **632** Abu Bakr, Muhammad's father-in-law, becomes the First Caliph; Shiite Muslims believe that Muhammad's cousin and son-in-law Ali was the rightful imam (leader). **635** Muslims conquer Damascus from the Byzantines.	**651** Caliph Uthman gathers the verses of the Koran into a single volume. **661** Civil war among Muslims ends with Muawiyah founding the Umayyad caliphate, with its capital at Damascus. **683** After war over the succession to the caliphate, Islam splits permanently between the majority Sunni, represented by the ruling Umayyad dynasty, and the Shiites, who support the claims to power of Muhammad's son-in-law Ali and his son, Husayn. **692** The Dome of the Rock is completed in Jerusalem.	**711** Muslim armies from North Africa invade Spain, where they begin to establish Islamic kingdoms. **725** Christian Copts in Egypt revolt unsuccessfully against their Islamic rulers. **747** In Khorasan, Iran, new converts to Islam begin a major rebellion to protest the tax benefits given to Arabic Muslims. **749** In the aftermath of the Khorasan Rebellion rebels proclaim as caliph Abu al-Abbas, founder of the Abbasid dynasty.	**750** Abu al-Abbas overthrows the Umayyad dynasty and establishes the Abbasid caliphate; he massacres most of the Umayyad family. **754** On the death of Abu al-Abbas, his brother Al-Mansur becomes the second Abbasid caliph; he founds Baghdad in Iraq as his capital. **787** The Second Council of Nicaea upholds the worship of icons, ending the Iconoclasm Controversy. **ca 790** According to Yoruba mythology, the world is created at Ife, a sacred city in modern-day Nigeria.	

800	850	900	925	950–1000
800 In Rome on Christmas Day, Pope Leo III crowns King Charlemagne of the Franks Holy Roman Emperor. **813** The Synod of Mainz decrees that Christmas should be marked by four days of public celebration. **837** In Córdoba, Spain, Jews and Christians launch an unsuccessful revolt against their Muslim rulers.	**ca 850** Jewish settlers in Germany develop a new language, now known as Yiddish. **ca 850** A system of modes is developed that establishes the harmony for church music; centuries later it leads to the development of major and minor scales. **863** The Cyrillic alphabet, traditionally attributed to Saint Cyril, is adopted in eastern Europe.	**ca 900** King Alfonso III of Castile begins the reconquest of Spain from the Islamic Moors. **910** The Benedictine abbey is founded at Cluny, France; it becomes a center of monastic reform.	**929** Emir Abdurrahman III of Córdoba, Spain, proclaims himself caliph, claiming supreme civil and religious authority in the Muslim world. **ca 930** Córdoba becomes the center of Islamic culture in Spain. **939** The kingdom of León captures Madrid, Spain, from the Moors.	**964** Monasticism begins to revive in England after the Danish invasions. **976** At Córdoba in Spain the Great Mosque is completed; it is notable for its 70 libraries of hand-copied books (one library alone holds 500,000 volumes).
ca 800 The Mississippians of eastern North America begin a tradition of building large, flat-topped earthworks known as temple mounds.	**ca 850** The ceremonial center of Chichén Itzá is founded in the northern Yucatán Peninsula, in Mexico.	**ca 900** The Anasazi (Pueblo) culture in what is now the southwestern United States build kivas—circular ritual spaces—at the heart of their settlements.		**ca 1000** Leif Eriksson, son of Erik the Red, establishes a settlement in Vinland on the coast of Newfoundland. The settlers are a mixture of Christians and pagans.
ca 800 On the island of Java in Indonesia, construction begins on a vast Buddhist monument known as Borobudur. **ca 804** Japanese monks found the Tendai and Shingon sects of Buddhism, both of which become popular in Japan. **843** Emperor Wuzong begins the Great Anti-Buddhist Persecution in China.	**868** The *Diamond Sutra*, the world's earliest known printed book, is produced in China; it is a Chinese translation of a short Buddhist sermon on the importance of avoiding extreme mental attachment to the world. **877** Indravarman I becomes king of the Khmer in Cambodia; his temple-mountain, Bakong, founds the tradition of religious architecture later continued by Angkor Wat.	**ca 900** Under the Chola dynasty of India, craftsmen produce spectacular bronze sculptures for use in religious processions. **ca 900** The Buddhist temples at Nara become one of Japan's main centers of artistic activity.	**930** The first-known written example of the Telgulu language of southern India appears in the dedication of a temple to Shiva. **ca 935** The beginning of the Koryo period marks the greatest influence of Buddhism in Korea.	**962** A Turkic Islamic kingdom is founded at Ghazni in Afghanistan; the Ghaznavids rule the region for the next two centuries. **999** The conquest of northern India and Central Asia by Turkic peoples bring those regions under Islamic control.
ca 800 A third school of Islamic law, the Shafi'i school, is established. **ca 820** Al-Mamun founds the House of Wisdom in Baghdad, an academy that translates key Greek and Indian philosophical and scientific works. **831** A final revolt by Coptic Christians in Egypt is defeated; many Copts convert to Islam. **ca 840** Thomas, the Nestorian bishop of Marga, writes *The Book of Governors*, a history of Christians in Iraq.	**ca 850** The mystic tradition of Sufi Islam is founded by the Egyptian Duhl Nul. **865** The *Sahih Bhukari*, a book of hadith (the sayings of Muhammad) is published; five more books follow in the next five years. **873** Muhammad al-Muntazar, the 12th imam of the Shiite Imami sect, disappears after going for a walk; his followers, the Twelver Shiites, still await his return. **ca 895** The earliest-known Hebrew copy of the Old Testament is created.	**ca 900** The Jewish Book of Creation, the Sepher Yetzirah, is written down; its author is said to be the prophet Abraham. **909** Taking its name from Fatima, daughter of the Prophet and wife of Ali, the Shiite Fatimid dynasty is established in Tunisia. **916** The Codex Babylonicus Petropolitanus is produced, the earliest-known complete Old Testament.	**930** Rebels sack the Muslim holy city of Mecca. **ca 950** The nature of the Islamic world is changed when the weakness of the Abbasids allows Turks from Central Asia to invade Muslim lands; many adopt the faith of their new territory.	**953** The al-Azhar University is founded in Cairo; its reputation as a center of Islamic learning grows rapidly. **977** Shiite Muslims build a shrine at the burial place of Ali, son-in-law of Muhammad, in Najaf, Iraq; the shrine becomes one of the holiest places in Shiism. **ca 985** Islam begins to make advances in the Christian regions of Nubia. **996** In Egypt, Caliph el-Hakim begins a 25-year persecution of Coptic Christians.

PEOPLE & PLACES	DOCUMENTS, ART, & ARTIFACTS	WORSHIP & DOCTRINE

EUROPE

543 The abbey of St. Germain-des-Pres is built in Paris, France.

ca 563 Columba leaves Ireland with 12 disciples and builds a monastery on the Scottish island of Iona.

573 Gregory becomes bishop of Tours (▤ facing page).

590 Gregory I becomes pope.

597 St. Augustine arrives in Britain, where he has been sent on a mission by Pope Gregory, and founds a Benedictine monastery at Canterbury.

ca 550 Crucifixes first appear as ornaments and decorative items in Europe.

570 The Arian cathedral of Sant'Apollinaire Nuovo in Ravenna is converted to a Catholic church. It contains many outstanding early examples of Byzantine mosaics of the life of Christ and of Catholic saints.

ca 550 Church bells are used for the first time, in France.

563 Christianity makes many converts among the Saxons of England.

589 King Recared converts and makes Christianity the official religion of Spain.

ca 590 Columbanus introduces the Celtic Church from Ireland to Gaul.

THE AMERICAS

553 Moon-Jaguar, ruler of the Mayan city of Copán, builds a temple named the Rosalila in honor of the sacred maize plant (▤ pages 74–75).

Empress Theodora, shown in a Byzantine mosaic from Ravenna, Italy, rose from prostitution to marry the Emperor Justinian and became a saint of the Catholic Church.

ASIA & OCEANIA

557 Luoyang becomes the capital of China and the center of Chinese Buddhism, with more than 1,000 temples and monasteries (▤ pages 42–43).

For so holy indeed is this Saint held throughout the whole earth, that always, by all and everywhere, he is called St. Gregory. Wherefore in the litanies, by which we implore the Lord for our excesses and innumerable sins by which we offend Him, we call St. Gregory to our aid.

LIFE OF SAINT GREGORY [POPE GREGORY I], CA 700.

ca 500 China is home to an estimated 14,000 Buddhist temples.

552 Buddhism arrives in Japan from Korea.

ca 570 The Chinese monk Zhiyi attempts a comprehensive classification of the teachings of Buddhism, stressing its symbolic and mystical qualities; his work helps develop a distinctive strand of Chinese Buddhism separate from Indian Buddhism.

AFRICA & THE MIDDLE EAST

ca 570 The Prophet Muhammad is born to a merchant family in the city of Mecca, a thriving commercial center on the Arabian Peninsula (▤ pages 90–91).

ca 550 The Byzantine empress Theodora sends Christian missionaries to North Africa.

553 The Second Council of Constantinople is held to try to reconcile the Eastern and Western churches; it ends with the excommunication and banishment of Pope Vigilius for refusing to condemn Nestorianism.

ca 570 Makurra, one of the kingdoms of Nubia (Sudan), converts to Christianity.

ca 580 The missionary Longinus converts Makurra's neighbor, Alwa.

RELIGION IN THE WORLD	WORLD EVENTS	

ca 550 Missionaries sent by the Byzantine emperor Justinian smuggle silk worms from China; the worms and the missionaries' knowledge of silk production become the basis of the European silk industry.

578 On a diplomatic mission to Constantinople to enlist Byzantine help against the Lombards, the future Pope Gregory decides that Rome must become independent of the Eastern Church.

561 A 50-year civil war breaks out among the Merovingians in France.

568 Refugees from Lombard invasions of northern Italy found the city of Venice on islands in a coastal lagoon.

ca 550 Native Americans in what is now Colorado begin to construct pit houses.

562 In the Mayan lowlands of Mexico, Tikal is defeated by its rival, Calakmul.

594 Calakmul defeats another Mayan center, Palenque.

GREGORY THE GREAT

Gregory the Great was a monk, pope, and scholar. He is considered one of the most important figures in the history of Christianity.

Gregory was born in Rome in around 540 to a very wealthy family. He received a comprehensive education and became a government official soon after leaving law school. After his father's death in 575, Gregory decided to dedicate his life to the church. He converted his family's mansion into a monastery, and founded several others elsewhere in the country. He intended to remain a monk until he died, but he was drawn back into worldly politics by the threat of war.

ca 580 Buddhist missionaries introduce the practice of flower arranging to Japan.

562 The kingdom of Silla expels the Japanese from Korea.

581 Yang Jian founds the Sui dynasty in China and rules as Sui Wendi.

589 Sui Wendi reunifies China.

590 Chosroes II comes to the Persian throne.

Augustine of Canterbury

In 595 Pope Gregory I decided that a mission should be sent to the British Isles to convert its people to Christianity. For this task, Gregory chose Augustine, the prior of a Benedictine monastery in Rome and a close friend. Augustine left Rome in early 596 with about 40 monks from his monastery. After arriving in Canterbury (a town in southeastern England) Augustine met with the local ruler, Aethelbert, and persuaded him to convert to Christianity. Augustine then established a monastery in the town and began educating missionaries to spread the religion throughout the country. He died in 604, and was canonized soon after.

553 The Byzantine emperor Justinian reconquers former Roman territory in North Africa.

ca 570 A Christian army is driven back from the city of Mecca in Arabia.

The Lombards, who held all of northern Italy, were poised to invade Rome. Gregory was sent to Constantinople to try to secure aid against them. Although he failed in this mission, success in other areas demonstrated his abilities, and he was elected pope in 590.

As pope, Gregory strengthened the position of the pope against that of the patriarch of Constantinople, leader of the Eastern Church. He brought tribes such as the Franks and Visigoths under the religious control of Rome, and organized successful missionary expeditions to England.

In the name of Allah, the Beneficent, the Merciful.

Praise be to Allah, Lord of the Worlds,

The Beneficent, the Merciful,

Master of the Day of Judgment.

KORAN SURA I:1–4

THE LIFE OF MUHAMMAD

THE FOUNDER OF THE ISLAMIC FAITH, THE PROPHET Muhammad, is a towering figure in world history. Muhammad was born in Mecca, Arabia, in 570; his father had died before he was born, and his mother died when he was still a child. Muhammad was raised by his extended family, mainly by his uncle, Abu Hamza. As a young man, Muhammad became a merchant and made many trips across the Arabian desert. At the age of 25, he married Khadijah, a wealthy woman several years his senior. By the time he was in his 30s, Muhammad was a successful businessman with a growing family.

All this would change, however, when in 610 he began seeing visions. In the years that followed, the Angel Gabriel appeared to Muhammad again and again, dictating to him the word of Allah—God. The name of the new religion, *Islam*, meant "surrender" to the divine will. It resembled Judaism and Christianity in many respects, most notably its monotheism, or worship of a single deity.

Inspired by religious zeal and a message of charity for the poor, Muhammad and his followers inevitably found themselves at odds with the Quraysh, Mecca's wealthy elite. In 622 they fled for the neighboring city of Medina, an event known as the Hegira, or "emigration." The Hegira marks the start of the Islamic calendar. In Medina, Muhammad was forced to act as a political as well as a spiritual leader, governing the growing Muslim community. After the death of Khadijah he took multiple wives, often to cement alliances with other local tribal leaders. He also acted as a military leader, organizing a Muslim army that defended the city against attacks by the Meccans.

In time the Muslims gained control of Mecca, and their victory marked the start of one of the most remarkable campaigns of conquest the world has ever seen. By the time the Prophet died in 632, to be controversially succeeded by his father-in-law, the Arabs had already carried the word of Islam through much of West Asia by force of arms—and by inspiration. After Muhammad's death, many of his sayings and actions were recorded and passed on by his wives and friends. These accounts—the hadith—form an important part of Muslim scripture.

This Islamic illustration shows the Prophet Muhammad praying at the Kaaba in Mecca. Muslims believe that the Kaaba contains a fragment of the first altar on Earth.

This 18th-century Turkish miniature depicts the Archangel Gabriel with Muhammad in Medina. The depiction of Muhammad's face has always been forbidden in Islamic culture.

600–649

PEOPLE & PLACES	DOCUMENTS, ART, & ARTIFACTS	WORSHIP & DOCTRINE

EUROPE

ca 600 Gregorian chant, a plainsong style of vocal church music, is introduced and named for Pope Gregory.

ca 600 Isidore becomes bishop of Seville in Spain.

603 The first church is built on the site of St. Paul's Cathedral in London.

609 In Rome, the domed ancient temple known as the Pantheon is consecrated as a Christian church, Santa Maria Rotunda.

612 Monasteries are founded at St. Gall in Switzerland and Bobbio in Italy.

626 The abbey of St. Denis is built in Paris.

635 Aidan becomes bishop of Iona, Scotland.

610 Bishops begin wearing episcopal rings as badges of authority and as a sign of their "marriage" to Christ; the rings also act as seals for stamping official documents and occasionally as repositories for holy relics.

ca 600 Pope Gregory founds the Schola Cantorum as a papal choir; the choir is influential in the spread of plainsong church music throughout Europe.

THE AMERICAS

615 In the Mayan city of Palenque, the ruler Pacal begins to build a lavish temple.

FAITH AND LIFE

The Third Caliph

Uthman, the Third Caliph, is an important figure in the history of Islam. Born in Mecca, he was one of the first converts to Islam and was married to Ruqayyah, one of Muhammad's daughters. He became a trusted deputy of Muhammad and of his first two successors, Abu Bakr and Umar. On the death of Umar in 644, Uthman was chosen as the new caliph by the elders of the Muslim community. He assumed control of a vast empire that now stretched from North Africa to Persia. Concerned about the possible effect of incorrect or inconsistent versions of Muhammad's teachings being propagated in the fringes of his empire, Uthman ordered the compilation of a standardized scripture and had copies sent to every Muslim city. He was assassinated in 656.

ASIA & OCEANIA

606 Former Gupta general Harsha comes to power over much of northern India; he converts to Mahayana Buddhism and becomes an important patron of the Buddhist university at Nalanda.

629 The Chinese pilgrim Xuanzang begins 16 years traveling in India and elsewhere recording Buddhist sacred texts, temples, and monuments: his records of his journey help preserve Buddhist texts after the decline of Buddhism in India.

ca 600 Sculptors in northern India create statues of Buddha in classic yoga postures.

607 The Horyuji Temple is completed in Japan; today it is the world's oldest wooden building.

607 Japanese rulers send envoys to China to obtain copies of Buddhist scriptures.

623 At the Kondo in Japan an altarpiece is carved showing Buddha flanked by two bodhisattvas.

604 Japanese prince Shotoko Taishi issues a law code that calls for the veneration of Buddha, his priests, and his laws.

625 The first shrine to Amaterasu is established at Ise in Japan, which remains one of the foremost Shinto holy places.

642 In northern India, Harsha summons a Buddhist convocation at Kanauj, attended by many pilgrims and local rulers.

645 Buddhism arrives in Tibet.

AFRICA & THE MIDDLE EAST

610 Muhammad undergoes a spiritual transformation and becomes a prophet.

610 The former slave Bilal becomes the first muezzin, charged with summoning Muslims to prayer.

632 Death of the Prophet Muhammad.

632 Abu Bakr, Muhammad's father-in-law, becomes the First Caliph; Shiite Muslims believe that Muhammad's cousin and son-in-law Ali was the rightful imam (leader) (pages 94–95).

634 Umar becomes the Second Caliph.

644 Uthman becomes the Third Caliph after Umar is assassinated.

If anyone among you used to worship Muhammad, then Muhammad is dead, but if any of you used to worship Allah, then Allah is alive and shall never die.

ABU BAKR, 632

RELIGION IN THE WORLD

The Umayyad Mosque in Damascus, Syria, was constructed on the site of a Christian church around 80 years after the city was conquered by a Muslim army.

636 Zoroastrians, originally from Persia (Iran), settle in central India.

622 The Hegira, year 0 of the Muslim calendar, is dated from Muhammad's flight from Mecca to Medina.

627 Muhammad punishes local Jews in Medina for conspiring with the Meccans.

630 The Muslims conquer Mecca and march north to raid the borders of Byzantine Syria.

632 The Byzantine emperor Heraclius I orders the forced conversion of Jews, whom he suspects of conspiring with the Persians against the empire.

635 Muslims conquer Damascus from the Byzantines.

638 Muslims conquer Jerusalem.

641 Muslims conquer Egypt and found a new capital, Fustat (later Cairo).

WORLD EVENTS

ca 615 The Anglo-Saxons complete their conquest of England.

620 Viking seafarers from Scandinavia raid Ireland.

ca 600 The Hohokam spread across what is now the southwestern United States.

ca 600 The Athabaskans arrive in the Great Plains from Canada.

ca 600 The Huari build a powerful empire in northern Peru.

ca 600 The Mon migrate from western China to Thailand.

ca 600 Japanese scribes begin to use Chinese characters.

618 Li Yuan founds the Tang dynasty.

610 Heraclius of Carthage usurps the throne of Byzantium.

614 Jerusalem falls into Sassanian hands. The "True Cross" of Jesus is seized and carried off to Persia.

630 The Byzantine and Persian empires agree on a truce.

HOLY RELICS

In the Christian church, relics are the bodily remains of a saint or any object that came into contact with Christ, the Virgin Mary, a saint, or a martyr. Such relics were carefully preserved and became a focus of worship and adoration in both the Roman Catholic and Eastern Orthodox churches.

Possession of relics was very profitable to a church, which could then become a center of pilgrimage. Relics also played an important role in trade and travel. Pilgrimages to the shrines of saints such as Thomas Becket in Canterbury, England, or Saint James in Compostela, Spain, promoted economic activity along the pilgrim routes. Pilgrims to the Holy Land bought sacred objects at premium prices: Records relate that some Venetian merchants paid the king of Jerusalem 20,000 gold coins for a piece of the True Cross.

Exaggerated claims, combined with the sheer number of relics, brought the cult of relics and the church itself into disrepute. The church insisted that the large number of relics was a miracle, but others accused the church of fraud. Doubt increased, even among believers. In the 16th century church reformers cast great numbers of relics on bonfires.

SUNNIS AND SHIITES

EXPLOSIVE IN ITS IMPACT, ISLAM SEEMED TO CARRY ALL before it as it spread from its Arab heartlands in the seventh century. The power of faith was backed up by force of arms. The skill of its mounted warriors, their military prowess, and their sense of destiny: Everything conspired to make the Arab advance irresistible. Yet there were an increasing number of conflicts within Islam itself, creating tensions that would ultimately split the entire Muslim community.

The Prophet's death in the summer of 632 left the elders of the Muslim community with a difficult decision. Muhammad had left no son and no specific instructions as to who should succeed him. The seeds of future division were sown when the elders chose Abu Bakr, the Prophet's father-in-law, as *khalifah*, or caliph—a title that implied both spiritual authority and political rule. Their choice passed over Muhammad's cousin and son-in-law, Ali, whose moral rigidity and religious fervor seem to have made the elders nervous.

A group of Pakistani boys strike their chests as part of traditional Shiite rituals on the day of Ashura—the anniversary of the death of imam Husayn.

In a series of civil wars fought over the next 53 years, first Ali himself and then his sons attempted to wrest back the succession that they saw as rightly theirs. Over time doctrinal differences further separated the rival groups. Those who followed Abu Bakr and the succession of "rightly guided" caliphs who came after him called themselves Sunni Muslims, because they followed the *sunnah*, or "customs," established by the Prophet. Shiites (named from the Arabic for "followers of Ali") argued that the ruling succession had been corrupted from the start, and that Islamic tradition should have flowed directly through Ali to the line of imams, or "teachers," who came after him.

In 680 Ali's son Husayn and a small band of partisans were on their way to join rebels in Iran when they were killed by Sunnis near Karbala in what is now Iraq. The deaths gave Shiism its first martyrs and lent the movement a new impetus. By 750 the Sunnis of the Umayyad dynasty had been swept away by the Abbasid caliphs, based in Baghdad, who were supported by Shiite scholars. Divisions between Sunni and Shiite Islam have persisted to this day, a source of distrust and at times of open warfare.

The Imam Ali shrine in Najaf, Iraq, draws millions of Shiite pilgrims every year to what they believe is the burial place of Muhammad's son-in-law, Ali.

PEOPLE & PLACES	DOCUMENTS, ART, & ARTIFACTS	WORSHIP & DOCTRINE

EUROPE

ca 650 The French bishop Emmeram founds a monastery at Ratisbon in Bavaria to combat pagan worship among the Germans.

652 After taking the blame for the extramarital pregnancy of a German princess, Emmeram is martyred by being tied to a ladder and cut to pieces.

660 The English noblewoman Hilda of Whitby runs a double monastery, one for monks and the other for nuns.

676 St. Cuthbert moves to live as a hermit in a cave on the Farne Islands in northern England; while there he passes the world's first bird preservation laws to protect the islands' nesting seabirds and ducks.

ca 650 At Lindisfarne Priory in northern England the monk Eadfrith copies and illuminates the Lindisfarne Gospels.

674 Glass windows are used for the first time in English churches.

664 In England the Synod of Whitby rejects practices of the Celtic churches of Ireland, Scotland, and Wales and places the English church under the control of the Pope.

673 The first synod of the independent English Church is held at Hertford.

ca 690 English missionaries are spreading Christianity in the Netherlands and Scandinavia.

THE AMERICAS

682 Ah Cacao becomes ruler of Tikal in Guatemala; Temple I in the Great Plaza will be built as his monument.

683 Pacal, lord of Palenque, is buried in a pyramid rediscovered in 1952.

The ruins of Whitby Cathedral, England, mark the site where the Synod of Whitby rejected the Celtic Church and embraced the Roman Catholic Church.

ASIA & OCEANIA

ca 650 King Srong-btsan-sgam-po dies; his two wives are instrumental in establishing Buddhism as a major faith in Tibet.

ca 670 Birth of the Buddhist monk Gyogi, who will argue that Japan's Shinto gods are manifestations of the Buddha, helping Buddhism gain a popular hold in Japan.

ca 650 Japanese craftsmen create the Tamamushi Shrine, a portable shrine illustrated with oil paintings of the Buddha's life.

ca 650 The Chinese monk Shan-tao begins to popularize Amida or Pure Land Buddhism over the more mystical form of the beliefs promoted by Zhiyi.

690 The Chinese monk and traveler I-Ching visits Mahayana Buddhists in Palembang, Sumatra (he has to make a long journey back to China to get ink and paper to copy scriptures, as Sumatra has none).

AFRICA & THE MIDDLE EAST

656 Uthman, the third caliph, is assassinated.

656 Muhammad's cousin and son-in-law Ali is elected caliph but is murdered in 661 after fighting a rival claimant, Muawiyah, governor of Syria.

661 Muawiyah becomes caliph and founds the Umayyad dynasty.

680 Husayn, the son of Ali, is defeated and killed at Karbala in an unsuccessful attempt to seize the caliphate.

683 Abd al-Malik becomes caliph; his rule provokes great resentment among Shiites.

651 Caliph Uthman gathers the verses of the Koran into a single volume.

692 The Dome of the Rock is completed in Jerusalem, where it is believed to mark the spot from which Muhammad ascended to heaven; according to Jews, this is also where Abraham prepared to sacrifice his son Isaac to God in the Old Testament.

692 The Quinisext Council of Constantinople settles the biblical canon—the accepted scripture—of the Eastern Church; the Roman Catholic Church rejects its decisions.

ca 650 Maritime trade carries the influence of Islam down the East African coast.

681 The Third Council of Constantinople affirms that Christ has "two natural wills."

683 After war over the succession to the caliphate, Islam splits permanently between the majority Sunni, represented by the ruling Umayyad dynasty, and the Shiites, who support the claims to power of Muhammad's son-in-law Ali and his son, Husayn (pages 94–95).

692 Abd al-Malik introduces coins with Arabic calligraphy for use throughout the Muslim world, helping move Islam beyond the religious sphere to the social and economic order.

RELIGION IN THE WORLD

ca 650 Benedictine monks in monasteries in Europe become very successful farmers, clearing forests, draining low-lying land, and learning to rotate crops.

In the late seventh century, Tikal was at the center of a large and prosperous Mayan city-state with numerous pyramid temples.

651 Arab traders introduce Islam to China.

651 The Muslim capture of Merv (Turkmenistan) brings Islam to Central Asia.

654 Muslims begin to enter Anatolia.

661 Civil war among Muslims ends with Muawiyah founding the Umayyad caliphate, with its capital at Damascus.

670 Muslim forces begin campaigning in North Africa.

678 The Byzantines raise a five-year Muslim siege of Constantinople, a first setback for the Muslims.

683 The Muslims and Byzantines agree on a border between their empires.

WORLD EVENTS

ca 650 Visigothic rule in Spain is weakened by internal power struggles.

681 Bulgars establish a kingdom south of the Danube.

687 Pepin, a high-ranking official known as the mayor of the palace, takes power from the Frankish Merovingian kings.

687 Venetians make their city a republic and elect a "doge," or leader.

ca 650 The ceremonial center at Teotihuacan in Mexico is sacked; it is later abandoned.

ca 650 The Hopewell begin to settle along the upper Mississippi River.

694 The accession of 18 Rabbit begins a new cultural age at Copán in Honduras.

695 Having recovered its power, Tikal defeats its longstanding enemy Calakmul and begins a golden age.

ca 650 India fragments into anarchy after the death of Harsha Vardhana.

659 The Tang defeat the Turks to extend Chinese control of the Silk Road westward.

670 The Tibetans temporarily fight off Chinese forces.

676 Having united Korea, Silla drives Chinese forces from the peninsula.

690 Empress Wu usurps the Chinese throne and establishes the Zhou dynasty.

ca 650 The Bantu migration from West Africa ends after several centuries with Bantu speakers now settled throughout east and southern Africa.

THE ARAB ADVANCE

When the Prophet Muhammad died in 632, he left behind a small Muslim community and no immediate successor. His followers were principally Bedouin tribes drawn from across Arabia. A small group of leaders, many of them companions of Muhammad, decided to use the idea of Islam to draw together the Arab tribes so they could provide a united front against potential enemies. United, they decided to expand their territory with bold campaigns that would eventually defeat the Byzantine and Sassanian empires.

The Arabs began their expansion with a series of raids on their neighbors. The Bedouin life was particularly well suited to fighting in the inhospitable desert terrain. Under the First Caliph, Abu Bakr, the Arabs began a two-year rampage across the Arabian Peninsula. The Arab tribes defeated the Byzantine and Persian Empires under Caliph Umar (ruled 634–644), an outstanding military strategist, and his successor Uthman (ruled 644–656). Within 25 years the Muslim Arab forces had created the first empire to permanently link West Asia with the Mediterranean.

The Arabs did not initially want the conquered people to convert to Islam. Not only did the decision have an economic element (non-Muslims paid higher taxes); the Arabs also believed that they alone belonged to a small elite chosen by the Prophet. That helped maintain their exclusive status as they imposed their own culture and language across their newly conquered lands.

Despite a civil war in the Muslim world in the 650s between the followers of Umar and those of Ali, and the subsequent division between Sunnis and Shiites, the Arab conquest continued. The victorious Umayyad dynasty took control for the next 70 years and continued the Islamic expansion into North Africa and the Iberian peninsula. In 685, Arabic was made the official language of the empire, causing the Greek language to disappear within a generation. The Arab expansion was complete.

PEOPLE & PLACES	DOCUMENTS, ART, & ARTIFACTS	WORSHIP & DOCTRINE

EUROPE

704 Aethelred, king of Mercia in England, abdicates his throne in favor of his son in order to become a monk.

735 The English monk Bede dies in his monastery; among his legacies are the dating system that classifies years into B.C. (before Christ) and A.D. (anno domini).

744 St. Boniface founds an abbey at Fulda in Germany that will become a great center of learning.

731 The Venerable Bede, a monk working in a monastery in northern England, completes his *Ecclesiastical History of the English People.*

740 The oldest known example in the West of a Crucifixion is painted in a chapel of the Santa Maria Antiqua Church in Rome.

ca 700 Easter eggs are used for the first time among Christians; already established as pagan symbols of springtime and fertility, eggs are for Christians symbols of the tomb from which Christ was resurrected.

711 The Muslim conquest of Spain ends religious intolerance of Jews.

719 Pope Gregory II sends the Anglo-Saxon monk Wynfrith, now known as St. Boniface, to convert the Germans.

723 St. Boniface fells an oak tree dedicated to Thor in Hesse, calling on the god to strike him down if the tree is sacred; when Boniface survives, many Germans abandon the worship of Thor and convert to Christianity.

THE AMERICAS

ca 700 The Caddo build large earthwork mounds in Texas and Oklahoma.

ca 700 Maya at Tikal build a carefully aligned observatory.

I have devoted my energies to the study of the scriptures, observing monastic discipline, and singing the daily services in church; study, teaching, and writing have always been my delight.

VENERABLE BEDE

ASIA & OCEANIA

ca 700 The Buddhist Taktsang monastery is founded in the Himalayan kingdom of Bhutan.

ca 700 In southern India the Pallava rulers build a Hindu temple complex at Mahabalipuram.

ca 700 Empress Wu commissions the Vairocana Buddha in the cave temple at Longmen.

713 Work begins on carving a 233-foot-tall Buddha in cliffs alongside a river near Leshan in Sichuan province, China, in order to calm the waters for vessels; due to lack of funds, the project is not completed until 803.

ca 700 Pamsukulikas ("rag wearers") begin to practice a strictly ascetic form of Buddhism in what is now Sri Lanka.

736 Huayan Buddhism arrives in Japan from Korea.

AFRICA & THE MIDDLE EAST

702 Kahina, "the Prophetess," a Berber princess who leads resistance to Arab rule, commits suicide after being defeated.

ca 730 John of Damascus is said to have had his right hand cut off for defending the veneration of icons; it is miraculously restored after the saint prays to an icon of the Virgin Mary.

749 In the aftermath of the Khorasan Rebellion rebels proclaim as caliph Abu al-Abbas, one of the Abbasid family descended from Muhammad's uncle, Abbas. (page 103)

710 Justinian II is the first emperor to kiss the pope's foot as a symbol of subservience to his spiritual authority.

The shore temple at Mahabalipuram, Tamil Nadu, India, was built in the early eighth century and dedicated to the gods Vishnu and Shiva.

RELIGION IN THE WORLD

711 Muslims conquer Spain as far north as the Pyrenees.

720 An uprising in Ravenna, Italy, against Leo III's decree against icons removes the region from Byzantine control.

720 Muslims settle on the Mediterranean island of Sardinia.

732 Charles Martel, the effective ruler of the Franks, defeats Muslim forces invading from Spain at the Battle of Tours in central France; the victory marks the farthest limit of the Muslim advance into Western Europe.

A manuscript illustration showing the Venerable Bede writing his history of the English Church.

WORLD EVENTS

725 Frankish ruler Charles Martel crosses the Rhine and conquers Bavaria.

ca 700 The Huari of northern Peru overthrow the Moche culture, which disappears from history.

---

ca 700 Zoroastrians fleeing the Islamic advance in Persia settle in western India, where they are known as Parsis.

710 The Japanese court moves to Nara, where Buddhism gains increased influence.

711 Muslim armies conquer Sind in India.

ca 740 Under Nagabhak I much of northern India is unified, which helps slow the Muslim advance into northwestern India.

710 Nara is built as the capital of Japan and becomes the country's first urban center.

712 Japan's oldest book, a history of the ruling dynasty, is written using Chinese characters.

738 In China, an imperial edict establishes schools in every prefecture and district.

---

702 Resistance to Muslim control ends in North Africa.

711 Muslim armies from North Africa invade Spain, where they begin to establish Islamic kingdoms.

725 Christian Copts in Egypt revolt unsuccessfully against their Islamic rulers.

739 In Morocco the Kharijite sect rebel against their Muslim rulers, but the revolt is suppressed in 742.

747 In Khorasan, Iran, new converts to Islam begin a major rebellion to protest the tax benefits given to Arabic Muslims.

ca 700 Arabic begins to become the common language of the Muslim world.

715 At its greatest extent, the Umayyad Empire stretches from Spain to Mongolia and south into Africa.

718 The Byzantine emperor Leo III defends Constantinople from an Arab fleet during a 13-month siege.

THE PARSIS

The small Parsi community of India has its origins in the Zoroastrian faith of the Persian Empire founded by the Achaemenid ruler Cyrus the Great. The Parsis have managed to maintain their unique ethnic and religious identity despite spending many centuries as a small and powerless ethnic group. Around 100,000 Parsis live in India today.

After the Arab invasion of Persia in the seventh century, Islam became the principal religion of what is now Iran. At the end of the ninth century, a number of Zoroastrians fled the country to escape persecution by its Muslim rulers. They arrived on the west coast of India in 936. The Indians called the newcomers Parsis, which meant Persians, and allowed them to practice their faith and to light the eternal fire that was at the heart of Zoroastrian ritual.

The Parsis originally worked as farmers and small traders. Over time, they settled along the Indian coastline. When the British arrived in India in the 17th century, the Parsis moved to urban centers and started to trade with the Europeans. They often became wealthy business people, particularly in Mumbai, where they contributed significantly to the city's wealth. The 19th and 20th centuries brought another wave of Zoroastrian immigration from Iran to India. These more recent immigrants are known as Iranis, and are considered to be a separate ethnic group from the Parsis.

The Parsis of India have always maintained links with the Zoroastrians who remained in Iran. For many centuries, Parsi leaders referred—and still refer—particular questions about doctrine or practice to senior Zoroastrian scholars in Iran.

A key Parsi belief is the need to avoid pollution of the environment with the bodies of the dead. This takes different forms but is most visible in the practice of exposing corpses on so-called "towers of silence" to be eaten by vultures, thus avoiding polluting either the earth by burial or the air by fire. In Mumbai, however, the number of vultures fell sharply in the 1990s. Parsis considered creating an aviary to sustain a program of breeding them in captivity.

TAOISM IN CHINA

TAOISM IS ONE OF THE THREE PRINCIPAL RELIGIONS OF China, along with Confucianism and Buddhism. Indigenous to China, Taoism is notable for its complexity and for its flexibility. It has adapted itself constantly to changes in Chinese culture. It has no single founder and no single message. Broadly, Taoism splits into two parts: religion and philosophy. The aim of both is to learn and practice "the way" (Tao), which Taoists believe is the path to discovering the truth to the universe

Taoism can trace its roots back to the sixth century B.C., when it is thought the Chinese philosopher Lao-Tzu wrote a book that set out the basic principles of Tao, the Tao Te Jing. Comparatively short, the text runs to only 5,000 words and is one of the world's most translated texts. The earliest known version of the Tao Te Jing dates from the second century B.C. and was only discovered in 1973. Lao-Tzu's follower and successor, Zhuangzi, added to the first principles in the fourth century B.C. Both of these texts continue to cause debate. Historians cannot say definitively, for example, whether Lao-Tzu or Zhuangzi even existed.

As a religion, Taoism did not start until long after the sacred books were written. Around A.D. 100, the hermit Zhang Daoling founded a sect called the Way of the Celestial Matters. He wrote down many of the guiding principles of Taoism. From then the religion flourished. Between 200 and 700, many of its practices and rituals were organized as Buddhism started to take hold in China.

Taoist beliefs complement those of Confucianism, but unlike Confucianism, Taoism concentrates on the individual; unlike Buddhism, meanwhile, it does not propose that life is built on suffering. Instead, Taoists believe that life is happy if it is lived well and in balance. At its heart lies the concept of yin and yang, a concept that already existed in Chinese belief. Yin and yang is the union of opposites, of male and female, which rather than work against each other work together to create an harmonious and good universe.

Taoism focuses on nature and the natural order in the belief that all things are one. Underlying Taoism is the belief that it goes beyond any human understanding but is the reason that the world exists. As in Buddhism, Taoists believe that to be happy one must free oneself from desire and must allow things to happen rather than to seek them.

Taoism eventually synthesised with Buddhism to create another branch of Buddhism known in the West as Zen Buddhism.

This third-century-B.C. bronze vessel from the Han dynasty has the earliest known Taoist symbols: The peaks of the lid represent the Mountains of the Immortals.

This detail from a Chinese fresco shows a representation of Lao-Tzu, the founder of Taoism. Almost nothing is known about Lao-Tzu's life.

PEOPLE & PLACES	DOCUMENTS, ART, & ARTIFACTS	WORSHIP & DOCTRINE

EUROPE

750 Having escaped Abu al-Abbas' massacre of the Umayyads, Prince abd al Rahman flees to Córdoba in Spain, which becomes the new Umayyad capital.

752 Stephen II becomes pope but dies the same year.

754 The Christian missionary Boniface is martyred in Frisia, when he is killed by Frisians for destroying their pagan shrines.

ca 790 Irish monks sail into the North Atlantic, reaching the Faeroe Islands and Iceland.

WORDS OF DEVOTION

The Second Council of Nicaea

In 787 representatives from the Eastern and Western branches of the Christian Church met in the city of Nicaea (now Iznik, Turkey). The council had been convened to discuss the issue of iconoclasm (the destruction of icons and images used in worship). Although such images had long been a part of Christian worship, the eighth century saw the emergence of several iconoclastic Christian sects. In 726 the Byzantine king, Leo III, sided with the iconoclasts and banned the use of images in worship. At the Second Council of Nicaea it was agreed that the use of images was acceptable and that the iconoclasts were heretics.

THE AMERICAS

ca 750 The Zapotec ceremonial center at Monte Albán, Mexico, is abandoned.

757 At Copán, the Maya ruler Smoke Shell begins a huge building program of temples and monuments.

ASIA & OCEANIA

754 After 10 failed attempts over the previous decade, Chinese monk Jianzhen reaches Japan and founds the Ritus school of Buddhism, which lays down rules for monks.

758 Krishnaraja I of the Rashtrakuta dynasty in central India commissions the Kailasa rock-cut Hindu temple at Ellora.

788 Birth in India of Sankaracharya, who becomes an outstanding Hindu guru and scholar.

ca 750 Pagodas are introduced to Japan from China.

752 The strength of the Buddhist presence in Japan is confirmed by the erection of a giant statue of Buddha at Nara.

794 The beginning of the Heian period in Japan brings a rise in the numbers of *hiriji*, wandering holy men.

AFRICA & THE MIDDLE EAST

754 On the death of Abu al-Abbas, his brother Al-Mansur becomes the second Abbasid caliph; he founds Baghdad in Iraq as his capital (📖 facing page).

786 Harun al-Rashid becomes Abbasid caliph; he is remembered today as the caliph of the *Arabian Nights*, in which he appears.

ca 750 The Persian Ibn al-Muqaffa, a Muslim convert, becomes secretary to the early Abbasids: he writes advice for Islamic rulers and translates Sassanian literature from Persian to Arabic.

751 The Islamic world is split between the Abbasids and Umayyads.

783 Abbasid caliph Mahdi introduces an inquisition to seek out and punish heretics; he uses the institution to execute many perceived opponents of his rule.

787 The Second Council of Nicaea upholds the worship of icons, ending the Iconoclasm Controversy.

ca 790 According to Yoruba mythology, the world is created at Ife, a sacred city in modern-day Nigeria.

RELIGION IN THE WORLD

ca 750 Gregorian church music spreads to Germany, France, and England.

766 The English monks Ethelbert and Alcuin make York a center of learning.

782 Alcuin quits York and moves to Europe to help the revival of learning inspired by Charlemagne.

793 On their first major raid in Europe, Vikings sack the monastery on Holy Island in northeast England, carrying off many of its treasures.

To make our confession short, we keep unchanged all the ecclesiastical traditions handed down to us, whether in writing or verbally, one of which is the making of pictorial representations, agreeable to the history of the preaching of the Gospel.

DECREE OF THE SECOND COUNCIL OF NICAEA

750 Abu al-Abbas overthrows the Umayyad dynasty and establishes the Abbasid caliphate; he massacres most of the surviving Umayyad family.

ca 750 Islamic merchants are instrumental in expanding the African slave trade across the Sahara Desert.

786 After an unsuccessful revolt in Mecca, Arabia, many Shiites flee to Libya in North Africa.

789 The Shiite Idrisid dynasty founds an independent caliphate in Morocco.

WORLD EVENTS

787 Danish Vikings invade Britain and establish settlements there.

797 Having imprisoned and blinded her co-ruler and son Constantine VI, Irene becomes the first Byzantine empress.

799 The Vikings raid the French coast for the first time.

ca 760 Many lowland Mayan cities build defensive walls, suggesting an increase in warfare at about this time.

ca 790 Spectacular Mayan murals are painted at Bonampak in Mexico; they are rediscovered only in 1946.

755 An-Lushan leads a rebellion in China that weakens the Tang dynasty.

763 The western capital of the Tang at Chang'an is attacked by Tibetans.

791 The Tibetans defeat the Chinese at Tingzhou; the Chinese abandon their territorial gains in Central Asia.

794 Emperor Kammu moves the Japanese court to Heian, now known as Kyoto.

THE ABBASID CALIPHATE

The first golden age of Islamic civilization was established by the Abbasid caliphate, which ruled the Islamic world between the middle of the eighth and tenth centuries. The Abbasid rulers held sway over an empire that stretched from North Africa across the Middle East and Arabia to the frontiers of India.

The Abbasids overthrew the ruling Umayyad dynasty in 750, promising to return the caliphate to strict Islamic rule. They moved the heart of the Islamic world farther east by establishing their capital in Baghdad, Iraq. They turned the city into a globally important cultural and educational center that attracted scholars and artists from across the Islamic world.

Unlike previous conquerors, the Abbasids presided over a multicultural, sophisticated civilization. The caliph was an absolute ruler who claimed direct authority from God. However, the Abbasids were tolerant of other faiths and did not force people to convert to Islam. This was partly because they perceived themselves as a minority elite—but also because non-Muslims paid higher taxes than Muslims, and tax revenue was an important source of income.

A page from a ninth-century Abbasid Koran. Arabic calligraphers found many supportive and generous patrons among the Abbasid rulers.

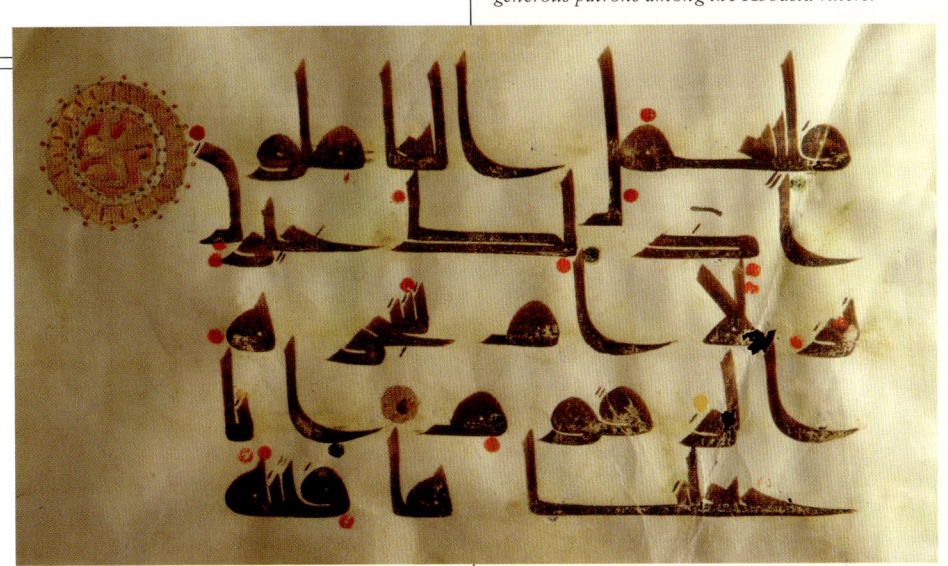

GLORIES OF BYZANTIUM

THE BYZANTINE EMPIRE EMERGED FROM THE DISINTEGRATING Roman Empire in the fourth century A.D. and lasted until the 15th century. At its greatest extent it controlled most of the eastern Mediterranean and what is now Turkey from Constantinople (previously known as Byzantium). The Greek-speaking empire was founded by Constantine, the first Christian Roman emperor, and throughout the empire's history Christianity exerted a strong influence on culture, politics, and society, most enduringly in art and architecture. In their icons, mosaics, and monumental structures, the Byzantines combined Christian inspiration with the technical sophistication of Roman and Greek art.

Icons—often stylized paintings or sculptures of religious figures—became popular in the sixth century. The Eastern Church taught that the icons symbolized the presence of the holy person they depicted. People revered images, praying before them and touching or kissing them as a way to share their mystical power. The Church split over the worship of icons and they were forbidden from 730 to 787, when the Second Council of Nicaea allowed their use again. The council laid down strict rules for icons. Images of saints had to be based on contemporary descriptions or portraits and each had to be clearly recognizable. The figure always looked directly out of the picture, ready to receive prayers from worshipers.

The Byzantine Empire was also renowned for its architecture, which again combined elements of Greek and early Roman styles with advanced engineering techniques developed in the late Roman period. The pinnacle of Byzantine architecture is the Hagia Sophia (Church of Holy Wisdom) in Constantinople. Construction took five years and

This Byzantine mosaic of Jesus and four angels comes from a church in the city of Ravenna, which was the capital of the Byzantine empire's lands in Italy from 535 to 751.

required an army of 10,000 masons, artists, and sculptors. When it was completed in 537, Hagia Sophia was the largest cathedral in the world. Its dome is 105 feet across and stands 180 feet high. The Emperor Justinian spared no expense on the interior, which was decorated with marvellous mosaics of gold, silver, and marble. The mosaics were created in the style of Byzantine icons, and depict biblical figures as well as numerous saints. After Constantinople fell to the Ottoman Turks in 1453, Hagia Sophia was turned into a mosque. The mosaics were plastered over and not revealed again until the 20th century.

This image of the Virgin Mary with the infant Jesus is typical of Byzantine icon painting, with highly stylized figures and facial features and the lavish use of gold paint.

PEOPLE & PLACES	DOCUMENTS, ART, & ARTIFACTS	WORSHIP & DOCTRINE

EUROPE

800 In Rome on Christmas Day, Pope Leo III crowns King Charlemagne of the Franks Holy Roman emperor.

814 On the death of Charlemagne the Frankish empire passes to his son, Louis the Pious, named for his deep religiosity as well as his campaigns against Muslims in Europe.

827 Pope Valentine dies after a reign of only 40 days.

848 Anskar becomes archbishop of Bremen; he makes missionary journeys to Denmark and Sweden over a period of some 35 years.

ca 800 Monks in Britain—possibly in Ireland—produce the illuminated *Book of Kells*, a Latin manuscript containing the four gospels named for the Abbey of Kells, where it is kept for many centuries.

832 In the Netherlands, the renowned *Utrecht Psalter* is completed with a lively pen-and-ink illustration accompanying every psalm: the artistic style influences Anglo-Saxon illustration for centuries.

800 Backed by Charlemagne, Pope Leo III separates from the Eastern Empire and becomes supreme bishop of the West.

813 The Synod of Mainz decrees that Christmas should be marked by four days of public celebration.

813 A hermit named Pelayo claims to find the tomb of St. James in northern Spain, beginning a tradition of pilgrimage to the spot, now known as Santiago (St. James) de Compostela.

ca 831 A bishopric is established in Hamburg, Germany, to provide a center for Christian missionary work among the Vikings.

THE AMERICAS

ca 800 The Mississippians of eastern North America begin a tradition of building large, flat-topped earthworks known as temple mounds.

This 14th-century manuscript illustration shows Pope Leo III crowning Charlemagne Holy Roman emperor in 800.

ASIA & OCEANIA

ca 838 The death of King Ralpacan, by either assassination or disease, marks the end of the first great period of Buddhist growth in Tibet (📄 facing page).

849 The city of Pagan (Bagan), later a major Buddhist center, is founded in Burma (Myanmar) (📄 pages 162–163).

ca 800 On the island of Java in Indonesia, construction begins on a vast Buddhist monument known as Borobudur, which eventually supports more than 70 small stupas.

ca 800 A populist form of Buddhism followed by the Amida sect is established in the kingdom of Silla in Korea.

ca 804 Japanese monks found the Tendai and Shingon sects of Buddhism, both of which become popular in Japan.

845 Confucianism is restored as the state ideology in China, where nonnative faiths such as Buddhism and Christianity are banned.

AFRICA & THE MIDDLE EAST

ca 800 Death of the first female Islamic mystic, Rabi'a the Mystic.

813 Al-Mamun becomes caliph in Baghdad; his 20-year reign marks an outstanding period in the history of the caliphate (📄 page 103).

ca 820 Al-Mamun founds the House of Wisdom in Baghdad, an academy that translates key Greek and Indian philosophical and scientific works.

ca 840 Thomas, the Nestorian bishop of Marga, writes *The Book of Governors*, a history of Christians in Iraq.

ca 800 A third school of Islamic law, the Shafi'i school, is established.

815 Iconoclasm—the destruction of religious images—reappears in the Byzantine Empire (it lasts until 842).

RELIGION IN THE WORLD	WORLD EVENTS
801 The Franks recapture Barcelona from the Muslims.	**803** Charlemagne and Nicephorus I agree the boundaries of the Frankish and Byzantine empires.
825 Muslims expelled from Spain conquer Crete.	**840** Viking settlers in Ireland found a trading center which will become the city of Dublin.
827 The Aghlabid rulers of northern Africa conquer Sicily.	**840** On the death of Louis the Pious, his sons fight for the Frankish crown.
837 In Córdoba, Spain, Jews and Christians launch an unsuccessful revolt against their Muslim rulers.	**843** The Treaty of Verdun formally divides up the Frankish empire among the three heirs of Louis the Pious.

A giant bronze statue of Buddha from Kamakura, Japan. Buddhism was introduced to Japan in the sixth century but did not become popular until the eighth and ninth centuries.

ca 800 The Toltec begin to move south into the Valley of Mexico.

ca 800 The Huari of Peru abandon their capital for reasons that are not known.

ca 800 The Anasazi build adobe villages in cliff sites in the American Southwest.

ca 820 Population levels fall in the lowlands of the Mayan Empire, marking the end of the Classic period.

838 The monk Ennin begins a nine-year visit to China, keeping a detailed record of Buddhism and its suppression by various emperors.

ca 840 King Langdarma is said to have begun a harsh persecution of Buddhists in Tibet, which dissolves into civil war after his death in 841.

843 Emperor Wuzong begins the Great Anti-Buddhist Persecution in China, which permanently weakens the faith's status in the country.

ca 800 Arab merchants found trading towns along the East African coast, increasing the Muslim presence in the region.

ca 800 The Aghlabid dynasty rules what are now Algeria and Tunisia, under the authority of the Abbasid caliph.

831 A final revolt by Coptic Christians in Egypt is defeated; many Copts convert to Islam.

836 Caliph al-Mutasim moves the capital of the caliphate from Baghdad to Samarra (in modern-day Iraq).

838 Al-Mutasim abandons an attack on Constantinople when a storm disrupts his fleet.

BUDDHISM IN TIBET

Tibet has its own form of Buddhism, which combines traditional belief in magic and spirit worship with Mahayana Buddhism. It is known as Vajrayana ("Vehicle of the Thunderbolt").

The earliest Mahayana scriptures were written in Sanskrit during the first century A.D. As Mahayana Buddhism spread to China, Japan, and Tibet, the works were translated and new scriptures were added. Vajrayana combines these texts (known as tantras) with ritual practices such as meditation and chanting mantras (words believed to have a powerful energy).

The Tibetan scriptures are divided into two separate parts. One is the *Bka-gyur* ("Translation of the Word of the Buddha"), which contains translations of Indian Buddhist scriptures. The second is *Bstan-gyur* ("Translation of Treatises"), which includes commentaries on the *Bka-gyur* and hymns and poems.

Offerings are a vital part of prayer in Tibetan Buddhism, a practice thought to have been adapted from earlier Tibetan religions. Tibetan Buddhists often place food and gifts in front of shrines to bodhisattvas or local gods. Unlike other forms of Buddhism, Tibetan Buddhism places a strong emphasis on the importance of ritual. The rituals and beliefs that surround death in particular are extremely important; they are contained in the *Bardo Thodol*, known as the Tibetan Book of the Dead.

Mount Kilas in Tibet is sacred to Tibetan Buddhists and is the traditional home of the Buddhist spiritual leader, the Dalai Lama. The role of the teacher or lama is sometimes seen as the key to passing on Buddhism. Tibetans believe that lamas are continuously reincarnated and dedicate themselves to Buddhist teaching from childhood until death.

The Chinese invaded Tibet in 1951 and the 14th Dalai Lama fled Tibet following a failed Tibetan revolt in 1959. Since then, the Chinese have worked to eradicate Buddhism. Tibetan Buddhists inside and outside Tibet struggle to keep their traditions alive.

PEOPLE & PLACES	DOCUMENTS, ART, & ARTIFACTS	WORSHIP & DOCTRINE

EUROPE

851 Execution of the first of the "Martyrs of Cordoba" in the Moorish kingdom of Al Andalus (now Andalusia, Spain). Some 48 Christians are executed over the next decade; they are mainly monks who deliberately set out to provoke the Muslim authorities to seek martyrdom.

851 Danish raiders sack Canterbury Cathedral in England (it is rebuilt ca 950).

865 Boris, king of the Bulgars, is baptized into the Orthodox Christian Church.

ca 850 A system of modes is developed that establishes the harmony for church music; centuries later it leads to the development of major and minor scales.

ca 860 An author publishes a collection of what purport to be letters by earlier popes establishing the supremacy of the pope and Catholic bishops over temporal rulers; these "False Decretals" are later revealed as forgeries.

873 A scribe at Christ Church, in Canterbury, England, creates a document so poorly written that a modern historian has suggested that he either knew no Latin or was blind and could not read his own words; English learning had suffered during years of Danish (Viking) invasion.

863 Pope Nicholas I begins the "Photian Schism" when he excommunicates Photius, who has illegally seized the patriarchate of Constantinople; the break between Rome and Constantinople lasts four years before a new emperor, Basil the Macedonian, deposes Photius and interns him in a monastery.

865 Byzantine Christianity becomes the official religion in Bulgaria.

THE AMERICAS

ca 850 The ceremonial center of Chichén Itzá is founded in the northern Yucatán Peninsula, in Mexico, marking a northward shift by the declining Mayan culture.

This Mayan chacmool, or ceremonial altar, at Chichén Itzá was designed to receive offerings to the gods, including the hearts of human sacrifices.

ASIA & OCEANIA

857 The wooden Foguang temple is built in Shanxi, China.

877 Indravarman I becomes king of the Khmer in Cambodia; his temple-mountain, Bakong, founds the tradition of religious architecture later continued by Angkor Wat.

889 The Khmer begin building a capital at Angkor in Cambodia.

868 The *Diamond Sutra*, the world's earliest known printed book, is produced in China; it is a Chinese translation of a short Buddhist sermon on the importance of avoiding extreme mental attachment to the world.

AFRICA & THE MIDDLE EAST

862 The Karaouine Mosque is built in Fez in what is now Morocco.

873 Muhammad al-Muntazar, the 12th imam of the Shiite Imami sect, disappears after going for a walk; his followers, the Twelver Shiites, still await his return.

876 The Tulunids build the Ibn Tulun Mosque in Cairo, Egypt.

ca 850 Patriarch Photius of Constantinople writes *Bibliotheca*, with extracts from ancient books that are now lost.

865 The *Sahih Bukhari*, a book of hadith (the sayings of Muhammad) is published; five more books follow in the next five years.

ca 871 Ibn Abd al-Hakam writes an account of the Arab conquest and the introduction of Islam to Egypt.

ca 895 The earliest-known Hebrew copy of the Old Testament is created.

ca 850 The mystic tradition of Sufi Islam is founded by the Egyptian Duhl Nul (📄 page 139).

869 The Eighth Council of Constantinople is called, mainly to consider disputes within the Orthodox Church.

882 At the Babylonian academy, Saadiah ben Joseph institutes a reform of the Jewish ritual calendar; it will take 60 years and will establish the date of Passover and other holy days.

RELIGION IN THE WORLD

ca 850 Jewish settlers in Germany develop a new language, now known as Yiddish.

855 King Ethelwulf of Wessex, England, begins to raise Peter's Pence, a tax paid to the Pope.

862 The Greek brothers Saints Cyril and Methodius are sent to convert the Slavs to Christianity.

863 The Cyrillic alphabet, traditionally attributed to Saint Cyril, is adopted in eastern Europe.

ca 880 Alfred the Great, king of Wessex, begins a program of education to revive Christian learning in England; among other works he translates Pope Gregory's *Pastoral Care*, a guide to the training of monks.

Convey my teachings to the people even if it is a single sentence, and tell others the stories of Bani Israel which have been taught to you, for it is not sinful to do so. Whoever ascribes to me what I have not said then let him occupy his seat in hell-fire.

SAHIH BUKHARI, VOLUME 4, BOOK 56, NUMBER 667

850 The Abbasids transform their capital at Samarra, in what is now Iraq, with a building program of mosques and palaces.

868 The independent Tulunid dynasty comes to power in Egypt.

871 The independent Arab Safavid dynasty comes to power in southeast Iran and Pakistan; it later conquers the whole of Iran.

881 The Abbasid capital is moved back to Baghdad.

WORLD EVENTS

859 Vikings raid coastal towns in the Mediterranean.

866 Danish Vikings invade England.

867 Basil I seizes the Byzantine throne from Michael the Drunkard, founding the Macedonian Dynasty, which will oversee a revival in the empire's fortunes.

874 Vikings start to settle Iceland.

878 The States of Novgorod and Kiev unite to form the first Russian state.

878 In England Alfred the Great defeats the Danes at the Battle of Edington; he will eventually confine the invaders to the eastern part of the country known as the Danelaw.

862 The long drought afflicting the Mayan lowlands peaks at about this time, contributing to massive population loss in the region.

889 The last dated inscriptions found in the Mayan lowlands date from this year.

ca 850 Maori sailors from Hawaii or Samoa land in New Zealand, where they settle and push the indigenous Moriois to the South Island.

This stained-glass window shows three saints from the Czech church: Ludmilla, Methodius, and Wenceslas. Ludmilla was a convert of Methodius; the famed "good king" Wenceslas was her grandson.

ISLAM IN INDIA

Islam arrived on the Subcontinent as early as 711, when Arab armies spilled across the mountains of the Hindu Kush onto the plains of the Indus Valley. There, in the region of Sind (now part of Pakistan), they established their own ruling dynasties which remained in power throughout the eighth and ninth centuries.

No concerted attempt at more systematic Islamization was made until 998, when the Afghan Mahmud of Ghazni came to power swearing jihad—holy war—for the conversion of India. By 1001 his forces were attacking in earnest. Nearly three decades of constant raiding culminated in the sack of the famous Hindu temple-city of Somnath. By his death in 1030 Mahmud had brought the entire northern Indian province of Punjab under Islamic rule.

Mahmud's empire did not long survive his death, although his successors kept his Ghaznavid dynasty alive in its original heartland around the Afghan city of Ghazni. In 1173, however, they were swept away by the forces of the Ghurid dynasty from eastern Iran. By 1193 Muhammad Ghuri's forces had captured Delhi. He made the city the capital of a rich and powerful Muslim sultanate that in time spanned the entire northern part of the subcontinent from the Indus River to the Bay of Bengal.

After Muhammad's death in 1206 the Delhi Sultanate was taken over by one of his generals, Qutbuddin Aibak, who had been born a slave. Qutubbin and his successors are known to history as the Slave dynasty. They were overthrown in 1290 by the Khalji, whose most illustrious ruler, Alauddin, conquered much of southern India. Yet, for all their military might, the sultans were living on borrowed time: A new and terrifying threat was looming in the steppes of the north. The sultanate survived the first wave of Mongol assaults, although in diminished form, but could not resist the invasion of Timur in 1398, which smashed the power of the Delhi sultans once and for all.

PEOPLE & PLACES	DOCUMENTS, ART, & ARTIFACTS	WORSHIP & DOCTRINE

EUROPE

910 The Benedictine abbey is founded at Cluny, France; it becomes a center of monastic reform (📄 facing page).

913 Lando becomes the last pope to take a name that has not already been used by a predecessor.

929 Emir Abdurrahman III of Córdoba, Spain, proclaims himself caliph, claiming supreme civil and religious authority in the Muslim world.

929 In Bohemia, the Christian duke Wenceslas is murdered by his pagan brother while on the way to church; he is later canonized as a martyr and miracle-worker and, in the mid-19th century, becomes the subject of the popular Christmas carol.

ca 900 Saint Tutlio, a monk at the Benedictine abbey of St. Gall in Switzerland, is a major artistic figure, painting, composing music, and writing poetry.

902 Construction begins of the campanile (bell tower) at St. Mark's in Venice, Italy; it collapses exactly 1,000 years later, in 1902.

ca 925 The dialogue of The Three Maries and the Angels at Christ's tomb is performed in churches on Easter morning, beginning the tradition of sacred drama.

These monumental stone sculptures of warriors stood in the Toltec capital of Tula.

917 The Bulgarian Church becomes independent of both Rome and Constantinople.

921 The Bohemians convert to Christianity.

927 Odo, bishop of Cluny, writes a code of discipline for Benedictine monks.

942 Christianity begins to be adopted in Hungary.

THE AMERICAS

ca 900 Anasazi builders at Chaco Canyon, New Mexico, construct a radiating network of roads so wide they are believed to have had a spiritual or ritual rather than practical purpose.

ca 900 The culture of the Cahokia reaches a peak near what is now St. Louis, with up to 100 mounds supporting ceremonial shrines or funerary temples.

ca 900 The Anasazi (Pueblo) culture in what is now the southwestern United States build kivas—circular subterranean ritual spaces—at the heart of their multistory settlements.

ASIA & OCEANIA

ca 900 The Buddhist temples at Nara become one of Japan's main centers of artistic activity.

ca 900 Under the Chola dynasty of India, craftsmen produce spectacular bronze sculptures for use in religious processions.

ca 900 At Ellora in India, Jains begin to excavate five cave-temples alongside numerous existing Hindu and Buddhist caves.

930 The first-known written example of the Telgulu language of southern India appears in the dedication of a temple to Shiva.

ca 935 The beginning of the Koryo period marks the greatest influence of Buddhism in Korea.

AFRICA & THE MIDDLE EAST

909 Taking its name from Fatima, daughter of the Prophet and wife of Ali, the Shiite Fatimid dynasty is established in Tunisia.

915 The Fatimids invade Egypt.

930 Rebels sack the Muslim holy city of Mecca.

ca 900 The Jewish Book of Creation, the Sepher Yetzirah, is written down; its author is said to be the prophet Abraham.

916 The Codex Babylonicus Petropolitanus is produced, the earliest-known complete Old Testament.

This 11th-century illustration shows a pair of Fatimid warriors, with their decorated swords and armor.

ca 900 King Alfonso III of Castile begins the reconquest of Spain from the Islamic Moors.

904 The election of Pope Sergius III begins a 60-year "dark age" of the papacy (also known as the Pornocracy or Rule of the Harlots) in which the papacy is shaped by corruption, conspiracy, affairs, and illegitimacy.

ca 930 Córdoba becomes the center of Islamic culture in Spain.

939 The kingdom of León captures Madrid, Spain, from the Moors.

911 The French king buys off Norman (Northmen) settlers by granting their leader, Rollo, the duchy of Normandy in northern France.

930 Norse settlers in Iceland establish the Althing, the world's oldest parliament.

ca 945 Gerbert of Aurillac, a French philosopher and future pope, introduces Hindu-Arabic numbers to Europe, but the new system does not at first catch on.

ca 900 Maya society finally collapses with the abandonment of the remaining lowland cities.

ca 900 The Toltec establish a capital at Tula, Mexico.

The central spire at the abbey of Cluny.

THE ABBEY AT CLUNY

Cluny was a Benedictine monastery founded in Burgundy in 910. It became famous for leading a movement for reform within the Roman Catholic Church that was a force for peace and progress in society for almost two centuries.

Duke William the Pious of Aquitaine established the abbey and installed a Burgundian nobleman, Berno, as its abbot. Berno and his monks initiated reform to address the troubling spiritual problems of their time: worldliness, immorality, and simony, or the purchasing of positions in the church. The monks renewed the Benedictine Rule of discipline and emphasized above all the need for worship and prayer.

Cluny was ruled by a remarkable series of abbots, many of whom were later canonized. They turned Cluny into a well-organized and productive institution that exerted a strong influence on European religion and politics.

As Cluny's reputation for piety and productivity grew, other monasteries wanted to be associated with it. The reformers instituted a congregational system of "daughter" houses. A prior was appointed for each monastery, but all were under the absolute control of the abbot of Cluny. The movement spread, until by the mid-1100s there was a network of 314 houses.

Diligent labor brought prosperity to Cluniac monasteries, and they were also given generous gifts by noble families. The monasteries became famous for their elegant buildings and elaborate services of worship. This desire to enhance worship with ornate accessories stimulated the production of glassmaking, metalworking, and the weaving of fine fabric. Perhaps inevitably, this wealth led to moral and spiritual decline. In the 1200s Cluny came under the control of Louis IX, king of France, and from then on, it was subject to the French crown. Later it was given as a benefice, or financial privilege, to the powerful Guise family.

PEOPLE & PLACES	DOCUMENTS, ART, & ARTIFACTS	WORSHIP & DOCTRINE

EUROPE

955 Grand Duchess Olga of Russia is baptized in Constantinople.

961 In London, St. Paul's Cathedral is rebuilt after a fire.

962 In Greece, the monastery of Great Lavra is founded on a peninsula near Mount Athos.

972 Grand Prince Géza of Hungary becomes a Christian.

996 The first German pope, Gregory V, is elected.

999 The philosopher Gerbert of Aurillac becomes the first French pope, Sylvester II.

ca 970 The German abbess Hroswitha of Gandersheim begins writing a series of Latin poems and plays that celebrate Christianity and chastity.

976 At Córdoba in Spain the Great Mosque is completed; it is notable for its 70 libraries of hand-copied books (one library alone holds 500,000 volumes).

980 An organ with 400 pipes is built at Winchester Monastery in southern England.

993 Bernward becomes bishop of Hildesheim in Germany and begins a program of artistic patronage reflecting the city's high status in the Holy Roman Empire.

996 In newly Christianized Russia, the Church of the Tithes is built in Kiev.

964 Monasticism begins to revive in England after the Danish invasions.

965 St. Dunstan enforces celibacy among English clerics.

966 The Poles are converted to Christianity.

980 After Muslim rulers are expelled from Crete, Nikon reconverts islanders to Christianity.

988 Vladimir, ruler of Kiev in what is now Ukraine, is converted to Christianity, founding the Russian Orthodox Church (📄 page 131).

993 The first saints are canonized by the Pope (📄 facing page).

998 The feast of All Souls is celebrated for the first time, in the abbey at Cluny.

THE AMERICAS

The Hindu temples at Khajuraho are famous for their elaborate carvings of erotic, religious, and everyday scenes.

ASIA & OCEANIA

ca 950 The Chola queen Sembiyan Madhavi becomes an important patron of Hinduism, spending her life building temple and monasteries.

ca 990 The Chola queen Kundavi builds three temples in southern India: two are dedicated to Vishnu and Shiva, respectively; the third is a Jain temple.

998 Mahmud of Ghazni becomes ruler of the Islamic Ghaznavid kingdom and pledges to conquer Hindu India.

ca 950 In southern India the Hindu Chandella dynasty begins two centuries of building at Khajuraho, including Hindu and Jain temples famous for their erotic carvings.

971 The Song rulers of China commission the carving of more than 130,000 woodblocks in order to print the whole Buddhist canon; the work takes 12 years.

981 A free-standing 57-foot-tall statue of the Jain deity Lord Bahubali is built at Shravanabelagola in Karnataka State, India.

AFRICA & THE MIDDLE EAST

953 The al-Azhar University is founded in Cairo; its reputation as a center of Islamic learning grows rapidly.

977 Shiite Muslims build a shrine at the burial place of Ali, son-in-law of Muhammad, in Najaf, Iraq; the shrine becomes one of the holiest places in Shiism.

ca 985 Islam begins to make advances in the Christian regions of Nubia.

996 In Egypt, Caliph el-Hakim begins a 25-year persecution of Coptic Christians.

A monument to St. Vladimir, the "Baptizer of Russia," stands in Kiev, Ukraine.

RELIGION IN THE WORLD	WORLD EVENTS
959 St. Dunstan, a key church reformer and spiritual advisor to English kings, becomes archbishop of Canterbury.	**954** Eric Bloodaxe, the last Viking king of York, is killed; England is united under the Anglo-Saxon King Eadred.
962 Pope John XII crowns Otto of Saxony Holy Roman Emperor in return for Otto's protection of Christian lands in Italy, Germany, and central Europe.	**962** After conquering Italy, Otto I is crowned Holy Roman Emperor.
962 St. Bernard of Menthon founds a hospice for travelers at the top of the Alpine pass in Switzerland that now bears his name, the Great Saint Bernard.	**ca 982** Vikings led by Erik the Red set up camp on Greenland, establishing a larger colony four years later.
	ca 987 The Toltec leader Topiltzin is driven into exile in "Tlapallan"—probably the Yucatán Peninsula.
962 A Turkic Islamic kingdom is founded at Ghazni in Afghanistan; the Ghaznavids rule the region for the next two centuries.	**960** Taizu becomes the first emperor of the Song dynasty.
991 Korea's rulers are greatly impressed to receive a printed copy of the Song dynasty Buddhist canon.	**978** Chinese scholars begin compiling a 1,000-volume encyclopedia.
999 The conquest of northern India and Central Asia by Turkic peoples bring those regions under Islamic control.	
ca 950 The Arab-dominated nature of the Islamic world is changed when the weakness of the Abbasids allows Turks from Central Asia to invade Muslim lands; many adopt the faith of their new territory.	**980** Arab settlers found towns along the eastern coast of Africa.
969 The Fatimids make Cairo the capital of their empire.	

THE COMING OF THE SAINTS

The Christian Church has always recognized certain individuals as being particularly holy. When, in 993, Pope John XV made the first formal canonization (of Saint Udalric, bishop of Augsburg), he was in many ways simply formalizing a process that was already centuries old.

In the early centuries of the church the individuals who achieved special status were the martyrs who had given up their lives for their Christian faith. Stories soon emerged of miracles that occurred near their graves. Their relics were collected and venerated. Later—from about the fourth century—the same honor was accorded to "confessors," who demonstrated their piety and faith by the example of their lives.

The process by which individuals came to be venerated was somewhat haphazard. Local bishops tried to ensure that local congregations only venerated suitable individuals. They ensured that any claims to martyrdom were investigated thoroughly to confirm that the proposed martyr was indeed motivated by his or her faith. Christians could be censured for venerating unauthorized individuals.

Even after John XV instituted the role of the pope in the canonization, or official recognition, of a saint, other authorities continued to claim the right to proclaim saints. That right was ended by Pope Alexander III in 1173, who condemned bishops for canonizing an undeserving individual: "It is not lawful for you to venerate him without the authority of the Catholic Church."

Official canonization involves a long process of investigation based on proofs that an individual has lived or died in such a devout way that he or she is a worthy example to other Christians. A lesser form of recognition—beatification—allows saints to be venerated locally. Canonization, however, allows them to be venerated in church liturgy around the world, and confirms that the church acknowledges their sanctity.

O din is the highest and oldest of the gods. He rules all things, but the other gods, each according to his might, serve him as children a father.

SNORRI STURLSSON

GODS OF THE VIKINGS

THE VIKINGS CAME FROM SCANDINAVIA, THE COUNTRIES OF Denmark, Iceland, Sweden, and Norway. Although primarily a society of farmers and fisherman, from the late eighth century groups of Viking warriors began raiding European coastal settlements. The Vikings frequently looted monasteries and churches and acquired a fearsome reputation in Europe that colored Christian accounts of their culture and religion. Consequently, there is little reliable information on Viking religious practices.

It is known the Vikings were pagan when they first came into contact with other Europeans, and worshiped many different gods. The chief of the gods was Odin, god of war. His wife Frigg was said to be the equivalent of the Greek goddess Venus. Odin's son, Thor, god of thunder, was known for his strength. Considered stupid, he was the god who represented the ordinary man. He was worshiped for his ability to bring rain to water crops.

Other important gods included the twins, Freyja and Freyr. Freyja was the goddess of wealth, fertility, and love; her twin brother was the sun god. Loki was the trickster god who could change shape and sex at will. He was part god and part fire spirit. He both caused the other gods trouble and helped them.

According to legend, Viking warriors who fell in battle went to Valhalla, which was a great hall where the dead heroes were said to feast at a long table. The Valkyries, warrior maidens who rode through the skies, were responsible for retrieving the dead from the battlefield and transporting them to Valhalla.

Little remains of any places connected with Viking religious ceremonies. An 11th-century account describes a wooden temple that contained a wooden statue dedicated to three Viking gods. According to the account, sacrifices of men and animals were made to the deities around the spring equinox.

This seventh-century carving shows two Viking warriors wearing headdresses decorated with boars, symbols of Freyja, the goddess of wealth, love, and war.

This illustration from a 13th-century Icelandic manuscript depicts Odin riding Sleipnir, his eight-legged flying horse.

CHAPTER 4

AGE OF GODS AND KINGS

This 16th-century illustration from an Aztec codex shows an Aztec emperor watching human sacrifice on a pyramid temple. The horrified Spaniards who arrived in Mexico in 1519 recorded that victims lay on their backs over a stone; four priests held their arms and legs while a fifth cut out their heart so quickly that it was still beating. The body was rolled off the pyramid to bounce down to the bottom.

Previous pages Serene faces smile from the stones of the Bayon at Angkor, in Cambodia. Built in the 12th century, the Mahayana Buddhist temple was one of the last great monuments constructed at the religious capital of the Khmer during a period when Buddhism and Hinduism shaped state formation in Southeast Asia. The faces—there are 216 in total—may represent either King Jayavarman II, who had the monument built, or the bodhisattva Lokesvara: the Khmer saw their rulers as god-kings descended from either Shiva or Buddha, depending on whether they were Hindu or Buddhist.

THE MIDDLE AGES WERE A TIME OF CONTRASTS WHEN FORMAL RELIGION existed alongside a belief in witches and magic, when great learning rubbed shoulders with widespread illiteracy and superstition, and when passionate faith was the cause of unspeakable violence. For communities around the world, from the Buddhists of Japan to the Inca and Aztec who came to power in the Americas, faith lay at the heart of everyday life. In Europe, townspeople devoted vast resources to the construction of monuments that would declare the glory of God. In the Islamic world spectacular mosques and madrasahs were built in cities from northern India to North Africa. Pilgrims from China took years to make the arduous journey to Buddhist sites in India and Tibet. In the Valley of Mexico, the Aztec based their whole civilization on making human sacrifices to the gods, maintaining a martial society in order to produce the warriors necessary to maintain a steady supply of captives from neighboring peoples for the purpose. Meanwhile rulers explored the usefulness of organized religion not merely for its spiritual contribution but also because it could play a part in social organization and unification. A change of ruler might bring a new faith, when the population would be forced to convert or left free to follow their own religion—but possibly at the price of paying higher taxes or of being excluded from high office.

Everywhere religion inspired artistic excellence, from the subterranean churches carved out of solid rock in the Ethiopian highlands to the delicate mosaics and gilded icons in an Orthodox Church and the deceptive simplicity of rock gardens in Japanese temples. Scholarship flourished, too. Jewish rabbis questioned and interpreted the law and the Torah; mullahs read the Koran and the hadith, or sayings of Muhammad; monks in the libraries and scriptoria of European monasteries asked themselves questions about the meaning of faith and the nature of salvation that Christians are still asking today. Manuscripts were highly treasured, lovingly transcribed by Islamic calligraphers or illuminated by Christian monks. But whereas in Christian Europe reading the words was usually the privilege of the priestly hierarchy, Islam, Buddhism, and Hinduism were highly literate faiths.

Monasteries were the focus not only of scholarship and artistic production but also of economic life. Religious foundations and the towns that grew up around them grew wealthy on taxes or on the revenue generated or donated by pilgrims. Monks in Europe took the lead in clearing land for agriculture and in innovations in farming methods. But for some Catholics, the church was becoming altogether too worldly. They began to object to church organizations that preached poverty while accumulat-

ing riches or to clergy—even popes—who professed spiritual authority while living more like princes, enjoying luxuries, maintaining mistresses, and passing on power to their illegitimate children. Small groups of believers came together in religious orders, trying to rediscover the spiritual experience at the heart of Christianity. Their dissatisfaction was the forerunner of huge upheavals to come.

Internal corruption was only one threat to the Christian Church, however. Beliefs that rejected Catholic dogma—heresy—had to be rooted out to preserve the purity of the faith. So too did the constant threat of witchcraft, which was suppressed in vicious campaigns that now seem unnecessarily spiteful but which to late medieval Europeans were grim battles to ensure salvation. The growth of Islam meanwhile left Christendom threatened by the presence of a mighty empire on its borders. When the Catholic Church called on the continent's rulers to win back the holy places of the Bible Lands, the series of Christian-Muslim wars known as crusades began. Armies from Western Europe fell on the Holy Land (and on the Christian Byzantine Empire). Despite Christian success in carving out temporary "Crusader Kingdoms," the centuries-long struggles failed to alter permanently the balance of power. They did, however, encourage a rich cultural and technological exchange between the Islamic and Christian worlds on the one hand—but on the other a long legacy of bitterness whose effects are still sometimes felt today.

Notre Dame, which stands on an island in the Seine River in the heart of Paris, was completed in the middle of the 13th century. The cathedral began the Gothic tradition in European architecture, in which builders used thinner walls and columns and more stained glass to construct soaring palaces of heavenly light.

	1000	1040	1080	1120	1160	
EUROPE	**ca 1000** Christianity arrives in Greenland and Iceland. **ca 1000** Spain replaces Mesopotamia as the dominant center of Jewish culture. **1022** The Synod of Pavia insists that the senior clergy in the Roman Catholic Church must remain celibate.	**1054** The schism between the Western and Eastern churches begins at Constantinople, when papal and patriarchal representatives mutually excommunicate one another; the dispute begins centuries of separation and division. **1077** Emperor Henry IV travels to Canossa in Italy to do penance to the pope.	**1088** Building of the Great Church begins at the abbey of Cluny. **1095** In response to a plea from Byzantine emperor Alexius I, Pope Urban II proclaims the First Crusade at Clermont in central France; its aim is to win back control of the Holy Land from the Seljuk Turks.	**1122** The Concordat of Worms resolves the power struggle between the popes and the Holy Roman emperors. It gives the emperors temporal authority; spiritual authority lies with the popes. **1143** Under the auspices of Peter the Venerable, abbot of Cluny, the Koran is translated into Latin.	**1170** Thomas Becket, archbishop of Canterbury, is murdered in Canterbury Cathedral by knights loyal to King Henry II. **1189** The coronation of Richard I in London sparks the "Massacre of the Jews" in which Jewish homes are burned and Jews murdered; at York the following year some 150 Jews are murdered rather than renounce their faith.	
THE AMERICAS	**ca 1000** In the lower Mississippi Valley a Southern Cult of mound-building peoples emerge.	**ca 1050** The violent life of the Toltec is reflected in their warrior religion, based on human sacrifice.	**ca 1100** The Maya who live in the lowlands of the Yucatán Peninsula make sacrifices to their gods by throwing valuable artifacts—and people—into deep sinkholes known as cenotes.	**ca 1150** The Mixtec begin writing sacred books in the high style of pictographic writing to commemorate their rulers.		
ASIA & OCEANIA	**1021** The Vimal Vasahi temple is carved into marble cliff by Jains at Dilwara, Gujurat, India. **1023** Amidism, or worship of Amida Buddha, begins in Japan; its followers believe the Buddha will help them be reborn in the Pure Land.	**1044** The accession of Anawratha in Burma begins 200 years of religious building at Pagan. **1057** Military victories by King Anawratha of Burma strengthen Buddhism in northern Thailand.	**ca 1100** On Easter Island, natives begin to erect massive stone statues, or *moai*, which represent guardian ancestors. **ca 1100** New gods and goddesses are introduced from Tahiti to Hawaii. **1100** The Song ruler Huizong begins a persecution of Buddhists in China.	**1145** The Korean scholar Kim Pusik writes *Samguk Sagi*, a history of Korea that emphasizes the positive effect of Confucianism on the development of the country.	**ca 1170** The monk Honen establishes Pure Land Buddhism—already ancient in China—as the independent Jodo sect in Japan. **1197** In India, Buddhist monasteries are attacked by Ghurid forces eager to replace Buddhism with Islam.	
AFRICA & THE MIDDLE EAST	**1004** The House of Knowledge, a library and center of scientific learning, opens in Cairo. **1009** In Jerusalem, Caliph al-Hakim orders the destruction of the Church of the Holy Sepulcher. **1020** The Druze sect of Lebanon begins when followers of Caliph al-Hakim, who claims to be the Mahdi, or messiah, flee persecution in Egypt after his death. **1027** Jewish communities settle in North Africa.	**1055** The Seljuk Turks, Sunni Muslims, seize Baghdad from the Shiite Buyids and reinvigorate the caliphate. **1067** In Baghdad, the Seljuk vizier Nizam al-Mulk founds the Nizamiya madrasah, or religious college. **1076** The Almoravids introduce Islam to the western African empire of Ghana. **1076** In the African kingdom of Kanem, King Hummany is persuaded by his conversion to Islam to promote education and literacy.	**1083** The Almoravids complete the conquest of all of North Africa west of Algiers from the Fatimids. **1097** An army of crusaders arrive in the Holy Land and capture the Seljuk capital, Nicaea. **1099** Crusaders capture Jerusalem. **ca 1100** Islam arrives in the kingdom of Kanem-Bornu on the southern edge of the Sahara. **1109** The crusaders have created several "Latin" kingdoms in Palestine and Syria.	**1124** The crusaders capture the city of Tyre. **1130** The Egyptian Fatimid caliph al-Amir is murdered by the Nizari Ismailis (Assassins). **1138** Salah ad-Din (Saladin) is born to a Sunni family in what is now Kurdish Iraq. **1149** Nur ad-Din defeats the crusader Raymond of Antioch and reestablishes Muslim dominance in Syria. **1159** The triumphant march of Byzantine emperor Manuel I through Antioch proves premature when his crusader army is attacked by Turks on the way home.	**1166** Death of the wandering Sufi mystic Ahmad ibn Ibrahim al-Yasavi, who spread Islam among Turkic nomads in central Asia. **1174** Saladin captures Syria from the crusaders. **1180** The great Jewish commentator Moses Maimonides completes a law code, entitled Mishnah Torah. **1187** Saladin defeats the crusaders at the Battle of Hattin and goes on to capture Jerusalem. **1191** The Third Crusade ends in failure.	

1200	1240	1280	1300	1325–1350
1209 Francis of Assisi writes his first rule for his Franciscan friars. **1215** The Fourth Lateran Council strengthens the Catholic Church's response to heresy and orders Catholics to make annual confession. **1232** Pope Gregory IX introduces the papal inquisition, a church court to combat heresy.	**1242** Frederick II invades papal territory in his dispute with the Pope. **1252** After Pope Innocent IV authorizes the use of torture against heretics, the Inquisition begins to use instruments such as the rack. **1278** In London, 278 Jews found guilty of clipping metal from coins are hanged; Christians guilty of the same crime are merely fined.	**1280** In Spain, Moses de Leon writes the *Zohar*, the main work of the Castilian Kabala tradition. **1283** The Teutonic Knights complete their violent conquest of the pagan Prussians after more than 50 years. **1290** Edward I expels all Jews from England. **1296** Construction begins of Florence Cathedral, Italy.	**1302** In *Unam Sanctam*, Pope Boniface VIII proclaims that "every living creature" falls under the universal jurisdiction of the pope. **1306** Philip IV expels the Jews from France. **1312** The withdrawal of papal support ends the Knights Templar; their disappearance creates many myths and legends, some of which still continue today.	**1327** The Dominican monk "Meister" Eckhart dies in Germany after defending his mystical beliefs against charges of heresy before a Franciscan-led Inquisition ordered by Pope John XXII. **1333** The caliphate of Yusuf I marks the height of Islamic culture in Granada, Spain. **1349** Jews are subjected to a fierce persecution in Germany.
ca 1200 The Anasazi of Arizona and New Mexico divide the year into four seasons; each season is heralded by a particular pattern of light thrown on two spirals carved into an outcrop named Fajada Butte.	**1263** The Mayan city-state of Mayapán is founded in Yucatán in southeast Mexico.			**ca 1325** The Kachina cult develops in the American Southwest; it will later become central to cultures such as the Hopi.
1203 Muslim invaders sack the great Buddhist university at Vikramasila, Bihar state, India. **1206** Former slave Qutbuddin Aibak founds the Islamic Delhi Sultanate in northern India. **ca 1220** The Japanese monk Eisai introduces Zen Buddhism to Japan from China.	**1266** Sanjusangendo Temple is built in Japan. **1271** Governor Tughril Khan extends Muslim rule deep into eastern Bengal. **1277** The Pagan Empire is weakened after defeat by Kublai Khan's Mongols.	**1287** The Mongols conquer Pagan, which enters a permanent decline. **1296** Alauddin comes to the throne of the Delhi Sultanate; his 20-year reign marks a golden age of the sultanate.	**1307** An archbishopric is created in Beijing, China. **1320** Ghiyasuddin Tughluq replaces the Khalji rulers in Delhi and founds the Tughluq dynasty.	**ca 1340** Popular religious movements known as the Red Turbans and the White Lotus Society rebel in Yuan, China. **1345** The noble Bhaman Shah overthrows the Delhi Sultanate in the Deccan; the Muslim Bhamanid dynasty rules the region for nearly 200 years.
1204 Constantinople, seat of the Eastern Orthodox Church, falls to the forces of the Fourth Crusade. **1219** The Fifth Crusade has some success in Egypt, but fails to capture Cairo. **1229** In the Sixth Crusade, Europeans take control of Jerusalem under a diplomatic agreement.	**1244** A Muslim army recaptures Jerusalem. **1250** In Egypt the Ayyubid dynasty ends and is replaced by the Turkish Mamluk dynasty. **1254** The Seventh Crusade ends without capturing the Christian holy places. **1256** The Mongol commander Hulagu occupies Persia and founds the Ilkhan dynasty, which later converts to Islam. **1258** Hulagu sacks Baghdad, finally ending the Abbasid caliphate.	**1291** After a series of Mamluk victories over the previous decades, the capture of Acre marks the final end of the crusader presence in Syria and Palestine. **ca 1295** The conversion of the Mongols leads to the destruction of the Nestorian Church in much of Central Asia (the "Assyrian Christians" still survive in the mountains of Kurdistan).	**ca 1300** Amina is the Muslim queen of Zazzau in Africa at about this time. **1324** Ruler of Mali Mansa Musa makes a pilgrimage to Mecca; he spends so much gold that it destabilizes the economy of the states through which he passes, astonishing Western rulers with stories of his wealth.	**1325** The Muslim traveler Ibn Battuta makes a pilgrimage from Egypt to Arabia, beginning his celebrated travels through the Islamic world. **1331** Ibn Battuta visits the wealthy Muslim trading cities of East Africa. **1346** Theodora, daughter of the Byzantine emperor, marries the Ottoman sultan Orhan in return for military aid.

PEOPLE & PLACES	DOCUMENTS, ART, & ARTIFACTS	WORSHIP & DOCTRINE

EUROPE

1009 The missionary Bruno of Querfurt becomes a Christian martyr when he is beheaded while on a mission to convert the Prussians.

1027 The Jewish community in Granada, Spain, gains its first leader, or *nagid*, Samuel Ibn Nagela.

1049 Leo IX becomes pope and begins a period of effective papal reform.

1011 The Handkerchief of St. Veronica, which is said to have been left with a miraculous image of Jesus after she wiped his face with it, is placed in a special altar in Rome.

1018 Construction begins of the cathedral at Strasbourg, France.

1037 The Cathedral of St. Sophia is completed in Kiev.

ca 1000 Christianity arrives in Greenland and Iceland.

ca 1000 Spain replaces Mesopotamia as the dominant center of Jewish culture.

1022 The Synod of Pavia insists that the senior clergy in the Roman Catholic Church must remain celibate.

1038 St. John Gualbert founds the Order of Vallombrosa near Florence.

1045 A school is founded that draws scholars from all over Europe to the Abbey of Bec in Normandy.

1046 Henry III of Germany calls the Council of Sutri in Italy to end the confusion that has seen three men claiming to be pope simultaneously: Clement II is elected pope and, in his first action in his new position, crowns Henry Holy Roman emperor.

Cairo's Al-Hakim Mosque was remodeled in the early 11th century and named for the sixth Fatimid caliph Al-Hakim bi-Amr Allah.

THE AMERICAS

ca 1000 In the lower Mississippi Valley a Southern Cult of mound-building peoples emerge.

ca 1000 The Maya develop two calendar cycles, which coincide every two years.

ca 1000 The Maya believe the universe has three horizontal layers: the earthly world is in the middle, beneath the celestial world; Xibalba, the underworld, lies below (📄 pages 74–75).

ca 1000 Among North American peoples, the Mandan and Hidatsa create origin myths that reflect their reliance on corn.

ca 1030 Mandan women, who grow the community's corn, make offerings to the geese whose return from migration is the signal to plant the new crop.

ASIA & OCEANIA

1018 Mahmud of Ghazni sacks the sacred Hindu city of Mathura in northern India.

1025 Raids by the Hindu Chola kingdom permanently weaken the Buddhist kingdom of Srivijaya in Sumatra, Indonesia.

1030 Mahmud of Ghazni dies; he is interred in an elaborate mausoleum.

1044 Anawratha becomes king of Pagan in Burma; he uses Sri Lankan monks to convert Burma to Theravada Buddhism.

1010 Printing of the Buddhist canon begins in Korea; because carving woodblocks is slow and texts are constantly being imported from China, the task is never completed.

1021 The Vimal Vasahi temple is carved into marble cliff by Jains at Dilwara, Gujarat, India.

1023 Mahmud of Ghazni raids the wealthy Hindu temple at Somnath in Gujarat.

1044 The accession of Anawratha in Burma begins 200 years of religious building at Pagan (📄 pages 162–163).

1017 Invasion and warfare end the tradition of Bhikkhuni (Buddhist nuns) in Sri Lanka.

1023 Amidism, or worship of Amida Buddha, begins in Japan; its followers believe the Buddha will help them be reborn in the Pure Land.

1042 The invitation to the Indian teacher Atisa to preach in Tibet marks the beginning of Buddhism's second period of growth there.

AFRICA & THE MIDDLE EAST

1048 The Almoravids, a clan of Berbers, begin a military campaign that will eventually bring them to power in much of North Africa.

1004 The House of Knowledge, a library and center of scientific learning, opens in Cairo.

1009 In Jerusalem, Caliph al-Hakim orders the destruction of the Church of the Holy Sepulcher.

1020 The Druze sect of Lebanon begins when followers of the Fatimid Caliph al-Hakim, who claims to be the Mahdi, or messiah, flee persecution in Egypt after his death.

1027 Jewish communities settle in North Africa.

RELIGION IN THE WORLD

1004 Muslim raiders sack the Italian city of Pisa.

1028 In Spain, Christians capture Castile from the Muslims.

1031 The caliphate of Córdoba in Spain fragments into smaller states.

1037 The Christian kingdoms of Aragon and Castile are united in Spain.

MONUMENTS OF FAITH

Holy Mountain

Rising at the heart of the Kandariya Mahadeva in Madhya Pradesh in southern India is a 102-foot spire representing Mount Meru, the holy mountain of Shiva, the Hindu god to which the temple is dedicated. Surrounding the central spire or shikara are 84 smaller spires decorated with ornate carvings, including erotic depictions of apsaras, the god's female consorts. The temple was built by the monarch Vidyahara, a famed ruler of the Chandela dynasty who resisted the advance of Islam from Pakistan.

1008 Islamic ruler Mahmud of Ghazni defeats Hindu leaders in present-day Pakistan.

1009 In Vietnam, Buddhist monks help the rise to power of the Ly dynasty, who combine Buddhism with traditional spirit worship.

Completed in about 1050, the Kandariya Mahadeva temple in Madhya Pradesh is a highpoint of medieval Hindu architecture.

WORLD EVENTS

1000 Venice takes control of the Adriatic Sea.

1016 England is united under the Danish king Canute.

1019 Yaroslav the Wise deposes his brother to seize the throne of Kievan Rus; he will become its greatest ruler.

1035 On the death of King Canute, his kingdom in Britain and Scandinavia is divided among his sons.

1040 The Earl of Moray murders Duncan I to become king of Scotland; Shakespeare later retells the story in a play named for the earl: *Macbeth*.

ROCK CHURCHES OF ETHIOPIA

Lalibela, who came to the throne of Christian Ethiopia in the late 12th century, had traveled to the Holy Land and visited the great Christian sites of Jerusalem. When that city was captured by Muslims in 1187, the devout monarch set out to reconstruct a new Jerusalem in the highlands of his kingdom at a city now known by his name: Lalibela.

Building continued throughout the king's reign until 13 churches stood around the city, clustered in four main groups. The most striking were monolithic structures hewn from the bedrock. The earlier Ethiopian kingdom of Axum had become Christian in the 300s (the first country in the world, it claimed to be home to the Ark of the Convenant) so Lalibela was following a long tradition; his architects incorporated elements of Axumite style. The largest of the churches—and the largest monolithic church in the world—Bete Medhane Alem was modeled on the church of Saint Mary of Zion at Axum. Local myths claimed that, when the builders finished work each night, angels came to continue their work: perhaps the angels also painted the rich murals that decorate many of the interior walls. As for Lalibela himself, he abandoned his throne to become a hermit and remains the most venerated of all Ethiopian saints.

THE ORTHODOX CHURCH

THE ORTHODOX CHURCH SEES ITSELF AS THE UNBROKEN continuation of the church established by Christ and his apostles, a legacy expressed in its very name: "orthodoxy" means "right doctrine." The Orthodox Church—in full the Holy Orthodox Catholic Apostolic Eastern Church—is unified by its sacraments rather than by a centralized organization.

The center of the Orthodox Church was Constantinople, the "new Rome" established as the capital of the Roman empire in 330 by Emperor Constantine. Constantine and his successors were heads of the Eastern Church, responsible for appointing the patriarch—chief bishop—of Constantinople and summoning councils to define basic doctrine for the whole of the Christian church. The Orthodox Church stressed the sacraments as the means of achieving salvation. It celebrated the Eucharist (Mass) and baptism with highly symbolic ritual, pomp, and processions. Its worship was essentially mystical; it appealed to the senses and imagination with icons—images of Christ and sacred figures—lamps, and incense.

Golden panels of an iconostasis—a screen decorated with icons—separate the altar from the congregation in this chapel on a Greek island. The iconostasis of Orthodox churches may be highly elaborate, with dozens of icons set in ornate wooden frames.

The Eastern Church was split by disputes. In the fifth century the patriarch Nestorius was exiled for his emphasis on Christ's human rather than divine nature; his followers founded the Nestorian Church in Baghdad. In the eighth century the church was again riven when four successive emperors outlawed the use of icons; restored in 843, icons played a central role in Orthodox worship.

The division between Constantinople and Rome grew, largely over the authority of the pope. In 858 the patriarch and pope excommunicated one another over a point of doctrine. Language had also become a barrier between the churches. Latin was the official language of the Roman Catholic Church, while the Orthodox Church used vernacular, or local, languages. Differences had also developed in ritual and clerical practices. For example, married men could become priests in the Orthodox Church but not in the Roman Catholic Church.

As friction intensified, the Byzantine emperor invited a papal delegation to Constantinople to discuss the issues in 1054. The church leaders ended their talks by excommunicating each other. The once-united Christian church split irrevocably in a torrent of curses.

In 1453 the Ottoman Turks conquered Constantinople, ending the great Byzantine Empire. Missionaries had long since spread Orthodox Christianity to the east. After the fall of Constantinople, Russia became the next great center of the Orthodox Church.

Candles flicker before a Byzantine-style icon of Mary and Jesus in the dark interior of an Orthodox cathedral on the Greek mainland.

PEOPLE & PLACES	DOCUMENTS, ART, & ARTIFACTS	WORSHIP & DOCTRINE

EUROPE

1054 Pope Leo IX quotes the (forged) Donation of Constantine to assert his supremacy over the Patriarch Michael Cerularius.

1073 Gregory VII becomes pope.

1077 Emperor Henry IV travels to Canossa in Italy to do penance to the pope, who makes the visitor wait three days in the snow before receiving him.

1093 Anselm becomes archbishop of Canterbury.

1098 Birth of Hildegard of Bingen, later a renowned German nun (📄facing page).

1099 Rodrigo Díaz de Vivar, better known as El Cid, dies in Valencia, Spain; he is a Spanish hero for his leading role in fighting the Muslims.

ca 1050 Monks in England become expert embroiderers.

ca 1051 The Monastery of the Caves is founded in Kiev, Ukraine; its caves are later supplemented by grand buildings and the monastery becomes the leading center of the Eastern Orthodox Church in Eastern Europe.

1060 Greeks at Daphne create a mosaic in Byzantine style, *Christ as Ruler of the World*.

1088 Building of the Great Church begins at the abbey of Cluny.

1094 The Basilica of St. Mark is consecrated in Venice.

1098 Anselm writes *Cur Deus Homo* (*Why God Became Man*) to explain how Christ's crucifixion atoned for man's sins.

1054 The schism between the Western and Eastern churches begins at Constantinople, when papal and patriarchal representatives mutually excommunicate one another; the dispute begins centuries of separation and division (📄pages 124–125).

1056 The Patarini movement begins in Milan, Italy; its members, many of whom are tradesmen, call for clerical reform such as the outlawing of simony (buying church offices) and clerical marriages.

1059 The college of cardinals becomes responsible for electing the pope.

1073 Elected pope, Gregory VII (Hildebrand) denies Europe's rulers the right to make clerical appointments.

1084 Bruno founds the Carthusian Order.

1098 The Cistercian Order begins with the foundation of the abbey of Cîteaux, France; it spreads rapidly and has more than 600 monasteries by the end of the 13th century.

THE AMERICAS

ASIA & OCEANIA

1084 Kyanzittha succeeds his father Anawratha as king of Burma; he is referred to as a bodhisattva from Buddhism; a chakravartin (a spiritual ruler in Buddhism and Jainism); and an incarnation of the Hindu god Vishnu.

1091 The construction of stone-built temples and pagodas is underway in Pagan, Burma; eventually the city is home to 13,000 religious buildings and palaces (📄pages 162–163).

Be not lazy in the festive service of God. Be ablaze with enthusiasm. Let us be a living, burning offering before the altar of God.

Hildegard of Bingen

AFRICA & THE MIDDLE EAST

1062 The Almoravids found the city of Marrakech in Morocco as their capital.

1067 In Baghdad, the Seljuk vizier Nizam al-Mulk founds the Nizamiya madrasah, or religious college.

1072 Malik Shah becomes ruler of the Seljuk Turks; "shah" means king in both Arabic and Persian, indicating the range of his ambition.

1092 Malik Shah's death begins the break-up of the Seljuk Empire.

1050 In West Africa, the Mossi of what is now Burkina Faso resist the spread of Islam.

1076 The Almoravids introduce Islam to the western African empire of Ghana.

1076 In the African kingdom of Kanem, King Hummany is persuaded by his conversion to Islam to promote education and literacy.

RELIGION IN THE WORLD

1075 The Investiture Crisis begins when Holy Roman emperor Henry IV challenges the pope's ban on lay appointments to the church.

1076 The Synod of Worms deposes Gregory VII as pope; Gregory responds by excommunicating Emperor Henry IV.

ca 1080 The Order of the Hospital of St. John of Jerusalem is founded to take care of Christian pilgrims; today it provides medical volunteers to important public events.

1086 With the help of Almoravids from North Africa, Muslims reestablish dominion over much of Spain.

1092 Roger I triumphs in a 30-year struggle to recapture Sicily from the Muslims.

1095 In response to a plea from Byzantine emperor Alexius I, Pope Urban II proclaims the First Crusade at Clermont in central France; its aim is to win back control of the Holy Land from the Seljuk Turks (📖 pages 132–133).

ca 1050 The violent life of the Toltec is reflected in their warrior religion, based on human sacrifice.

The Byodo-in Temple near Kyoto was founded in 1052 and houses a renowned wooden statue of the buddha Amitabha.

1057 Military victories by King Anawratha of Burma strengthen Buddhism in northern Thailand.

1090 The Nizaria Ismaili Shiites, known in the West as the Assassins, establish a stronghold in the Elburz Mountains of Persia to resist Seljuk rule.

1055 The Seljuk Turks, Sunni Muslims, seize Baghdad from the Shiite Buyids and reinvigorate the caliphate.

1071 At the Battle of Manzikert in Anatolia Seljuk Turks rout the Byzantines.

1097 An army of crusaders arrive in the Holy Land and capture the Seljuk capital, Nicaea.

1099 Crusaders capture Jerusalem.

WORLD EVENTS

ca 1050 The city of Oslo is founded in Norway.

1054 Kiev is torn apart by civil war after the death of Yaroslav the Wise.

1066 William, duke of Normandy, invades England, killing King Harold and taking the throne to begin Norman rule.

1083 The army of Henry IV captures Rome.

1086 William I orders a survey of his kingdom in England that is recorded in a document known as the Domesday Book.

1088 The first university in Europe is founded at Bologna in Italy.

1091 The Norman adventurer Roger de Hauteville conquers Sicily.

Pope Urban II preaches the First Crusade at the Council of Clermont in 1095.

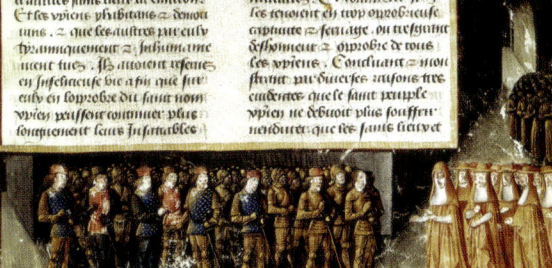

1083 The Almoravids complete the conquest of all of North Africa west of Algiers from the Fatimids.

1092 The Seljuk sultanate begins to fragment after the death of its ruler, Malik Shah.

HILDEGARD OF BINGEN

Hildegard of Bingen was a German nun and visionary. Her contributions to medieval literature, science, and music made her one of the most influential figures of her time.

Hildegard was born in 1098, the 10th child of a noble family. At age 14 she entered the Benedictine monastery at Disibodenberg, where in 1136 she became abbess. Since early childhood Hildegard had experienced visions that she interpreted as revelations from God, and in 1141 she was finally persuaded to write them down in a collection called *Scivias* (*Scito vias dominus* or "Know the Ways of the Lord").

The book brought Hildegard to the attention of the archbishop of Mainz, who in 1148 asked a committee of church scholars to investigate Hildegard's visions. The committee declared that they were indeed divine. Official acceptance gave Hildegard great authority, and she was soon corresponding with contemporary religious and political leaders such as Saint Bernard of Clairvaux and Frederick I Barbarossa.

In 1147 Hildegard established a new convent at Rupertsberg near Bingen, where she wrote two important medical texts. *Physica* (Medicine) and *Causa et curae* (Causes and Cures) demonstrate a powerful imagination and sound scientific observation that were rare in the Middle Ages. In these books Hildegard listed numerous medicinal herbs and drugs, made the connection between sugar and diabetes, and wrote about the relationship between the brain and the nervous system. Hildegard was also a gifted musician and composer.

Following Hildegard's death in 1179, numerous miracles were reported to have taken place at her tomb. Although she was never officially made a saint by the Roman Catholic church, Hildegard is still revered as one in some towns in Germany, where her feast day is celebrated on September 17.

GOTHIC CATHEDRALS

THE GREAT CATHEDRALS OF WESTERN EUROPE ARE AWE-inspiring reminders of a world in thrall to the glory of God. Cathedrals—named for the Greek word for the throne of a bishop—were primers in stone to teach a largely illiterate congregation about the means of salvation. Even the collapse of a cathedral—a frequent occurrence during construction—was taken as a sign of God's displeasure: Chartres Cathedral in France had to be rebuilt six times.

Between about 1000 and 1150 cathedrals were based on Roman architecture, with vaults, rounded arches, and massive walls. But Saint Augustine had described light as a sign of God's presence, and so builders sought to let more light into churches. In about 1150 a new style arose that would dominate the next three centuries. It used pointed arches, ribs, and buttresses to construct buildings that were much taller and lighter. In the 15th century disapproving Renaissance historians dubbed the style Gothic, in the mistaken belief that it came from the Goths, barbarians from northern Europe.

The first great Gothic cathedrals were built in France in the late 12th century, including Notre Dame in Paris, Chartres, Reims, and Amiens. Their soaring height reflects the confidence of the townspeople who paid for them. Slender piers rise to roof vaults, and walls give way to large windows. French cathedrals were characterized by magnificent western facades, with towers, statues, and huge rose-shaped stained-glass windows marking the main entrance.

Meanwhile a distinctively English tradition developed, at Canterbury, Wells, and Lincoln. These cathedrals were longer, lower, and more spread out than in France because they were set in spacious "closes" rather than being squeezed among houses and shops. They still boasted dizzying towers and spires, however. The tallest cathedral spire in medieval Europe was built in England at Salisbury: 404 feet.

Gothic cathedrals came later in other parts of Europe, such as Germany and Spain, where the style varied slightly according to local customs. The design of Seville (begun in 1402), the largest medieval cathedral in Europe, was dictated by the mosque already on the site: its minaret became the cathedral's bell tower.

While the last great Gothic cathedrals were being built in Spain, elsewhere in Europe the main period of cathedral building had already come to an end. Another style of building was beginning to take over from Gothic: the Classical style, encapsulated by the Renaissance dome topping the Gothic walls of the Duomo in Florence.

Salisbury in southern England boasted the tallest spire in medieval Europe. Its nave walls are supported by flying buttresses, load-bearing struts that allow the walls themselves to be a delicate tracery of stone and glass.

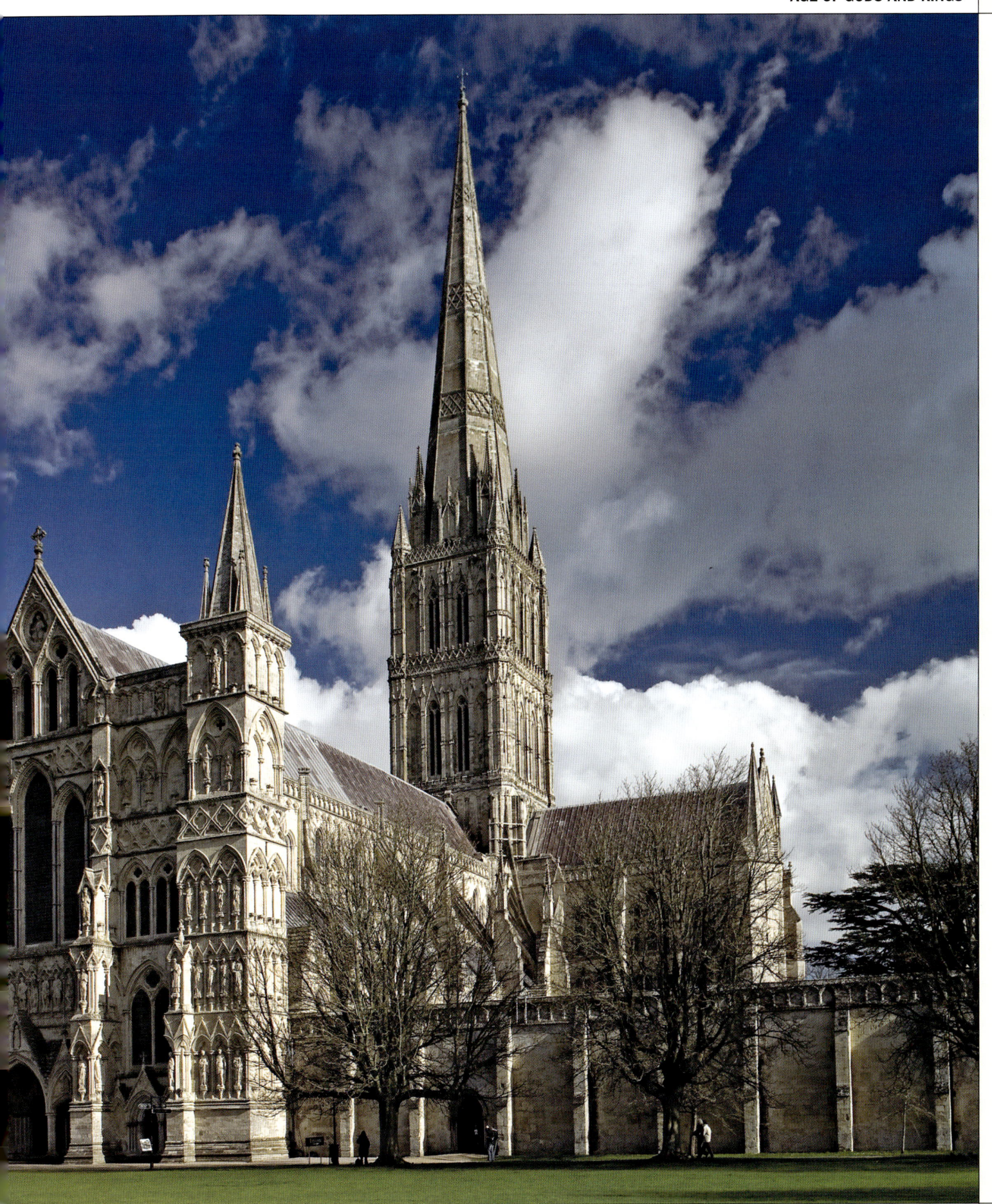

PEOPLE & PLACES	DOCUMENTS, ART, & ARTIFACTS	WORSHIP & DOCTRINE

EUROPE

1112 Bernard, later St. Bernard of Clairvaux, becomes a monk at the abbey of Cîteaux, France.

ca 1116 Renowned French theologian Peter Abelard begins teaching at Notre Dame in Paris; his doomed love affair with the canon's daughter, Héloïse, for which she is ordered into a nunnery and he is castrated, becomes a popular romance of the Middle Ages.

1122 Suger is elected abbot of Saint-Denis in France; he is noted as the first patron of the Gothic style of architecture.

1130 A disputed papal election in Rome leaves both Innocent II and the anitpope Anacletus II claiming the pontificate.

1143 Roger II, the Norman ruler under whom Sicily is enjoying a cultural flowering, raids Islamic states in northern Africa.

1110 The first recorded Miracle Play, a dramatic enactment of an episode from Christ's life, is staged at Dunstable, England.

1113 In Novgorod, Russia, construction begins on the church of St. Nicholas, one of the first onion-domed churches.

1134 The celebrated western facade of Chartres Cathedral is built in France.

1143 Under the auspices of Peter the Venerable, abbot of Cluny, the Koran is translated into Latin.

1122 The Concordat of Worms resolves the power struggle between the popes and the Holy Roman emperors. It gives the emperors temporal authority; spiritual authority lies with the popes.

1123 Pope Callixtus II convenes the First Lateran Council to underline the assertion of papal supremacy in spiritual matters.

1139 The Second Lateran Council is called to resolve the schism that began with the election of the antipope Anacletus II.

ca 1140 The jurist Gratian writes *Decretum* (*Concordance of Discordant Canons*), in which he unifies canon law from a range of sources to produce a document whose authority lasts in the Roman Catholic Church until 1917.

1143 Catholic authorities in Cologne, Germany, report the presence of heretics who support Catharism, a type of Christianity influenced by eastern beliefs.

THE AMERICAS

In this 17th-century painting by Giuseppe Passeri, Saint Stephen welcomes the young noble Bernard (now Saint Bernard) to the Benedictine monastery of Cîteaux in 1113. Three years later, Stephen sent Bernard to found the monastery of Clairvaux.

ca 1100 The Maya who live in the lowlands of the Yucatán Peninsula make sacrifices to their gods by throwing valuable artifacts—and people—into deep sinkholes known as cenotes.

ASIA & OCEANIA

1123 The Tibetan Buddhist poet Milaraspa dies; he is said to have written some 100,000 songs and performed many miracles as a wandering monk.

1145 The Korean scholar Kim Pusik writes *Samguk Sagi*, a history of Korea that emphasizes the positive effect of Confucianism on the development of the country.

ca 1100 On Easter Island, natives begin to erect massive stone statues, or *moai*, which represent guardian ancestors: some 500 years later, the effort of producing the huge monuments precipitates the sudden collapse of Easter Island society.

ca 1100 New gods and goddesses are introduced from Tahiti to Hawaii.

1100 The Song ruler Huizong begins a persecution of Buddhists in China.

AFRICA & THE MIDDLE EAST

1106 The death of Yusuf Ibn Tashfin begins the decline of the Almoravid Empire in northern Africa.

1130 The Egyptian Fatimid caliph al-Amir is murdered by the Nizari Ismailis (Assassins).

1138 Salah ad-Din (Saladin) is born to a Sunni family in what is now Kurdish Iraq.

1149 Nur ad-Din defeats the crusader Raymond of Antioch and reestablishes Muslim dominance in Syria.

1107 Construction is completed of the Friday Mosque at Kizimkazi on the island of Zanzibar off East Africa.

ca 1100 Islam arrives in the kingdom of Kanem-Bornu on the southern edge of the Sahara.

1120 The religious reforms of Ibn Tumert inspire the formation of the Almohad dynasty in the Atlas Mountains of Morocco.

1118 The capture of Saragossa from the Muslims extends the Spanish kingdom of Aragon to the Mediterranean Sea.

1129 The Council of Troyes defines the order of the Knights Templar, otherwise known as the Poor Fellow-Soldiers of Christ and of the Temple of Solomon, one of the most famous of the medieval Christian military orders and a powerful force for two centuries, thanks in part to their role in the Crusades.

1146 Bernard of Clairvaux preaches the Second Crusade at Vézélay in France.

1147 En route to the Holy Land, crusaders from northern Europe liberate Lisbon, Portugal, from Muslim rule.

Shown in a contemporary Egyptian portrait, Salah ad-Din—better known in the West as Saladin—was a Kurdish general (born in 1138) and later Ayyubid sultan of Egypt who earned great respect throughout Europe for the chivalry with which he led the successful Islamic reconquest of Palestine from the crusaders in 1187.

1109 The crusaders have created several "Latin" kingdoms in Palestine and Syria.

1124 The crusaders capture the city of Tyre.

1146 The Second Crusade is proclaimed after the 1144 defeat of the crusaders at Edessa (📄 pages 132–133).

1147 The Almohads seize Marrakech and replace the Almoravids as the major power in North Africa.

ca 1100 The introduction of the padded horse-collar to Europe makes it possible for horses to pull heavier plows, improving agricultural production.

ca 1125 Economic activity increases and new towns are built as Europe experiences a period of prosperity.

1138 Conrad III of the Hohenstofen family becomes German emperor on the death of the Guelf Lothair II.

1143 Having secured independence from the Spanish kingdom of León, Afonso Henriques becomes the first king of Portugal.

ca 1100 Anasazi farmers build cliff dwellings in southern Colorado and Arizona.

ca 1125 Cahokia, Illinois, is the urban center of the mound-builders of the Mississippi Valley.

ca 1125 Pueblo towns in New Mexico are linked by roads into a widespread trade network.

ca 1130 Abd al-Mumin becomes leader of the Almohads on the death of Ibn Tumart.

1143 Sicily's Norman ruler, Roger II, launches raids on the coast of North Africa.

THE RUSSIAN CHURCH

After the split between the western (Roman) and eastern (Greek) branches of Christianity in 1054, the Eastern Church—also known as the Orthodox Church—went its own way. Based on the patriarchate of Constantinople (modern-day Istanbul, in Turkey), it had a liturgy that emphasized the worship of icons. From its heartlands, it spread across the Balkans to eastern Europe.

To the east, the state of Kievan Rus had been founded in the ninth century covering parts of what are now Belorussia, Ukraine, and Russia. Thanks to missions from Constantinople, by the mid-10th century much of the nobility—including the royal Princess Olga—had converted to Christianity, although paganism remained dominant among the masses. Olga's grandson, Grand Prince Vladimir of Kiev, made Kievan Rus a Christian state when he held a mass baptism of his subjects in 989.

Vladimir's motivation for adopting a faith was a desire to forge international contacts and expand trade. He sent out emissaries to study the various faiths available. They reported that Islam forbade alcohol, that Judaism had no homeland, and that Catholicism was highly restrained. Only in the theatrical ritual of the Eastern Orthodox Church did they find a spectacle worth recommending to the grand prince. Vladimir's Russian Orthodox Church took its structure from Roman Catholicism, but its rituals came from the Eastern Church.

At the heart of the new church was the Virgin of Vladimir. This painted icon of Mary and the baby Jesus was sent from the patriarch of Constantinople in 1131 to the ruler of Kiev. Where the horses carrying the icon refused to go any farther, the Kievans erected a new religious capital named for Vladimir, and built the Great Assumption Cathedral there to house the icon. Many people believed that the icon performed miracles; the Virgin of Vladimir remains the most venerated of all the Russian saints.

THE CRUSADES

BETWEEN 1095 AND 1291, ARMIES FROM WESTERN EUROPE fought a series of wars known as Crusades to recapture Palestine from Muslim control and to protect the holy places of Christianity. Crusaders wore a cross (the word "crusade" derives from *crux*, the Latin for "cross"). While many crusaders were motivated by religious zeal, others saw the Crusades as a way of acquiring land and plunder. In the long run the campaigns failed, and Palestine was reclaimed by the forces of Islam.

Pope Urban II launched the First Crusade in 1095 in response to an appeal from the Byzantine Emperor Alexius for help against the Islamic Seljuk Turks, who had recently overrun Anatolia and Syria. An army consisting mostly of French and Norman knights fought its way overland to Jerusalem, which it captured in 1099. Fulcher of Chartres, a Frenchman who wrote an account of the crusade, left a vivid account of the bloody massacre of Muslims that followed the storming of the city.

One reason for the crusaders' success was that the Seljuk Turks, divided by internal feuding, had ceased for the time being to be a military threat. Taking advantage of their divisions, the crusaders set up a number of states in Palestine and Syria known collectively as Outremer ("Overseas"). Commerce flourished as fleets of ships from Venice and Genoa carried a steady stream of pilgrims and supplies to Outremer and brought exotic goods such as silks and spices back to Europe.

The Seljuks did not remain weak for long, however. The Muslim reconquest of Outremer began with the fall of Edessa in 1144. The Second and Third Crusades sent from Europe failed to halt the Muslim advance, and by 1191 the crusader enclaves had been reduced to just the port of Acre on the Syrian coast.

By that time the Byzantines had come to resent the crusaders bitterly. The final insult came in 1204, when the Fourth Crusade sacked Constantinople, massacred its inhabitants, and established a Latin empire in place of the Greek-speaking Byzantine Empire (it lasted until 1261). Although four more expeditions were sent to the Holy Land during the 13th century, the Crusades had largely lost their purpose and impetus.

The Christian ventures to the Holy Land were only part of a wider crusading movement in Europe, which paralleled the Roman Catholic Church's reaction to perceived threats to its power. In the Reconquista, Christian armies gradually reconquered Spain and Portugal from the Muslims, ending in 1492. The Teutonic Knights, meanwhile, a German and Danish crusading order, were active in converting the pagan Slavs and Balts of the eastern Baltic to Christianity. And in 1208 Pope Innocent III declared a crusade against the Albigensians, followers of a heretic sect based in southern France that was wiped out amid much bloodshed over the next two decades.

This 14th-century French illustration depicts Islamic defenders fighting off Christian forces in the Siege of Antioch during the First Crusade. The Europeans captured the Anatolian city after a two-year siege and established it as the center of a crusader state.

PEOPLE & PLACES	DOCUMENTS, ART, & ARTIFACTS	WORSHIP & DOCTRINE

EUROPE

ca 1150 The work of the Islamic scholar Averröes in Córdoba, Spain, helps reintroduce the philosophy of the ancient Greek thinker Aristotle to western Europe (📖 facing page).

1159 Alexander III becomes pope; he is one of the most respected holders of the office.

1161 Edward the Confessor, king of England, is canonized.

1165 Emperor Charlemagne is canonized as a saint (in the 18th century he is reduced to being "blessed").

1170 Thomas Becket, archbishop of Canterbury, is murdered in Canterbury Cathedral by knights loyal to King Henry II; the two had fallen out when Becket excommunicated bishops who crowned Henry's son "junior king" of England; Henry is popularly reported to have complained "Will no-one rid me of this turbulent priest?"

1174 Thomas Becket is canonized as a martyr.

1198 Innocent III becomes pope.

ca 1150 Bernard of Clairvaux writes *De Consideratione* (*On Consideration*), including an apology to the pope for the failure of the Second Crusade (in support of which Bernard had performed miracles) which he blames on the sins of the crusaders.

ca 1157 Peter Lombard writes *The Four Books of Sentences*, for 400 years one of the most important books of Christian theology.

1159 The election of Pope Alexander III causes the Alexandrine Schism in the Roman Catholic Church, which lasts until 1178; the dispute concerns the foreign policy of the Holy See.

1160 Emperor Frederick I Barbarossa declares his support for Antipope Victor IV, deepening the schism.

ca 1174 Wealthy French merchant Peter Waldo forms the "poor men of Lyons," or Waldensians, preaching poverty, public preaching, and personal study of the scriptures; the Waldensians are persecuted as heretics for nearly 500 years.

FAITH AND LIFE

Thomas Becket

The 12th-century English churchman Thomas Becket is venerated by both Catholics and Anglicans for his martyrdom in defense of the church. As England's senior clergyman, archbishop of Canterbury, Becket clashed with Henry II's efforts to establish his own spiritual as well as political primacy. Becket began to excommunicate Henry's supporters. When the king complained, four knights went to Canterbury, where they murdered Becket in the cathedral. Becket's shrine became a major pilgrimage destination until the Reformation of the 16th century, when Henry VIII had the shrine destroyed and Becket's bones disposed of.

THE AMERICAS

Innocent III, who became pope in 1198, excommunicates the Cathars for heresy in this early 14th-century illustration from France, sparking the Albigensian Crusade in 1209.

ca 1150 The Mixtec begin writing sacred books in the high style of pictographic writing to commemorate their rulers.

ASIA & OCEANIA

ca 1150 Buddhist art enters a golden age in Burma.

1197 The great Buddhist university at Nalanda in India is sacked by Muslims.

ca 1170 The monk Honen establishes Pure Land Buddhism—already ancient in China—as the independent Jodo sect in Japan.

1181 The devout Buddhist Jayavarman VII becomes king of the Khmer in modern-day Cambodia; he builds the Buddhist Bayon temple in Angkor, itself a predominantly Hindu monument.

1197 In India, Buddhist monasteries are attacked by Ghurid forces eager to replace Buddhism with Islam.

AFRICA & THE MIDDLE EAST

1157 The death of Sultan Sanjar marks the beginning of the decline of the Seljuk Turks.

1180 Caliph al-Nasir attempts to restore the power of the Abbasid dynasty in Baghdad.

1166 Saladin builds a cathedral in Cairo, Egypt.

1180 The great Jewish commentator Moses Maimonides completes a law code, entitled Mishnah Torah.

1166 Death of the wandering Sufi mystic Ahmad ibn Ibrahim al-Yasavi, who spread Islam among Turkic nomads in Central Asia.

1198 Muslims in Yemen force Jews to convert to Islam.

1164 Henry II of England introduces the Councils of Clarendon to increase the power of the crown at the expense of the church; the argument ends with the exile of the archbishop of Canterbury, Thomas Becket.

1177 At the Treaty of Venice, Alexander III and Frederick I Barbarossa agree to end the schism.

1182 Jews are expelled from France.

1189 Muslims in Sicily begin a 57-year period of rebellions against their Christian rulers.

1189 The coronation of Richard I in London sparks the "Massacre of the Jews" in which Jewish homes are burned and Jews murdered; at York the following year some 150 Jews are murdered rather than renounce their faith.

Built in the late 12th or early 13th century, the last of the 13 rock-cut churches of Lalibela, Ethiopia, the Church of Saint George (Bet Giyorgis) was carved from pink tuff rock in the shape of a Greek cross with four arms of equal length.

1185 The beginning of the Kamakura period marks the emergence of further forms of Japanese Buddhism.

1186 Muhammad Ghuri occupies the Punjab and establishes a Muslim power base in northern India.

1190 After a period of anarchy, Pagan returns to Theravada Buddhist rule.

1159 The triumphant march of Byzantine emperor Manuel I through Antioch proves premature when his crusader army is attacked by Turks on the way home.

1174 Saladin captures Syria from the crusaders.

1187 Saladin defeats the crusaders at the Battle of Hattin and goes on to capture Jerusalem.

1191 The Third Crusade ends in failure.

1152 Eleanor of Aquitaine marries Henry of Anjou, who becomes ruler of much of western France.

1154 Henry of Anjou inherits the Engish throne as Henry II, founding the Plantagenet dynasty.

1171 The English begin the conquest and colonization of Ireland.

1176 At the Battle of Legnano, Italy's merchant cities retain their independence from the Holy Roman Empire.

1189 Three European rulers—Richard I of England, Philip II of France, and Holy Roman emperor Frederick I Barbarossa—proclaim the Third Crusade (Frederick drowns en route to the Holy Land).

ca 1150 The Seljuk sultanate of Rum ("Rome") extends deep into Byzantine territory in what is now Turkey.

1169 Saladin becomes vizier of Egypt on behalf of the Fatimid sultans.

1171 Saladin overthrows the Fatimid dynasty in Egypt and becomes the first Ayyubid sultan.

1194 The Khwarazmian Turks begin to campaign in eastern Iran and Iraq.

AVERROËS

Averroës, the westernized name of Ibn Rushd (1126–1198), was one of the most influential thinkers of the Middle Ages. Latin translations of his commentaries on the works of the ancient Greek Aristotle had a profound influence on Christian and Jewish philosophy.

Born in Córdoba, in Muslim Spain, Averroës studied science, medicine, and philosophy, but eventually became a judge. In 1182 he became the personal physician of the Almohad caliph and moved to the royal court of Marrakech in North Africa.

Averroës studied the works of Aristotle over some 25 years, translating them into Arabic and writing commentaries on them. Italian poet Dante called those commentaries the finest ever written. Not everyone was happy with Averroës' ideas, however. Aristotle had lived before the coming of both Christianity and Islam and had attempted to explain the natural world without any reference to a creator or an all-powerful God. Averroës followed in Aristotle's footsteps. He argued that there was no need to make the world of faith and the world of reason come together. They were different worlds and were therefore not in conflict.

Many Islamic and Christian leaders in Europe and West Asia, who argued that God governed all things, were disturbed by that argument. They condemned Averroës for suggesting that philosophical truths about the meaning of life could be discovered by human reason without the assistance of faith.

In 1195 Averroës was forced into exile, and many of his works were burned. The caliph soon recalled him to court, however, and he died highly respected once more. His writings were studied at the University of Paris in the 13th century, where his followers became known as Averroists. Averroës became so popular that in 1263 Pope Urban IV banned the study of his work. However, his theories continued to influence thinkers in the 14th and 15th centuries.

*You should study not only that
you become a mother when
your child is born, but also that
you become a child.*

DOGEN

ZEN BUDDHISM

ORIGINATING IN CHINA IN THE SEVENTH CENTURY, Zen brings together strands of Mahayana Buddhism and Taoism. Spreading to Korea, Japan, and Vietnam in the medieval period, it became popular in the West in the latter part of the 20th century. Zen—the name comes ultimately from the Sanskrit word *dhyana*, or "meditation"—is best understood as a practical form of Buddhism. It is based on meditation and practice, as taught by a Zen master, rather than doctrine.

At its heart, Zen is based on the belief that everyone is a buddha who is capable of discovering the truth of existence inside themselves. The questions posed by existence can be answered from within, which is why Zen Buddhists spend much of their time in meditation. Words and logical thought are unnecessary: a Zen practitioner uses meditation to free the mind from the intellect to achieve Enlightenment.

In 1004, the Chinese Buddhist monk Daoyun described how the spiritual awakening of one buddha was transmitted to the next generation, concluding with Bodhidharma, who brought Buddhism from India to China in the sixth century. In China, Buddhism absorbed Taoist philosophy and flourished from around the middle of the seventh century until the Buddhist persecution in the middle of the ninth century. Most of the important Zen masters came from this period.

The ideas of Zen arrived in the West in the first half of the 20th century through the books of Japanese Buddhist scholar Daisetsu T. Suzuki. Suzuki set out a vision of Buddhism that was based on the religious and cultural value of irrational intuition. He suggested that the clearest example of Zen Buddhism's achievements might be seen in the precision of the traditional tea ceremony or the symmetry of a Japanese rock garden.

Suzuki's ideas found a receptive audience in the United States and Great Britain after World War II. Servicemen who had visited Japan and experienced its culture were attracted to the idea that a person could, through his or her own efforts at meditation, achieve a new pure experience untainted by logical thought.

As a philosophy, Zen Buddhism acquired new followers after it was embraced by the Beat Generation of writers such as Jack Kerouac during the 1950s. Their interpretation of Zen came to refer to any spontaneous activity and became removed from its original religious meanings. Perhaps the best example of this was Robert M. Pirsig's 1974 novel, *Zen and the Art of Motorcycle Maintenance*. As Pirsig noted, the book had little to do with either Zen Buddhism or motorcycle maintenance, but it did bring the concept of Zen to a huge audience. Pirsig tried to show that a rational approach to life could be successfully combined with what he termed a zenlike approach of living in the moment.

The famous golden pavilion of the Kinkaku-ji Zen temple in Kyoto was rebuilt in 1955 after fire destroyed the original, constructed as a villa in 1397 and converted to a Zen temple shortly afterward by the shogun Ashikaga Yoshimochi.

PEOPLE & PLACES	DOCUMENTS, ART, & ARTIFACTS	WORSHIP & DOCTRINE

EUROPE

1202 Joachim of Fiore, revered as a mystic and founder of the monastic order of San Giovanni in Fiore—a stricter form of Cistercianism—dies while awaiting the pope's judgment on his many writings.

1226 Francis of Assisi dies, three years after Pope Honorius III approves his Franciscan rule.

1228 Francis of Assisi is canonized.

1239 Emperor Frederick II is excommunicated by Pope Gregory IX as part of the ongoing struggle between the popes and the emperors.

1201 The western facade of Notre Dame is built in Paris, France.

1227 Building of Toledo Cathedral begins in Spain.

In 1224, St. Francis of Assisi receives the stigmata while praying: the miracle is the first description of the miraculous appearance of Christ's wounds on a believer's body.

1200 Jewish Kabalistic philosophy emerges in southern Europe.

1209 Francis of Assisi writes his first rule for his Franciscan friars.

1215 The Fourth Lateran Council strengthens the Catholic Church's response to heresy and orders Catholics to make annual confession.

1216 The order of Dominican friars is established by the Spanish priest Dominic.

1232 Pope Gregory IX introduces the papal inquisition, a church court to combat heresy.

1233 A popular penitential movement, the "Great Alleluia," sweeps northern Italy.

THE AMERICAS

ca 1200 The Anasazi of Arizona and New Mexico divide their ceremonial year into four seasons; each season is heralded by a particular pattern of light and shadow thrown on two spirals carved into an outcrop named Fajada Butte.

ASIA & OCEANIA

1203 Muslim invaders sack the great Buddhist university at Vikramasila, Bihar state, India.

1206 Former slave Qutbuddin Aibak founds the Islamic Delhi Sultanate in northern India.

ca 1220 The Japanese monk Eisai introduces Zen Buddhism to Japan from China.

1236 Raziya succeeds to the throne of the Delhi Sultanate; she is the only Muslim woman to rule in India.

1230 Two Jain brothers carve the elaborate Luna Vashi temple into the marble cliffs at Dilwara, Gujarat, India, already the site of a Jain shrine.

1232 In Delhi, the new Islamic rulers complete the building of the 240-foot-tall Qutb Minar minaret.

AFRICA & THE MIDDLE EAST

1204 Constantinople, seat of the Eastern Orthodox Church, falls to the forces of the Fourth Crusade.

At 238 feet, the towering Qutb Minar in Delhi was built in the 13th century (work began in 1193) as a symbol of the power and grandeur of India's new Islamic rulers.

RELIGION IN THE WORLD	WORLD EVENTS

1209 Pope Innocent III launches the Albigensian Crusade against the Cathars of southern France (📄 pages 132–133).

1212 Victory over the Almohads at the battle of Las Navas de Tolosa lends impetus to the Christian reconquest of Spain.

1229 In Toulouse, France, the Inquisition forbids laymen to read the Bible.

1236 Ferdinand III of Castile begins a 10-year campaign to conquer the Moorish kingdom of Al Andalus (Andalusia) in southern Spain.

1242 Frederick II invades papal territory in his dispute with the Pope.

1245 The First Council of Lyon formally deposes Emperor Frederick II for heresy; the new pope, Innocent IV, flees imperial troops in Rome.

1248 An imperial army is routed by papal troops at the Battle of Parma.

1215 Rebellious English barons force King John to limit the monarchy's powers by signing the Magna Carta.

1220 Frederick II becomes Holy Roman emperor and ruler of southern Italy.

1230 Wenceslas I ascends the throne of Bohemia.

1230 Crusaders returning from the Holy Land bring leprosy to Europe.

1238 The Mongols invade Russia; in 1240 they overthrow Kiev and establish the Khanate of the Golden Horde.

1240 Alexander Nevsky, ruler of Novgorod, defeats the Swedes at the Battle of the Neva River.

1240 Mongol Tatars complete their conquest of Kievan Rus.

1241 The German ports of Lübeck and Hamburg form an alliance that will eventually grow into the Hanseatic League.

The minute I heard my first love story, I started looking for you, not knowing how blind that was. Lovers don't finally meet somewhere. They're in each other all along.

JALAL UL-DIN (RUMI)

RUMI AND SUFISM

The Persian poet Jalal ad-Din Muhammad Balkhi is known in the West as Rumi, because he spent most of his life in the Sultanate of Rum in what is now Turkey. His masterpiece, the 35,000 couplets of the *Diwan e-Kabir* (*Great Work*), was inspired by and dedicated to his teacher, Shams e-Tabrizi, who disappeared in mysterious circumstances in 1248.

Rumi's poetry expressed a regret that humans have become separated from God, whom he treats in romantic terms, and a wistful longing for a reunion with him. Like other Sufis, Rumi believed that Muslims should seek various ways to become immersed in the love of God. They reject many of the rituals of orthodox Islam in favor of solitary meditation, ascetism, and dancing to achieve a trancelike state. Rumi was closely associated with dancing.

After his death in 1273 Rumi's tomb became a shrine of pilgrimage. His teachings inspired the creation of the Malawi, a Sufi order known today as the Whirling Dervishes. Their spinning dance enacts a Muslim's spiritual ascent toward reunion with God.

1215 A period of Mongol rule introduces Tantric Buddhism to China from Tibet.

ca 1238 Theravada Buddhism is the state religion of the new Thai kingdom of Sukhothai.

1277 The Pagan Empire is weakened after defeat by Kublai Khan's Mongols.

1287 The Mongols conquer Pagan, which enters a permanent decline (📄 pages 162–163).

1204 The Fourth Crusade sacks Constantinople.

1212 The Children's Crusade ends in failure.

1219 The Fifth Crusade has some success in Egypt, but fails to capture Cairo.

1229 In the Sixth Crusade, the crusaders take control of Jerusalem under a diplomatic agreement.

1244 A Muslim army recaptures Jersualem.

The white gowns of the dervishes are symbols of death; their characteristic brown hats represent tombstones.

THOMAS AQUINAS

THOMAS AQUINAS WAS ONE OF THE GREATEST CHRISTIAN thinkers of the late Middle Ages. He tackled the main intellectual problem of the time—how to reconcile faith with reason—in a long series of writings, and his answers provided a firm basis for Christian doctrine that remained influential for centuries. In 1323 he was made a saint: the Catholic Church regards him as one of the greatest of all theologians.

Aquinas (1225–1274) was born at Aquino near Naples, Italy, into a noble family. As a teenager, despite the objections of his family, he joined the Dominicans, a teaching order of monks. Because Aquinas was large and quiet, his fellow students nicknamed him "dumb ox," but his later studies at the universities of Naples, Paris, and Cologne revealed his genius. He received a master's degree and taught in Italy, Spain, and Paris.

Aquinas guided Catholics through a turbulent time when Christianity came into contact with influences from around the world, such as reports brought from East Asia by Marco Polo, seen here with his brother praying with Teobaldi Visconti (later Pope Gregory X).

Aquinas wrote many commentaries on scripture and on Greek philosophy, but two of his works are especially renowned. *Summa Contra Gentiles* explains Christian doctrine—vital for Dominican missionaries in particular. The *Summa Theologica* is a systematic presentation of knowledge, with explanations of how it is acquired. Aquinas approached more than 600 topics by asking questions, then posing and considering 10,000 possible responses.

The problems Aquinas tackled had arisen when works written by the influential ancient Greek philosopher Aristotle were translated into Latin in the 12th century. Aristotle had written long before the appearance of Christianity, but was still considered a great spiritual authority. He had taught that all knowledge, or truth, is based on what we experience with our senses and explain with reason. The church, on the other hand, taught that truth comes from God's revelation and is accepted by faith. These two systems seemed to be incompatible.

Aquinas's great achievement was to explain reason and faith in such a way that those who adopted Aristotle's system could integrate it with Christianity. He believed that the human mind perceives truth in nature through the senses and reason, but supernatural truth by faith. The meeting point between the two hinges on knowledge of the existence of God, which can come through faith or through reason. Aquinas argued that many other spiritual truths were also provable through logical reasoning, thus making reason and faith compatible. His work provoked great controversy, and after his death some of his writings were condemned by the church.

Thomas Aquinas—portrayed here in an illustration from a primer of Catholic saints published in 1928—is one of the greatest Christian theologians for his reconciliation of faith with classical philosophy.

PEOPLE & PLACES	DOCUMENTS, ART, & ARTIFACTS	WORSHIP & DOCTRINE

EUROPE

1254 In Paris, court chaplin Robert de Sorbon founds a school of theology, later to become known as the Sorbonne University.

ca 1255 Thomas Aquinas is teaching in Paris.

1270 Louis IX dies on crusade in Tunis.

1271 Gregory X becomes pope; he is later beatified.

1274 Thomas Aquinas dies after establishing himself as the leading theological scholar of western Christendom.

1276 Four men hold the papacy successively within the year: Gregory X, Innocent V, Hadrian V, and John XXI.

1294 When the college of cardinals elects the hermit Pietro di Morone as Pope Celestine V, he holds office for only a few months before abdicating to return to his ascetic way of life.

ca 1250 The first choral Passions—musical settings of the story of the Crucifixion—appear.

1273 Thomas Aquinas writes *Summa Theologica* (📄 pages 140–141).

1278 The church of Santa Maria Novella is built in Florence.

1280 In Spain, Moses de Leon writes the *Zohar*, the main work of the Castilian Kabala tradition.

1295 At Assisi, Italy, the early Renaissance painter Cimabue paints *Madonna with St. Francis of Assisi*.

1295 *The Harrowing of Hell*, an early mystery play, is performed in England.

1296 Construction begins of Florence Cathedral, Italy.

1260 Flagellant movements emerge in southern Germany and northern Italy; participants use whips to punish themselves for the sins of humankind.

1268 A three-year vacancy begins in which there is no pope.

1274 The Second Council of Lyon decrees the union of the Roman and Orthodox churches; however, the union is rejected by many Greeks and Slavs.

THE AMERICAS

Only a quarter-century after his death, King Louis IX of France was canonized in 1297 for a life of exemplary devotion—illustrated in this contemporary manuscript—during which he led two crusades, dying in the course of the second.

ASIA & OCEANIA

1296 Alauddin comes to the throne of the Delhi Sultanate; his 20-year reign marks a golden age of the sultanate.

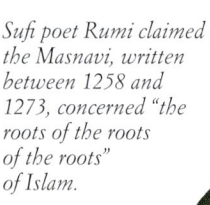

Sufi poet Rumi claimed that the Masnavi, written between 1258 and 1273, concerned "the roots of the roots of the roots" of Islam.

ca 1250 Jains build finely carved temples at Mount Abu, India.

1266 Sanjusangendo Temple is built in Japan.

1295 A pilgrim from Tibet reports finding a small Buddhist school still teaching within the ruins of the former university at Nalanda in India.

1271 Governor Tughril Khan extends Muslim rule deep into eastern Bengal.

1283 The Tibetan Black Hat Buddhist sect begins the tradition of seeking the reincarnations of office holders, later the method of identifying a new Dalai Lama.

AFRICA & THE MIDDLE EAST

1256 The Mongol commander Hulagu occupies Persia and founds the Ilkhan dynasty, which later converts to Islam.

1269 Abu Yaqub overthrows the Almohads in Morroco and establishes the Marinid dynasty.

1280 The Ilkhan ruler of Persia, Teguder Ahmed, converts to Islam.

1280 Al-Mansur Qalawun becomes the Mamluk sultan of Egypt.

1295 Under the reign of the Ilkhanid ruler Mahmud Ghazan, many Mongols convert to Islam.

ca 1295 The conversion of the Mongols leads to the destruction of the Nestorian church in much of Central Asia (the "Assyrian Christians" still survive in the mountains of Kurdistan).

ca 1200 Venetian laws forbid prostitutes in Venice from having intercourse with Jews or Muslims.

1250 On the death of Frederick II the territory he has conquered is returned to the church, ending the power struggle between the papacy and the Hohenstaufen of Germany; the emperor dies wearing the robes of a Cistercian monk.

1252 After Pope Innocent IV authorizes the use of torture against heretics, the Inquisition begins to use instruments such as the rack and the *strappado*.

1278 In London, 278 Jews found guilty of clipping metal from coins are hanged; Christians guilty of the same crime are merely fined.

1283 The Teutonic Knights complete their violent conquest of the pagan Prussians after more than 50 years.

1290 Edward I expels all Jews from England.

Marco Polo and his family present letters from Pope Gregory X to Kublai Khan, Mongol emperor of China, in around 1271.

1287 The death of Balban plunges the Delhi Sultanate into a period of instability, ended in 1290 by the establishment of the Khalji dynasty.

1295 The Mongol leader Ghazan Khan converts to Islam, ending the Mongols' tradition of Tantric Buddhism.

1250 In Egypt the Ayyubid dynasty ends and is replaced by the Turkish Mamluk dynasty.

1254 The Seventh Crusade ends without capturing the Christian holy places.

1258 Hulagu sacks Baghdad, finally ending the Abbasid caliphate.

1291 After a series of Mamluk victories over the previous decades, the capture of Acre marks the final end of the crusader presence in Syria and Palestine.

1260 At the Battle of Montaperti, the Ghibillines (who support the emperor) defeat the Guelfs (supporters of the pope).

1264 The English Parliament is taken over by rebel barons led by Simon de Montfort, Earl of Leicester; the rebellion is defeated the following year.

1273 Rudolf of Habsburg's election to the Holy Roman throne ends the Great Interregnum, a 19-year gap without an emperor.

1284 After an eight-year campaign, Edward I of England completes the subjection of Wales.

1293 The Ordinances of Justice pass control of Florence in Italy from the city's nobles to its craft guilds, inspiring an outpouring of civic pride.

1297 William Wallace ("Braveheart") leads an initially successful Scots revolt against the English.

1263 The Mayan city-state of Mayapán is founded in Yucatán in southeast Mexico.

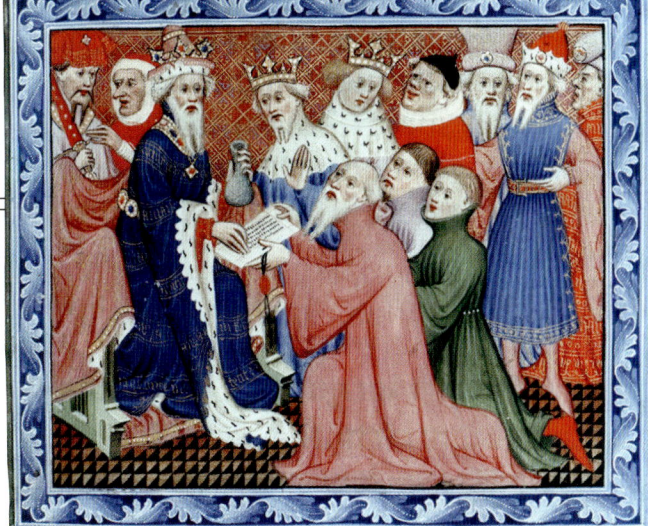

1260 The Mamluks halt the Mongol advance at the Battle of Ayn Jalut in Palestine.

1270 In Ethiopia, Yekuno Amlak seizes the throne from the last Zagwe ruler and founds the Solomonid dynasty, claiming descent from the biblical Solomon.

1281 The Ottoman dynasty is founded when Osman takes control of a small territory in Anatolia.

SCHOLASTICISM

Scholasticism describes a process by which medieval theologians attempted to reconcile faith and reason through logical questions and answers. The methods of the Scholastics led them into esoteric debates—"How many angels can dance on the head of pin?"—but ultimately they were exploring the nature of Christian truths. Did Christians simply have to believe them (faith) or could the truths be proved by logical argument (reason)? The Scholastics sought to fulfill an injunction by the sixth-century scholar Boethius: "As far as you are able, join faith to reason." In the 11th century Anselm, archbishop of Canterbury, also argued that a Christian had a duty to understand faith through reason.

Scholastic method consisted of asking a question (such as, "Is the world created or eternal?"), citing authorities who gave different answers (the Bible or ancient philosophers), and then reconciling apparently contradictory answers through logic. Above all, the Scholastics focused on Aristotle, particularly after a number of his works and Arabic commentaries on them were translated into Latin around 1200.

Aristotle taught that human knowledge is based on experience, and that we build up an understanding of truth from our power of reason. Many of his ideas directly challenged Christian beliefs based on the Bible.

Two Dominican scholars set out to reconcile Christianity and Aristotle: Albertus Magnus and his student, Thomas Aquinas. If knowledge is based on what we experience physically, how can we know God, who is not physical? Their answer was that truths can be reached through both faith and reason. That conclusion was opposed by Franciscans such as John Duns Scotus and William of Ockham, who argued that knowledge and faith were separate and that bringing them together was not possible or even desirable. Eventually most scholars agreed with this view—and by the 15th century scholasticism had been replaced by new problems and questions.

RELIGION IN THE INCA EMPIRE

Inca worship the sun from the top of a pyramid temple in this 16th-century Italian woodcut, which illustrated one of the earliest histories of the New World.

AT THE SPIRITUAL HEART OF of the Empire that dominated Peru in the 15th and 16th centuries was the worship of the sun, the ancestral father of the Inca (the moon was their mother). The emperor represented the sun god on Earth, and linked worship of the sun with ancestor worship.

The Inca Empire had grown to stretch from Ecuador in the north to Chile in the south. As the empire grew, the Inca absorbed the religions of the people they conquered, who for their part had to practice Inca state religion and worship its gods. Those gods included the creator god Viracocha; Viracocha's son, Inti; Inti's wife, Mama Kilya, the moon goddess; and Ilapu, the weather god, who sent the rain to grow the corn on which the Inca depended as their staple food.

Inca sacred sites included not only shrines and temples maintained by priests who ranked second only to the nobility in the social hierarchy, but also *huacas*. A huaca might be a natural feature such as a mountain or river, or even the mummy of a dead ancestor. All places and objects had spiritual power. Archaeologists have found the mummies of dead children sacrificed to the gods high on towering Andean peaks. The children were led up the mountains by priests, then drugged and left to die of exposure.

Sacrifice was key to worship, although human sacrifice was reserved for special occasions. Usually sacrifice took the form of food and drink offered to the gods. During an annual festival dedicated to Inti, the emperor and his family processed to the Temple of the Sun to make offerings of gold and silver and to sacrifice llamas in the god's honor.

Before the Inca took any action they consulted oracles to learn the will of the gods. They consulted many different forms of oracles, from the pattern of the leaves of the coca plants in a dish to a spider's trail, to learn which path of action to take. Every aspect of life was subjected to divination, from personal illness to warfare.

After the Spanish conquest of the Inca in 1532, Christianity became the state religion. The practice of Inca religion survived briefly only in the remote "lost cities" of the Andes before it withered and died there, too.

Built high above the Urubamba River of Peru's Sacred Valley, Machu Picchu was a ceremonial city—it is thought never to have housed a permanent population—whose Hitching Post of the Sun may have been the center of ritual based on astronomical alignments with the surrounding peaks.

PEOPLE & PLACES

1303 Having quarreled with and excommunicated King Philip IV of France, Pope Boniface VIII dies a prisoner in the Vatican.

1305 After the election of Pope Clement V, the papacy moves to Avignon in France (1309), the beginning of the "Babylonian captivity."

1308 The theologian and Church Father John Duns Scotus, probably of English or Irish birth, dies at Cologne in Germany; his nuanced analysis of theological problems has earned him the nickname "Doctor Subtilis."

1324 The Church Father Thomas Aquinas is canonized.

DOCUMENTS, ART, & ARTIFACTS

1301 Giovanni Pisano sculpts the pulpit in Pisa Cathedral.

1305 At Padua in Italy, Giotto decorates the church of St. Maria dell' Arena with a cycle of frescoes illustrating the Life of Jesus and the Life of the Virgin, to whom the chapel is dedicated.

1307 The Italian poet Dante Alighieri begins writing his *Divine Comedy* (📄 facing page).

1314 Old St. Paul's Cathedral is completed in London with the construction of the spire (today's building dates from 1708).

1324 Marsilius of Padua writes *Defensor pacis* (*Defender of the Peace*), which controversially asserts the power of the state and of secular rulers, severely limiting the power of the papacy.

WORSHIP & DOCTRINE

1302 In *Unam Sanctam*, Pope Boniface VIII proclaims that "every living creature" falls under the universal jurisdiction of the pope; many European rulers are offended by his assertion of the superiority of spiritual over secular power.

1312 The Council of Vienna withdraws church support for the Knights Templar and decides in favor of tight rules on poverty for Franciscan monks.

1314 Jacques de Molay, grand master of the Knights Templar, is burned at the stake in Paris for alleged heresy.

1322 The pope forbids the use of counterpoint rather than plainsong in church music; the complex melodies are feared to obscure the meaning of the words.

God is always ready, but we are very unready;

God is near to us, but we are far from Him;

God is within, but we are without;

God is at home, but we are strangers.

MEISTER ECKHART, GERMAN MYSTIC

A Tibetan monk gazes over the Himalaya from the Buddhist monastery at Drepung, near Lhasa.

EUROPE

THE AMERICAS

ASIA & OCEANIA

AFRICA & THE MIDDLE EAST

RELIGION IN THE WORLD

1306 Philip IV expels the Jews from France.

1312 The withdrawal of papal support ends the Knights Templar; their disappearance creates many myths and legends, some of which still survive today.

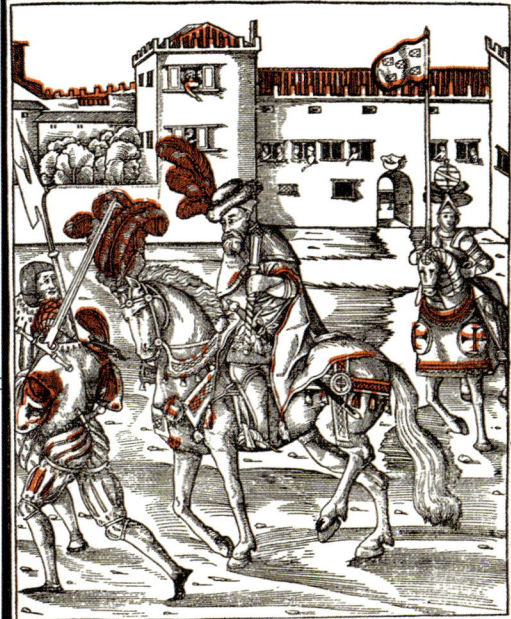

1307 An archbishopric is created in Beijing, China.

1320 Ghiyasuddin Tughluq replaces the Khalji rulers in Delhi and founds the Tughluq dynasty.

ca 1300 Amina is the Muslim queen of Zazzau in Africa at about this time.

1324 Ruler of Mali Mansa Musa makes a pilgrimage to Mecca; he spends so much gold that it destablizes the economy of the states through which he passes, astonishing Western rulers with reports of his wealth (📄 pages 166–167).

WORLD EVENTS

1302 In Paris, the Estates-General meets for the first time, with representatives from the three "estates": nobility, clergy, and commoners.

1308 The Ottomans cross the Bosporus and invade Europe.

1314 Scots led by Robert Bruce defeat the English at the Battle of Bannockburn and establish Scottish independence.

1323 The Flemish inhabitants of the Low Countries rebel against their French rulers.

Prester John, legendary ruler of Africa, is depicted in a 1540 woodcut. Stories of the Christian monarch intrigued Europeans with the prospect of an ally against Islam. The legends may have been based on the Christian kings of Ethiopia.

THE DIVINE COMEDY

The most enduring expression of medieval Christian belief was written by Italian poet Dante Alighieri in the early 14th century. In three parts—Inferno (Hell), Purgatorio (Purgatory), and Paradiso (Paradise)—*The Divine Comedy* records a journey through the Christian afterlife (Dante's poem is based closely on the teachings on St. Thomas Aquinas). The overall structure of the allegory can be read as a description of the soul's progression toward God.

The Roman poet Virgil guides Dante through Hell and Purgatory to witness the sufferings of those who had sinned during their lives. In Paradise, Dante's guide is his ideal woman, Beatrice (a real woman he idealized at a distance from her childhood until her death at age 24).

The poem remains the greatest masterpiece of Italian literature (it was the poet Boccaccio who added the word "divine" to its original title of *Comedy*). It stands as a powerful testament to how medieval Europeans saw the world.

Dante presents The Divine Comedy *in front of his native city of Florence; his poem helped establish Tuscan as the dominant form of Italian.*

PEOPLE & PLACES	DOCUMENTS, ART, & ARTIFACTS	WORSHIP & DOCTRINE

EUROPE

1327 The English theologian William of Ockham writes his first polemic against the power of the papacy; Ockham is famous for "Occam's Razor," a methodological approach that argues, broadly speaking, that the simplest explanation or answer is likely to be the best one.

1327 The Dominican monk "Meister" Eckhart dies in Germany after defending his mystical beliefs against charges of heresy before a Franciscan-led Inquisition ordered by Pope John XXII.

1333 Caliph Yusuf I oversees a flowering of Islamic culture in Granada, Spain.

1334 The artist Giotto begins building the campanile (bell tower) at Florence.

ca 1340 Sergei of Razdonezh founds the monastery of the Holy Trinity near Moscow.

1344 Matthew of Arras begins building St. Vitus's Cathedral in Prague.

1344 Construction begins on the Palace of the Popes in Avignon, France.

1325 The "Tournai Mass," the earliest polyphonic mass still extant, is composed in France.

1337 The Hesychast Controversy begins when Barlaam of Calabria argues that monks living lives of quiet contemplation and prayer (*hesychasm*, or "prayer of the heart") at Mount Athos in Greece are wasting their time and should seek God through study and learning; Gregory Palamas defends the monks in teachings that are affirmed by a series of councils in Constantinople.

THE AMERICAS

*When all the world
is the eye of the lord,
onlooking everywhere,
what can you cover
and conceal?*

MAHADEVIYAKKA, HINDU MYSTIC

The Alhambra, built in the early 14th century overlooking Granada, was one of the last expressions of Muslim culture in Spain: already, the Christian kingdoms had reduced the Islamic lands to a fraction of their previous extent.

ASIA & OCEANIA

1325 Muhammad Ibn Tughluq comes to the throne in Delhi; he brings the sultanate to its greatest extent.

1346 In southern India the monumental city of Vijayanagar becomes the center of a Hindu empire.

AFRICA & THE MIDDLE EAST

1325 The Muslim traveler Ibn Battuta makes a pilgrimage from Egypt to Arabia, beginning his celebrated travels through the Islamic world (📄 box, this page).

1331 Ibn Battuta visits the wealthy Muslim trading cities of East Africa.

1335 The death of Khan Abu Said ends the Mongol Ilkhan dynasty of Persia.

FAITH AND LIFE

Ibn Battuta

O riginally from Morocco, the Islamic legal scholar Ibn Battuta saw little of his homeland after he quit in 1325, age 21, to make his first hajj to Mecca. Instead of returning home, he resolved to travel throughout the whole Islamic world. So began a journey of nearly 30 years that took him through Central and South Asia to China, across North Africa and south of the Sahara, and throughout South and East Europe. Wherever he went, the traveler visited shrines and commented on religious practices at a time when Islam was changing rapidly: orthodox himself, he was upset by the relaxed attitudes of the Muslims in newly converted India, for example. The account Ibn Battuta later wrote, although known to be unreliable in parts, is our main record of the medieval Islamic world.

1333 The caliphate of Yusuf I marks the height of Islamic culture in Granada, Spain.

1349 Jews are subjected to a fierce persecution in Germany.

ca 1325 The Kachina cult develops in the American Southwest; it will later become central to cultures such as the Hopi.

The kachina cult spread among the peoples of the American Southwest in the 13th or 14th centuries, offering a connection with the spirits through ritual dances and dolls.

ca 1340 Popular religious movements known as the Red Turbans and the White Lotus Society rebel in Yuan, China.

1345 The noble Bhaman Shah overthrows the Delhi Sultanate in the Deccan; the Muslim Bhamanid dynasty rules the region for nearly 200 years.

1346 Hindu temples in the Valley of Kathmandu in Nepal are raided by Muslim attackers.

1346 Theodora, daughter of the Byzantine emperor, marries the Ottoman sultan Orhan in return for military aid.

1328 Under Grand Duke Ivan I, Muscovy rises to prominence.

1340 An English fleet destroys the French navy off the port of Sluys in Flanders in what will prove the first battle of the Hundred Years' War.

1347 The Black Death reaches Europe from Asia.

1327 China's Grand Canal is completed after some 1,250 years; it is 1,100 miles long.

1333 In the Kemmu Restoration, Japan's Emperor Go-Daigo overthrows the Kamakura Shogunate.

1349 Chinese emigrants found the first settlement at Singapore.

1333 The Ottoman capture of Nicomedia leaves the Byzantines with only a toehold in Anatolia.

1335 The Mongol Ilkhan dynasty of Persia ends with the death of the last khan.

1347 The Marinids of Morocco capture Tunisia from its Hafsid rulers.

1348 Egypt is devastated by the Black Death.

KINGDOM OF IFE

The city-state of Ife-Ife was well established in what is now the West African country of Nigeria before the early 11th century and from the 12th to the 15th centuries dominated the region. For the Yoruba people, the city was sacred. They believed that it was the birthplace of the Yoruba themselves—and also the place where the Earth was created. In Yoruba myth, the city had been founded by the son of their most important god, Olodumare. Olodumare had lowered an iron chain from the sky, down which his son Oduduwa had climbed. Oduduwa carried a gourd full of sand, from which he made the Earth. He also carried the nut of an oil palm and a chicken, which provided food. According to myth, other Yoruba cities were traditionally founded by princes from Ife. They were symbolized by the many leaves of the palm tree that grew from the nut. The city and the kingdom that grew around it were probably named for Ifa, the god of divination.

Ife had originally grown wealthy from trade; it had a highly developed artisan community that started to develop from about 700 onward. Its artists created striking terracotta, bronze, and stone sculptures of the heads of important people, reflecting the Yoruba belief that the head contained a person's power and energy. The Yoruba believed that the more powerful an individual was, the bigger was his or her head.

Ife started to decline after the 1400s as its economic importance shifted to the neighboring kingdom of Benin. However, the city remained the most important religious center for the Yoruba. All new kings of the Yoruba state of Oyo, for example, had to promise not to attack Ife. However, Ife's sacred importance could not protect it forever. It was attacked and weakened by slave raiders in the 18th and early 19th centuries. The city was finally destroyed in 1882 after Ife declared war on a neighboring state and was defeated.

I am created in the one and only God; I sing sweet songs among the flowers; I chant songs and rejoice in my heart. The fuming dewdrops from the flowers in the fields intoxicate my soul. I grieve to myself that ever this dwelling on Earth should end.

NEZAHUALCOYOTL, 15TH-CENTURY KING OF TEXCOCO

SACRIFICE AND THE AZTEC

THE SPANIARDS WHO ENCOUNTERED THE AZTEC IN 1519 reported that their empire was built on human sacrifice. Hundreds of victims had their hearts ripped out by priests atop temple pyramids, and their bodies thrown down the steep sides. The Europeans were horrified, but the Aztec saw bloodshed as vital to appease the vengeful gods who might otherwise destroy the world. The Aztec waged war on their neighbors to capture sacrificial victims to feed the appetites of the gods … and when the Spaniards arrived, those same resentful neighbors would help the newcomers overthrow the Aztec.

It had taken just under two hundred years for the Aztec to rise to rule what is now central Mexico. Originally from the north, they had settled at a site prophesied by the god Huitzilopochtli where they found an eagle sitting on a cactus with a snake in its mouth. They founded a city–state, Tenochtitlan, in 1325; by the time the Spanish conquerors arrived in 1519, it was a thriving metropolis.

The Aztec's many gods included those they appropriated from their defeated enemies, a process that helped strengthen their position as victors. Such gods included the creator god Quetzalcoatl, the plumed serpent, whom the Aztec inherited from the Toltec. The chief gods were Huitzilopochtli, god of the sun and of war, and Tlaloc, the rain god who ensured the agriculture on which the wealth of the empire was based. Each god had a temple–pyramid in the heart of Tenochtitlan: that of Huitzilopochtli was painted blood red, that of Tlaloc, azure blue.

The Aztec believed in the significance of certain dates based on a complex sacred calendar; every 52 years a coincidence of inauspicious dates put the world in particular peril. Prophecies were also an integral part of their beliefs. A prophecy had founded the empire—and another may have allowed it to be easily overthrown. In some accounts, the conquistador Hernán Cortés was welcomed by the Aztec because of a prophecy that Quetzalcoatl would return in the guise of a fair-skinned man arriving from the sea.

A mosaic of turquoise and lignite covers a human skull to make a mask of the Aztec god Tezcatlipoca, the Smoking Mirror, crafted in Central Mexico in about 1500.

A 16th-century illustration from an Aztec codex shows a priest brandishing the heart of a sacrifice; the horrified Spaniards reported that the hearts were still beating when they were removed from the victims.

Built between 1555 and 1561 at the geographical heart of Moscow, St. Basil's Cathedral (officially known as the Cathedral of Intercession of Theotokos on the Moat) was commissioned by Ivan IV (the Terrible) to celebrate the Russian capture of the neighboring states of Kazan and Astrakhan. The design drew on Islamic and traditional Russian sources: originally the onion domes were probably embellished with gold leaf.

Modern Native Americans re-create a dance in traditional costumes. Many American peoples used dance, masks, and costume as a way to overcome the barriers between the daily world and the world of the spirits that shaped their lives.

IN 1517 AN OBSCURE PRIEST IN A MINOR GERMAN CITY NAILED A DOCUMENT TO THE door of the cathedral. Martin Luther was using an accepted means of starting an academic debate. In 95 points, he listed what he saw as faults of the Catholic Church. They included corruption among the clergy, who were more interested in temporal comfort than spiritual salvation, and the sale of indulgences. These paper certificates absolved the purchaser of his or her sins, promising to shorten the length of time the soul spent in purgatory after death and bringing paradise closer. This was, for Luther, selling salvation.

Luther was not the only Catholic to object to how the church was administered. People throughout Europe had turned to purer forms of the faith, forming religious orders to practice the will of God by living lives of poverty and labor. But Luther's protest had the merit of timing. Seized upon by European princes and nobles eager to increase their own political power at the expense of the great Catholic rulers, particularly the Holy Roman Emperor, Luther's teachings eventually led to the creation of a new branch of Christianity: Protestantism.

In response to the upheaval—the Reformation—the Catholic Church began a period of intense introspection. It faced many problems. The papacy had seen the absolute authority it had enjoyed for nearly a thousand years undermined by a period of political intrigues in which more than one pope had claimed to be God's sole representative on Earth, the heir to St. Peter. The rise and fall of the antipopes reflected the princely struggles in Europe, where the changing mosaic of alliances made politics highly fluid. For nearly 40 years from 1378, the papacy was based not in Rome but in Avignon in France. (The sale of indulgences to which Martin Luther particularly objected was part of the Vatican's program to raise funds to build a new basilica to mark the papacy's return to Rome—now the renowned St. Peter's).

The Catholic reaction to the rise of Protestantism—the Counter-Reformation—was directed by a great church council at Trent in northern Italy. The council overhauled the faith, clarifying its beliefs, laying down instructions for rituals, and tackling worldliness in the clergy. Meanwhile, a medieval church court known as the Inquisition was revived in Rome and later in Spain, using torture and execution to root out heresy. The church enlisted leading artists and architects to produce spectacular artworks that proclaimed the glory of the Catholic faith.

Spain's "Catholic monarchs" Ferdinand and Isabella were at the forefront of protecting the church, expelling Muslims and Jews from their reunified kingdom or forcing them to convert. The Spanish also took the lead in sending missionaries to the "New World" that Christopher Columbus had reached in 1492. The peoples of Precolumbian America had well-established religions of their own, but while elements of Inca faith survived the arrival of the Conquistadors, the temples where the Aztec of Mexico practiced human sacrifice were levelled to make way for Christian churches. After the initial conquest, a few priests emerged to speak out for the rights of native peoples and against the excesses of the colonialists. Farther north, meanwhile, other Native Americans presented European settlers with a variety of religious beliefs, rooted in a spiritual closeness to the natural world that Europeans largely dismissed as pagan superstition.

Monks of the Spanish Inquisition torture Jews in this 1475 woodcut. As Spain was slowly recaptured from the Islamic Moors, authorities forced Muslims and Jews to convert to Christianity. Those who converted became the focus of intense suspicion, both from their fellow religionists, who distrusted them for converting, and from Christians, who suspected that their conversion was not genuine.

In Africa, Islam inspired the rise and fall of great empires. The pilgrimage of Mali's emperor Mansa Musa to Mecca in 1324 had become notorious for its extravagance. The ruler spent so much gold in Egypt that he devalued the local currency. After the upheaval of the Crusades, the cultural border between Christianity and Islam was more peaceful, with free exchange not just of trade but also of cultural ideas: The great works of classical Greece filtered back into Europe from the Islamic libraries where they were preserved, while the Republic of Venice sent the official painter, Gentile Bellini, to work for the Ottoman sultan in Constantinople.

Meanwhile Buddhism enjoyed mixed fortunes in Southeast Asia. The Khmer abandoned their great capital at Angkor, while in Burma (Myanmar) the great empire that had flourished at Pagan reached its peak and then began to decline. In Tibet, meanwhile, the first Dalai Lama became the spiritual head of the Gelug sect of Buddhists—although he was only awarded the title decades after his death—founding a tradition of reincarnation that Tibetans believe has carried on unbroken until today.

Previous pages *The touch of God gives life to Adam in an iconic scene from the ceiling of the Sistine Chapel, painted by Michelangelo for Pope Julius II from 1508 to 1512.*

CONCISE HISTORY OF WORLD RELIGIONS

	1350	1375	1400	1425	1450
EUROPE	**1371** Bulgaria and all of Macedonia, with the exception of Salonika, come under the control of the Islamic Ottoman Turks. **1374** Dutch preacher Gerhard Groote renounces worldly enjoyment and begins a process that will eventually lead to found the Brethren of the Common Life, inspiring religious reform throughout Germany.	**1375** English reformer John Wycliffe begins a long attack on clerical wealth, monasticism, and the authority of the pope. **1378** The Great Schism opens when cardinals elect two different candidates as pope: Urban VI and Clement VII. **1382** John Wycliffe is expelled from Oxford University	**1413** In *De Ecclesia*, Jan Hus calls for church reform along the same lines as John Wycliffe. **1417** Pope Benedict XIII is deposed by the Council of Constance and replaced by Martin V, marking the end of the Great Schism.	**1428** Inspired by religious visions, Joan of Arc leads the French in battle against the English. **1431** Captured by the Burgundians and passed to the English, Joan of Arc is burned to death for heresy in Rouen. **1444** A papal crusade against the Ottomans is decisively defeated at Varna on the Black Sea.	**1453** Johannes Gutenberg prints the Mazarin Bible at Mainz, Germany. **1474** Isabella, wife of Ferdinand I of Aragon, becomes queen of Castile, uniting the two largest Spanish kingdoms and laying the foundation for the campaign to drive the Islamic Moors from Spain.
THE AMERICAS	**ca 1350** In Mexico, priests are among the elite of Aztec society; some rise to become rulers of the empire.	**ca 1400** The Upper and Middle Mississippi phases of Mound Builders develop in North America.		**1440** Moctezuma I becomes emperor of the Aztec.	**ca 1450** The Aztec capital Tenochtitlan has around 300,000 citizens, who worship at pyramid temples that rise above the city.
ASIA & OCEANIA	**1368** The Ming dynasty is established in China; its foundation is linked with the promised coming of a new bodhisattva. **1369** Timur (Tamerlane) takes control of the Mongols.	**1384** King Lu Thai of Thailand takes full ordination as a Buddhist monk. **1391** Birth of Gedun Drupa, the first Dalai Lama of Tibet. **1393** Timur occupies Baghdad. **1398** Led by Timur, Mongols invade India and sack Delhi, ending the Delhi Sultanate.	**ca 1415** Sultan Firuz Shah Bahmani makes the kingdom of Bahmani a center of Muslim culture in India's Deccan region. **1420** Korean scholars begin studying in the new Chiphyonjon, a royal academy.	**1431** In Cambodia the Khmer abandon their capital at Angkor and move to Phnom Penh; the old city is overgrown by the jungle. **1443** Visiting the Hindu city of Vijayanagar in India, a Persian visitor claims that it has "no equal in all the world."	**ca 1450** The Ryoanji Zen temple is built at Kyoto, Japan, with a famous drystone landscape garden. **1469** Nanak, the first guru of Sikhism, is born in the Punjab region of northwestern India. **1472** Birth of Wang Yangming, whose Neo-Confucian ideas will influence Chinese thought for generations.
AFRICA & THE MIDDLE EAST	**1352** The Coptic Patriarch Marco is imprisoned by Muslims during the persecution of Christians in Cairo, Egypt. **1352** The Moroccan traveler Ibn Battuta visits Mali, where he is shocked by the lack of Islamic tradition, believing the empire to be motivated only by trade and wealth. **1360** The death of Mansa Suleiman marks the beginning of the decline of the mighty Islamic empire of Mali.	**1382** David I becomes king of Christian Ethiopia and makes contact with Christian nations beyond Africa. **1382** Arab theologian and scholar Ibn Khaldun becomes a judge in Cairo, Egypt.	**ca 1410** In southern Africa, most of the stone buildings at Great Zimbabwe have been completed by now: the settlement may have been a ceremonial center. **1415** An Ethiopian Christian army kills the Muslim ruler of Seylac during a raid on the Arab port on the Red Sea.	**1427** The Ethiopian emperor Yeshaq sends ambassadors to Spain to try to find allies against the Muslims of North Africa. **ca 1440** Emperor Zara Jacob reforms the Ethiopian Church. **1445** Zara Jacob of Ethiopia invades and defeats the neighboring Islamic state of Ifat.	**1450** In Ethiopia, emperor Zara Jacob persecutes Falasha Jews. **1463** Muhammed Rumfa, king of Kano, turns the traditional monarchy into an Islamic sultanate, paving the way for Kano's emergence as a major trading power. **1468** The Mamluk sultan Qa'itbay begins a 28-year-reign during which he extensively restores the Islamic shrines of Mecca and Medina.

1475	1500	1525	1550	1560–1574
1487 *Malleus maleficarum* (*The Hammer of Witches*) is published by two German monks as a handbook for witch hunters. **1492** The Inquisitor General Tomás Torquemada gives Spain's Jews three months to either convert to Christianity or leave the country.	**1501** A papal bull orders the burning of books that question the authority of the church. **1514** The Fugger bank is granted the right to sell papal indulgences in Germany. **1517** Martin Luther nails his 95 Theses to the door of the cathedral in Wittenberg, Germany, detailing his criticisms of the Catholic Church.	**1531** Henry VIII declares England free from the authority of the Catholic Church. **1536** John Calvin writes *The Institutes of the Christian Religion*, establishing him as a leader of the Reformation. **1541** John Calvin becomes chief pastor of Geneva, Switzerland.	**1553** The Catholic "Bloody" Mary Tudor becomes queen of England and begins a five-year suppression of Protestants. **1557** In Rome, the Catholic Church publishes the first *Index Librorum Prohibitorum*, listing banned books.	**1560** Puritanism emerges in England. **1572** In the Massacre of St. Bartholomew's Day, more than 2,500 leading Protestants are murdered in Paris. **1572** St. Teresa of Avila experiences an ecstasy of mystical religious experience.
1487 In Tenochtitlan, up to 80,000 human sacrifices mark the dedication of the temple of the Aztec god Huitzilopochtli.	**1508** Pope Julius II gives the Spanish crown the right to control missionary activity in the Americas.	**1531** The first Spanish archbishop in Mexico reports that the Spaniards have destroyed more than 500 Aztec temples.	**1552** Bartolomé De las Casas publishes *A Brief Relation of the Destruction of the Indies*, an account of the cruel treatment of indigenous American peoples.	**1569** The Spanish Inquisition begins in the Americas when King Philip II sets up tribunals in Mexico City and Lima, Peru.
1488 In Japan, Buddhists of the True Pure Land sect kill a feudal landowner in the first of what will be a long series of clashes with Japan's ruling classes. **1497** The Iranian Safavid dynasty begin their rise to power in Persia, promoting the "Twelver" form of Shiite Islam.	**1504** The Mogul ruler Babur begins a series of conquests in Afghanistan which will eventually bring almost the whole Indian subcontinent under Islamic rule. **1512** Shiite Islam becomes the state religion in Persia. **1526** Led by Babur, the Moguls defeat the Sultan of Delhi.	**1539** Death of Guru Nanak, the founder of the Sikh religion. **1542** Religious reforms introduced by the Emperor Akbar aim to unite the Muslim rulers of the Mogul Empire with their Hindu subjects. **1542** Jesuit St. Francis Xavier begins his mission to Goa in southern India.	**1552** Jesuit missionary Francis Xavier dies on a small island off Macao after many failed attempts to reach the Chinese mainland. **1556** Akbar begins the conquest of nearly the whole Indian subcontinent, spreading religious toleration and encouraging the integration of Muslims and Hindus.	**1562** Spain introduces Catholicism to the Philippines. **1565** An alliance of Muslim sultanates overthrows the Hindu Vijayanagar Empire in India.
1485 The first Portuguese missionaries arrive in Angola. **1490** King Nzinga Nkuwu of Kongo is converted to Christianity by Portuguese missionaries. **1492** Many Jewish and Muslim exiles arrive in North Africa after the fall of Moorish Spain. **ca 1500** Timbuktu in Mali has become a center of Islamic education, with a university and schools dedicated to the study of the Koran.	**1504** In Sudan, the Muslim Funj defeat a Christian kingdom in Sennar, between the Blue and White Niles. **1508** The new Ethiopian emperor Lebna Dengel struggles to limit growing Islamic influence in his Christian kingdom. **1520** Portuguese priest Francisco Alvarez begins a six-year mission to Ethiopia. **1520** Henry, a prince of Kongo who has studied in Lisbon and Rome, becomes the first sub-Saharan African to be consecrated as a Catholic bishop.	**1531** Muslim leader Ahmad Gran goes to war with Christian Ethiopia. **1535** Ahmad Gran controls most of Ethiopia, but Christian resistance continues in the highlands. **1543** Ahmad Gran is defeated and killed by Ethiopian Christians with Portuguese assistance. **1548** At the invitation of the king, Jesuit missionaries arrive in Kongo.	**ca 1550** Building is completed of the great stone structures at Great Zimbabwe. **1551** The Ottoman Turks capture Tripoli from the Knights Hospitallers. **1556** Süleyman's mosque in Istanbul, designed by the architect Sinan, is completed.	**ca 1560** A wealthy Jewish woman, Dona Gracia Nasi, settles in Istanbul and uses her extensive business contacts and wealth to encourage widespread Jewish settlement in the Ottoman Empire. **1571** At the Battle of Lepanto, the Spanish and their allies defeat the Ottoman fleet, in a landmark victory of Christians over Muslims.

PEOPLE & PLACES	DOCUMENTS, ART, & ARTIFACTS	WORSHIP & DOCTRINE

EUROPE

1352 Corpus Christi College is founded in Cambridge, England, by two medieval guilds; scholars at the new institution are required to pray for guild members killed by the Black Death.

1359 In Vienna, Austria, work begins on the nave of St. Stephen's Cathedral.

1366 After a vision, St. Catherine of Siena begins to work among the poor in the Tuscan city where she was born.

ca 1362 English poet William Langland begins writing *Piers Plowman*, an allegorical poem in which he experiences a vision of heaven.

1374 Dutch preacher Gerhard Groote renounces worldly enjoyment and begins a process that will eventually lead to founding the Brethren of the Common Life, inspiring religious reform throughout Germany.

1375 John Wycliffe begins preaching at the University of Oxford.

Timur's Mongols fight the Knights of Saint John in a battle for Smyrna.

THE AMERICAS

ASIA & OCEANIA

ca 1360 King Rajasanagara oversees a golden age of the Buddhist kingdom of Majapahit in Indonesia.

1369 Timur (Tamerlane) takes control of the Mongols.

ca 1350 Cambodia adopts the Theravada form of Buddhism and changes its liturgical language from Sanskrit to Pali.

AFRICA & THE MIDDLE EAST

O immeasurable love! O gentle love! Eternal fire! You are that fire ever blazing, O high eternal Trinity. You are direct without twisting, genuine without any duplicity, open without any pretense. Turn the eye of your mercy on your creatures. I know that mercy is your hallmark, and no matter where I turn I find nothing but your mercy. This is why I run crying to your mercy to have mercy on the world.

CATHERINE OF SIENA, 1370s

RELIGION IN THE WORLD

1371 Bulgaria and all of Macedonia, with the exception of Salonika, come under the control of the Islamic Ottoman Turks.

WORLD EVENTS

1351 The Black Death begins to recede in Europe: around 75 million people have died since 1347.

1356 The English defeat the French at Poitiers, a clash in the Hundred Years' War.

ca 1370 Germany's Hanseatic League reaches the height of its power, dominating trade in the Baltic Sea.

1372 The French defeat the English navy in the Atlantic Ocean off La Rochelle.

At Meteora monasteries perch on the rock columns where they were built for safety.

WORDS OF DEVOTION

St. Catherine's Prayer

The daughter of a lower-class family in Siena, Catherine (1347–1380) lived as a nun within her family home before, in 1366, a mystical spiritual experience persuaded her to work among the sick and the poor. She became renowned for her piety and an influential voice in Italian politics. Catherine wrote moving letters to many prominent individuals, including the pope. Her prayers and other spiritual commentaries, written in her native Tuscan dialect, are among the classics of vernacular Italian literature of the 14th century.

ca 1350 In Mexico, priests are among the elite of Aztec society; some rise to become rulers of the empire (📄 pages 150–151).

ca 1350 The Hohokam begin to abandon many of their villages in Arizona.

ca 1350 The Aztec extend their control over neighboring peoples in central Mexico.

1351 Binyau, king of Burma, requests a relic of Buddha from Sri Lanka in order to build a stupa to mark a military victory.

1351 U Thong establishes a capital at Ayutthaya in Thailand and introduces Brahminism alongside Buddhism.

1368 The Ming dynasty is established in China; its foundation is linked with the promised coming of a new bodhisattva.

1351 Firoz Shah becomes the sultan of Delhi.

1355 In China, rebels led by Zhu Yuanzhang seize Nanjing from Mongol control and found the Ming dynasty.

ca 1360 The Indianized Buddhist kingdom of Majapahit in Java begins a golden age under the rule of Rajasanagara.

ca 1370 Vijayanagar becomes the dominant state of southern India.

1352 The Coptic Patriarch Marco is imprisoned by Muslims during a persecution of Christians in Cairo, Egypt.

1352 The Moroccan traveler Ibn Battuta visits Mali, where he is shocked by the lack of Islamic tradition, believing the empire to be motivated only by trade and wealth.

1360 The death of Mansa Suleiman marks the beginning of the decline of the mighty Islamic empire of Mali.

1352 The Marinid dynasty takes control of Algeria.

1360 Murhad becomes emperor of the Ottomans and puts down a revolt in Ankara, in Turkey.

1365 The Christian ruler of Makurra (Nubia) is killed by Arab raiders.

THE MONASTERIES OF METEORA

The valley of the Piniós River in central Thessaly, Greece, is home to a remarkable collection of monasteries perching atop giddy sandstone pinnacles that rise up to 1,600 feet above the plain.

The first hermits arrived in the valley in about 1000, seeking a place to practice a strict, ascetic form of Christianity. As more hermits arrived, they formed a monastery. In 1382 building began on top of the tallest rocky outcrop. The Byzantine Empire was losing its power, and Christians were facing persecution by foreign invaders. St. Athanasios, a refugee from the monastery at Mount Athos, began the construction of Megálou Meteórou ("Meteora" comes from a Greek word meaning "suspended in the air"). The stone, and the builders themselves, had to be hoisted up to the rock in baskets. Building took 300 years, during which some 23 other monasteries were also built to accommodate hermits, under first Serbian and then Ottoman rule. The monasteries contain important religious frescoes in the late Byzantine style from the 16th and 17th centuries.

PEOPLE & PLACES	DOCUMENTS, ART, & ARTIFACTS	WORSHIP & DOCTRINE

EUROPE

1375 English reformer John Wycliffe begins a long attack on clerical wealth, monasticism, and the authority of the pope.

1382 John Wycliffe is expelled from Oxford University after being condemned by the London Synod.

1387 Florentius Radewyns, a follower of Gerhard Groote, founds the Monastery of Windesheim in the Netherlands.

1377 The return of the papal musicians makes Rome a musical center.

1384 John Wycliffe completes the translation of the Bible into English shortly before his death.

ca 1387 English poet Geoffrey Chaucer begins writing *The Canterbury Tales*, recounted by pilgrims traveling to the shrine of Saint Thomas Becket in Canterbury Cathedral.

1388 Building work begins on Milan Cathedral.

1390 John Wycliffe's teachings reach Bohemia, where they will influence the reformer Jan Hus.

1398 Jan Hus lectures on theology at Prague University.

FAITH AND LIFE

The Canterbury Tales

Geoffrey Chaucer's long poem, written between 1387 and 1400, was an early English masterpiece. Chaucer conceived it as a collection of tales told by pilgrims to entertain one another as they traveled from Southwark, in London, to Canterbury Cathedral to pray at the shrine of St. Thomas Becket, the archbishop who was martyred there in 1170. Religion figures highly in the tales. A number of the pilgrims belong to the church establishment, such as the Monk, the Prioress, and the Nun's Priest. Others—the Pardoner, who sells "indulgences" or pardons, and the Summoner, who identifies sinners for possible excommunication—represented a more controversial side of Catholicism during the upheaval of the Great Schism.

THE AMERICAS

ASIA & OCEANIA

1384 King Lu Thai of Thailand takes full ordination as a Buddhist monk.

1391 Birth of Gedun Drupa, the first Dalai Lama of Tibet (page 165).

AFRICA & THE MIDDLE EAST

1382 David I becomes king of Christian Ethiopia and makes contact with Christian nations beyond Africa.

1382 Arab theologian and scholar Ibn Khaldun becomes a judge in Cairo, Egypt.

This 14th-century manuscript shows the poet Geoffrey Chaucer in the guise of a pilgrim on the journey from London to Canterbury Cathedral.

RELIGION IN THE WORLD	WORLD EVENTS
1377 Pope Gregory XI returns to Rome after the papacy's "Babylonian captivity" in Avignon.	**1379** The Venetians defeat their rivals from Genoa in the naval Battle of Chioggia.
1378 The Great Schism opens when cardinals elect two different candidates as pope: Urban VI and Clement VII (📄 box, right).	**1381** In England, a short-lived Peasants' Revolt is suppressed and its leader, Wat Tyler, is executed.
1387 Lithuania converts to Christianity a year after being united with Poland.	**1389** The Ottoman sultan Murad I defeats the Serbs at the Battle of Kosovo, although he is killed during the clash.
1393 The Czech churchman John of Nepmuk is drowned in Prague on the orders of King Wenceslas, reputedly for refusing to tell the king secrets from the queen's confessional (but probably for opposing Wenceslas's appointments to the clergy). Nepmuk later becomes a Czech national saint.	**1395** In southern Russia, Timur defeats another Mongol empire, the Golden Horde.
	1396 Sigismund of Hungary leads a Christian army against the Muslim forces advancing into Europe under the Ottoman sultan Bayezid, but is defeated at Nicopolis.
	1399 In England Henry Bolingbroke overthrows Richard II and takes the throne as King Henry IV.

THE GREAT SCHISM

The Great Schism (1378–1417) was a division in the Catholic Church during which there were two rival popes, one in the French city of Avignon and the other in Rome. When Pope Urban VI attacked wealth in the church in 1378, a group of cardinals moved to Avignon (seat of the papacy from 1309 until 1377) and elected another pope, Clement VII. The split had serious implications for the

The papacy had been centered at Avignon, France, during an exile from Rome before the Great Schism, so it was the logical site for the antipope to establish his court.

idea that the pope was God's sole representative on Earth.

In 1409 the cardinals called a council at Pisa in Italy to resolve the schism. The council deposed both popes and elected Alexander V. Gregory and Benedict refused to leave office, so there were now three popes (Alexander soon died and was succeeded by John XXIII).

John called another council in Constance in 1414. It instructed all three popes to abdicate. John refused and fled in disguise. The council deposed and ordered the arrest of John, who was imprisoned. Gregory agreed to resign, while Benedict found himself isolated. The council then elected Martin V, who ruled in Rome as the one true pope. At last the schism was over.

RELIGION IN THE WORLD	WORLD EVENTS
ca 1382 After Muslim raids on the Malla kingdom in Tibet, Jaya Sthiti repairs damaged temples and introduces a legal and social code based on Hindu principles.	**1393** Timur occupies Baghdad.
	1398 Led by Timur, Mongols invade India and sack Delhi, ending the Delhi Sultanate.

	1375 In Africa Gao secedes from Mali and eventually becomes the Islamic Songhai Empire.
	ca 1380 The Kongo Kingdom is founded near the mouth of the Congo River in Central Africa.
	1390 The Byzantines lose their last territory in Asia Minor to the Ottomans.

THE GLORY OF PAGAN

A T DAWN GOLDEN LIGHT CATCHES HUNDREDS OF SPIRES rising above a dusty plain on the Irrawaddy River in Myanmar (Burma). The ruins mark the site of Pagan, a holy city that once contained thousands of Buddhist temples and stupas built between the 11th and 13th centuries. All the stone structures at Pagan—except the city walls—had a religious purpose. Despite Myanmar's international isolation, the location is still a popular destination for Buddhist pilgrimage.

Pagan was founded in 849 and became the capital city of the first Burmese empire a few decades later, supported by thriving trade on the river. In the 11th century King Anawrahta unified northern and southern Burma, conquering the Mon and using Mon monks, scholars, and artists to create a new capital at Pagan. He dedicated the city in about 1056 to Theravada Buddhism, introduced by monks from Sri Lanka. Under Anawrahta and later King Kyanzittha, Theravada Buddhism became virtually the exclusive faith; other forms of Buddhism and other religions were suppressed.

Anawrahta's patronage began a golden age that would last for another two hundred years. The king built five stupas to mark out the limits of his new capital: one in each corner, with a fifth at the heart of the city. The two most splendid stupas housed relics of the Buddha himself: one held a hair, the other a tooth.

After Anawrahta, later kings were more inclined to build temples rather than stupas. They include the Ananda Temple, which has been in constant use for worship since it was completed in 1091. Meanwhile, Pagan became an educational center, attracting Buddhist students from India and Sri Lanka, as well as the Thai and Khmer regions. The golden age of building came to an end in 1274, with the completion of the Mingalarzedi Stupa.

Pagan's influence ended when the Mongols invaded in 1287. The invaders destroyed thousands of pagodas and temples; the defenders of Pagan may also have destroyed their own religious structures in order to reuse their stones to build a fort. With Burmese political unity shattered, the complex was abandoned and left to decay and ruin.

Of the 13,000 religious buildings that stood in the city's heyday, fewer than 2,500 still stand, including 911 temples, 524 stupas, and 415 monasteries, as well as other structures and unexcavated mounds.

The golden early morning sun lights up the ruined temples scattered on the plain at Pagan in Myanmar.

EUROPE

PEOPLE & PLACES

1400 The Alt-Neu Synagogue is built in Prague, Bohemia.

1402 Work begins on Seville Cathedral, Spain.

1405 In England, building starts on Bath Abbey.

1415 Jan Hus is executed for heresy by order of the Council of Constance.

1420 Architect Filippo Brunelleschi begins to build the cupola of Florence Cathedral.

DOCUMENTS, ART, & ARTIFACTS

ca 1400 Ecclesiastical drama in the style of English mystery plays flourishes in Italy.

1413 In *De Ecclesia*, Jan Hus calls for church reform along the same lines as John Wycliffe.

1418 The *Imitatio Christi* appears; its author is often claimed to be Thomas à Kempis.

1425 Lorenzo Ghiberti begins sculpting panels for the doors of the Baptistery in Florence.

WORSHIP & DOCTRINE

1413 Christians and Jews debate doctrinal matters in the Disputation of Tortosa, Spain.

1414 The Council of Constance begins its four-year meeting which will proclaim that general councils of the church have authority over popes.

1417 Pope Benedict XIII is deposed by the Council of Constance and replaced by Martin V, marking the end of the Great Schism (📄 page 161).

1423 Pope Martin V summons a general council at Pavia and Sienna, but poor attendance leads him to suspend it for seven years.

Ghiberti's panel from the Baptistery doors in Florence shows Abraham preparing to sacrifice his son, Isaac.

THE AMERICAS

ca 1400 The Upper and Middle Mississippi phases of Mound Builders develop in North America.

ASIA & OCEANIA

1409 In Tibet, Tsong-kha-pa founds the first of three major Buddhist monasteries he will create in the next decade.

AFRICA & THE MIDDLE EAST

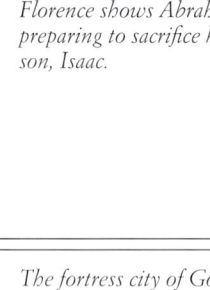

The fortress city of Golconda was a center of Muslim power in southern India under the Bahmani Sultanate, which ruled from 1347 to 1527.

RELIGION IN THE WORLD

1410 Jan Hus and his followers are excommunicated by the Archbishop of Prague.

1410 The Medici family of Florence increase their political influence when their favored candidate is elected antipope as John XXIII.

1414 The Medici become bankers to the papacy.

1420 Followers of Jan Hus begin a 13-year war against the authority of the emperor in Bohemia (now the Czech Republic).

WORLD EVENTS

1410 The Jagiellon dynasty is established in Poland after a Polish–Lithuanian army defeats the Teutonic Knights at the Battle of Tannenberg (Grunwald).

1415 King Henry V of England invades France and wins a major victory at the Battle of Agincourt.

1419 The Portuguese prince Henry (the Navigator) begins to study navigation.

1420 Henry V marries a French princess, becoming heir to the French throne.

The statue of Jan Hus stands in the Bohemian capital at Prague.

ca 1415 Sultan Firuz Shah Bahmani makes the kingdom of Bahmani a center of Muslim culture in India's Deccan region.

1420 Korean scholars begin studying in the new Chiphyonjon, a royal academy.

1402 A usurper overthrows the second Ming emperor, Jianwen, and rules China as the Yongle emperor.

1405 On the death of the Mongol leader Timur, his empire is divided between his sons.

1407 The capital of the Timurid Empire is moved to Herat in Afghanistan.

1420 In China the Yongle emperor moves his capital to Dadu, which he renames Beijing.

ca 1410 In southern Africa, most of the stone buildings at Great Zimbabwe have been completed by now: the settlement may have been a ceremonial center.

1415 An Ethiopian Christian army kills the Muslim ruler of Seylac during a raid on the Arab port on the Red Sea.

1413 The Ottomans win back control of Anatolia from the heirs of Timur.

1415 The Portuguese capture Ceuta on the Moroccan coast from its Muslim rulers, gaining a foothold in North Africa.

1416 A Chinese fleet under Admiral Cheng Ho visits ports on Africa's east coast; it takes back a giraffe as a gift for the emperor.

1421 Murad II becomes Ottoman sultan and resumes a policy of expanding the empire.

THE FIRST DALAI LAMA

In about 1411 a former nomadic shepherd named Gedun Drupa was ordained as a Buddhist monk at Narthang monastery in Tibet. He went on to study with the reformer Tsong-kha-pa, who made the young man his principal disciple. Tsong-kha-pa gave Gedun a set of new robes as a sign that he should spread Buddhist teachings throughout Tibet. Gedun founded three monasteries, including the great monastery at Tashilhunpo, where he lived until his death in 1474.

Gedun is now recognized as the first Dalai Lama, the spiritual leader of the Gelug ("Yellow Hat") Buddhists of Tibet. The title was conferred on the third Dalai Lama, Sonam Gyatso, by the Mongol king Altan Khan in 1578. The title, which means "Ocean of Wisdom," was bestowed retrospectively on Gedun Drupa and his successor, Gedun Gyatso. The lamas are believed to be reincarnations of Avalokiteshvara, the bohisattva of compassion, a spiritual being who has chosen to be reborn on Earth in order to enlighten others. Although the Dalai Lama is primarily a spiritual leader, from the 17th century until the Chinese took control in 1959 he also led the Tibetan government.

Tibetan Buddhists believe that each Dalai Lama is a reincarnation of his predecessor. When a Dalai Lama dies, senior lamas spend two or three years searching Tibet for the young boy as whom he has been reincarnated. They seek guidance from the spirit of the holy lake, Lhamo La-tso. The spirit, Palden Lhamo, was said to have promised Gedun Drupa to watch over the reincarnation of his line. Patterns on the surface of the lake might indicate the direction in which to seek the new Dalai Lama; visions might also direct the searchers. When they find a likely candidate, the boy is given a series of tests, such as identifying objects that belonged to the previous Dalai Lama. The current Dalai Lama, Tenzin Gyatso, born in 1935, is the 14th successor to Gedun Drupa.

ISLAM IN AFRICA

WHILE THE RENAISSANCE WAS UNDER WAY IN Europe, powerful and influential civilizations arose in Africa. Many were inspired by Islam, introduced to the continent by Arab traders from about 1000 onward. Important centers of Islamic learning and culture emerged and grew wealthy through trade and conquest. In the 14th and 15th centuries African scholars such as the Islamic historian Ibn Khaldun furthered people's understanding of the world. At the same time, tales of the riches of African kings spread throughout both the Islamic and Christian worlds.

Europe and North Africa had had close links for hundreds of years. From the early eighth century until 1492 Muslims from northern Africa—Europeans knew them as Moors—controlled parts of Spain. During the 16th century North Africa increasingly fell under the control of Turks. By 1570 the Islamic empire of the Ottomans covered all of the continent's Mediterranean coast apart from Morocco.

Farther south the scrub and grasslands of Sudan were home to the great empire of Mali, which prospered thanks to its control of lucrative trade routes across the Sahara Desert. In 1324 Mansa Musa, Mali's most famous ruler, made a pilgrimage to Mecca that became such an extravagant display of wealth that chroniclers wrote about it for years. Each of his 500 servants carried a golden staff, while a caravan of 100 elephants carried 10,000 pounds of gold. On a stopover in Cairo, he spent so much money that he devalued the Egyptian currency. During his reign the Sankoré mosque in Timbuktu became a center of Islamic learning and the foundations for the University of Sankoré were laid. In the middle of the 15th century Mali began to be overshadowed by another Islamic state, Songhai, which lay to the east. Both Mali and Songhai had walled cities with spectacular mosques, like the famous one at Djénné.

Along the coast of eastern Africa centuries of trade with Arabs, Persians, Indians, and other Africans had allowed Islamic Swahili city-states such as Kilwa, Mogadishu, and Mombasa to prosper by the early 13th century. Goods from inland, as well as local exports such as silk and timber, were traded for luxury goods from Asia and Arabia. The Swahili merchants lived in fine houses made from stone and coral. Their towns were encircled by stone walls and ruled by sheikhs or sultans.

Northwest of the Swahili city-states lay the Christian kingdom of Ethiopia, whose rulers claimed descent from the biblical King Solomon. Ethiopia often came under threat from its Islamic neighbors, in particular in 1526 when the ruler of the Muslim kingdom of Adal launched a holy war. However, with aid from Portugal, Emperor Lebna Dengel managed to defeat his Islamic enemies and keep his kingdom Christian.

The mosque at Djénné in Mali is the largest of Africa's mud-built Islamic buildings and a popular pilgrimage destination. The wooden struts are built into the walls to act as scaffolding during maintenance work.

PEOPLE & PLACES	DOCUMENTS, ART, & ARTIFACTS	WORSHIP & DOCTRINE

EUROPE

1425 The Duomo, or cathedral, is completed in Florence, Italy.

1428 By command of Pope Martin V, the remains of the English reformer John Wycliffe are dug up and burned, and the ashes scattered in a river.

1446 Building begins on King's College Chapel, Cambridge, England.

1447 Nicholas V is elected pope; he is a renowned scholar.

1448 Jonas becomes metropolitan of Moscow and All Rus without the authority of Constantinople.

1436 Fra Angelico paints at the San Marco Monastery in Florence.

1445 Fra Angelico paints a series of frescoes for the Saint Nicholas Chapel in the Vatican, Rome.

1431 The opening of the Council of Basel coincides with the death of Martin V and the election of Pope Eugene IV. The council sits until 1449.

1436 The Compacts of Prague, negotiated with the Pope, allow most of the Hussites, followers of executed Czech reformer Jan Hus, back into the church.

1438–39 The Council of Ferrara–Florence proclaims the reunion of the Catholic and Orthodox churches, but is rejected by Orthodox Christians.

THE AMERICAS

1440 Moctezuma I becomes emperor of the Aztec (📄 pages 150–151).

Joan of Arc became a French national heroine for her role in leading the fight against the English.

ASIA & OCEANIA

1440 Birth of the Indian mystic Kabir, the future master of Nanak, founder of Sikhism.

1431 In Cambodia the Khmer abandon their capital at Angkor and move to Phnom Penh; the old city is overgrown by the jungle (📄 pages 260–261).

1438 The Jamma Musjid Mosque of Husain is built in Jaunpur, India.

1443 Visiting the Hindu city of Vijayanagar in India, a Persian visitor claims that it has "no equal in all the world."

AFRICA & THE MIDDLE EAST

ca 1440 Emperor Zara Jacob reforms the Ethiopian Church.

Ta Prohm in Angkor is one of the temples that were overgrown by the jungle after the capital was abandoned by the Khmer.

RELIGION IN THE WORLD

1419 War breaks out between the Hussites and imperial forces.

1428 Inspired by religious visions, Joan of Arc leads the French in battle against the English.

1431 Captured by the Burgundians and passed to the English, Joan of Arc is burned to death for heresy in Rouen.

1433 Nicholas of Cusa proposes a program of reform for the church and the Holy Roman Empire.

1434 A revolt in Rome forces Pope Eugene IV to flee to Florence.

1436 The Compact of Iglau ends the Hussite Wars and declares Emperor Sigismund as king of Bohemia.

1444 A papal crusade against the Ottomans is decisively defeated at Varna on the Black Sea.

WORLD EVENTS

1434 The Medici family, led by Cosimo de Medici, become the effective rulers of Florence.

1437 A Portuguese expedition led by Prince Henry the Navigator fails badly in an attempt to capture Tangiers in Islamic North Africa.

1438 The title of Holy Roman emperor becomes a hereditary possession of the Habsburg dynasty.

1428 The Aztec defeat the city-state of Azcapotzalco and take its place as the dominant power in the Valley of Mexico.

1438 Pachacutec begins Inca rule in Peru.

If I made the seven seas
my ink and the trees of the
forest my pen,
If the whole expanse of
Earth were my paper,
Still I could not write the
greatness of Ram!

KABIR, INDIAN MYSTIC POET

The ruins of Vijayanagar—"City of Victory"—include this stone monument in the shape of a chariot. The city reached is peak in the early 15th century, serving as a bulwark of Hindu culture against Islam from the north.

1427 The Ethiopian emperor Yeshaq sends ambassadors to Spain to try to find allies against the Muslims of North Africa.

1445 Zara Jacob of Ethiopia invades and defeats the neighboring Islamic state of Ifat.

THE RUSSIAN ORTHODOX CHURCH

Russians date the creation of the Russian Orthodox Church to 988, when Prince Vladimir of Kiev was baptized into Christianity, which he made the religion of his state. The metropolitanate of Kiev—and its successors in Vladimir and Moscow—were subordinate to Constantinople, seat of the Orthodox Church, until 1448. After a long disagreement with Constantinople over concessions to the Catholic Church, Russian bishops elected their own metropolitan, Jonas, without consulting Constantinople. Jonas became metropolitan of Moscow and All Rus, ranking below only the patriarchs of Constantinople, Alexandria, Antioch, and Jerusalem. When the Ottoman Turks conquered Constantinople in 1453, Russian Christians saw Moscow as the legitimate successor to Rome and Constantinople as the seat of the true Christian faith.

The emergence of the Russian church coincided with a key period of history as Tsars Ivan III and his son, Vasily III, consolidated the monarchy and expanded Russian territory. Although there were protests that monasteries should have their land taken away, they thrived with imperial support. Monasteries and new sects satisfied an appetite for spiritual growth. Followers of St. Sergius from the Monastery of the Trinity at Radonezh founded hundreds of monasteries throughout northern Russia. Their efforts helped attract settlers to colonize the region, reinforcing the state.

Russia's new power was acknowledged in 1589, when Metropolitan Job became the patriarch of Moscow and All Rus. This meant that not only was the Russian church self-governing: it also meant that the patriarchs were almost as powerful as the tsars. On some occasions they ran the state when the government was weak.

RELIGIOUS ART IN THE RENAISSANCE

MOST RENAISSANCE PAINTINGS AND SCULPTURES HAD religious themes. They showed events from the Bible or told stories of the life of the Virgin Mary and the saints. The most important function of such works was to teach people about the beliefs of Christianity. Artists used conventions that made the images easy to recognize, such as using a halo to indicate a saint or deep-blue robes to show Mary.

Events from the life of Christ, particularly his birth and death, were often depicted as part of an altarpiece (a structure behind an altar) so they were at the center of Catholic worship and ritual. Paintings of the Nativity showed the Virgin and Child in a stable, often with the shepherds or kings, angels, and animals. Images of the Crucifixion portrayed Christ's suffering for humankind. Artists in northern Europe drew particular attention to his pain, showing blood spurting out of his wounds.

Renaissance artists also showed other stages of Christ's Passion. The Deposition portrayed Christ's followers taking his body down from the cross. The Lamentation showed Christ's family and followers weeping over his body. In contrast, pictures of the Resurrection show Jesus as triumphant and godlike.

Most homes had a small image of the Madonna (Italian for "My Lady"). The most common image of the Virgin showed her with the Christ Child, often in a lifelike way that made Mary appear almost like an ordinary mother with her child. Other pictures show Mary's grief at her son's death. In a *pietà* (Italian for "pity"), the Virgin supports the dead Christ in her lap. Other popular scenes from the life of the Virgin included the Annunciation, when the angel Gabriel announces to Mary that God has chosen her to be the mother of Christ, and the Assumption, or Mary's ascent to heaven.

The Protestant religion placed more emphasis on the word of the Bible rather than images. Protestant churches contained few works of art. The Catholic Church also introduced stricter guidelines for artists. It specified which subjects artists could show—those not actually described in the Bible were discouraged—and also how they should be portrayed. Nude figures were discouraged. Authorities instructed that draperies should be painted over the nudes in Michelangelo's painting of the *Last Judgment* in the Sistine Chapel.

Mary cradles the body of her son in a pietà sculpted by Michelangelo in 1499, the first of his treatments of the subject.

The Last Judgment by Fra Angelico (painted ca 1435) shows the souls of the dead emerging from their tombs to face judgment.

PEOPLE & PLACES	DOCUMENTS, ART, & ARTIFACTS	WORSHIP & DOCTRINE

EUROPE

1450 The Vatican Library is founded.

1453 After capturing Constantinople from the Byzantine Empire, the Ottoman Turks convert the Hagia Sophia Basilica into a mosque.

1458 Turkish troops sack the ancient temples of the Acropolis, Athens, Greece.

1460 Winchester Cathedral is completed in England.

1463 The architect Sinan begins building the mosque of Sultan Mohammad II in Constantinople (📄 pages 204–205).

1471 The German monk Thomas à Kempis, author of the influential *Imitatio Christi*, dies.

1450 Johannes Gutenberg prints the *Constance Mass Book*.

1452 Lorenzo Ghiberti completes *The Gates of Paradise*, his panels for the doors of the Baptistery in Florence.

1453 Johannes Gutenberg prints the Mazarin Bible at Mainz, Germany.

1466 Johann Mentel prints the first German Bible, in Strasbourg.

1472 The first printed version appears of Dante's *Divine Comedy*.

1468 The bishopric of Vienna is established.

This basalt statue of Coyolxauhqui, the Aztec moon goddess and daughter of Coatlicue, was carved in Mexico in about 1400.

THE AMERICAS

ca 1450 The Aztec capital Tenochtitlan has around 300,000 citizens, who worship at pyramid temples that rise above the city (📄 pages 150–151).

ca 1450 Aztec craftsmen use the green feathers of the quetzal, a bird from Central America, to create luxury goods for nobles and priests.

ca 1450 The creator god Viracocha emerges as the most important deity of the Inca world, followed by the sun god (📄 pages 144–145).

ASIA & OCEANIA

ca 1450 The Ryoanji Zen temple is built at Kyoto, Japan, with a famous drystone landscape garden.

1469 Nanak, the first guru of Sikhism, is born in the Punjab region of northwestern India.

1472 Birth of Wang Yangming, whose Neo-Confucian ideas will influence Chinese thought for generations.

The garden at Ryoanji is a re-creation in stone of a landscape with fields and mountains. Such rock gardens were built in order to encourage spiritual contemplation.

AFRICA & THE MIDDLE EAST

1468 The Mamluk sultan Qa'itbay begins a 28-year reign during which he extensively restores the Islamic shrines of Mecca and Medina.

1450 In Ethiopia, emperor Zara Jacob imposes reforms on the church and persecutes Falasha Jews.

1463 Muhammed Rumfa, king of Kano, turns the traditional monarchy into an Islamic sultanate, paving the way for Kano's emergence as a major trading power.

RELIGION IN THE WORLD	WORLD EVENTS
1474 Isabella, wife of Ferdinand I of Aragon, becomes queen of Castile, uniting the two largest Spanish kingdoms and laying the foundation for the campaign to drive the Islamic Moors from Spain.	**1453** The Ottoman Turks conquer Constantinople, which they rename Istanbul, marking the end of the Byzantine Empire. **1453** The French defeat of the English at Castillon ends the Hundred Year's War (the conflict has actually lasted, with interruptions, 116 years). **1455** England is ravaged by the Wars of the Roses, a dynastic feud between the Lancasters and the Yorks (the families' emblems are, respectively, a red and a white rose). **1474** William Caxton prints the first book in English.
	1461 The Maya abandon the once-mighty city of Mayapán. **1470** The Inca defeat the coastal Chimu empire, extending their influence and religion.

ALEXANDER VI

Pope Alexander VI (1431–1503) was an influential figure in late 15th-century Italy and a great patron of the arts. A member of the powerful Borgia family, he was proclaimed pope in 1492.

Alexander's taste for women and displays of wealth caused great resentment. Equally controversial was the energy he spent guaranteeing the power of his numerous children. However, he also proved to have considerable skills as an administrator. He restored law and order in Rome, reformed the papal finances, and formed an international "Holy Alliance" of Venice, Milan, the King of Spain, and the Holy Roman Emperor to expel French invaders from Italy. At the request of the monarchs of Spain, Alexander also negotiated the 1494 Treaty of Tordesillas, which divided colonial discoveries in the "New World" between Spain and Portugal.

Alexander was also a major patron of the arts. Under his guidance the Castel Sant'Angelo (an ancient fortress in the Vatican) was restored, and the University of Rome was rebuilt. He also commissioned the artist Pinturicchio to decorate the Castel and the Vatican apartments with frescoes.

Now know I well how that fond fantasy
Which made my soul the worshiper and thrall
Of earthly art, is vain; how criminal
Is that which all men seek unwillingly.
Those amorous thoughts which were so lightly dressed,
What are they when the double death is nigh?
The one I know for sure, the other dread.
Painting nor sculpture now can lull to rest
My soul that turns to His great love on high,
Whose arms to clasp us on the cross were spread.

MICHELANGELO, "ON THE BRINK OF DEATH"

PEOPLE & PLACES	DOCUMENTS, ART, & ARTIFACTS	WORSHIP & DOCTRINE

EUROPE

1492 Donato Bramante begins construction of the choir and cupola of Santa Maria della Grazie in Milan.

1493 Cesare Borgia is appointed a cardinal by his father, Pope Alexander VI.

1494 Dominican priest Girolamo Savonarola becomes leader of a republic in Florence, Italy.

1498 The humanist Erasmus of Rotterdam lectures at the University of Oxford.

1498 Excommunicated by the Pope, Savonarola is executed in Florence.

1477 William Caxton prints Chaucer's *Canterbury Tales*.

1477 Michael Pacher creates the altar at Saint Wolfgang, Austria.

1481 Artists including Botticelli, Ghirlandaio, and Perugino paint frescoes in the Sistine Chapel, Rome (📄 pages 170–171).

1487 *Malleus maleficarum* (*The Hammer of Witches*) is published by two German monks as a handbook for witch hunters.

1494 Sebastian Brant, a German theologian, publishes *The Ship of Fools*, a satire about the state of the Catholic Church.

1494 Leonardo da Vinci completes his painting *Madonna of the Rocks* 11 years after beginning it.

1495 Leonardo begins three years' work painting *The Last Supper*.

1498 Michelangelo sculpts a *pietà* for Saint Peter's in Rome.

1478 In Spain, Ferdinand and Isabella begin the Spanish Inquisition to seek out heresy among converted Jews (📄 facing page).

1484 Pope Innocent VIII issues the papal bull *Summis desiderantes*, which recognizes the existence of witches and lends church authority to efforts to seek them out and punish them.

1497 In the Bonfire of the Vanities in Florence, Savonarola orders the confiscation and burning of all possessions he associates with immorality and vanity, including many books and works of art.

THE AMERICAS

1487 In Tenochtitlan, up to 80,000 human sacrifices mark the dedication of the temple of the Aztec god Huitzilopochtli.

In anguish everyone prays to Him, in joy does none; To One who prays in happiness, how sorrow can come.

KABIR, ISLAMIC MYSTIC POET

ASIA & OCEANIA

1484 In Japan, Shogun Yoshimasa introduces the famous tea ceremony, heavily influenced by the teachings and rituals of Zen Buddhism (📄 pages 136–137).

AFRICA & THE MIDDLE EAST

1493 Askiya Muhammad founds the Askiya dynasty, under which the Songhai Empire will become a major power and the Sankoré Mosque at Timbuktu will become a major center of Islamic learning.

This English engraving from the 18th century shows Amida, or Amitabha, principal buddha of the Pure Land Sect of Buddhism.

AMIDA, a DEITY of JAPAN, with the manner in which his Votaries drown themselves to his honour.

RELIGION IN THE WORLD	WORLD EVENTS

1492 The Inquisitor General Tomás de Torquemada gives Spain's Jews three months to either convert to Christianity or leave the country.

1495 The Jews are expelled from Portugal.

1496 The Pope dubs Ferdinand and Isabella "los reyes catolicos"—"the Catholic sovereigns."

1499 The forced conversion of Moors in Spain causes a Moorish revolt in Granada.

1492 The Reconquista (Reconquest): Spain is reunited under Ferdinand and Isabella and the Moors are expelled.

1495 Pope Alexander VI forms the Holy League to drive Charles VIII of France out of Italy, but the league is defeated in battle.

Tuareg visit the mosque at Sankoré, Timbuktu, in what is now Mali.

1492 Christopher Columbus lands in the Bahamas, marking the first modern European contact with the "New World."

1493 Pope Alexander VI divides up the "New World" between Spain and Portugal; the division is the basis for the Treaty of Tordesillas (1494).

1497 John Cabot, sailing on behalf of the English monarch, reaches Newfoundland, in modern Canada.

THE SPANISH INQUISITION

In 1231 Pope Gregory IX set up the Inquisition in Rome. Inquisitors—usually Franciscan or Dominican friars—sought out heretics who did not follow official church doctrine. Those who confessed often received a mild punishment, such as being sent on a pilgrimage. Those who were put on trial and found guilty, however, could be imprisoned or handed to civic authorities to be burned at the stake.

In 1478 a second form of Inquisition was set up in Spain. Led by a friar named Tomás de Torquemada (1420–1498), it was notorious for the use of torture. Under Torquemada about 2,000 victims were burned to death. The Spanish Inquisition was aimed mainly at Jews and Muslims who had become Christians to avoid exile, but who were thought to be practicing their old religion in secret. Later, Protestants were also targeted. Tribunals were set up all around Spain and in Spanish colonies in Mexico and Peru. The accused were sentenced at an auto-da-fé ("act of faith"), a public declaration of the sentence, which was usually death by burning.

A third form of the Inquisition was established in 1542 in Rome to target Protestants in Italy.

1488 In Japan, Buddhists of the True Pure Land sect kill a feudal landowner in the first of what will be a long series of clashes with Japan's ruling classes.

1492 The Delhi sultanate annexes Bihar.

1497 The Iranian Safavid dynasty begin their rise to power in Persia, promoting the "Twelver" form of Shiite Islam.

1498 Portuguese navigator Vasco da Gama lands in Calicut, India, having established a sea route around the Cape of Good Hope from Europe.

1485 The first Portuguese missionaries arrive in Angola.

1490 King Nzinga Nkuwu of Kongo is converted to Christianity by Portuguese missionaries.

1492 Many Jewish and Muslim exiles arrive in North Africa after the fall of Moorish Spain.

1491 The Mamluks and Ottomans end six years of war with a peace settlement.

This woodcut from 1485 shows friars of the Spanish Inquisition torturing and killing Spanish Jews.

NATIVE RELIGIONS OF NORTH AMERICA

NATIVE AMERICANS HAD A DEEPLY SPIRITUAL VIEW OF the world. Their beliefs reflected the close links that bound people and nature together, the value and sacredness of life, and the continuity between the present and the past. Ghosts, visions, shamans, and totems, or revered symbols, all helped Native Americans understand the world around them.

There was no single religion in North America, but most separate faiths shared many aspects, most importantly the belief that divine power manifested itself in every detail of the natural world. Humans and animals, plants and rocks, heavenly bodies and the spirits of the dead: everything was connected, even things that had died and no longer existed in the visible world.

The sacred creation that linked everything was presided over by the One Great Spirit. Northeastern peoples saw this deity as a supernatural power that could attach itself to people and things like an invisible force. Farther south, in Florida, peoples connected the supreme being with the sun. The importance of the sun was reflected in the prominence of the circle in ritual and art. The sun and moon, the wheeling stars, and the rotating seasons all confirmed that existence was circular. Dances around the fire or the pole, the passing of a pipe around a group of people, and the decoration of shields all emphasized the power of the circle.

This shaman from Roanoke Island, now in North Carolina, was painted in the early 16th century by the English colonist and artist John White, who titled his image "The Flyer."

The souls of the dead, symbolized in a tribe's totem, were treated with respect and fear. They fertilized the ground and assisted in the growth of crops; they blessed hunting parties; they watched over childbirth and ensured health and prosperity.

Dreams and visions were a common way of contacting the spirits and influenced important decisions: An early colonial settler observed, "The dream is God of this country." Waking visions, induced by achieving a trancelike state, were particularly important among the tribes of the western Plains. Young braves would undertake a vision quest in order to make contact with a guardian spirit that would watch over their lives.

Guiding the religious life of the community was the shaman. Usually male, the shaman organized community worship and made sure that its rituals were correctly observed. He was a medium for communication with the spirit world and was skilled at interpreting omens; and he was also a moral guide, warning against behavior that would offend the gods and bring the tribe into danger. His role as a healer combined a practical knowledge of herbs and their medicinal powers with an ability to channel spiritual forces to aid the sick.

In the American Southwest, the Pueblo built kivas—circular, often underground structures for prayers centered on a sipapu, *an indentation or hole that connected the living to the world of their ancestors.*

PEOPLE & PLACES	DOCUMENTS, ART, & ARTIFACTS	WORSHIP & DOCTRINE

EUROPE

1500 Antwerp Cathedral is completed.

1503 Canterbury Cathedral is completed after 433 years of building.

1503 Martin Luther enters an Augustinian monastery in Erfurt, Germany (📄 page 181).

1504 Pope Julius II orders the founding of the University of Santiago de Compostela, Spain.

1505 Pope Julius II calls Michelangelo to work for him in Rome.

1506 Dominican monk Johann Tetzel sells indulgences in Germany.

1506 Pope Julius II lays the foundation stone of a new church at St. Peter's in Rome; it will be designed by Donato Bramante.

1508 The painter Raphael enters the service of the pope.

1514 In England, Thomas Wolsey becomes cardinal and Lord Chancellor.

1500 Hieronymus Bosch paints *Ship of Fools*.

1501 Michelangelo sculpts *David*.

1502 French composer Josquin des Prez publishes his *First Book of Masses*.

1508 Michelangelo begins five years' work painting the ceiling of the Sistine Chapel in Rome.

1512 Michelangelo completes the ceiling of the Sistine Chapel.

1501 A papal bull orders the burning of books that question the authority of the church.

1508 In Germany the emperor authorizes the persecution of Jews and the destruction of all Jewish books, especially the Talmud.

1509 Dutch scholar Desiderius Erasmus attacks corruption in the church.

1512 The Fifth Lateran Council begins: it pronounces the "Immortality of the Soul" as Roman Catholic dogma.

1512 Polish astronomer Nicolaus Copernicus publishes his theory that the Earth and other planets orbit the sun, contrary to Christian teaching (📄 page 203).

Ruins in the desert in Xinjiang province, China, mark the course of the ancient Silk Road, the main artery for the eastward transmission of Buddhism and later Islam across Asia.

THE AMERICAS

1502 Moctezuma II becomes king of the Aztec.

1514 While preaching on Ecclesiastes chapter 34—"The sacrifice of an offering unjustly acquired is a mockery"—Bishop Bartolomé de las Casas, who accompanied Christopher Columbus on his second voyage to the New World, converts to the cause of supporting Indians in the Spanish Empire.

1501 The first bishopric in the Americas is established on Hispaniola (📄 pages 186–187).

1508 Pope Julius II gives the Spanish crown the right to control missionary activity in the Americas.

ASIA & OCEANIA

1504 The Mogul ruler Babur begins a series of conquests in Afghanistan which will eventually bring the whole Indian subcontinent under Islamic rule.

AFRICA & THE MIDDLE EAST

ca 1500 Timbuktu in Mali has become a center of Islamic education, with a university and schools dedicated to the study of the Koran.

MONUMENTS OF FAITH

The Sistine Chapel

Built for Sixtus IV in 1481, the pope's personal chapel in the Vatican is rather nondescript—until worshipers get inside. The walls are covered with colorful murals by the greatest artists of the day, including scenes from the lives of Christ and Moses painted by Botticelli, Perugino, Ghirlandaio, and Signorelli. Tapestries by Raphael of the Acts of the Apostles were hung on ceremonial occasions. The greatest masterpieces, however, are the paintings of Michelangelo. The ceiling features scenes from the Old Testament while the west wall has the huge Last Judgment, painted for Pope Paul III between 1534 and 1541.

RELIGION IN THE WORLD	WORLD EVENTS
1500 Pope Alexander VI declares a Year of Jubilee and imposes a tax to raise money for a crusade against the Turks. **1500** Ferdinand of Aragon puts down a revolt among Spain's Moors. **1501** Henry VII of England refuses the pope's request to lead a crusade against the Turks. **1508** The pope excommunicates Venice as part of the League of Cambrai's campaign against the Venetian republic. **1514** The Fugger bank is granted the right to sell papal indulgences in Germany.	**1508** Pope Julius II crowns Maximilian I as Holy Roman emperor and decrees that the title will now be hereditary for the kings of Germany. **1509** Henry VIII becomes king of England and marries his brother's widow, Catherine of Aragon. **1511** Julius II forms the Holy League with Venice to force the French out of Italy.

1509 Mexican bishop Bartolomé de las Casas suggests that settlers in the New World should bring African slaves with them. **1511** Antonio de Montesinos preaches against the harsh treatment of indigenous peoples in Hispaniola.	**ca 1500** The Inca Empire reaches a highpoint under Huayna Capac (📄 pages 144–145). **1503** The Spanish establish a colonial office to deal with American affairs.
ca 1500 The spread of Islam to Borneo and Java weakens the Hindu–Buddhist kingdom of Majapahit. **ca 1500** Muslim khanates develop in the major cities along the Silk Road that links Europe with East Asia. **1514** Islam comes to dominate the Taklamakan Desert region under Khan Sayid of Kashgar.	**1506** In Korea the tyrant Yonsangun is deposed by a rebellion that brings Chungjong to the throne; he embarks on a program of political reform.
1504 In Sudan, the Muslim Funj defeat a Christian kingdom in Sennar, between the Blue and White Niles. **1508** The new Ethiopian emperor Lebna Dengel struggles to limit growing Islamic influence in his Christian kingdom. **1512** Shiite Islam becomes the state religion in Persia.	**1501** Ismail I conquers Persia and founds the Safavid dynasty. **1505** Portuguese troops sack Kilwa, on the coast of East Africa. **1508** Mozambique becomes the first Portuguese colony in Africa. **1514** The Ottomans defeat the Persians at the Battle of Chaldiran; the Ottoman Empire expands south and east.

THE HINDU SANT TRADITION

Hinduism has always been a highly literary faith. Its early development was based on the written accounts of the epic poems known as the Vedas. Later epics such as the *Bhagavad Gita* and the *Ramayana* recounted the exploits of Hindu deities as a guide for worshipers.

In the mid-15th and early 16th centuries a tradition emerged in northern India of *sants*, teachers and poets who used poetry as a form of worshiping God. The *Bhagavad Gita* had described the concept of *bhakti*, or active devotion, which suggested that worship could take the form of yoga or poetry. The poet-sants continued that tradition through composing verses that followed oral folk tradition in the Hindi dialects of northern India and the archaic Marathi dialects of the south. Unlike orthodox Hinduism as promoted by the brahmins, or priests, the sants rejected the caste system in favor of a more egalitarian view of society. They also rejected religious rituals as a means to achieve salvation, instead arguing that it could be found by surrendering to the "divine name," which dwelled within the heart of the individual.

The sant tradition, known as the Sant Mat, drew on historical roots but was particularly influenced by the late 14th-century figure Ramananda, who was renowned for accepting students from any caste. It was for that reason that the sant traditionally attracted followers among the lower castes, including Untouchables, and among women. One of the most famous Sant poets, Mirabai, was a female devotee of Krishna.

The importance of the sant tradition extended beyond Hinduism and beyond India. In Persia it merged with the mystical sufi form of Islam and influenced poets such as Kabir and Jalal al-Din Muhammad Rumi. In northern India today the Radhasoami movement claims to be continuing the sant tradition, a claim also made by other groups.

PEOPLE & PLACES	DOCUMENTS, ART, & ARTIFACTS	WORSHIP & DOCTRINE

EUROPE

1515 German artist Matthias Grünewald completes the Isenheim Altar for an abbey near Colmar in Germany (now in France).

1515 Raphael becomes the chief architect at St. Peter's in Rome.

1517 Seville Cathedral is completed in Spain.

1515 The Catholic Church forbids the printing of books without approval from church authorities.

1516 Dutch scholar Erasmus publishes a new edition of the New Testament in Greek and Latin.

1518 Raphael paints a portrait of Pope Leo X and his cardinals.

1522 Luther completes and publishes his translation of the New Testament into German.

1522 The University of Alcala, Spain, publishes the Polyglot Bible, in Latin, Greek, Hebrew, and Aramaic.

1523 Ignatius Loyola completes *The Spiritual Exercises*, which will provide the basis of Jesuitism.

1525 An English translation of the New Testament by William Tyndale is published in Cologne and Worms.

1517 Martin Luther nails his 95 Theses to the door of the cathedral in Wittenberg, Germany, detailing his criticisms of the Catholic Church. The event is traditionally seen as the start of the Reformation (📄 facing page; pages 182–183).

1521 The Diet of Worms meets; it declares Luther a heretic.

1521 Martin Luther is excommunicated by the papal bull *Decet Romanum Pontificem*.

1525 Matteo Bassi founds the Capuchin ("Hooded") Order of monks.

1529 At the Diet of Speyer, the states of the Holy Roman Empire split into Catholic and reforming members. The reformers make a formal protest (*protestatio*) against the majority Catholics, creating the term "Protestant."

THE AMERICAS

1529 The Franciscan friar Bernardino de Sahagún starts his mission in Mexico.

1527 The Dominican monk Francisco de Vitoria begins a decade-long series of lectures justifying the morality of Spanish conquest in the Indies.

ASIA & OCEANIA

This illustration from the 1540 Codex Fiorentino, compiled under the direction of Bernardino de Sahagún, shows Aztec priests carrying out a religious ceremony on a lake.

AFRICA & THE MIDDLE EAST

This 16th-century illustration by an Ottoman artist shows Sultan Süleyman the Magnificent, who became the Ottoman sultan in 1520 and whose reign would mark a golden age of political power and cultural achievement.

1520 Portuguese priest Francisco Alvarez begins a six-year mission to Ethiopia.

1520 Henry, a prince of Kongo who has studied in Lisbon and Rome, becomes the first sub-Saharan African to be consecrated as a Catholic bishop.

RELIGION IN THE WORLD	WORLD EVENTS
1516 In Venice, all Jews are forced to live in a separate, walled area: the first ghetto.	**1519** Charles I of Spain becomes Holy Roman Emperor as Charles V.
1516 The pope grants the French king independence in ecclesiastical appointments.	**1524** German peasants begin a revolt, partly in the hope that they will be backed by Martin Luther; he condemns them and the revolt ends in failure after two years.
1518 Huldrych Zwingli preaches the Reformation in Switzerland and persuades the council in Zurich to ban the sale of indulgences.	**1524** At Ulm, Protestant German princes meet to resist the authority of Emperor Charles.
1525 In Germany, princes form the Catholic League to resist the spread of Lutheranism.	**1525** The Teutonic Knights make Prussia the secular duchy of Brandenburg.
1525 Anabaptist leader Thomas Münzer is executed in Germany for his role in the Peasants' Revolt.	**1526** Jews are persecuted in Hungary.
1526 The Anabaptists settle in Moravia as the "Moravian Brothers."	**1527** Imperial troops sack Rome and imprison the pope.
1527 The Reformation is adopted in Sweden.	**1528** The English king Henry VIII seeks to divorce Catherine of Aragon in oder to marry Anne Boleyn.
1527 The first Protestant university is founded at Marburg, Germany.	**1529** The Ottomans unsuccessfuly besiege Vienna.
1528 The Reformation arrives in Scotland.	
1528 Finland adopts Lutheranism.	
1515 Bartolomé de las Casas actively campaigns for the rights of indigenous peoples in the Spanish colonies.	**1519** Spanish navigator Ferdinand Magellan sails into the Pacific Ocean.
1524 Franciscan monks arrive in Mexico; they will spearhead European exploration northward into what is now the U.S. Southwest.	**1519** Hernán Cortés lands in Mexico and encounters the Aztec Empire.
	1527 The Inca Empire is weakened by civil war over the succession to the throne.
1515 Sultan Selim I makes Sunni Islam the state religion of the Ottoman Empire, in direct opposition to Shiite Persia, and begins persecuting Shiites.	**1520** Süleyman "the Magnificent" becomes sultan of Turkey.
1526 Led by Babur, the Moguls defeat the Sultan of Delhi.	

Few souls understand what God would accomplish in them if they were to abandon themselves unreservedly to Him and if they were to allow His grace to mold them accordingly.

SAINT IGNATIUS OF LOYOLA

MARTIN LUTHER

The German Martin Luther (1483–1546) was the main leader of the Reformation and founder of the Protestant faith. He became a monk in 1505; in 1512 he became professor of biblical theology at Wittenberg University.

Luther believed that people find favor with God by their faith in his promise that Christ died for their sins. This "justification by faith" differed from the Catholic belief that believers earn God's favor by doing good works. Luther also disagreed with the sale of indulgences, which released people from suffering for their sins after death. Luther argued that forgiveness could not be bought; it was a gift from God.

In 1515 Pope Leo X authorized the sale of indulgences to pay for the building of St. Peter's in Rome. Luther protested by listing his criticisms in his 95 Theses (articles) and went on to attack the whole church. In 1521 Pope Leo X excommunicated Luther, who was also condemned by the Emperor Charles V.

Luther's supporters hid him for eight months for his own safety. In his absence, however, other reformers pressed for both social and religious reform. Luther opposed this development. Despite his religious views, Luther was politically conservative. Although Catholic reformers pointed out the similarities between Lutheran and Catholic beliefs, the Reformation soon made its way across northern Europe. Luther continued to lecture at Wittenberg, and in 1534 he and his colleagues completed a German translation of the Old Testament. He also wrote and translated a number of hymns. With the Reformation in full swing, Luther died in 1546.

This statue of Martin Luther stands in Worms, Germany.

THE REFORMATION

P ROTESTANTISM WAS BORN OF MARTIN LUTHER'S ATTEMPT to reform the Roman Catholic Church, which in his eyes was corrupt. The religious upheavals that followed split the unity of Western Christendom and unleashed a century and a half of warfare and persecution. At a time when religion was an essential part of everyday life, the turmoil in the church affected the whole of Europe.

The Catholic Church had been in a state of rolling reformation since its earliest times: There was no shortage of reformers in the medieval period. But the crisis that began when the German monk Martin Luther nailed a list of alleged church abuses to the door of Wittenberg Cathedral in 1517 represented a new scale of protest. Outraged at the sale of indulgences—documents sold to purchase the forgiveness of sins—Luther boiled over in anger at a church that seemed more concerned with earthly wealth and power than heavenly salvation.

Luther is seen as the first "Protestant," a catch-all name given to the various groups and individuals who eventually broke with the Catholic Church. Luther's belief that the structures of the church only interfered between individuals and their God struck a chord throughout Germany and much of northern Europe. The spirit of revolt spread like wildfire. Luther's attack on the pope's authority quickly broadened into a split.

Many of the reformers were sincere believers like Luther himself, shocked by clerical misconduct. Others were more opportunistic. Henry VIII of England first denounced Luther's views, then underwent a change of heart when the pope refused to grant him a divorce from his marriage. The Church of England he established was at first Catholic in everything but its obedience to Rome, which Henry renounced.

Luther's own objections were to the institutions of the church; his faith in its central tenets remained unchanged. In Geneva, however, French preacher John Calvin rethought Christian theology, promoting a severe Bible-based theological system. In his view the faithful, or "elect," would be saved, but sinners would be cast into hell. Calvin argued that God knew which group was which, and that some people were thus predestined to be damned. In English-speaking countries his followers became known as Puritans, famed for their strict personal morality and their intolerance of those who did not share their beliefs.

The Reformation split Europe and other parts of the world into opposing camps. Protestants were persecuted in Catholic lands, Catholics in the growing number of Protestant ones; many followers of both braved torture and death rather than give up their beliefs. Meanwhile, some Catholics acknowledged the justice in Luther's complaints. Loyal to the pope, they sought to combat the Protestants by cleansing the church of abuses from within in the spiritual movement called the Counter-Reformation.

This Protestant etching shows Martin Luther dressed as a knight standing in front of the city of Worms, where in 1521 his refusal to recant his views led to his condemnation by the Pope and Emperor Charles V, forcing Luther into hiding with his supporters.

The ruins of the Cistercian abbey at Tintern, on England's Welsh border, are eloquent testimony to the consequences of Henry VIII's dissolution of the monasteries, a crucial step in the Anglican Reformation.

PEOPLE & PLACES	DOCUMENTS, ART, & ARTIFACTS	WORSHIP & DOCTRINE

EUROPE

1530 Charles V is crowned Holy Roman Emperor by the pope in Bologna; he is the last emperor to have a papal coronation.

1533 Henry VIII of England divorces his first wife and marries Anne Boleyn; he is excommunicated by the pope.

1534 Work begins building St. Basil's Cathedral in Moscow, Russia.

1536 In England, 376 Roman Catholic monasteries, abbeys, and convents are dissolved by royal command.

1537 Expelled from Geneva, John Calvin settles in Strasbourg.

1538 Shrines and relics destroyed in southern England include Thomas Becket's shrine at Canterbury.

1539 Strasbourg Cathedral erects the first recorded Christmas tree.

1534 Martin Luther completes his German translation of the Bible.

1536 William Tyndale, translator of the Bible into English, is executed for heresy.

1536 Michelangelo paints the *Last Judgment* on the wall of the Sistine Chapel in Rome.

1536 John Calvin writes *The Institutes of the Christian Religion*, establishing him as a leader of the Reformation (pages 182–183).

1539 In England the Great Bible is published by order of Henry VIII.

1543 Nicolaus Copernicus publishes *De Revolutionibus Orbium Coelestium* (*On the Revolution of Heavenly Bodies*), explaining his conclusion that the planets orbit the sun (page 203).

1530 Denmark adopts a Lutheran creed.

1531 Henry VIII declares England free from the authority of the Catholic Church.

1532 John Calvin introduces the Reformation in France.

1535 Henry VIII's former chancellor Thomas More is executed after refusing to take an oath declaring the king's authority over that of the pope.

1535 Angela Merici founds the Order of the Ursulines in Brescia, Italy.

1535 Henry VIII becomes supreme governor of the Church of England.

1540 Pope Paul III recognizes the Society of Jesus (the Jesuit order) (facing page).

1543 Pope Paul III issues a list of forbidden works.

1544 Paul III summons a general council to meet at Trent in 1545 to clarify the church's response to the Reformation (pages 192–193).

THE AMERICAS

1531 Saint Juan Diego sees a vision of Mary near Mexico City: an image of the lady miraculously appears on his cloak while he is trying to persuade the local bishop of the truth of his story; today the Virgin of Guadalupe is the most clebrated icon in Mexico.

1531 The first Spanish archbishop in Mexico reports that the Spaniards have destroyed more than 500 Aztec temples.

1538 The Spanish found a bishopric at Bogotá, Colombia, the first in South America.

1539 Eight priests and four friars arrive in Tampa Bay, Florida, with the conquistador Hernando de Soto, but fail to restrain the harsh treatment of native peoples during his expedition through what is now the southeastern United States.

ASIA & OCEANIA

1539 Sinan, the outstanding Islamic architect of the day, becomes chief of the Ottoman Corps of Royal Architects (pages 204–205).

1539 Death of Guru Nanak, the founder of the Sikh religion.

1542 Sunan Gunung Jati founds an Islamic state, Banten, on the Sunda Strait; it soon comes to dominate the neighboring Hindu state of Java.

1542 Religious reforms introduced by the Emperor Akbar aim to unify the Muslim rulers of the Mogul Empire with their Hindu subjects (page 207).

1542 Jesuit St. Francis Xavier begins his mission to Goa in southern India.

The Virgin of Guadalupe is Mexico's most famous religious icon and her shrine remains the destination of millions of pilgrims every year.

AFRICA & THE MIDDLE EAST

> *I perceived how that it was impossible to establish the lay people in any truth except the Scripture were plainly laid before their eyes in their mother tongue.*
>
> WILLIAM TYNDALE, ENGLISH TRANSLATOR OF THE BIBLE

1531 Muslim leader Ahmad Gran goes to war with Christian Ethiopia.

1535 Ahmad Gran controls most of Ethiopia, but Christian resistance continues in the highlands.

1543 Ahmad Gran is defeated and killed by Ethiopian Christians with Portuguese assistance.

RELIGION IN THE WORLD	WORLD EVENTS

1531 Catholic Swiss defeat the Protestants of Zurich; Huldrych Zwingli is among the dead.

1531 Protestant German princes from the Schmalkaldic League resist attempts by Charles V to reintroduce Catholicism.

1531 The Inquisition begins work in Portugal.

1533 Anabaptists take control of Munster in Germany and prophesy the end of the world.

1535 The Anabaptists in Munster are overthrown and their leaders executed.

1541 John Calvin becomes chief pastor of Geneva, Switzerland.

1541 John Knox leads the Calvinist Reformation in Scotland.

1541 Pope Paul III establishes the Inquisition in Rome.

1543 The Spanish Inquisition burns its first Protestants at the stake (page 175).

1530 Holy Roman Emperor Charles V is also crowned king of Italy.

1531 The appearance of the "Great Comet" (now called Halley's comet) causes fear and superstition throughout Europe.

1536 In England, the Pilgrimage of Grace is a popular revolt against the dissolution of the monasteries; it is put down the next year.

1537 Cosimo de Medici becomes duke of Florence; he will establish a reputation as a great patron of the arts.

1533 Pope Clement VII favors France and encourages French exploration of North America.

1537 Pope Paul III declares that indigenous peoples in the Americas are entitled to liberty and the right to own property.

1530 The Portuguese colonize Brazil.

1530 Spanish influence now extends into Ecuador, Paraguay, and Chile.

1533 Francisco Pizarro executes the ruler of the Inca, Atahualpa.

1534 French explorer Jacques Cartier sails up the St. Lawrence River, Canada, as far as the site of modern Quebec.

1535 A viceroy arrives from Madrid to rule New Spain from Mexico City.

ca 1530 In southern India, the Nayaka dynasty becomes independent of the Vijayanagar Empire and becomes a great patron of Hindu temple building.

1533 Vietnam splits into two independent kingdoms: Tonking and Annan.

1534 The Ottomans capture Baghdad from Persia.

1536 Akbar becomes emperor of India.

1534 The Ottoman admiral Khayr ad-Din Barbarossa captures the North African stronghold of Tunis.

1543 The death of King Afonso leaves the kingdom of Kongo vulnerable to the activities of African and European slave traders.

The colorful Meenakshi Amman temple at Madurai in Tamil Nadu in southern India—dedicated to the Hindu god Shiva—was built by the Nayaka dynasty in about 1600.

SOLDIERS OF CHRIST

The Catholic Church's reaction to the Reformation was led by the Society of Jesus, or Jesuits. The founder of the order, Ignatius Loyola, was a soldier who was injured in 1521 and underwent a spiritual transformation. He wrote his *Spiritual Exercises* and began to lead a holy life.

Six disciples joined Loyola in taking vows of poverty, chastity, and obedience. In 1538 they created the Society of Jesus, whose stated tasks were to undertake missions to foreign lands to educate children and adults, and to help the sick and others in need. By the time Loyola died in 1556, the society had more than a thousand members.

Loyola had aimed to defend Catholicism against the spread of Islam. In fact, the Reformation proved a greater threat. To combat new forms of Christianity, Jesuits traveled around Europe and to Africa and Asia. Francis Xavier became one of the greatest Catholic missionaries, helping establish Christianity in India, Malaysia, and Japan. The Jesuits also reached China. In Japan they made many converts before the government restricted Christianity in 1612. The Jesuits followed the Portuguese to America, where they preached against the enslavement of native peoples.

The Flemish artist Peter Paul Rubens painted this portrait of St. Ignatius of Loyola as part of the Catholic Church's response to the Reformation.

CATHOLICISM IN LATIN AMERICA

THE EUROPEANS WHO SAILED TO THE SO-CALLED NEW World at the end of the 15th century were not only seeking riches. Many also sought to convert "heathens" to Christianity, a goal which ensured the church's blessing for their expeditions. On Christopher Columbus's second voyage to the Americas in 1493, the Spanish monarchs sent their personal chaplain to start the conversion of the indigenous people. The Spaniards had recently fought to drive out the Islamic Moors and reunite Spain; they saw little contradiction in conquering with the sword in one hand and the cross in the other.

By the time Hernán Cortés conquered Mexico in 1521, the Spaniards had already established colonies in the Caribbean. The first bishop arrived in Hispaniola (now Haiti and the Dominican Republic) in 1512. A church or cathedral stood at the heart of every colonial town as an immediate and visible symbol of the Catholic Church. In Mexico the conquerors built churches atop the ruins of destroyed Aztec temples. In Peru, the cathedral in Cuzco was built on a foundation of massive stone blocks laid by the Inca. Meanwhile, riches sent back by the conquerors paid for the construction of striking palaces and churches in Spain and Portugal.

The Catholic Church was integral to Spanish settlement. Each estate had a Catholic friar—most were Dominicans, Franciscans, or Jesuits—to make converts. One Franciscan claimed to have converted 14,000 Mexicans in one day. Many of these converts embraced Catholicism thoroughly; others incorporated elements of traditional rituals into the new faith, a process known as syncretism. Catholic friars built hospitals and schools, and led protests against the harsh treatment of native peoples. In Brazil, Jesuit priests defended native peoples against their Portuguese masters.

As Catholicism spread—in part as more and more Spaniards were born in the Americas—so the American church began to develop its own character. A vision of the Virgin of Guadalupe appeared to a peasant in 1531 and became—and remains—Mexico's most important religious icon. The Peruvian nun, Rose of Lima (1586–1617), was the first Catholic saint to be born in the Americas.

Local converts adapted Christian ritual to their own cultures. In this painting from the wall of a 16th-century monastery in Lima, Peru, Christ and the disciples enjoy a Last Supper of a local delicacy: roast guinea pig.

Throughout their Latin American empire, Spanish settlers built traditional Catholic churches and monasteries at the heart of their towns, using architectural styles familiar from their homeland.

PEOPLE & PLACES	DOCUMENTS, ART, & ARTIFACTS	WORSHIP & DOCTRINE

EUROPE

PEOPLE & PLACES

1546 Death of Martin Luther (📄 page 181).

1547 In France the astrologer Nostradamus makes his first predictions of future events.

1551 Giovanni Pierluigi da Palestrina becomes director of music at St. Peter's, Rome (📄 page 191).

1553 Michael Servetus, author of *Chrisitanismi restitutio* (*Restitution of Christianity*), is executed for heresy after denying the existence of the Holy Trinity in favor of belief in the oneness of God.

1559 The mystical experiences of Teresa of Avila climax when the saint feels a flaming spear pierce her heart (📄 facing page).

DOCUMENTS, ART, & ARTIFACTS

1546 Michelangelo undertakes the completion of St. Peter's in Rome.

1548 *The Spiritual Exercises* by Ignatius Loyola is published 27 years after it was written (📄 page 185).

1550 Michelangelo paints the *Deposition from the Cross*.

1550 Thomas Cranmer publishes *A Defence of the Catholic Doctrine of the Sacrament*.

1550 The first musical setting of the English liturgy is published.

1554 Palestrina dedicates his first *Book of Masses* to Pope Julius III.

1557 In Rome, the Catholic Church publishes the first *Index Librorum Prohibitorum*, listing banned books.

1558 *The Zohar*, a 13th-century cabbalist work of Jewish mysticism, is printed in Italy.

1559 The *Elizabethan Prayer Book* is published in England.

WORSHIP & DOCTRINE

1545 The Council of Trent meets in northern Italy to begin a session that will last, with interruptions, for 19 years; it lays the basis for the Counter-Reformation, the Catholic Church's response to the Reformation (📄 pages 192–193).

1549 The first *Book of Common Prayer* becomes the only prayer book permissible in English churches.

1549 John Calvin and supporters of Huldrych Zwingli agree the *Consensus Tigurinus*, on the form of Holy Communion.

1552 In England the second *Book of Common Prayer* is published.

1559 French Protestants (Huguenots) hold their first national synod (📄 page 223).

THE AMERICAS

PEOPLE & PLACES

1544 Missionary Fray Juan de Padilla is killed by Indians in New Mexico, becoming the first Christian martyr in the Americas.

1545 Bartolomé de las Casas founds a utopian community at Verapaz in modern-day Honduras based on partnership between Europeans and native peoples.

ca 1555 Mexican converts to Christianity build churches and monasteries in a distinctive style based on local ceramic designs (📄 pages 186–187).

DOCUMENTS, ART, & ARTIFACTS

1552 De las Casas publishes *A Brief Relation of the Destruction of the Indies*, an account of the cruel treatment of indigenous American peoples.

WORSHIP & DOCTRINE

1549 Jesuit missionaries begin work in South America.

1549 The first Jesuit mission in Brazil is founded by Manoel da Nobrega.

1551 Brazil's first bishop is installed at Bahia; he is answerable to the archbishop of Lisbon.

ASIA & OCEANIA

PEOPLE & PLACES

ca 1550 Under King Anga Chan, the Cambodians rediscover the Khmer capital of Angkor and try to restore it to its former glory.

1552 Jesuit missionary Francis Xavier dies on a small island off Macao after many failed attempts to reach the Chinese mainland.

WORSHIP & DOCTRINE

1548 Francis Xavier founds a Jesuit mission in Japan.

AFRICA & THE MIDDLE EAST

PEOPLE & PLACES

ca 1550 Building of the great stone structures is completed at Great Zimbabwe.

1556 Süleyman's mosque in Istanbul, designed by the architect Sinan, is completed (📄 pages 204–205).

Istanbul's Süleymanie Mosque is one of the masterpieces of the outstanding architect of the Ottoman Empire, Sinan.

RELIGION IN THE WORLD	WORLD EVENTS
1546 The Protestant Schmalkaldic League goes to war against Emperor Charles V in Germany.	**1547** Ivan IV becomes tsar of Russia; he is known as "the Terrible," meaning "awesome."
1547 France creates *La chambre ardente* to try heretics.	**1547** On the death of Henry VIII, the English throne passes to his nine-year-old son Edward VI.
1550 Jews are persecuted in Bavaria.	**1553** When Edward dies, the English throne passes to his half-sister, the Catholic Mary Tudor.
1551 The Jesuits found a university in Rome.	
1553 The Catholic "Bloody" Mary Tudor becomes queen of England and begins a five-year suppression of Protestants.	**1556** Charles V abdicates and retires to a monastery at Yuste; his son becomes King Philip II of Spain.
1554 Mary I restores Catholicism in England.	**1558** Mary Tudor dies; Elizabeth I becomes queen of England and sets out to restore religious toleration.
1555 The Peace of Augsburg ends religious fighting in Germany by giving Lutheran states equal rights with Catholic states.	**1559** The Treaty of Cateau–Cambrésis ends 70 years of intermittent warfare between France and the Habsburgs and France and England.
1556 Senior Anglican archbishop Thomas Cramner is burned at the stake.	

1542 Don Francisco Vasquez de Coronado plants a cross in Witchita territory in modern-day Kansas, marking the limit of his mission in the American Southwest.	**1555** The French build a settlement at the site of what is now Rio de Janeiro, Brazil.
1550 In Vallodolid, Spain, De las Casas debates the treatment of indigenous Americans with theologian Juan de Gines.	**1556** New methods of separating silver from its ore are adopted in the Spanish Empire, allowing an expansion of the mining industry.
1554 Jesuit priests leave Bahia and move to São Vincente, where they found what later becomes São Paulo.	

1556 Akbar begins the conquest of nearly the whole Indian subcontinent, spreading religious toleration and encouraging the integration of Muslims and Hindus (📄page 207).	**1550** Mongols from Central Asia raid northern China and attack Beijing.
	ca 1550 Japanese warlords—the daimyo—begin a decade of chronic warfare.
	1555 The Mogul emperor Humayun conquers Lahore and reestablishes Mogul power in Delhi.
	1555 On his death, Humayun is succeeded by his 13-year-old son Akbar.

1545 The Ottomans' chief religious authority, Mehmet Ebussuud, begins nearly 30 years' work to reconcile the empire's law code with Islamic law.	**1550** The Saadi dynasty become rulers of Morocco.
1548 At the invitation of the king, Jesuit missionaries arrive in Kongo.	**1553** Süleyman I leads an Ottoman invasion of Persia, ended by a peace treaty in 1555.
1551 The Ottoman Turks capture Tripoli from the Knights Hospitallers.	**1555** Kongo's Christian king, Diogo I, expels his former Portuguese allies.
	1559 Bayezid and Selim, sons of Suleyman I, fight over the Ottoman succession, even though their father is still alive.

The spiritual ecstacy of St. Teresa was a popular subject for Renaissance painters and sculptors.

St. Teresa of Avila

Spanish nun Teresa of Avila (1515–1582) was a great figure of the Roman Catholic Church; she was canonized in 1622. Born in Avila in central Spain, she ran away in 1535 to join a Carmelite convent. In 1539 Teresa attributed her recovery from serious illness to St. Joseph.

In 1554 Teresa was praying in front of a statue of Christ when she felt a spiritual warmth: she saw the episode as a "second conversion." The nun began to experience mystical visions and voices, which came to a climax in 1559. She fell into a state of ecstasy and felt an angel pierce her heart with a flaming spear.

Teresa now concentrated on creating a more disciplined form of the Carmelite Order. In 1562 she started a new convent at Avila; it was the first of a number. The nuns were known as the Discalced (shoeless) Carmelites because they wore sandals or went barefoot.

The discalced foundations reinvigorated the religious life of Spain, although some members of the Spanish church objected to the changes Teresa was making. In 1580 the disputes were brought to an end when King Philip II gave the order his support. By this time Teresa's health was declining. She founded three more convents before she died in October 1582.

PEOPLE & PLACES	DOCUMENTS, ART, & ARTIFACTS	WORSHIP & DOCTRINE

EUROPE

1561 St. Basil's Cathedral in Moscow is completed.

1561 St. Paul's Cathedral in London is badly damaged by fire.

1563 Philip II begins to build the Escorial outside Madrid as a palace-monastery and royal mausoleum for Spanish kings.

1564 Death of Protestant reformer John Calvin.

1561 John Knox and other Scottish ministers draw up the *Confessions of Faith*.

1563 The first English edition appears of John Foxe's *Book of Martyrs*.

1567 An English translation appears of Thomas a Kempis's *The Imitation of Christ*.

1574 Italian poet Torquato Tasso writes his religious epic *Jerusalem Delivered*.

1560 Puritanism emerges in England (📄 pages 208–209).

1562 St. Teresa of Avila receives the church's blessing to found the order of Discalced Carmelite nuns, based at the Convent of St. Joseph in Spain (📄 page 189).

1562 Faustus Socinus begins to preach the Unitarian doctrine in Poland: there is only one God, rather than the Trinity of the father, the son, and the Holy Ghost taught by the Orthodox Church.

1563 The Council of Trent ends.

1567 Maximilian II sets up a monastery council to control the clergy in the Holy Roman Empire.

THE AMERICAS

1562 Captain Jean Ribault builds a Protestant settlement at Charlesfort on Port Royal Island, South Carolina; it survives only two years.

1573 Construction begins on the cathedral in Mexico City, the first cathedral in North America (📄 pages 186–187).

ca 1570 Maya scribes write the *Popol Vuh*, a collection of Mayan myths written using the Roman alphabet (📄 pages 74–75).

ca 1575 Dominican friar Bernardino de Sahagún compiles an illustrated account of Aztec myths and rituals.

1569 The Spanish Inquisition begins in the Americas when King Philip II sets up tribunals in Mexico City and Lima, Peru.

1572 Franciscans begin missionary activities on the northern edges of New Spain, which is increasingly dominated at its center by Jesuits.

ASIA & OCEANIA

1562 Spain introduces Catholicism to the Philippines.

AFRICA & THE MIDDLE EAST

The defeat of the Turks by the Holy League at the naval Battle of Lepanto was ascribed by Europeans to the intercession of the Virgin Mary.

1561 Calvinist refugees from the civil war in the Netherlands arrive in England.

1561 The Edict of Nantes halts the persecution of Protestants in France.

1562 The First War of Religion starts in France; it ends the following year.

1564 The Counter-Reformation begins in Poland.

1566 Calvinists in the Netherlands provoke suppressive measures from their Spanish rulers, sparking a war.

1567 The Catholic Mary Queen of Scots is dethroned by a confederacy of Protestant nobles.

1569 Moriscos (Spanish Muslims who have nominally converted to Christianity) rebel against government attempts to make them abandon their language and culture.

1572 In the Massacre of St. Bartholomew's Day, more than 2,500 leading Protestants are murdered in Paris.

1570 A Jesuit mission travels to Chesapeake Bay with an Algonquin captive named Opechancanough: in Virginia, the captive leads a native uprising that kills the missionaries.

This 18th-century Persian miniature illustrates a scene from the Shahname, or "Book of Kings," Persia's national epic.

ca 1560 A wealthy Jewish woman, Dona Gracia Nasi, settles in Istanbul and uses her extensive business contacts and wealth to encourage widespread Jewish settlement in the Ottoman Empire.

1562 A Huguenot (Protestant) revolt breaks out in western France.

1572 The Dutch War of Independence intensifies as the Dutch revolt against the Spanish governor of the Netherlands, the Duke of Alba.

ca 1560 Portuguese in Brazil relocate more than 40,000 pacified Brazilian Indians to reserves named *aldeias*.

1567 An epidemic of typhoid kills millions of Americans, who have no natural immunity to the disease.

1573 Spain gives up expansion in the Americas to concentrate on the challenge from Protestantism in its European empire, particularly in the Netherlands.

1565 An alliance of Muslim sultanates overthrows the Hindu Vijayanagar Empire in India.

1568 Pope Gregory XIII proposes that Persia and Russia combine forces in a crusade against the Ottoman Turks.

1569 The Ayutthaya kingdom in modern-day Thailand is conquered by the Burmese.

1560 The Ottoman emperor Selim II receives from the shah of Persia a magnificent illuminated copy of the *Shahname* (*Book of Kings*), the Persian national epic.

1567 The Shiite Zeydis in Yemen begin a brief but unsuccessful uprising against the Ottomans.

1571 At the Battle of Lepanto, the Spanish and their allies defeat the Ottoman fleet in a landmark victory of Christians over Muslims.

CHANGING MUSIC

The Italian composer Giovanni Pierluigi da Palestrina (about 1525–1594) played a major role in changing church music in line with Counter-Reformation ideas. In doing so, he created compositions of great clarity and beauty.

Summoned to Rome by Pope Julius III, Palestrina served as music director at the churches of Saint John Laterano and Great Saint Mary's, and from 1571 at Saint Peter's Basilica. His duties included writing music for church services and religious holidays.

In his many hymns and other sacred compositions, Palestrina responded to the church's desire to purge sacred music of secular (nonreligious) influences. The Council of Trent debated banning the fashionable polyphonic ("many-voiced") style of music, which blended two or more melodic lines, for fear that it made the sacred text too difficult to understand at a time when the church was eager to communicate its message clearly. Gregory XIII (pope 1572–1585) directed Palestrina to restore the purity of sacred music and to rid it of anything that might hinder understanding of the words. In 1577 the pope asked Palestrina to edit and rewrite the church's books of plainsong in accordance with the new guidelines.

Palestrina did not do away completely with polyphony, but his compositions wove melodic lines in a clear musical texture that listeners could easily follow. In his most famous work, the *Pope Marcellus Mass*, the music, which is performed *a cappella* (unaccompanied), is in a polyphonic texture in six parts but in which each part is perfectly balanced.

The Vatican endorsed Palestrina's new style music, and with the support of the church he became the most celebrated composer of his day. His controlled, precise style reflects the mystic and contemplative rather than dramatic and flamboyant aspects of the Counter-Reformation. When he died in 1594, his body lay in state in Saint Peter's in honor of his service to the Catholic Church.

The Spirit of our Lord Jesus Christ, and
the Spirit of the Orthodox Church His
Spouse, by which Spirit we are governed
and directed to Salvation, is the same.

IGNATIUS LOYOLA

THE COUNTER-REFORMATION

E VEN BEFORE LUTHER SPARKED THE REFORMATION IN 1517, many Catholics had recognized the problems facing the church. During the papacy of Paul III (1534–1546), a commission investigated—and echoed—many Protestant criticisms. In 1542 a harsher way to fight Protestantism arrived when the Roman Inquisition revived a medieval means of stamping out heresy, using torture and execution against heretics.

If heresy was to be combated, it was essential to define the official beliefs of the Roman Catholic Church. The pope called a church council at the Italian town of Trent in 1545 to draw a clear line between Catholic and Protestant doctrine. Among its most important decisions was the belief that people achieved salvation through a combination of faith in God and good works, rather than by faith alone, as Protestants believed. The council also set up procedures to combat abuse and corruption.

A more energetic church emerged from the Council of Trent, ready to win back Protestant converts. The fight was led by the Jesuits, one of many new religious orders that sprang up in the first half of the 16th century. Groups such as the Ursulines and the Capuchins tried to reinvigorate the church by living in the spirit of Christ's teachings, while the Jesuits set out to spread the Catholic faith around the world. Meanwhile, while many of the men who held the papacy in the 15th century led lives like Renaissance princes, the popes of the 16th century were far more concerned with spiritual matters.

By 1600 the advance of Protestantism had been halted; by 1660 it had been reversed. Although reformed churches had been established in parts of northern Europe, including Scandinavia, Scotland, England, the Netherlands, and most of Germany, Catholicism had been restored to Poland, southern Germany, Hungary, Austria, Bohemia, and much of France. In southern European countries such as Spain and Italy the threat of Protestantism had been almost completely wiped out. In many ways the Catholic Church had emerged from the upheaval stronger than it had been for centuries.

The interior of the Jesuit Church in Vienna, Austria, built at the height of the Counter-Reformation in the 1620s, is an extravagant demonstration of the dynamism and confidence of the resurgent Roman Catholic Church.

Lord, haue mercy

on London

I follow.

We fly.

Wee dye.

Keepe out.

This contemporary woodcut shows death rising in the center of London during the "Great Plague" of 1665. Some 100,000 Londoners died—about a fifth of the city's population. Churches were overwhelmed as their graveyards filled so rapidly that the tradition of individual funerals and burial was abandoned and the dead were interred in mass plague pits (though the pits were usually dug on consecrated ground).

Previous pages *Built in the 1550s on the order of Sultan Süleyman the Magnificent, the Süleymaniye Mosque in Istanbul is one of the masterpieces of the Islamic architect Sinan.*

NORTH AMERICA OFFERED EUROPE'S CHRISTIANS BOTH A CHALLENGE AND A BLANK slate. The challenge was the presence of millions of Native Americans, pagans to be converted to the one true God. Spanish Catholics were already at work in the south and west; the French also found some converts to the north, in what is now Canada. Protestants from England and the Netherlands complained meanwhile at their own slowness to gain converts among the peoples they encountered on the east coast.

Despite the presence of native peoples, the vast "empty" continent also seemed to offer Christians the opportunity to create religious communities outside the influence of established churches or centralized governments. Protestants who found it difficult to gain acceptance for their unorthodox views within Europe were among those who responded most enthusiastically to the chance to cross the Atlantic. Many were dissenters or nonconformists, whose refusal to acknowledge the authority of the Protestant Church or of national governments earned them persecution at home.

The Puritans who settled in Massachusetts Bay were renowned—and feared—for their rejection of the established church and its hierarchy, and for their piety, sobriety, and emphasis on personal interpretation of the Bible. The Puritans gathered in homes to read the Bible and sing hymns: lacking musical instruments, each individual simply made up his or her own tune. John Winthrop, the governor of Massachusetts Bay colony, argued in a renowned sermon that his fellow Puritans had a duty to create "a city on the hill" that would serve as an example of what a truly Christian community could achieve.

The intensity of faith in colonial communities ultimately became destructive, however. Growing intolerance led to the persecution and exile of individuals, even in Pennsylvania. The increased involvement of the English government led to the establishment of official churches. Suspicion and fear led to the remarkable episode remembered today as the Salem witch trials.

The Europe that colonial Americans left behind was still split by the upheaval that followed the Reformation. The continent was ravaged by warfare. In France the Huguenots (the Protestant minority) were first persecuted, then accepted, and then expelled after a civil war fought between rival families for the French crown. Nowhere was the violence worse than in the German lands, where the Thirty Years' War saw the princes of the Holy Roman Empire divide into Protestant and Catholic alliances to wage a series of conflicts that left Central Europe devastated and depopulated.

In India, the Islamic Mogul Empire reached its zenith under the reign of the enlightened monarch Akbar, whose theological investigations produced a syncretic "divine faith," which represented an early attempt to combine the most worthwhile elements from a number of religions. Islam was far more than a faith, however. It was a culture that bound together a huge area, from North Africa, Egypt, and Turkey in the west to India and Southeast Asia in the east. The language of worship and the Koran were universal, as was the architectural style of the mosque, brought to a celebrated perfection by the Ottoman architect Sinan.

The Taj Mahal, a garden tomb built in the mid-17th century by an Islamic ruler for his beloved wife, remains today one of the great national symbols of India, a country with a large Hindu majority.

CONCISE HISTORY OF WORLD RELIGIONS

	1575	1590	1605	1620	1635
EUROPE	**1580** Edmund Campion starts a Jesuit mission to England; he is arrested, tried, and executed for treason. **1582** Pope Gregory XIII reforms the Julian calendar to make it more accurate; the Gregorian calendar is adopted in Catholic countries but more slowly in Protestant countries.	**1593** In France, King Henry IV converts to Catholicism in order to unify his country. **1598** Henry IV guarantees the rights of French Protestants in the Edict of Nantes. **1600** Italian Dominican friar Giordano Bruno is burned at the stake for arguing that the universe is infinite and that the sun is one among many heavenly stars.	**1605** A group of Catholics is foiled in the Gunpowder Plot, a plan to blow up the English Parliament. **1607** The appearance of what is now known as Halley's comet is seen as an evil omen all over Europe. **1611** The King James Bible (authorized version) is published in England	**1624** When French cardinal Armand Jean du Plessis de Richelieu becomes first minister of Louis XIII, he becomes the most powerful man in France. **1633** Galileo Galilei is found guilty by the Inquisition of teaching Copernican doctrine (that the Earth orbits the sun).	**1642** Civil war breaks out in England between the Royalists, who are supported by the established church, and the Parliamentarians, who are supported by Puritan groups. **1648** English preacher George Fox founds the Society of Friends (Quakers).
THE AMERICAS	**ca 1580** The Spanish crown begins to use the Catholic Church and missionaries as a means to bring the colonial population under Spanish control. **1584** Reverend Richard Hakluyt bemoans the fact that the English have not converted a single Native American to Protestantism, in contrast to the "millions" converted by Catholic missionaries.	**1595** In Mexico City, the Inquisition condemns many *conversos* (converted Jews) to execution. **ca 1600** Franciscans in Florida and New Mexico not only preach Catholic doctrine to native peoples, but also introduce European styles of dress, food, and farming.	**1607** When English settlers arrive at Jamestown, Virginia, the Reverend Robert Hunt holds the first Anglican communion in the New World. **1612** The Spaniard Francisco de Parejo publishes a bilingual catechism in Castilian and the indigenous Timucuan language of Florida.	**1620** The Pilgrims on board the *Mayflower* land at New Plymouth. **1632** Preaching in Algonquian, John Eliot converts native peoples in New England and settles them in Christian villages. **1633** Protestant Roger Williams becomes minister at Salem, Massachusetts, where he causes controversy by questioning the accepted teachings of the church.	**1639** The Maryland Assembly passes laws to increase religious freedom. **1645** Catholic missionaries claim to have baptized 300,000 native converts in Mexico and the Southwest. **1649** Maryland outlaws Jews and blasphemers as nonlegitimate members of the colony.
ASIA & OCEANIA	**1576** Emperor Akbar pays for the first great annual pilgrimage caravan from India to Mecca and Medina. **1577** The Sikhs found a holy city at Amritsar. **1582** Akbar sets out the *Din-I Ilahi* (Divine Faith); it incorporates ideas from Islam and Indian religions such as Hinduism and Jainism.	**1595** In China, Jesuit missionary Matteo Ricci becomes the first Westerner ever permitted to enter the Forbidden City. **ca 1600** The practice of building huge stone heads dies out quite suddenly on Easter Island; the islands are abandoned shortly after.	**1605** The fifth Sikh guru, Arjun, is executed on the orders of Jahangir. **1614** In Japan, Christian worship is outlawed.	**1626** Jesuit missionaries open the first Christian church in Tibet. **1629** The Ching promote the translation of Buddhist texts for the first time into Mongolian. **1632** The most renowned of the Mogul garden tombs, the Taj Mahal, is built by Shah Jahan for his wife, Mumtaz Mahal.	**1635** An Italian Jesuit, Giulio Alenio, publishes the first life of Jesus in Chinese. **1644** Jesuits reform the Chinese calendar and use the telescope in Chinese observatories. **1645** The Dalai Lama's residence, the Potola Palace, is begun in Lhasa, Tibet.
AFRICA & THE MIDDLE EAST		**1593** The Portuguese build a stronghold, Fort Jesus, on the coast of East Africa near the historic Islamic port of Mombasa, which they sack.	**1616** Emperor Sarsa Dengel has Ethiopia's Falasha (Jews) massacred.	**ca 1630** In the Ottoman Empire the influence grows of ideologically and legalistically strict preachers known as Kadizadelis; they will remain a power for some 50 years. **1632** Ottoman emperor Murad IV begins a morality campaign during which people with unorthodox opinions are executed.	**1642** Shah Abbas II ascends to the throne of the Safavid dynasty, beginning a period of religious intolerance in Persia.

1650	1665	1680	1695	1710–1724
1654 In an attempt to weaken nonconformist groups, the English Parliament passes the Conventicle Act, which forbids religious gatherings of more than five people. **1655** Oliver Cromwell, Lord Protector of England, readmits Jews to the country.	**1666** The Old Believers split from the Orthodox church in Russia. **1667** English poet John Milton writes *Paradise Lost*, including the story of the fall of the angels. **1675** Building begins on a new St. Paul's Cathedral to replace the building destroyed in the Great Fire of London; it is designed by architect Christopher Wren.	**1682** In France, 38,000 Huguenots are forced to convert to Catholicism. Many more are forced into exile. **1689** English philosopher John Locke writes *Letters Concerning Toleration*. **1689** The English parliament passes the Toleration Act, granting freedom of worship to nonconformists but not to Roman Catholics or Quakers.	**1695** English philosopher John Locke writes *The Reasonableness of Christianity*, arguing that the doctrines of the faith are compatible with reason. **1706** English theologian Matthew Tindal publishes *The Rights of the Christian Church*, an influential assertion of the rights of the state over the church.	**1717** The Grand Lodge of Freemasonry is established in London. Members are called upon to believe in the "Glorious Architect of Heaven and Earth." **1721** In Russia, Peter the Great abolishes the Moscow patriarchate in favor of the "Holy Synod," effectively bringing the Russian church under government control.
1656 The Dutch government orders New Amsterdam to grant Jews freedom of worship. **1658** Jacob Lumbrozo stands trial for heresy in Maryland on the grounds of professing Judaism. **1660** Quaker Mary Dyer is hanged in Boston for heresy. **1661** John Eliot translates the Bible into Algonquian.	**1665** French priest Claude Jean Allouez begins converting Nipissing native peoples in the region of Lake Superior. **1678** Jews from Barbados arrive in Rhode Island after English colonists on the Caribbean island have attacked their synagogues.	**1680** The shaman Popé leads the Tewa Pueblo in a revolt against Spanish rule in New Mexico, burning Catholic missions. **1682** Quaker William Penn founds Pennsylvania, a colony he bases on religious toleration. **1692** Salem, Massachusetts, becomes the center of witch trials that convict and execute 19 people.	**1695** The first synagogue in the English colonies, Shearith Israel, is established in rented quarters in New York; its first building is constructed in 1730. **1700** In a unique outbreak of violence, Hopi who have links with Spanish priests are massacred by Hopi who are loyal to traditional beliefs.	**1710** In New England, preacher Cotton Mather writes *Essays to Do Good*. **1711** The Portuguese ban any religious orders from the region that contains the Brazilian gold fields. **1723** Families from the German Palatinate join other German settlers in Pennsylvania by way of New York.
1650 The first Roman Catholic church is built in Beijing, China. **1658** Aurangzeb becomes Mogul emperor when he deposes his father Shah Jahan; he sets out to enforce strict Sunni orthodoxy and represses other Islamic groups, along with Hindus and Sikhs.	**1669** The Mogul emperor Aurangzeb becomes increasingly intolerant, outlawing Hindu worship in India. **1675** Goband Singh becomes the last of the Ten Gurus of the Sikhs, after his predecessor has been executed by the Moguls for refusing to embrace Islam.	**ca 1690** The Mogul emperor Aurangzeb dispatches a large army to subdue the Sikhs. His forces are defeated by an army led by the tenth guru, Goband Singh, at the Battle of Nadaun. **1692** In China, an imperial decree permits Christian worship.	**1698** England's East India Company is founded; its charter allows for the provision of Anglican chaplains in India. **1699** The Tenth Guru, Goband Singh, founds the Khalsa ("Pure") brotherhood of Sikhs. **1704** The pope sends a legate to Asia to prevent Jesuit compromises with Chinese and Indian traditions.	**1710** Banda Bahadur founds an independent Sikh nation in Punjab (he is executed by the Moguls in 1715). **1720** When the Japanese Shogun Yoshimune permits the import of Western books to Japan to promote knowledge, religious books are still excluded.
ca 1650 In West Africa, Muslims begin settling among the Fulani. **ca 1660** The Islamic leader Nasir al-Din begins a jihad (holy war) in northern Senegambia to resist growing Western influence between the Senegal and Gambia rivers.	**1665** Shabbetai Tsevi is proclaimed as the Jewish messiah and attracts numerous followers, mainly among Jews; arrested for sedition, however, he converts to Islam, as do his followers, who form the Donme sect of Turkey. **1666** Suleiman comes to the Safavid throne; he continues to persecute non-Muslims in Persia.	**1682** The Christian Iyasu I becomes king of Ethiopia. **1688** French Protestants (Huguenots) arrive as refugees in the Dutch colony of South Africa.	**ca 1695** In Ethiopia, King Isayu I builds many churches in his capital, Gondar. **1704** In Kongo, the Antonians seek to combine Christianity with traditional African religious practices.	**1711** The Druze of Lebanon split; Yamani Druze move to Syria, leaving a largely Maronite Druze population in Lebanon. **1714** The Jesuits begin a mission in Sierra Leone.

PEOPLE & PLACES	DOCUMENTS, ART, & ARTIFACTS	WORSHIP & DOCTRINE

EUROPE

1580 Edmund Campion starts a Jesuit mission to England; he is arrested, tried, and executed for treason.

1581 King James VI of Scotland signs the Second Confession of Faith.

1589 The Protestant Bourbon prince Henry of Navarre becomes King Henry IV of France.

1577 In Spain, Greek-born artist El Greco begins painting his most important works, which are a remarkable expression of the energy of the Counter-Reformation.

1579 Spanish Carmelite monk St. John of the Cross writes his poem "Dark Night of the Soul."

1584 Reginald Scot condemns superstition in *The Discoverie of Witchcraft.*

1587 *History of the Reformation in Scotland*, written by Scottish reformer John Knox, is published posthumously.

1588 William Morgan translates the Bible into Welsh.

1577 The Formula of Concord provides a definitive statement of the Lutheran Confession.

1586 Pope Sixtus fixes the number of Catholic cardinals at 70; he also forbids usury.

1588 The Spanish Jesuit priest Luis de Molina argues that humans have free will and that salvation does not come by predestination.

1589 The Church of Russia becomes a patriarchate of the Eastern Orthodox Church.

THE AMERICAS

ca 1580 In New Spain, Simón Perenyns and Baltasar de Echave Orio design magnificent paintings and altarpieces.

1584 Reverend Richard Hakluyt bemoans the fact that the English have not converted a single Native American to Protestantism, in contrast to the "millions" converted by Catholic missionaries.

ASIA & OCEANIA

1577 The Sikhs found a holy city at Amritsar (📄 facing page).

A contemporary illustration shows the killing of Huguenots in the 1572 St. Bartholomew's Day massacre, the bloodiest episode in the Wars of Religion that came to an end with Henry IV's accession to the French throne in 1589.

ca 1577 Tibetan monk Sonam Gyatso is recognized as a spiritual authority by the Mongols; he is seen as the third incarnation of the Dalai Lama.

1582 Akbar sets out the *Din-I Ilahi* (Divine Faith), using ideas from Islam, Hinduism, and Jainism (📄 page 207).

AFRICA & THE MIDDLE EAST

It is natural to unnatural people, and particularly witchmongers, to pursue the poor, to accuse the simple, and to kill the innocent; supplying in rigor and malice toward others, that which they themselves lack in proof and discretion.

REGINALD SCOT, *DISCOVERIE OF WITCHCRAFT*

1579 In the Union of Utrecht, the seven mainly Protestant northern provinces of the Netherlands reject the control of their monarch, Philip II of Spain; the mainly Catholic southern provinces make peace with him.

1582 Pope Gregory XIII reforms the Julian calendar to make it more accurate; the Gregorian calendar is adopted in Catholic countries but more slowly in Protestant countries.

1589 Patriarch Jeremias II of Constantinople visits Moscow.

1588 An English fleet commanded by Sir Francis Drake defeats the Spanish Armada, an invasion fleet.

1589 Philip II of Spain declares war on France in support of Catholics who oppose the new king.

FAITH AND LIFE

Matteo Ricci

Italian Jesuit missionary Matteo Ricci was one of the first Westerners to study Chinese language and culture. In 1578 Ricci arrived at the Jesuit mission in the Portuguese colony of Macau, an island off the coast of China. Here Ricci learned Chinese and Chinese script from Christian converts, before establishing a mission in China in 1583. Through his work as a missionary and translator, Ricci was the first Westerner to experience many aspects of Chinese culture, including being the first to visit the Forbidden City. He compiled the earliest Chinese-Portuguese dictionary and translated many important Confucian texts. Ricci taught that Christianity was compatible with Confucian philosophy and encouraged converts to maintain their traditional cultural practices. He remained in China until his death in 1610.

ca 1580 The Spanish crown begins to use the Catholic Church and missionaries as a means to bring the colonial population under Spanish control.

1576 Emperor Akbar pays for the first great annual pilgrimage caravan from India to Mecca and Medina.

1579 Jesuit missionaries visit the Mogul court in India.

ca 1580 Matteo Ricci and other Jesuits arrive in China.

1588 Shah Abbas becomes ruler of the Safavid empire in Persia and rebuilds a capital at Esfahan (pages 246–247).

HOLY CITY OF THE SIKHS

The city of Amritsar in northwestern India was founded by the Sikh gurus Ram Das and Arjun Dev in the late 16th century. It is the cultural and spiritual center of the Sikh religion, home to its holiest shrine, the Harmandir Sahib (known in English as the Golden Temple), as well as many other important sites.

The Golden Temple is a small structure built in the center of an artificial lake, known as the *Amrit sar* (Pool of Nectar). Although there has been a temple on the site since the city's founding, the actual building was destroyed and rebuilt many times during the turbulent early history of Sikhism.

The Golden Temple's location at the center of the pool creates a mirror image of the temple in the water, which symbolizes the connection between the spiritual and temporal planes of existence. Inside the Golden Temple lies the Guru Granth Sahib, the holy scripture of the Sikhs, which is traditionally venerated and treated as if it is a living guru.

Every year many thousands of Sikh pilgrims visit Amritsar. They tour the temple complex before bathing in the Pool of Nectar.

The Harmandir Sahib (known in English as the Golden Temple) in Amritsar is one of the oldest and most important holy sites for Sikhs.

	PEOPLE & PLACES	DOCUMENTS, ART, & ARTIFACTS	WORSHIP & DOCTRINE

EUROPE

1590 Pope Urban VII dies after the shortest-ever papal reign: 13 days; his brief achievements include the first known smoking ban (on tobacco in church).

1594 Italian Domincan friar Giordano Bruno is imprisoned by the Vatican for his heretical views, which include arguing that the universe is infinite and that the sun is one among many heavenly stars.

1600 Giordano Bruno is burned to death in Rome.

1594 Anglican theologian Richard Hooker publishes *Treatise on the Laws of Ecclesiastical Polity*.

1600 Caravaggio paints *Doubting Thomas*, controversial for its use of realistic peasant faces for a holy scene.

1593 Sweden adopts the Lutheran Augsburg Confession.

1596 At the Council of Brest-Litovsk, most Orthodox Christians in Ukraine join the Roman Catholic Church.

THE AMERICAS

I believe you who pronounce my sentence are in greater fear than I who receive it.

GIORDANO BRUNO

This carving shows the heretic Giordano Bruno preaching in Florence. Some modern scholars believe that Bruno was sentenced to death primarily for his pantheist beliefs, rather than the cosmological theories for which he was actually condemned.

1595 In Mexico City, the Inquisition condemns many *conversos* (converted Jews) to execution.

ca 1600 Franciscans in Florida and New Mexico not only preach Catholic doctrine to native peoples, but also introduce European styles of dress, food, and farming.

ASIA & OCEANIA

1595 In China, Jesuit missionary Matteo Ricci begins wearing the clothes of a Confucian scholar.

1601 Matteo Ricci arrives at the Chinese capital in Beijing after years of seeking access; after he presents the Chinese emperor with a chiming clock, Ricci becomes the first Westerner ever permitted to enter the Forbidden City.

ca 1590 The Royal Mosque is built in Esfahan; Persian Shiism meanwhile becomes more moderate and tolerant in its character.

1592 The Chinese novel *Journey to the West* describes the pilgrimage of a Buddhist monk.

1599 At the Synod of Udayamperur, the Malabar Christians of southwestern India accept the authority of the Roman Catholic Church.

ca 1600 Under the Moguls, Indian Hindus are granted religious tolerance and not forced to convert to Islam.

AFRICA & THE MIDDLE EAST

The Royal Mosque at Esfahan was built on the southern end of the Nagsh-i Jahan square, a public park surrounded by palaces, mosques, and bazaars.

RELIGION IN THE WORLD	WORLD EVENTS
1593 In France, King Henry IV converts to Catholicism in order to unify his country; he reportedly remarks "Paris is worth a mass." The conversion marks the end of the Wars of Religion.	**1595** Hugh O'Neill, earl of Tyrone, leads a rebellion in Ireland against English rule.
1595 The Pope recognizes Henry IV as king of France.	**1596** The Spanish crown is bankrupt, and the country's population falls as a result of several years of famine and plague.
1598 Henry IV guarantees the rights of French Protestants in the Edict of Nantes (📄 page 223).	**1598** Boris Godunov is elected tsar of Russia on the death of Fyodor.
1600 Charles IX of Sweden persecutes Catholics.	
1602 Habsburg emperor Rudolf II suppresses meetings of the Moravian Brethren, part of the ongoing persecution of Protestants in the Habsburg Empire.	

1591 John White, governor of Roanoke Island, returns with supplies for the struggling colony but finds it abandoned.

ca 1600 The practice of building huge stone heads dies out quite suddenly on Easter Island; the islands are abandoned shortly after.

King Henry IV of France converted from Protestantism to Catholicism to put an end to the religious wars that had divided France for decades.

1593 The Portuguese build a stonghold, Fort Jesus, on the coast of East Africa near the historic Islamic port of Mombasa, which they sack.

1594 The Portuguese have by now established control over most of coastal Angola but are unable to penetrate far into the interior because of disease.

COPERNICUS AND THE UNIVERSE

The Polish astronomer Nicolaus Copernicus (1473–1543) is remembered for developing the theory that the Earth and other planets move around the sun.

Copernicus was born in Torun, Poland. He studied at the University of Krakow, and later traveled to Italy to study church law, Greek philosophy, and medicine. When he returned to Poland Copernicus became a canon, or church official, at the cathedral of Frombork. His duties left him plenty of time to continue his studies of the stars.

In 1514 Copernicus was asked by the pope to look at ways of reforming the flawed Julian calendar. To get enough information to be able devise a new system, Copernicus undertook further studies that led him to a revolutionary conclusion. He concluded that the Earth turned on its axis once every day as it went on a yearly orbit around the sun. By 1540 his original ideas had grown into a six-part work entitled *The Revolutions of the Heavenly Spheres,* which was printed in Leipzig in 1543.

Although today this idea is taken for granted, Copernicus's ideas met with fierce opposition when they were first published. At the time people believed that the sun and the planets moved around the Earth, which was stationary at the center of the universe. This was regarded as an indisputable fact, supported by the highest authority of the time—the Bible. Passages such as Psalm 104:5, which states "He set the earth on its foundations; it can never be moved," and Ecclesiastes 1:5—"The sun rises and the sun sets, and hurries back to where it rises"—were seen as proof that the sun orbited the Earth.

For its contradiction of holy scripture, Copernicus's heliocentric model was strongly opposed by both the Catholic Church and the leaders of the Protestant community. Martin Luther described Copernicus as "a fool who went against Holy Writ," and the Catholic Church prohibited the publication or sale of his works until the 19th century.

THE MOSQUES OF SINAN

MIMAR SINAN (CA 1490–1588) WAS THE OTTOMAN EMPIRE'S chief architect and civil engineer from around 1538 until his death. During this time Sinan designed hundreds of structures, ranging from bridges and aqueducts to the monumental mosques for which he is known today. He established a distinctive style of Islamic architecture that was preserved and developed by his students after his death.

Not much is known about Sinan's origins—the name Mimar Sinan means simply "Sinan the Architect"—but it is thought that he was from a Christian family, probably in the Balkans, and converted to Islam after he joined the Ottoman army. He became a military engineer and rose up through the ranks. When one of his former commanders, Çelebi Lutfi Pasha, became grand vizier in 1538, he hired the 50-year-old Sinan as chief architect to the Sultan. Sinan then embarked on an ambitious building program that stretched over the reigns of Süleyman II (reigned 1566–1574) and Murad III (reigned 1574–1595) until Sinan's death in 1588.

Sinan was working during the period when the Ottoman Empire was at its height. His great mosques were funded by triumphant sultans and military leaders who wanted to give thanks to God for their successes. The Ottoman leaders also wanted to win favor with the people of the empire and so Sinan's mosques were typically built within complexes that comprised several schools, hospitals, baths, and other public buildings. Sinan and his team built mosques across the Ottoman Empire and the progression in his design can be traced from his earliest mosques until its peak, the Mosque of Süleyman (1557) in Istanbul and the Mosque of Selimiye (1575) in Edirne.

Sinan studied the techniques employed by Roman and Byzantine engineers, particularly those used in the construction of the Hagia Sophia in Istanbul, and applied them to the construction of mosques. His new mosques were designed around a massive, well-lit prayer hall that allowed everyone to have an uninterrupted view of the minbar (pulpit). To make such a space possible, his mosques had a large central dome supported by a structure of arches and half-domes that distributed the weight away from the center of the building. To give the mosque a sense of balance he used tall slender minarets in each corner to frame the building and to maintain the symmetry of the domed shape. His mosques and their surrounding complexes were each carefully designed around the landscape of the chosen site. The interior of the mosque was decorated with calligraphic inscriptions, multicolored stonework, and ornate patterned tiles.

Although it is not the largest or most prestigious of his projects, Mimar Sinan considered the Selimiye Mosque in Edirne—completed in 1574 when he was around 84 years old—to be his greatest work.

PEOPLE & PLACES	DOCUMENTS, ART, & ARTIFACTS	WORSHIP & DOCTRINE

EUROPE

1613 Composer Claudio Monteverdi becomes master of the chapel at St. Mark's, Venice.

1616 Condemned as a heretic, Galileo Galilei is barred by the Catholic Church from pursuing any scientific studies (📄 page 213).

1618 English courtier, poet, and adventurer Walter Raleigh is executed for piracy; a poem he writes shortly before his death concludes, "I have a long journey to make and must bid the company farewell."

1609 The Roman Catholic bishop of Geneva Francis de Sales writes his spiritual guide, *Introduction à la vie dévote* (*Introduction to the Devout Life*).

1611 The King James Bible (Authorized Version) is published in England; its highly literary language remains popular, and people still use it as their preferred version of the Bible.

1611 Peter Paul Rubens paints *Descent from the Cross*.

1610 The women-only Roman Catholic Order of the Visitation is founded by Jeanne de Chantal and Francis de Sales.

1611 In Paris, Pierre de Bérulle founds the French Oratory, a Catholic congregation that is highly influential in France in the 17th century.

1618 At the Synod of Dort, the Dutch Reformed Church condemns Arminianism as a heresy.

THE AMERICAS

1612 The Spaniard Francisco de Parejo publishes a bilingual catechism in Castilian and the indigenous Timucuan language of Florida.

WORDS OF DEVOTION

King James Bible

King James I of England presided over an important conference at Hampton Court in January 1604. James had summoned Puritan leaders and the bishops of the Church of England in an attempt to reconcile their religious differences. During the meeting, James appointed a committee of scholars to create the Authorized or King James Version of the Bible. The committee translated the text from Greek and Hebrew sources, using earlier English translations for reference. English Protestants embraced the new translation when it was published in 1611. The new Bible was noteworthy for its simple, clear, and eloquent language. The Authorized Version of the Bible is still widely read today.

The Holy Bible
Containing the Old and New Testaments translated out of the original tongues : and with the former translations diligently compared and revised, by His Majesty's special command

Authorized King James Version

ASIA & OCEANIA

1605 Jahangir becomes emperor of India; he follows the teachings of both Muslim and Hindu holy men.

1614 In Japan, Christian worship is outlawed.

Shogun Iyeyasu Tokugawa prohibited Christian worship and expelled all Christian missionaries from Japan.

AFRICA & THE MIDDLE EAST

1616 Emperor Sarsa Dengel has Ethiopia's Falasha (Jews) massacred.

RELIGION IN THE WORLD	WORLD EVENTS
1605 A group of Catholics is foiled in the Gunpowder Plot, a plan to blow up the English Parliament.	**1605** In Spain Miguel de Cervantes publishes the first part of his masterpiece *Don Quixote*.
1607 The appearance of what is now known as Halley's comet is seen as an evil omen all over Europe.	**1609** German astronomer Johannes Kepler publishes his first two laws of planetary motion, which show that the planets travel in elliptical paths around the sun.
1609 Philip II of Spain expels the Moriscos (Christian descendants of Arab settlers); some 300,000 people are forcibly deported in the next five years.	
1609 Rudolf II allows freedom of worship in Bohemia.	
1612 Authorities in England burn heretics for the last time.	
1607 When English settlers arrive at Jamestown, Virginia, the Reverend Robert Hunt holds the first Anglican communion in the New World.	**1608** French explorer Samuel de Champlain founds a colony at Quebec.
	1609 Henry Hudson enters New York Bay and sails up the river that will later be named for him as far as the future site of Albany.

King Phillip III of Spain was responsible for the expulsion of over 300,000 Moriscos, Christian converts from Islam.

1605 The fifth Sikh guru, Arjun, is executed on the orders of Jahangir.

Akbar's Divine Faith

Akbar the Great was the third and most significant of the Mogul emperors—the Muslim rulers who controlled most of India between the early 15th and 18th centuries. When he came to the throne as a 13-year-old, the Mogul state was relatively weak and unstable. During his long reign, from 1556 to 1605, Akbar turned it into one of the most powerful empires in the world.

In addition to his military and political achievements, Akbar was also a religious scholar. As a young man his tutors included Sunni, Shiite, and Sufi Muslims, who impressed on him the importance of religious tolerance. This tolerant attitude was an important part of his success as a ruler. By abolishing the tax traditionally levied on non-Muslims and appointing Hindus to government positions, Akbar secured the trust and approval of his Hindu subjects.

In his later life Akbar became interested in finding a set of theological principles on which all religious leaders could agree. In his capital city, Fatehpur Sikri, Akbar built what he called the House of Worship. There he began to host debates between religious scholars. At first these involved only Muslims, but soon Akbar began to invite representatives of other faiths, including Hindus, Jains, Zoroastrians, and even Christians from the Portuguese colony of Goa.

Eventually, after years of debates had failed to produce any meaningful agreement, Akbar decided to found his own religion, the *Din-e Ilahi* (Divine Faith). Combining elements of Islam, Hinduism, and Christianity, the Divine Faith never really caught on except with a few courtiers. Akbar, who had declared himself the head of this new cult, did not try to enforce it on his people. After his death, the Divine Faith quickly evaporated. Its benevolent spirit of tolerance, however, is a reminder of its founder's ambition to unify his people under a religion that would transcend their spiritual differences.

PURITANS AND DISSENTERS

IN 1534 THE ENGLISH KING HENRY VIII CREATED THE CHURCH OF England, removing his country's church from the authority of the pope in Italy. Although this occurred at around the same time as the Protestant Reformation in Europe, the decision was made for purely political reasons. Henry was not a Protestant, and was in fact a fierce critic of Protestant theology. Although the Church of England was reestablished on Protestant principles under Henry's successors, it retained many doctrinal and organizational similarities with the Catholic Church.

Those who opposed the new church were divided into two broad groups. The first group were known as Puritans, for the purity of their biblical zeal. The Puritans aimed to create a religious community "purified" of Catholic influence and strictly obedient to the word of God, the Bible. Rather than practicing faith through the rituals of the Church of England, the Puritans emphasized personal study and Bible-centered sermons that probed issues of faith, morality, and behavior. Puritans organized their church on a system of elders rather than the hierarchy of priests and bishops in the Church of England.

Although fierce critics of the Church of England, the Puritans were not necessarily opposed to the idea of a state-backed religion. In the Puritan colonies of New England, for example, the religious authorities exercised absolute control over the practice of religion in the region. Jews, Catholics, and even other Protestant groups were forbidden from establishing congregations or trying to win converts. Those who defied these rules faced severe punishments including exile or execution.

The second group were a diverse collection of smaller religious communities collectively known as "Dissenters." Dissenters were typically followers of less orthodox Christian doctrines, ranging from the radical egalitarianism of the Quakers to the mystical pantheism of the Ranters. Dissenters were supporters of freedom of religion and objected to the idea that anyone—whether a king, a bishop, or a pope—could claim authority over what people chose to believe. In North America, Dissenters established communities in which freedom of religion was a founding principle. Colonies such as Rhode Island and Pennsylvania were settled by dissenting groups from across Europe, including Moravians from Germany, Mennonites from the Netherlands, and Baptists from Britain. The ideas of the Dissenters, particularly their emphasis on equality and freedom of religion, were an important influence on the United States Constitution.

This painting shows a 17th-century Puritan preacher interrupting Christmas celebrations in Massachusetts. Festivals such as Christmas and Easter were seen as unchristian by Puritans.

PEOPLE & PLACES	DOCUMENTS, ART, & ARTIFACTS	WORSHIP & DOCTRINE

EUROPE

1622 Philip Neri, founder of the Congregation of the Oratory who died in 1595, is canonized by Pope Gregory XV.

1624 The German mystic Jakob Boehme dies after a lifetime of asserting a mystical form of Catholicism which is widely condemned by church authorities.

1624 When French cardinal Armand Jean du Plessis de Richelieu becomes first minister of Louis XIII, he becomes the most powerful man in France.

1628 Pope Gregory XV canonizes Ignatius Loyola, founder of the Jesuits.

1632 The Italian composer Claudio Monteverdi takes holy orders to become a priest.

1622 Dutch jurist Hugo Grotius writes *On the Truth of the Christian Religion*; he uses legalistic arguments to assert the truth of Protestant Christianity.

1628 Spanish artist Diego Velázquez paints *Christ on the Cross*.

1629 Gianlorenzo Bernini takes over direction of building works at St. Peter's, Rome (pages 218–219).

1622 A papal bull issued by Gregory XV creates the *Congregation de Propaganda Fide*, the church department responsible for the spread of Catholicism and its exercise in non-Catholic lands.

1629 In Constantinople, Patriarch Cyril Loukaris issues a Confession of Faith that reflects Protestant influence.

1633 In France, Vincent de Paul and Louise de Marillac found the Sisters of Charity, a religious order for women who take simple vows and perform spiritual and physical acts of mercy for the poor; in France they are known as the "Gray Nuns," for the color of their habits.

THE AMERICAS

1620 The Pilgrims on board the *Mayflower* land at New Plymouth (facing page).

1625 George Calvert, first Lord Baltimore and founder of Maryland, converts to Catholicism.

1628 Jonas Michaelius becomes a priest to Dutch settlers in Manhattan; he gives up four years later.

1633 Protestant Roger Williams becomes minister at Salem, Massachusetts, where he quickly causes controversy by questioning the accepted teachings of the church.

1634 In Canada, Father Jean de Brébeuf begins a 15-year mission preaching to the Ontario Huron.

1624 The laws of Virginia colony are amended to include the establishment of the Church of England.

ca 1630 The Yaqui of Sonora settle in towns and convert to Catholicism.

1632 Preaching in Algonquian, John Eliot converts native peoples in New England and settles them in Christian villages.

1634 English Catholics celebrate their first Mass in the Americas, in Maryland.

ASIA & OCEANIA

1626 Jesuit missionaries open the first Christian church in Tibet.

1629 The Ching promote the translation of Buddhist texts for the first time into Mongolian.

AFRICA & THE MIDDLE EAST

ca 1630 In the Ottoman Empire the influence grows of ideologically and legalistically strict preachers known as Kadizadelis; they will remain a power for some 50 years.

1632 Ottoman emperor Murad IV begins a morality campaign during which people with unorthodox opinions are executed.

In 1627, two Jesuit missionaries became the first Westerners to visit the Buddhist kingdom of Bhutan, high in the Himalayas.

RELIGION IN THE WORLD	WORLD EVENTS

1625 Christian IV of Denmark joins the Protestant side in the Thirty Years' War; Denmark is forced to withdraw in 1629, following heavy defeats.

1633 Galileo Galilei is found guilty by the Inquisition of teaching Copernican doctrine (that the Earth orbits the sun) (page 213).

1625 James I of England dies and is succeeded by his son Charles I.

1629 Charles dissolves Parliament and rules as an absolute monarch.

1630 An outbreak of bubonic plague causes around 50,000 deaths in Venice.

THE MAYFLOWER

The Pilgrims were among the earliest of all the European colonists of North America, settling Plymouth, Massachusetts, in 1620. The ship they arrived on, the *Mayflower*, has become a cultural icon and symbol of the European settlement of North America.

1622 While English colonists along the James River in Virginia share a Good Friday breakfast, Native American attacks leave 347 dead.

1630 During the Atlantic voyage to Massachusetts, Puritan John Winthrop writes "A Model of Christian Charity," setting out his ideals for the Massachusetts Bay colony; he wants the colony to be an example, a "city on a hill" (pages 208–209).

1634 Puritan cleric Thomas Hooker petitions to leave Massachusetts Bay and found Connecticut.

This painting is an imagined depiction of the Pilgrims leaving Plymouth, England, in 1620.

1627 Two Jesuit missionaries become the first ever Westerners to visit Bhutan in the Himalayas.

1632 The most renowned of the Mogul garden tombs, the Taj Mahal, is built by Shah Jahan for his wife, Mumtaz Mahal.

1622 Persian forces in alliance with troops provided by the English East India Company capture the important trading base at Hormuz at the mouth of the Persian Gulf, under Portuguese control since 1507.

1636 As part of a campaign to eradicate Western influence in Japan, all foreigners are forced to live on the artificial island of Dejima in Nagasaki harbor.

The Pilgrims orginally set sail in two ships, the *Mayflower* and the *Speedwell*, from Southampton in southern England. A few days into the voyage, however, the *Speedwell* developed a serious leak and they were forced to return to port. All the Pilgrims set sail again on the *Mayflower*. Of the ship's 102 passengers, 37 were Separatists who intended to leave the Church of England; the remainder had been hired to protect the new colony. The *Mayflower* arrived at Cape Cod, Massachusetts, on November 9, but it was another six weeks before the Pilgrims decided on the place for their settlement, New Plymouth, which they reached on December 21. The first year was extremely harsh for the new settlers, who were exhausted from their months at sea, unused to the New England winter, and highly vulnerable to disease. By the end of 1621 nearly half had died.

For we must consider that we shall be as a city upon a hill. The eyes of all people are upon us. So that if we shall deal falsely with our God in this work ... we shall shame the faces of many of God's worthy servants.

JOHN WINTHROP, "A MODEL OF CHRISTIAN CHARITY"

PEOPLE & PLACES	DOCUMENTS, ART, & ARTIFACTS	WORSHIP & DOCTRINE

EUROPE

1638 Death of the Dutch theologian Cornelius Jansen, founder of Jansenism.

1639 The Italian cardinal Jules Mazarin enters the service of the French statesman Cardinal Richelieu.

1640 Portuguese-Jewish philosopher Uriel Acosta commits suicide after being punished for his rejection of orthodox Judaism by being whipped and having the congregation of the synagogue trample over him.

1644 French philosopher René Descartes reaches the famous basis of his Cartesian philosophy, "I think, therefore I am."

1645 Matthew Hopkins becomes witch-finder general in England.

1640 Published posthumously, *Augustinus,* by the Belgian Cornelius Jansen, bishop of Ypres, argues that St. Augustine of Hippo was chosen by God to reveal his doctrine; any later Catholic doctrine that contradicts Augustine should be revised. Jansenism becomes popular but is condemned by Rome as heresy.

1645 The Dutch painter Rembrandt paints *The Rabbi.*

1642 Under the influence of the Puritan Commonwealth, all England's theaters are closed on grounds of immorality.

1643 In France, Antoine Arnauld defends the teachings of Cornelius Jansen and condemns the Jesuits.

1648 English nonconformist preacher George Fox founds the Society of Friends (Quakers).

1649 Led by nonconformist Gerrard Winstanley, Diggers and Levellers found communal settlements in England.

THE AMERICAS

1636 French Jesuit Isaac Jogues begins preaching among Mohawk peoples in what is now New York State (📄 page 249).

1638 Anne Hutchinson is tried and banished from Massachusetts Bay Colony for preaching nonconformist views; she goes into exile in Maryland.

1643 Roger WIlliams, expelled from Massachusetts Bay Colony in 1635 for advocating religious freedom, sails back to England to obtain a charter to found the colony of Rhode Island.

1649 Jesuit missionary Jean de Brébeuf is tortured to death by Iroquois in Quebec during conflict between Iroquois and Huron.

MONUMENTS OF FAITH

Virgin of Guadalupe

The Virgin of Guadalupe, also known as Our Lady of Guadalupe, is a famous Catholic icon of the Virgin Mary venerated by Catholics in Mexico and Central America. According to legend, the image miraculously appeared on the cloak of a Mexican peasant, Juan Diego, in 1531, shortly after he had seen a vision of the Virgin Mary. A shrine was built on the site of the vision, and pilgrims came from across Mexico to view the image. The Virgin of Guadalupe quickly became a symbol of Mexican cultural identity—during the Mexican War of Independence, rebel armies used the image as their flag.

ASIA & OCEANIA

This painting shows the prayer meeting of a group of Quakers in Amsterdam.

1635 An Italian Jesuit, Giulio Alenio, publishes the first life of Jesus in Chinese.

1645 The Dalai Lama's residence, the Potola Palace, is begun in Lhasa, Tibet.

1637 In Japan, persecuted Catholic peasants rise up in the Shimabara Rebellion; they are put down by 125,000 troops of the Tokugawa shogunate, and Christianity is banned.

1642 The Qosot Mongols conquer Tibet; they make the fifth Dalai Lama the ruler of what from now on is a theocratic state.

1644 Jesuits reform the Chinese calendar and use the telescope in Chinese observatories.

AFRICA & THE MIDDLE EAST

1642 Shah Abbas II ascends to the throne of the Safavid dynasty, beginning a period of religious intolerance in Persia.

RELIGION IN THE WORLD	WORLD EVENTS
1637 The introduction of the *English Prayer Book* causes resentment and violence in Scotland, where nobles sign the National Covenant to express their opposition to the divine right of monarchs and English interference in Scottish religious affairs.	**1642** The English Civil War begins between Royalists and Parliamentarians, dominated by Puritans.
1641 Irish Catholics launch a rebellion against English government, killing some 4,000 to 12,000 Protestant settlers in the "Ulster massacres"; the Irish Confederate Wars continue into the 1650s.	**1648** The Treaty of Westphalia brings the Thirty Years' War to an end, guaranteeing independence for the Dutch republic, the Swiss Confederation, and some 250 German states.
1647 Defeated and captured after the civil war, England's king Charles I agrees to abolish episcopacy and restore Presbyterianism.	**1649** Charles I of England is beheaded.
1639 The Maryland Assembly passes laws to increase religious freedom.	**1642** French settlers found a colony at Ville de Marie in Canada, later to be called Montreal.
1642 In Massachusetts Bay, Thomas Graunger is executed for bestiality, according to the law laid down in the Book of Leviticus—the first settler to be executed in the North American colonies.	**1647** Peter Stuyvesant arrives to become governor of New Amsterdam.
1645 Catholic missionaries claim to have baptized 300,000 native converts in Mexico and the Southwest.	**1649** In Canada, the Iroquois destroy the neighboring Huron.
1649 Maryland outlaws Jews and blasphemers as nonlegitimate members of the colony.	

The Potala Palace, traditional home of tha Dalai Lama, rises majestically over the Tibetan capital of Lhasa.

GALILEO ON TRIAL

After the publication of Galileo's work *Dialogue of the Two Chief World Systems*, the church soon realized that its author was openly in favor of Copernicus' heliocentric system, which it considered to be heretical. The church stood by the model described in the Bible, in which the sun and planets orbit around the Earth. Pope Urban XIII therefore ordered the printing of the book to be halted while an investigation took place.

Galileo had been investigated by the Catholic Church before, when rumors of his research had reached the Holy Office, or Roman Inquisition, but no formal action was taken against him at the time. Galileo was initially given permission to publish *The Dialogue* because he said it would be a balanced discussion of the Copernican and biblical models. However, when the Inquisition received a copy of the book it soon decided that the text was biased strongly toward the Copernican model of the solar system.

In September 1632 Galileo was summoned to Rome and in the following year he was put on trial by the Roman Inquisition. Threatened with torture if he did not disown his support of Copernicus' ideas, Galileo was compelled to kneel in front of church officials and recant his views, declaring: "I am here to obey and I have not held this opinion." There is a story that after his declaration he whispered to himself "e pur si muove" ("and yet it [the earth] does move"), but this is probably a legend.

Despite his recantation, Galileo was sentenced to life imprisonment. Because of his age (he was 70 at the time) the sentence was reduced to house arrest. From 1633 to his death in 1642, Galileo continued to develop his ideas and frequently corresponded with his former pupils. He was prohibited, however, from publishing any further work and *The Dialogue* was put on the Vatican's *Index of Prohibited Books*. It was not removed until 1835.

The sight of this mansion creates sorrowing sighs;

And the sun and the moon shed tears from their eyes.

In this world this edifice has been made;

To display thereby the creator's glory.

SHAH JAHAN

THE TAJ MAHAL

THE MAGNIFICENT WHITE MARBLE MAUSOLEUM THAT stands on the banks of the Yamuna River in Agra, India, is a monument to the enduring power of love. Built by a Muslim emperor in memory of his wife, the Taj Mahal ("Crown Palace") has transcended the religious tensions of modern India to become a national symbol held in deep affection by both Muslims and Hindus.

For centuries India had been dominated by Hinduism and Buddhism, before in the 10th century it fell under the influence of the Islamic faith spreading east from its Arab homelands. A succession of Muslim invaders from the north expanded their control over the subcontinent, culminating in the Mogul dynasty, which ruled from 1526 to the early 18th century, when growing British influence slowly eroded its power. While nearly a quarter of Indians adopted Islam, it remained a minority faith. Some emperors attempted to integrate their non-Muslim subjects; others practiced intolerance and persecution.

The fifth Mogul emperor, Shah Jahan (reigned 1628–1658), commissioned the Taj Mahal in 1631 on the death in childbirth of his beloved wife, Mumtaz. Construction took around 20,000 workers some 22 years to complete. The complex reflects Persian influence: it is a garden tomb, in which the mausoleum stands within extensive walled grounds with pools of water that both reflect the mausoleum and symbolize the rivers of Jannah, the Islamic paradise. Along with the domed mausoleum, which holds the tombs of both Mumtaz and Shah Jahan, the complex also includes an elaborate gateway and a mosque, both of red sandstone, and minarets from which the muezzin calls the faithful to prayer. The interior decoration reflects both Islamic and Hindu influences in intricate floral patterns and calligraphy created with painting, carving, or inlays of semiprecious stones.

Shah Jahan's creation is widely acknowledged as the highpoint of Mughal architecture. It was not his only religious monument, however. He also constructed two magnificent mosques in Agra and the Great Mosque in Delhi.

The mausoleum is decorated with verses from the Koran inlaid in black marble. The passages on the outside of the monument warn of the doom that awaits unbelievers; those inside offer a more rewarding glimpse of paradise. The flowing script was signed by its Persian calligrapher: "Written by the insignificant being, Amanat Khan Shirazi."

The garden tomb is an earthly re-creation of the Islamic paradise. Visitors are greeted by the words "Return to the Lord at peace with Him, and He at peace with you."

PEOPLE & PLACES	DOCUMENTS, ART, & ARTIFACTS	WORSHIP & DOCTRINE

EUROPE

1650 Archbishop James Ussher of Ireland calculates from biblical texts that the world was created during the night preceding October 23, 4004 B.C.

1653 English Quaker James Naylor is heralded by followers as the new messiah.

1654 French mathematician and scientist Blaise Pascal experiences an intense religious vision some weeks after avoiding injury in a serious stagecoach accident; he records his "night of fire" in a document that he carries secretly with him at all times, sewn into the lining of his clothes. Pascal gives up science and devotes himself to Jansenist theology.

1655 Dutch philosopher Baruch Spinoza is excommunicated by his synagogue for heresy.

1653 English priest Brian Walton publishes a polyglot Bible, with text in nine languages: Hebrew, Chaldee, Samaritan, Syriac, Arabic, Persian, Ethiopic, Greek, and Latin.

1656 Blaise Pascal attacks the Jesuits in *Lettres provinciales*.

1656 Gianlorenzo Bernini designs the piazza of St. Peter's in Rome (📄 pages 218–219).

1661 The use of the organ to accompany hymns is revived in England, having been banned during the Commonwealth.

1662 In England, the *Book of Common Prayer* is revised.

1653 The Pope condemns Jansenist teachings, but Jansenists argue that the propositions he condemns do not appear in Jansen's works.

1661 The Trappist order of monks is founded in La Trappe, Normandy; they follow the rule of St. Benedict and place special emphasis on contemplation and silence (although they do not, as sometimes believed, take a vow of silence).

Bills of Mortality recorded the deaths in London during the plagues that drastically reduced the city's population in the 1660s.

THE AMERICAS

1652 Jesuit Antonio Vieira begins a 25-year mission among the native peoples in Brazil.

1658 Jacob Lumbrozo stands trial for heresy in Maryland on the grounds of professing Judaism.

1659 François-Xavier de Montmorency-Laval becomes the first Roman Catholic vicar apostolic of New France, based at Quebec (he becomes the first bishop in 1674).

1660 Quaker Mary Dyer is hanged in Boston for heresy.

1663 Italian-born Eusebio Kino becomes a Jesuit missionary on his recovery from a serious illness; he will make notable missions to northern Mexico.

1661 John Eliot translates the Bible into Algonquian.

1662 Solomon Stoddard promotes the Halfway Covenant to make Puritanism more relaxed, in the hopes of attracting members and maintaining Puritan influence in the colonies.

1660 Spaniards use the Inquisition against the Pueblo and against Spaniards who criticize missionary activity in the American Southwest.

ASIA & OCEANIA

1650 The first Roman Catholic church is built in Beijing, China.

1662 The Ching who rule China promote Buddhism in Tibet, partly as a means of political control.

AFRICA & THE MIDDLE EAST

ca 1650 In West Africa, Muslims begin settling among the Fulani.

The massive Badshahi Mosque in Lahore was constructed by Shah Jahan's son Aurangzeb, a devout Muslim, in 1673.

RELIGION IN THE WORLD	WORLD EVENTS
1654 In an attempt to weaken nonconformist groups, the English Parliament passes the Conventicle Act, which forbids religious gatherings of more than five people. **1655** Oliver Cromwell, Lord Protector of England, readmits Jews to the country. **1655** The Duke of Savoy, in France, persecutes the Vaudois (better known as the Waldenses). **1660** The Restoration of Charles II to the English monarchy ends the Puritan Commonwealth and restores the Anglican Church. **1661** In France, the Edict of Orleans tries to halt the persecution of Protestant Huguenots (📄 page 223).	**1652** The Dutch Republic declares war on England over a trade dispute. **1658** Leopold I is enthroned as Holy Roman Emperor. **1663** An Ottoman army is turned back in the Alps at St. Gothard, an apparent triumph for European power, but the Ottoman Empire comes off best in the ensuing negotiations.
1654 The first Jews arrive in New Amsterdam, intending to become traders and merchants. **1654** Authorities in New Amsterdam deny religious freedom to Dutch Lutherans. **1656** The Dutch government orders New Amsterdam to grant Jews freedom of worship (but only in private). **1657** The first ship of Quakers lands in New Amsterdam. **1658** In the Flushing Remonstrance, Quakers in Long Island petition New York Governor Peter Stuyvesant for freedom of worship. **1660** The Virginia House of Burgesses forbids ships' captains from importing Quakers.	**1655** New Amsterdam conquers the colony of New Sweden (in modern Delaware). **1662** The English colony of Virginia authorizes slavery.
1658 Aurangzeb becomes Mogul emperor when he deposes his father Shah Jahan; he sets out to enforce strict Sunni orthodoxy and represses other Islamic groups, along with Hindus and Sikhs. **1660** In India, Aurangzeb begins campaigning against neighboring Muslim states.	**1658** Fort St. George, the future city of Madras, becomes the English East India Company's headquarters in India.
ca 1660 The Islamic leader Nasir al-Din begins a jihad (holy war) in northern Senegambia to resist growing Western influence between the Senegal and Gambia rivers.	**1656** Mehmed Kiuprili becomes grand vizier of the Ottoman Empire and brings stability after a period of near anarchy. **1661** The post of grand vizier in the Ottoman Empire becomes hereditary, beginning a dynasty that lasts for over a century.

RUSSIA'S OLD BELIEVERS

The Old Believers is the name given to a group of religious protestors who objected to reforms introduced by Patriarch Nikon to the Russian Orthodox Church in 1652.

Over time, discrepancies emerged between Russian religious texts and their Greek originals as a result of translating and copying errors that had become absorbed into the Russian translations. In an effort to clarify the differences between the Russian and Greek Orthodox Churches, Patriarch Nikon ordered a revision of the texts and the use of the newly revised texts in all services.

The Old Believers objected to the new texts and to what they considered a lack of consultation. They wanted to carry on with the old liturgical practices, including using different fingers to make the sign of the cross, reciting certain prayers a different number of times, and using an alternate translation of the Bible in their services. With the help of the state, the Russian Church suppressed the Old Believers. As well as being excommunicated, those who did not follow the reforms were arrested. The leader of the Old Believers, Archpriest Avvakum Petrov, was executed in 1682, along with other Old Believers. Many others fled Russia after 1685 as torture and execution became common.

From the end of the 17th century to the start of the 20th century anyone who followed the old texts was persecuted. Persecution only ended in 1905 when Tsar Nicholas II granted Old Believers freedom of worship.

The Old Believers are still an active religious group with congregations across Russia.

Thou art Peter, and upon this rock I will build my church, and the gates of hell shall not prevail against it.

GOSPEL ACCORDING TO ST. MATTHEW, 16:18

BERNINI AND ST. PETER'S

GIANLORENZO BERNINI (1598–1680) WAS AN ARTIST whose sculptural and architectural additions to St. Peter's Basilica in Rome captured the devotional spirit of the baroque Counter-Reformation. During his lifetime he created numerous sculptures of saints and popes, many of which can still be seen in the Vatican City and in the public spaces and churches of Rome.

The son of sculptor Pietro Bernini, Gianlorenzo was born in Naples but moved to Rome with his father while he was still young. His first patron, Cardinal Scipione Borghese, belonged to the influential Borghese family. He introduced Bernini to his uncle, Camillo Borghese, later Pope Paul V. The Borghese family commissioned Bernini's early works to decorate their private residences. These were mostly scenes from classical mythology rather than religious pieces, but revealed Bernini's extraordinary talent.

Bernini's fame rests, however, on his later architectural and religious compositions, which made Italy the cultural center of the Counter-Reformation. Bernini designed a bronze canopy, the Baldacchino, for his most important patron, Pope Urban VIII. Situated in St. Peter's Basilica underneath Michaelangelo's dome and over the tomb of St. Peter, the first pope, the canopy rises over 100 feet and testifies to the enduring wealth and power of the Catholic Church. A symbol of religious zeal and faith, Bernini's Baldacchino celebrates the papacy and the Catholic Church. In 1656, Bernini received a commission from Pope Alexander VII to complete the open-air space, the piazza, in front of St. Peter's Basilica. In keeping with the baroque taste for grandiose display, Bernini enclosed the courtyard with 284 Doric columns and 140 statues of saints. The space holds approximately 250,000 people. Even today, the faithful still gather in the dramatic setting that Bernini created in front of St. Peter's.

The interior of St. Peter's Basilica is dominated by Gianlorenzo Bernini's vast bronze canopy, which can be seen to the right of this painting.

PEOPLE & PLACES	DOCUMENTS, ART, & ARTIFACTS	WORSHIP & DOCTRINE

EUROPE

1666 English preacher John Bunyan writes *Grace Abounding to the Chief of Sinners*, describing his conversion and doubts; such spiritual autobiographies are a highly popular literary genre at the time.

1669 The Austrian divine Abraham a Sancta Clara, famous for his coarse humor, is made court preacher by the Habsburgs in Vienna.

1667 Blind English poet John Milton writes *Paradise Lost*, including the story of the fall of the angels.

1675 Building begins on a new St. Paul's Cathedral to replace the building destroyed in the Great Fire of London; it is designed by architect Christopher Wren.

1678 French theologian Richard Simon publishes the *Histoire critique du Vieux Testament*, one of the first books to critically examine the Bible from a secular, historical perspective.

1678 Nonconformist preacher John Bunyan writes the first part of his *Pilgrim's Progress*; part of the allegorical story of a journey to heaven is written while he is in jail for preaching without a license (📄 facing page).

1666 The conservative Old Believers leave the Russian Orthodox Church to protest reforms (📄 page 217).

1675 German theologian Philipp Jakob Spener founds Pietism when he writes *Pia Desideria*.

THE AMERICAS

1666 French priest Jacques Marquette arrives in Canada.

1667 Mexican theologian Sor Juana Inés de la Cruz enters a convent after her learning brings her into conflict with church authorities.

1670 Solomon Stoddard becomes minister of Northampton, Massachusetts.

1671 Rose of Lima is canonized by the pope; the nun, daughter of Spanish settlers in Peru, is the first New World saint.

1673 Jacques Marquette sets off with Louis Jolliet to explore the Mississippi River, sailing south.

1675 Marquette dies in what is now southern Illinois.

ca 1670 Jesuits in Canada produce sketches and paintings of Native American life.

This fresco from the Church of San Francisco Javier in Tepotzotlán, Mexico, shows the Virgin Mary appearing before St. Juan Diego.

1665 French priest Claude Jean Allouez begins converting Nipissing native peoples in the region of Lake Superior.

1674 Missionary John Eliot oversees 14 "praying towns" of native converts to Christianity in Massachusetts; however, Metacomet of the Wampanoag, known to Europeans as King Philip, tells Eliot that he cares no more for his gospel than he does for a button of his coat.

ASIA & OCEANIA

1668 The Spanish Jesuit Diego Luis de San Vitores establishes a mission on Guam in the Pacific Marianas islands.

1669 The Mogul emperor Aurangzeb becomes increasingly intolerant, outlawing Hindu worship in India.

1675 Goband Singh becomes the last of the Ten Gurus of the Sikhs, after his predecessor has been executed by the Moguls for refusing to embrace Islam.

AFRICA & THE MIDDLE EAST

1665 Shabbetai Tsevi is proclaimed as the Jewish messiah and attracts numerous followers, mainly among Jews; arrested for sedition, however, he converts to Islam, as do his followers, who form the Donme sect of Turkey.

1666 Suleyman comes to the Safavid throne; he continues to persecute non-Muslims in Persia.

1673 The English parliament passes the Test Act; its purpose is to exclude any non-Anglicans, particularly Catholics and nonconformists, from holding high political office; the act remains in force until 1829.

1678 The discovery of the "Popish Plot" in England leads to the trials of many leading Roman Catholics; Catholics are excluded from the English Parliament.

1678 Jews from Barbados arrive in Rhode Island after English colonists on the Caribbean island have attacked their synagogues.

I saw in my dream, that just as Christian came up to the cross, his burden loosed from off his shoulders, and fell from off his back, and began to tumble, and so continued to do till it came to the mouth of the sepulcher, where it fell in, and I saw it no more.

JOHN BUNYAN, THE PILGRIM'S PROGRESS

1666 The Great Fire of London destroys over 13,000 houses and almost 90 churches.

1676 The Royal Observatory is founded in London, England.

1676 Fyodor III becomes tsar of Russia.

This illustration from the Pilgrim's Progress *depicts the moment when Christian reaches the Cavalry Cross and his heavy burden falls from him.*

1670 The Welsh pirate Henry Morgan captures Panama.

1674 The Treaty of Westminster confirms the English possession of New Amsterdam; the colony is renamed New York.

1679 The French begin to explore the upper Great Lakes and discover Niagara Falls.

1674 The French East India Company founds a base at Pondicherry, south of Madras in India.

1674 Sivaji, the Hindu leader of the Marathas of western India, has himself crowned king.

1672 Mulay Ismail succeeds Mulay Rashid as sultan of Morocco.

1678 Kara Mustafa, a brother-in-law of Mehmed Kiuprili, becomes grand vizier and effective ruler of the Ottoman Empire.

THE PILGRIM'S PROGRESS

The English preacher John Bunyan (1628–1688) wrote *The Pilgrim's Progress from This World to That which is to Come* in 1678. It is a Christian allegory, which Bunyan wrote while in prison in Bedfordshire, England, for preaching outside of a church.

The book is about the journey of Christian, an everyman character, from his home in the City of Destruction to the Celestial City on top of Mount Zion. Leaving his family behind, he journeys toward the Celestial City. Along the way, Christian meets many different characters with whom he has theological debates. Some represent the unchristian values of secular society, while others represent Christian virtues or biblical characters. Many of those he encounters try to tempt him away from his journey, but he rejects their offers and chooses the long, difficult journey that is the right path to salvation.

PEOPLE & PLACES	DOCUMENTS, ART, & ARTIFACTS	WORSHIP & DOCTRINE

EUROPE

1680 Composer Henry Purcell becomes organist at Westminster Abbey, London.

1690 At the Battle of the Boyne in Ireland, the deposed Catholic king of England James II is defeated by his successor, the Protestant William II.

This illustration shows William of Orange (on horseback, center) crossing the Boyne River during the Battle of the Boyne.

1688 *Medulla theologiae moralis*, a Jesuit moral handbook by Hermann Busenmann, argues that "The end justifies the means."

1689 English philosopher John Locke writes *Letters Concerning Toleration*.

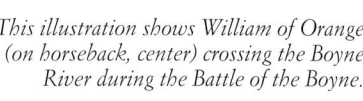

1682 The French clergy publish the Gallican Articles, which propose limiting the pope's authority over temporal affairs in favor of the state and the monarch; Pope Alexander VIII formally rejects the articles in 1690.

1682 In France, 38,000 Huguenots are forced to convert to Catholicism.

1687 Pope Innocent XI formally condemns Quietism, a Christian philosophy focused on internal peace and stillness, and its founder Miguel de Molinos.

1693 In Italy a secret society—the Knights of the Apocalypse—is founded to defend the Roman Catholic Church against the Antichrist.

THE AMERICAS

1680 The shaman Popé leads the Tewa Pueblo in a revolt against Spanish rule in New Mexico, burning Catholic missions.

1682 Quaker William Penn founds Pennsylvania, a colony he bases on religious toleration.

1687 An earthquake devastates Lima in Peru; Jesuits there introduce the Three Hours Service for Good Friday.

1687 Eusebio Kino, now a Jesuit priest, begins his mission in Arizona and California (📄 page 249).

1692 Salem, Massachusetts, becomes the center of witch trials that convict and execute 19 people (📄 pages 224–225).

ca 1680 The first Jesuit missionaries begin to arrive in the American Southwest.

1691 King William annuls Lord Calvert's charters for Maryland, marking the beginning of a period of persecution of the colony's Catholics.

1692 In Pennsylvania, Quakers found the Christian Quakers to protest compromise with other faiths.

ASIA & OCEANIA

ca 1690 The Mogul emperor Aurangzeb dispatches a large army to subdue the Sikhs. His forces are defeated by an army led by the tenth guru, Goband Singh, at the Battle of Nadaun.

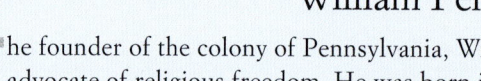

FAITH AND LIFE

William Penn

The founder of the colony of Pennsylvania, William Penn, was an important advocate of religious freedom. He was born into a powerful and wealthy English family in 1644 and received a conventional Anglican upbringing. As a young man he became attracted to nonconformist Christianity, particularly the Quaker movement. Penn became an outspoken advocate of Quakerism, and was jailed several times for criticizing the Anglican Church. As the persecution of Quakers in Britain grew more severe, Penn appealed directly to the king for permission to establish a colony where Quakers and other nonconformists could practice their religion freely. In 1677 this was granted, and Penn became the proprietor of a province he called Pennsylvania. The new province's constitution placed a strong emphasis on freedom of religion. This soon attracted immigrants from persecuted groups across Europe, including Jews, Huguenots, and Amish.

AFRICA & THE MIDDLE EAST

1682 The Christian Iyasu I becomes king of Ethiopia.

1688 French Protestants (Huguenots) arrive as refugees in the Dutch colony of South Africa.

RELIGION IN THE WORLD	WORLD EVENTS
1683 The Second Siege of Vienna marks the limit of the Ottoman advance into Europe.	**1684** The Pope forms the Holy League (Poland, Venice, and Habsburg Austria) to free Europe from the Ottomans.
1685 French King Louis XIV revokes the 1598 Edict of Nantes, which had guaranteed rights to French Protestants (📄 box right).	
1688 In the "Glorious Revolution" the English drive the Catholic James II from the throne, which is offered to the Dutch Protestant Prince William of Orange.	
1689 The English parliament passes the Toleration Act, granting freedom of worship to nonconformists but not to Roman Catholics or Quakers.	

If any man err from the right way, it is his own misfortune, no injury to thee; nor art thou to punish him in the things of this life because thou supposest he will be miserable in that which is to come.

JOHN LOCKE, *A LETTER CONCERNING TOLERATION*

1683 Dutch and English pirates sack Veracruz, Mexico.

1689 War between England and France in Europe spreads to North America as King William's War, the first of the French and Indian Wars, which set settlers from the two nations against one another.

1690 A Puritan force from Massachusetts lays unsuccessful siege to the city of Quebec during King William's War.

1681 Jesuits introduce Western farming techniques to China.

1692 In China, an imperial decree permits Christian worship.

Fasiladas Palace, near the town of Gondar, Ethiopia, was the home of Christian King Iyasu I.

1684 The Dutch East India Company occupies the Sultanate of Bantam on Java.

FLIGHT OF THE HUGUENOTS

The Huguenots were a French Protestant group that emerged during the religious wars of the 16th and 17th centuries. Although relatively small, the community included powerful aristocratic families, and posed a potential threat to the Catholic monarchy.

The Huguenot population was primarily drawn from the ranks of France's middle classes and included many businessmen, merchants, and skilled workers. As a result, Huguenot communities became important manufacturing centers and made significant contributions to the French economy. By the late 17th century industries such as silk weaving were controlled almost exclusively by Huguenot firms. With their own churches and means of economic support, Huguenot communities were separate and distinct from the Catholic populace that surrounded them, a fact that often generated resentment.

Throughout the second half of the 16th century, the Huguenots were involved in a bitter conflict with France's Catholic monarchy. During this time there were several massacres of Huguenot communities, most notably the St. Bartholomew's Day Massacre in the summer of 1572, in which thousands of Huguenots died. This conflict was brought to an end in 1598 by the Edict of Nantes, which guaranteed Huguenots the right to live and worship in France.

The Huguenot population continued to grow throughout the 17th century, as the faith attracted more converts. In 1685, however, King Louis XIV revoked the Edict of Nantes. Many Huguenots reacted by fleeing into exile. Over the next few years, the Huguenots migrated to the commercial centers of Europe, such as Amsterdam, Berlin, and London, where they reestablished their businesses. Others settled in more distant locations, including South Africa and colonial North America. Regardless of where they settled, the Huguenot communities retained their distinctive culture and language.

THE SALEM WITCH TRIALS

IN 1692 IN THE SMALL VILLAGE OF SALEM, MASSACHUSETTS, THERE occurred some of the strangest events in American colonial history. These events became known as the Salem witch trials. In the course of eight months in Salem and a number of surrounding villages, more than 100 people were accused of witchcraft. Fifty of them "confessed," 26 were found guilty by trial and jury, and 19 were put to death.

The trouble began in February 1692, when the daughter and the niece of Samuel Parris, the village minister, began having seizures that doctors in the town described as "bewitchment." The proof of this, they said, was that the two girls were friends with the Parris' slave girl, Tituba, who admitted using charms to foretell the future. Soon other young girls began having seizures, blaming not only Tituba but also two local widows, Sarah Osburn and Sarah Good. By May more than 25 people had been accused of witchcraft, including several men and a former minister of Salem, George Burroughs.

The governor of Massachusetts decided to appoint a special court to try the cases. There the accusers often screamed and fainted when they saw the accused, and juries were coerced into handing out guilty verdicts. If the accused "confessed" to avoid execution, they had to name those who helped them "do the devil's work."

By June the trouble had spread to the neighboring villages of Andover, Haverhill, Topsfield, and Gloucester. By the fall some church ministers at last began to be concerned about the so-called evidence against the accused. However, action was taken only when the accusers turned on the wives of eminent men in the district, including that of the governor himself. Then even Samuel Parris, who had been most determined to hunt down those who had "bewitched" his girls, began to think better of the trials—while the judge himself now publicly expressed his doubts about the accusers. By early 1693 the court refused to hear any more charges of witchcraft. However, it was not until 1711 that any compensation was paid to the surviving victims.

There are several theories about what caused the Salem witch trials. Many historians believe that the Puritan obsession with sin and strong belief in the devil created the perfect conditions for charges of witchcraft, while personal grudges, childish attention-seeking, and the social structure of these religious communities also played a role.

The Salem witch trials became widely known as a result of the account written by Cotton Mather, a minister and writer who was present at the trials as an advisor to the judges.

The Wonders of the Invisible World:

Being an Account of the

TRYALS

OF

Several Witches,

Lately Excuted in

NEW-ENGLAND:

And of several remarkable. Curiosities therein Occurring.

Together with,

I. Observations upon the Nature, the Number, and the Operations of the Devils.

II. A short Narrative of a late outrage committed by a knot of Witches in *Swede-Land*, very much resembling, and so far explaining, that under which *New-England* has laboured.

III. Some Councels directing a due Improvement of the Terrible things lately done by the unusual and amazing Range of *Evil-Spirits in New-England*.

IV. A brief Discourse upon those *Temptations* which are the more ordinary Devices of Satan.

By *COTTON MATHER.*

Published by the Special Command of his EXCELLENCY the Governour of the Province of the *Massachusetts-Bay* in *New-England.*

Printed first, at *Boston* in *New-England*; and Reprinted at *London*, for *John Dunton*, at the *Raven* in the *Poultry.* 1693.

Many of those convicted of witchcraft were elderly women of low social status whom no one in the community was willing to risk defending publicly.

	PEOPLE & PLACES	DOCUMENTS, ART, & ARTIFACTS	WORSHIP & DOCTRINE
EUROPE	**1702** Architect Fischer von Erlach completes the Church of the Holy Trinity in Salzburg, Austria. **1704** The French philosopher Voltaire joins a Jesuit college. **1705** The young German composer Johann Sebastian Bach walks 20 miles to hear the celebrated church organist and composer Dietrich Buxtehude. **1709** Louis XIV of France begins the destruction of the Jansenist stronghold at Port-Royal.	**1695** English philosopher John Locke writes *The Reasonableness of Christianity*, arguing that the doctrines of the faith are compatible with reason. **1702** English satirist Daniel Defoe writes *The Shortest Way With Dissenters*, a parody on church attacks on nonconformists; a Dissenter himself, Defoe is put in the pillory and jailed. **1704** George Friedrich Handel composes his *Saint John Passion* (pages 242–243). **1708** Christopher Wren's St. Paul's Cathedral is completed in London.	**1698** In London, philanthropist Thomas Bray founds the Society for Promoting Christian Knowledge (SPCK), still functioning today. **1699** The Pope again condemns quietism. **1701** The Society for the Propagation of the Gospel in Foreign Parts is founded in London. **1706** English theologian Matthew Tindal publishes *The Rights of the Christian Church*, an influential assertion of the rights of the state over the church.
THE AMERICAS	**1695** The first synagogue in the English colonies, Shearith Israel, is established in rented quarters in New York; its first building is constructed in 1730. **1697** In the Yucatán, Mexico, Spaniards destroy the last remains of Maya cilivization, including their temples. **1700** In a unique outbreak of violence, Hopi who have links with Spanish priests are massacred by Hopi who are loyal to traditional beliefs. **1706** Francis Makemie forms the first American presbytery in Philadelphia.	**1701** The *Popul Vuh*, the sacred book of the Quiché Maya of Guatemala, is translated by the Spanish priest Francisco Ximénes. **1702** Cotton Mather publishes *Magnalia Christi Americana*, a rather gloomy view of Christianity in the Americas (facing page).	*The New Englanders are a people of god settled in those which were once the Devil's territories.* COTTON MATHER, *THE WONDERS OF THE INVISIBLE WORLD*
ASIA & OCEANIA	**ca 1695** In Ethiopia, King Isayu I builds many churches in his capital, Gondar. **1698** England's East India Company is founded; its charter allows for the provision of Anglican chaplains in India. **1699** The Tenth Guru, Goband Singh, founds the Khalsa ("Pure") brotherhood of Sikhs. **1704** The pope sends a legate to Asia to prevent Jesuit compromises with Chinese and Indian traditions.		
AFRICA & THE MIDDLE EAST	*The English East India Company gained its first foothold in India during the early 18th century, beginning a period of military expansion that would see it control most of the country by the mid-19th century.*		

1699 The Treaty of Karlowitz ends fighting between the Holy League and the Ottomans, who cede most of Hungary to the Habsburgs.

1701 In England, the Act of Settlement excludes Catholics from succeeding to the throne.

1697 Peter the Great, Tsar of Russia, makes a grand tour of Europe; traveling incognito, he visits shipyards in England and the Netherlands.

1702 The first English-language daily newspaper, *The Daily Courant,* starts publication in England.

1707 The Act of Union brings England and Scotland together in the United Kingdom of Great Britain.

New England minister Cotton Mather was one of the first internationally known writers from North America.

COTTON MATHER

Cotton Mather was an influential religious leader in colonial America. Born in Boston, Massachusetts, in 1663, Mather received his education at Harvard before going on to become a preacher in Boston. Working alongside his father, Increase Mather, he was involved in some of the defining events of his time.

While still a young man, Mather played a significant role in the Salem witchcraft trials. In 1692 he wrote the minister's statement concerning the case, which called for cautious judgment and public prayer as a solution. As the trials progressed, Mather became more supportive of Salem's witch hunters and wrote several essays denouncing the practice of witchcraft. The works spread the news of events in Salem widely.

In his later life Mather wrote more than 450 books on topics as diverse as church history, the effectiveness of vaccination, and plant science. Thanks to his books, Mather became better known in Europe than any other American of his time. His most celebrated work was a religious history of New England entitled *Magnalia Christi Americana,* published in 1702. Cotton Mather died in 1728. He had 15 children by three wives, but only two survived him.

1696 In Philadelphia, the Yearly Meeting of Quakers criticizes slave owners.

1702 The Church of England is established in Maryland by law.

This illustration shows Port-Royal, the Jansenist sect's stronghold southwest of Paris. The complex was destroyed on the orders of King Louis XIV

1704 In Kongo, the Antonians seek to combine Christianity with traditional African religious practices.

1706 Doña Beatriz, leader of the Kongolese Antonians, is tried and executed by the Dutch authorities for heresy.

1706 Ethiopian emperor Susenyos becomes a Roman Catholic.

1701 Osei Tutu embarks on a program of expansion that will unite the small principalities of the Gold Coast (modern Ghana) into a single Ashanti kingdom.

1708 Algerian forces take Oran from Spain.

PEOPLE & PLACES	DOCUMENTS, ART, & ARTIFACTS	WORSHIP & DOCTRINE

EUROPE

1719 The first Lutheran missionary to India, Bartholomäus Ziegenbalg, dies in Tamil Nadu after working there for 13 years and translating scripture into Tamil.

1722 The German count Nicolaus Ludwig Zinzendorf founds the hamlet of Herrnhut in Saxony as a sanctuary for nonconformist Protestants.

1723 The German composer Johann Sebastian Bach becomes cantor at Leipzig, where he composes his great religious works over the next 27 years.

1724 The English towns of Gloucester, Hereford, and Worcester form the Three Choirs Festival, a celebration of sacred choral music that still continues.

1710 In *Theodicy*, German philosopher Gottfried Leibniz argues that God has created "the best of all possible worlds."

1720 In London, building begins on St. George's Church, Bloomsbury, the last of the six parish churches designed by the architect Nicholas Hawksmoor, former pupil of Christopher Wren.

1720 Giam Battista Tiepolo paints the *Martyrdom of St. Bartholomew*.

1723 Johann Sebastian Bach writes his *St. John Passion*.

1713 The papal bull *Unigenitus* condemns 101 propositions of the Jansenists; the Jansenists appeal to a general council of the church in France.

1717 The Bangorian Controversy divides the Church of England; it is caused when Benjamin Hoadly, bishop of Bangor, suggests that churches should have no government or organization.

1719 The Jesuits are expelled from Russia.

1724 The Jansenist Church of Utrecht splits from the Roman Catholic Church.

THE AMERICAS

1711 Father Eusebio Kino dies after having made at least 50 known missionary journeys through northern Mexico and the Southwest, a total of over 8,000 miles.

1712 British governor and slaveholder Christopher Codrington leaves his wealthy estates on Barbados to the Society for the Propagation of the Gospel in Foreign Parts.

1710 Preacher Cotton Mather writes *Essays to Do Good*.

1724 The Convent of Corpus Christi, the first religious house for native women, opens in Mexico.

1711 The Portuguese ban any religious orders from the region that holds the Brazilian gold fields.

1712 A cult dedicated to Mary begins among Mayans in Chiapas, Mexico, inspired by a young girl's vision of the saint.

ASIA & OCEANIA

1715 The Jesuit missionary Giuseppe Castiglione arrives in China, where he influences local styles of painting.

1720 When the Japanese Shogun Yoshimune permits the import of Western books to Japan to promote knowledge, religious books are still excluded.

AFRICA & THE MIDDLE EAST

Johnann Sebastian Bach wrote many of his most famous works for religious events and ceremonies.

FAITH AND LIFE

Eusebio Kino

Eusebio Kino was an Italian Jesuit missionary who traveled widely across Northern Mexico and what is now California and Arizona. Kino lived for several years among the Pima people of the Sonoran Desert, attempting to convert them to Christianity. He also established one of the first missions in Baja California in 1683, although it was soon abandoned due to a drought. In addition to his missionary activities, Kino was a well-known advocate of the rights of Native Americans. His views frequently brought him into conflict with the religious authorities in Mexico, who tolerated the brutality with which native groups, including Christian converts, were treated.

RELIGION IN THE WORLD

1717 The Grand Lodge of Freemasonry is established in London; it soon spreads through Europe and North America. Members are called upon to believe in the "Glorious Architect of Heaven and Earth."

1717 Armenian Mekhitarist monks settle on one of the Venetian islands.

1721 In Russia, Peter the Great abolishes the Moscow patriarchate in favor of the "Holy Synod," effectively bringing the Russian church under government control.

... offensive to pious ears, scandalous, pernicious, rash, injurious to the Church and her practice, impious, blasphemous, suspected of heresy, and smacking of heresy itself.

UNIGENITUS, DESCRIPTION OF JANSENISM

1710 Banda Bahadur founds an independent Sikh nation in Punjab (he is executed by the Moguls in 1715).

1719 A conspiracy of Spanish friars murder the Spanish governor of the Philippines in retaliation for his financial reforms.

1723 The accession to the Chinese throne of Yung Chêng begins three years of the persecution of Christians and the expulsion of Christian missionaries from the country.

1711 The Druze of Lebanon split; Yamani Druze move to Syria, leaving a largely Maronite Druze population in Lebanon.

1714 The Jesuits begin a mission in Sierra Leone.

WORLD EVENTS

1713 The War of the Spanish Succession ends with the Peace of Utrecht and the crowning of France's favored candidate, Phillip V, as King of Spain.

1715 Louis XV, age five, succeeds to the French throne on the death of his great grandfather Louis XIV.

1720 The collapse of the Britain's South Sea Company ruins thousands of investors in the financial scandal known as the "South Sea Bubble."

1715 New immigrants and established settlers start to push west into the Piedmont region of eastern Appalachia.

1720 A Spanish expeditionary force from Mexico occupies what is now Texas.

This 18th century painting shows the Moravian community of Bethlehem, Pennsylvania. Many Moravians settled in the colony, where nonconformist religious groups were tolerated.

GERMAN SECTS IN AMERICA

Beginning in 1681 thousands of German-speaking immigrants flowed into Pennsylvania. They brought with them the diverse religious principles, which were largely Protestant in nature, for which they had been persecuted in Europe. These sects created a land of rich spiritual variety, helping make colonial Pennsylvania famous for its religious diversity.

Most of the immigrants were either Lutherans or members of the German Reformed Church, but there were many other groups, each with unique doctrines and practices. The Mennonites, and their more conservative offshoot, the Amish, were known for their simple dress and rural lifestyle. They avoided politics and concentrated on farming. The Moravians, by contrast, dedicated themselves to missionary work, especially among the Native Americans.

While most of these sects remained small and isolated, the larger German groups did influence American religious life. They founded many churches and colleges which preserved their beliefs and ensured that they would survive for future generations.

YORUBA KINGDOMS OF AFRICA

THE YORUBA ARE ONE OF THE THREE largest ethnic groups of West Africa. The Yoruba are principally from southwestern Nigeria, with smaller groups in Benin and northern Togo. Today, there are estimated to be around twenty-one million Yoruba. Unlike other African ethnic groups, the Yoruba settled in urban centers during the first millennium A.D. Each Yoruba kingdom had its own capital city ruled over by a hereditary king (oba). By the ninth century the city of Ife-Ife was a thriving urban center where artists created the distinctive terracotta and bronze sculptures that are linked to the Yoruba.

Masks such as this one were used in the ritual practices of the Yoruba people.

Probably one of the oldest religions in the world, the Yoruba religion had many creation myths and gods (orisa) that differed from community to community. However, some were popular across the entire Yoruba peoples. One common creation myth told of Oduduwa, the first king and the founder of the Yoruba. According to some accounts, his son created life in Ife-Ife, which then became the seat of the kingdom. When the Yoruba were forcibly shipped to the New World to be slaves in the 16th century, they took their religious beliefs with them. Their beliefs became the basis of New World slave religions such as Santería in Cuba.

According to Yoruba legends, there were 401 orisa or gods that lined the path to heaven. At one point, they were all humans who became gods because of the important deeds they did when alive. Sango, the god of thunder, for example, was the king of Oyo before he became an orisa. So for the people of Oyo, Sango was their patron god and was worshiped in the area that made up the Oyo Empire. By contrast, Sango was an insignificant god to the people of the kingdom of Ife.

Worship of the orisa involved sacrifice, which could be the offering of food, prayer, or the killing of an animal. For the Yoruba, sacrifice was an acknowledgment of powerful forces at work that must be kept appeased at all times.

The Niger River was an important trade route and source of water for the Yoruba people, and the gods that represented it were commonly worshipped.

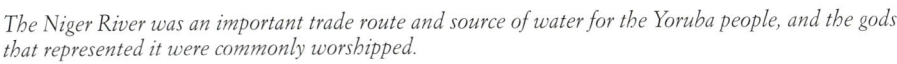

THE FAITH OF HUMANS IN THEIR ABILITY TO UNDERSTAND THE WORLD WITH-OUT resorting to religion and superstition reached a high point in the middle of the 18th century. A generation of European intellectuals believed that reason was the only tool necessary to explain all kinds of phenomena formerly ascribed to supernatural causes, from the flash of lightning to the eruption of a volcano. Many of the leaders of this movement, often termed the Enlightenment, remained highly devout—but the god they believed in tended to have created the universe and then left it alone, largely indifferent to human prayers or actions. Such a belief was termed "deism."

In part this Age of Reason echoed the emergence of an understanding of the world based on the observation, experimentation, and deduction of enthusiastic amateur scientists, known at the time as "natural philosophers." It also encouraged further investigation—and greater ambition. There seemed to be nothing that was beyond human ingenuity to explain. The French writer Denis Diderot summed up the ambition of the age with his plan to create an encyclopedia of all human knowledge in the 35 volumes of the *Encyclopedie*.

The trend toward rationalism inspired the revolutions that swept the Americas and France. In 1763 the Founders chose not to have an established church in the United States. The separation of church and state remains a core element of the Constitution, though one that has come under much scrutiny with the political rise of the religious right. In France, the 1789 revolution was rooted in anticlerical sentiment: Many church leaders were also members of the aristocratic *ancién regime*; the church was effectively dismantled and monks and priests killed or turned out. The revolutionary Robespierre attempted to create a religion based entirely on reason—but it did not

Previous pages *The colonial cathedral built by the Spaniards on top of the palace of the former Inca ruler dominates the Plaza de Armas in Cuzco, Peru. The Catholic Church spread effectively through South America, where every colonial town had its cathedral or church on the main square.*

Christmas lights illuminate the Assembly Hall in Temple Square, Salt Lake City, built by Mormons in 1877. The square is home to the Salt Lake Temple—the largest Mormon temple in the world—and to the domed Tabernacle, home to the world-famous Mormon Tabernacle Choir.

survive its creator's appointment with the guillotine in 1794. Still, efforts persisted to find spiritual fulfillment beyond the parameters of established faith. Such was the inspiration behind the Romantic movement, which sought in untamed nature an emotional counterpoint to the ills of the industrial world.

In the United States the westward expansion of settlement provided many opportunities for missionaries. Some received a favorable welcome from native populations (particularly where they covered ground previously trodden by early Spanish friars); others met only hardship and martyrdom. Victory over Mexico, which made California and the Southwest part of the United States, created many Roman Catholic Americans. Meanwhile, among the Americans heading west were the Mormons, a controversial home-grown Christian sect who only found freedom from persecution on the banks of the Great Salt Lake in the Utah desert.

Elsewhere, imperialism brought Europeans into contact with the religions of Oceania, including the Australian Aborigines and their belief in a mythical Dreamtime when the world was created. Europeans also encountered the great monuments of the Buddhist and Hindu past of South and Southeast Asia—reminders that great civilizations had clearly once existed where imperial eyes tended to see only mud huts and natives. While the Mogul Empire in India declined under pressure from competing colonial newcomers—and from its Islamic and Hindu neighbors—Islam grew stronger in its heartland in the Arabian peninsula, where the Wahhabi sect inspired the Saud clan to create the Saudi Arabian state that their descendants still rule.

This lithograph from about 1800 shows a Hindu widow being thrown onto her husband's funeral pyre, a practice known as suttee. The British banned the practice in various states in 1828 and in Bengal the campaigner Raja Rammohan Roy marshalled a native protest against it—although in places such as Nepal it survived into the 20th century.

The wild hills and still lakes of England's Lake District attracted a generation of Romantic writers, including William Wordsworth, Samuel Taylor Coleridge, and Thomas de Quincey.

CONCISE HISTORY OF WORLD RELIGIONS

	1725	1740	1755	1770	1785
EUROPE	**1727** At the Yearly Meeting in London, Quakers call for the abolition of the transatlantic slave trade. **1727** Empress Catherine the Great of Russia expels Jews from Ukraine. **1734** French philosopher Voltaire writes *Lettres philosophiques*, calling for religious and political toleration.	**1743** Anti-Jewish pogroms break out in Russia. **1750** Johann Sebastian Bach dies, having composed more than sacred 750 choral and organ works. **1753** An act of Parliament allows Jews to become naturalized in England.	**1755** New British laws are passed to allow Jews to become naturalized citizens. **1759** Voltaire writes *Candide*, a major work in developing Enlightenment philosophy. **1766** Catherine the Great grants religious freedom in Russia.	**1772** The Roman Catholic Inquisition is abolished in France. **1773** Pope Clement XIV suppresses the Jesuit Order. **1783** In Germany, Moses Mendelssohn writes *Jerusalem*, calling for civil rights for Jews in Europe.	**1785** British MP William Wilberforce undergoes a conversion experience and becomes an evangelical Christian. **1791** Half of the French clergy reject the Civil Constitution of the Clergy, which subordinates the church to the revolutionary government and abolishes all religious orders.
THE AMERICAS	**1733** The hellfire preaching of Jonathan Edwards inspires the Great Awakening, a wave of religious fervor in the British colonies. **1738** British Anglican George Whitefield makes his first visit to North America, where his preaching is instrumental in spreading the Great Awakening. **1739** The Moravian Church is founded in the United States by August Gottleib Spangenberg.	**1740** Preaching in North America, George Whitefield criticizes the established church there. **1741** American Presbyterians split into conservative and revivalist factions, the "Old Side" and the "New Side." **1743** Ministers in Connecticut protest preaching by laymen. **1743** The Quaker John Woolman begins preaching against slavery in North America.	**1758** At the Yearly Meeting in Philadelphia, Quakers vote to exclude slave traders and appoint a committee to lead an abolition campaign. **1763** Touro Synagogue, in Newport, Rhode Island, becomes the first major Jewish center to open in North America. **1764** Penoboscot Native Americans petition the governor of Massachusetts to send them a priest.	**1773** The First Methodist Conference is held in North America. **1774** Mother Ann Lee moves to North America, where she founds the Shaker movement. **1779** In response to moves to make Christianity the established faith in Virginia, Thomas Jefferson proposes a bill in favor of religious freedom and against tax support for churches.	**1789** President George Washington receives an appeal from Baptists to prevent taxes being used to support other churches. **1790** John Carroll of Baltimore is the first Roman Catholic bishop to be consecrated in North America. **1798** Politician Thomas Jefferson conceives of a new kind of Bible, which removes its supernatural elements and treats its message as a philosophical system.
ASIA & OCEANIA	**1725** In Japan, many urban dwellers adopt a new religion, Shingaku, whose founder Isida Baigan has drawn on Shinto, Buddhist, and Confucian elements. **1739** Persian ruler Nadir Shah sacks Delhi and loots Mogul palaces throughout the Punjab.	**1742** The papal bull *Ex Quo Singulari* condemns the "Chinese rites," the practice of some Catholic orders in East Asia of adopting local customs such as making offerings to the Emperor; the bull greatly reduces missionary activity in China.	**1762** The Mogul ruler of Bengal goes to war against the increasing activity of the British East India Company. **1767** The Muslim ruler Hyder Ali begins the First Mysore War against British forces in southern India.	**1781** The Qing rulers of China put down a Muslim rebellion in Gansu province. **1784** Tipu Sultan imprisons up to 60,000 Christians from Mangalore in southwestern India, mainly for supporting his British enemies, and destroys many Christian churches.	**1785** Korean authorities ban Catholicism. **1797** The first Christian missionaries arrive in the Pacific islands of Tahiti and Tonga. **1798** A Sikh kingdom is founded in India by Ranjit Singh, known as the Lion of the Punjab.
AFRICA & THE MIDDLE EAST	**1730** The Janissaries take effective control of the Ottoman Empire: they are traditionally recruited from Christian subject peoples but are forced to convert to Islam (not least because Christians are forbidden from carrying weapons throughout the empire).	**1740** Arab scholar Muhammad ibn Abd al-Wahhab is banished from his home town, Uyayna, for preaching that all innovation in Islam should be forbidden and undone; he forms an alliance with neighboring ruler Muhammad ibn Saud, ancestor of the Saud dynasty of modern Saudi Arabia.	**1762** The Hamadj dynasty become rulers of the Sultanate of Funj in northern Sudan. **1765** Abd al-Aziz becomes emir after the death of his father Muhammad Ibn Saud, and extends Saudi rule in the Arabian peninsula.	**1772** In Morocco, the ruler Sidi Muhammad II gives Jews senior positions in his diplomatic service. **1777** In Morocco, the enslavement of Christians is abolished.	**1790** Jews are persecuted in Morocco, mainly as a reaction to their privileged status under the previous ruler, Sidi Muhammad II. **1793** The Wahhabi conquer Riyadh in Arabia, where clerics fill judicial and teaching posts.

1800	1810	1820	1830	1840–1849
1804 The Christian Serbs rebel against their Muslim Ottoman rulers. **1807** The British Parliament makes the slave trade illegal after lobbying led by evangelical Christian William Wilberforce. **1808** Napoleon abolishes the Inquisition in Spain and Italy.	**1811** In the "Great Schism," two-thirds of Welsh Protestants leave the Anglican Church. **1814** Pope Pius VII is freed from virtual captivity after the fall of Napoleon I; he returns to Rome, reinstitutes the Inquisition and the *Index of Prohibited Books*, brings back the Jesuits, and condemns Protestant missionary activity.	**1820** Scottish aristocrat and theologian Thomas Erskine tries to reform Calvinism to create a doctrine closer to Calvin's intentions. **1829** In Britain the Catholic Relief Act completes the process of Roman Catholic emancipation: Catholics can now become members of Parliament (although they cannot become monarchs).	**1833** The Oxford Movement in Britain begins to introduce reforms to the Anglican Church. **1839** Pope Gregory XVI issues a bull condemning slavery.	**1840** The first Mormon missionaries arrive in England. **1844** German political philosopher Karl Marx observes "Religion is the opium of the people." **1845** A potato blight causes famine in Ireland that will last until 1851, killing about a million and driving far more Catholic emigrants to the United States and elsewhere.
1800 Elihu Palmer, a former Presbyterian preacher struck blind by yellow fever in 1793, founds *The Temple of Reason*, a newspaper that reflects his deist views. **1801** The Second Great Awakening begins in Kentucky; it draws scattered rural worshipers together at long revivalist "camp meetings." **1805** Joseph Smith, the founder of the Mormons, is born in Vermont.	**1810** The Grito de Dolores: Mexican priest Miguel Hidalgo de Costilla declares Mexican independence (September 16); he is defeated and executed the following year. **1810** Nationalist rebels in Mexico use the Virgin of Guadalupe as their standard, proclaiming her the patron saint of the oppressed.	**1823** Joseph Smith has his first vision of the angel Moroni, the messenger of God who will guide him to found the Church of the Latter Day Saints (Mormons). **1823** African American missionary Betsey Jackson begins preaching in the Sandwich Islands. **1829** Catholics begin to found parochial schools throughout the American West.	**1830** Joseph Smith and his supporters form the Church of Jesus Christ of Latter-day Saints (Mormons). **1834** Students quit Lane Theological Seminary over Lyman Beecher's refusal to admit African Americans. **1836** Ralph Waldo Emerson writes *Nature*, the founding document of the Transcendentalists.	**1842** Nativists in Philadelphia riot for three days to protest Catholics being given the right to translate their own Bible. **1843** Joseph Smith announces that God has instructed him to practice polygamy. **1846** Bohemian rabbi Isaac Mayer Wise arrives in the United States, where he becomes a leader of Reform Judaism. **1846** Hoping to escape persecution, Brigham Young leads the Mormons westward.
1801 The first major persecution begins of Roman Catholics in Korea. **1807** Robert Morrison becomes the first Protestant missionary in China, although it is still illegal to spread Christianity there.	**1813** The renewed charter of the British East India Company makes it easier for missionaries to enter India. **1819** Sikh forces led by Ranjit Singh capture Kashmir from Muslim rule.	**1821** Joshua Marshman publishes the first Chinese translation of the Bible, after 15 years' work. **1828** The British in India forbid the Hindu practice of *suttee*, the forced cremation of a living widow with her husband's body.	**1834** Sikhs in northern India capture the city of Peshawar in the Northwest Frontier from the Afghans. **1836** The first bishops arrive in Australia, representing the Roman Catholic and Anglican churches.	**1844** An imperial edict allows the Catholic Church to start operating again in China. **1845** The first Anglo–Sikh War breaks out when Sikh forces invade British territory in northern India; the conflict ends in 1846.
1803 With their occupation of the Hejaz in Arabia, the Wahhabi sect take control of the Muslim holy cities of Mecca and Medina. **1804** In western Sudan, the Fulani religious leader Usman dan Fodio is proclaimed commander of the faithful; he declares jihad—holy war—against neighboring kingdoms.	**1811** The Ottoman emperor sends Muhammad Ali of Egypt to confront the Saudi dynasty in the Arabian peninsula. **1814** The Muslim Omanis strengthen their control over the Swahili coast of East Africa.	**1821** Patriarch Gregory V of Constantinople is hanged by the Ottoman Turks for his failure to prevent a violent Greek uprising against Ottoman rule.	**1834** The Egyptian governor of Syria, Ibrahim Pasha, provokes a Muslim revolt when he extends conscription into the army, previously limited to poorer sections of society. **1835** Ibrahim Pasha orders the rebuilding of synagogues in Jerusalem.	**1840** Western missionaries, including the renowned German Johann Ludwig Krapf, are expelled from Ethiopia. **1841** The Africa Civilization Society begins a mission along the Niger River. **1847** The Catholic archbishopric of Abyssinia is created.

PEOPLE & PLACES	DOCUMENTS, ART, & ARTIFACTS	WORSHIP & DOCTRINE

EUROPE

1726 Sixteenth-century Spanish mystic John of the Cross is canonized.

1734 French philosopher Voltaire flees the scandal caused by his *Lettres philosophiques* by escaping to the castle of his lover in the remote French countryside.

1738 Preacher John Wesley undergoes a spiritual conversion at a Moravian meeting in London on May 24; he writes, "I felt my heart strangely warmed."

1728 William Law writes *A Serious Call to a Devout and Holy Life*.

1729 German composer Johann Sebastian Bach writes the *Saint Matthew Passion*.

1730 In *Christianity as Old as the Creation*, English deist Matthew Tyndale attacks the supernatural element in organized religion.

1734 British orientalist George Sale translates the Koran into English.

1734 French philosopher Voltaire writes *Lettres philosophiques*, calling for religious and political toleration.

1736 Joseph Butler writes *The Analogy of Religion*.

1732 Some 12,000 Protestants expelled from Salzburg, Austria, resettle in East Prussia.

1735 The Bible is translated into Lithuanian.

1736 The English repeal anti-witchcraft laws originally enacted in the Middle Ages.

1739 John Wesley breaks with his Moravian colleagues over their support for quietism and founds the Methodist Society.

THE AMERICAS

1725 Jonathan Edwards becomes assistant to his grandfather, Solomon Stoddard, the influential Puritan minister in Connecticut.

1729 Solomon Stoddard dies after 55 years as minister at Northampton, Connecticut.

1738 British Anglican George Whitefield makes his first visit to North America, where his preaching is instrumental in spreading the Great Awakening (📄facing page).

1739 The Moravian Church is founded in the United States by August Gottleib Spangenberg (📄 page 229).

ASIA & OCEANIA

ca 1730 Bajirao I, Hindu ruler of Maharashtra in central India, expands his territory at the expense of the declining Mogul Empire.

1736 Nadir Shah becomes ruler of Persia.

1739 Persian ruler Nadir Shah sacks Delhi and loots Mogul palaces throughout the Punjab.

This illustration shows John Wesley preaching to Native Americans in Georgia. Wesley came to North America with a Moravian community, but returned to England to found his own church.

1725 In Japan, many urban dwellers adopt a new religion, Shingaku, whose founder Isida Baigan has drawn on Shinto, Buddhist, and Confucian elements.

AFRICA & THE MIDDLE EAST

1730 In Istanbul, the elite Janissary army corps depose the emperor Ahmed III and place Mahmud I on the Ottoman throne.

You have heard, brethren, the eternity of hell-torments plainly proved, from the express declarations of holy scriptures, and consequences naturally drawn from them. And now there seems to need no great art of rhetoric to persuade any understanding person to avoid and abhor those sins.

GEORGE WHITEFIELD

RELIGION IN THE WORLD	WORLD EVENTS
1727 At the Yearly Meeting in London, Quakers call for the abolition of the transatlantic slave trade. **1727** Empress Catherine the Great of Russia expels Jews from Ukraine. **1728** In Madrid, the Spanish Inquisition suppresses the Freemason's Lodge. **1738** Pope Clement XII publishes an edict against Freemasonry. **1739** When the Ottomans advance on Belgrade, Holy Roman emperor Charles VI returns northern Serbia to Muslim rule.	**1726** Irish writer Jonathan Swift writes his famous satire *Gulliver's Travels*. **1735** English clockmaker John Harrison builds the first accurate marine chronometer; his invention makes position plotting and navigation at sea far more accurate and safe. **1735** Sewdish botanist Karl Linné (Carolus Linneaus) publishes his first major work, *Systema Naturae*, which introduces a new system of plant classifcation.
1732 Johann Conrad Beissel founds the Ephrata Community, a sect of Seventh-Day Baptists (so-called for their stress on Saturday as the Sabbath) in Germantown, Pennsylvania (page 229). **1733** The hellfire preaching of Jonathan Edwards inspires the Great Awakening, a wave of religious fervor in the British colonies (box, right).	**1726** Spanish colonists found the city of Montevideo at the mouth of the Rio de la Plata. **1729** The city of Baltimore is founded as a center for shipbuilding. **1731** In Philadelphia Benjamin Franklin establishes the first subscription library in North America. **1733** The Molasses Act, passed by the British Parliament, effectively prohibits direct trade between the American colonies and the French West Indies by imposing high tariffs.
	1726 The Safavids retake the key Persian city of Esfahan from the Afghans. **1729** Emperor Shizu bans opium smoking in China. **1738** Nadir Shah of Persia embarks on a campaign of eastward expansion, capturing the city of Kandahar in Afghanistan.
1730 The Janissaries take effective control of the Ottoman Empire: they are traditionally recruited from Christian peoples but are forced to convert to Islam (not least because Christians are forbidden from carrying weapons throughout the empire).	**1731** The Persian and Ottoman empires agree on a peace treaty. **1732** A slave revolt forces the Dutch to abandon their slave trading post at Maputo in Mozambique.

THE GREAT AWAKENING

Beginning in 1739 a period of religious revival swept over the British colonies in the Americas. This Great Awakening rekindled the spiritual fire of Christian churches, as both old members and new converts were reinvigorated by a new enthusiasm. Preachers such as George Whitefield and Jonathan Edwards attracted large audiences with their emotionally charged, theatrical sermons.

The Awakening replaced formal services with more passionate, emotional forms of worship. In the process it not only divided congregations, some of whose members objected to changes in traditional church authority; it also began a wider process of reducing the influence of state-controlled churches in the Americas. After the Great Awakening, it was no longer seen as important that a minister had a university education or even any detailed knowledge of theology: passion and enthusiasm were enough. In turn, that helped the growth of a wider range of Christian denominations. Baptists, Methodists, and Presbyterians all began to increase in number and influence.

George Whitefield was one of the key figures of the Great Awakening whose open-air sermons attracted thousands of people.

PEOPLE & PLACES	DOCUMENTS, ART, & ARTIFACTS	WORSHIP & DOCTRINE

EUROPE

1740 Benedict XIV, the outstanding pope of the 18th century, is elected pontiff.

1750 Baal Shem—Israel ben Eliezer—founds the Jewish Hasidic sect in towns in Ukraine, where he preaches a version of Judaism that combines mystical folk wisdom with Cabalistic scholarship.

1750 Johann Sebastian Bach dies having composed more than sacred 750 choral and organ works.

1742 *Messiah*, an oratorio composed by George Frideric Handel in less than a month, is performed for the first time in Dublin. During its first London performance it is said that King George II rises to his feet during the Hallelujah Chorus, followed as protocol requires by the orchestra and audience; the custom lasts in some places to the current day (🖹 pages 242–243).

1747 French author Denis Diderot begins to compile his famous *Encyclopedie*, often seen as the major work of the rationalist Enlightenment.

THE AMERICAS

1740 Preaching in North America, George Whitefield criticizes the established church there.

1741 Count Zinzendorf arrives in the American colonies to encourage Moravian settlers there.

1747 Isaac Backus forms the First Baptist Church in Marlborough, Massachusetts.

1750 After losing popularity for his old-style views—he is by now limited to preaching sermons on Thursday afternoons—Jonathan Edwards is fired as minister of Northampton, Massachusetts.

1741 Jonathan Edwards preaches his famous sermon "Sinners in the Hands of an Angry God" at Enfield, Massachusetts.

1754 John Woolman publishes the first part of *Some Considerations on the Keeping of Negroes*, one of the first antislavery tracts.

Isaac Backus was a Baptist preacher from Malborough, Massachusetts, who campaigned against state-established churches.

1741 American Presbyterians split into conservative and revivalist factions, the "Old Side" and the "New Side."

1742 The Lutheran and Reformed churches both send official ministers to take up posts in Pennsylvania.

1746 The "New Light" Baptists form a separatist church.

ASIA & OCEANIA

1746 The German Christian Friedrich Schwartz arrives in India, where he makes more converts from both Hinduism and Islam than any other Protestant missionary.

1747 In China, Jesuit missionaries design the Summer Palace for the Emperor Qianlong.

1747 Nadir Shah of Persia is assassinated by his Afghan bodyguards.

1752 Parts of Muslim-controlled Hyderabad fall under Hindu control (🖹 facing page).

1742 The papal bull *Ex Quo Singulari* condemns the "Chinese rites," the practice of some Catholic orders in East Asia of adopting local customs such as making offerings to the Emperor; the bull greatly reduces missionary activity in China.

1751 The Qianlong emperor of China recognizes the Dalai Lama as leader of Tibet—and takes control of the succession; to make Chinese rule more popular in the Buddhist state, the emperor is portrayed in statues as a bodhisattva.

AFRICA & THE MIDDLE EAST

1740 Arab scholar Muhammad ibn Abd al-Wahhab is banished from his home town, Uyayna, for preaching that all innovation in Islam should be forbidden and undone; he forms an alliance with neighboring ruler Muhammad ibn Saud, ancestor of the Saud dynasty of modern Saudi Arabia.

Parts of the Summer Palace in Beijing were designed by the Jesuits Giuseppe Castiglione and Michel Benoist, who wanted to demonstrate to the Qianlong emperor the benefits of Western technology—and faith.

RELIGION IN THE WORLD	WORLD EVENTS
1743 Anti-Jewish pogroms break out in Russia.	**1740** Frederick William I of Prussia dies and is succeeded by his son Frederick II ("the Great").
1745 The Jacobites—Scots who support a Catholic succession to the British throne—launch a failed revolt led by Charles Edward Stuart, known as the Young Pretender.	**1748** Excavations begin on the site of the rediscovered ancient city of Pompeii, Italy, buried by an eruption of Mt. Vesuvius in A.D. 79.
1749 In Paris, France, the "Refusal of the Sacraments" crisis begins when a priest refuses to grant the last sacrament to a parishioner who cannot prove his loyalty to the Pope rather than to the Jansenists; the parliament supports the Jansenists, the monarchy the Pope.	
1753 The British Marriage Act forbids weddings by unauthorized officials.	
1753 An act of Parliament allows Jews to become naturalized in England.	
1743 Ministers in Connecticut protest preaching by laymen.	**1741** Hundreds of indentured servants and slaves are arrested after rumors of an impending slave rebellion grip New York. After a brief show trial, many are executed.
1743 The Quaker John Woolman begins preaching against slavery in North America.	**1742** British troops defending Georgia repel an attempted Spanish invasion.
1749 Benjamin Franklin argues for the necessity of a "publick religion" in the colonies.	**1746** The cities of Lima and Callao in Peru are destroyed by an earthquake that kills 18,000 people.
1750 Boston minister Johnathan Mayhew delivers a sermon on *A Discourse Concerning Unlimited Submission and Nonresistance to the Higher Power*; he argues that it would be just to execute an English king who failed to uphold English freedoms.	**1750** Spain and Portugal sign the Treaty of Madrid, which confirms the boundaries of Brazil.

There is no fortress that is any defense from the power of God.... We find it easy to tread on and crush a worm that we see crawling on the earth; thus easy is it for God when he pleases to cast his enemies down to hell.

JONATHAN EDWARDS, *SINNERS IN THE HANDS OF AN ANGRY GOD*

1744 Much of Arabia falls under the control of Muhammad Ibn Saud and Muhammad Ibn Abd al-Wahhab, founder of the Wahhabi Islamic sect.	**1743** The Ottomans and the Safavids of Persia resume hostilities.
	1745 Firearms are used for the first time in an African tribal war when the Ashanti defeat the neighboring state of Dagomba.
	1752 In the Sudan Sultan Abu al-Qasim of Darfur is killed resisting a Funj invasion force led by the Sultan of Kordofan.

THE END OF INDIA'S ISLAMIC EMPIRE

The Islamic Mogul dynasty ruled northern India for more than 300 years. At its peak in the 16th century it was noted for religious tolerance, but tensions between the Moguls and their Hindu subjects grew greater as the empire declined. The Mogul capital at Delhi was threatened by the dynasty's neighbors, who included both Hindu rulers in southern India and other Islamic rulers, such as Nadir Shah of Persia.

From the reign of Shah Jahan (1628–1658) cracks began to appear. Under his successor Aurangzeb, religious uprisings became common. Aurangzeb responded with increased intolerance, although many of his anti-Hindu policies were not enforced by his nobles.

The empire became increasingly vulnerable to internal and external attack. The Marathas took Mogul territory to create a Hindu empire, while the Moguls lost control of Punjab, Assam, and the Rajputs.

By the middle of the 18th century—the Moguls lost control of Hyderabad in 1752—the Mogul power base was effectively reduced to Delhi and its surroundings. Many Hindu states had evolved on former Mogul territory. Meanwhile the British East India Company, which had arrived in the 17th century to exploit the spice trade, offered financial and military support to Hindu rulers across India, further weakening the empire. After the Battle of Plassey in 1757, the East India Company became the de-facto ruler of India until control eventually passed to the British government.

HANDEL AND CHURCH MUSIC

GERMAN-BORN COMPOSER GEORGE FRIDERIC HANDEL (1685–1759) was one of the most influential composers of the 18th century. Over a long and successful career—Handel was a clever businessman and investor—he composed 42 operas, 29 oratorios, and hundreds of shorter works. Today he is best remembered for his sacred choral works, and specifically for the 1741 oratorio *Messiah*.

Born in Halle, Germany, Handel trained in keyboard and composition before traveling to Italy in 1706. During four years in Italy, Handel wrote operas for aristocratic audiences in Florence and Venice, as well as sacred music for the Roman Catholic Church. In 1710, his opera *Agrippina* attracted the patronage of the elector of Hanover, the future king of England, George I.

Handel himself settled in England in 1712. He continued to compose operas, but English audiences were increasingly turning away from an art form they considered morally suspect. Theater itself was notorious for the immorality of both the actors and the audiences. As opera's popularity declined, Handel made a commercial decision: for his conservative public among England's emerging middle classes, he turned to writing edifying oratorios—lengthy choral compositions that told a story without theatrical action or scenery. Handel's oratorios used biblical narratives and were sung in English.

His first oratorio, *Deborah and Atahalia*, was composed in 1733 with little success: Handel was soon declared bankrupt. He persisted, however, producing two of his most celebrated oratorios, *Saul* and *Israel in Egypt,* in 1739. His greatest oratorio, *Messiah*, was composed in less than a month during the summer of 1741 and first performed in Dublin, Ireland, in 1742. Handel continued to revise and alter the work as its popularity grew. *Messiah* is a meditation on the life of Christ with lyrics by Charles Jennens based on the different books of the Old and New Testament. The most famous movement of *Messiah* is the Hallelujah Chorus, with a text from the Book of Revelation.

In 1750 Handel arranged a special performance of *Messiah* to raise funds for the Foundling Hospital, an orphanage in London. The performance was a huge success—it was repeated every year—and Handel became closely involved with the orphanage. When Handel died in 1759, he left the Foundling Hospital an original copy of the score for *Messiah* in his will.

George Frideric Handel was one of the most popular composers of his time. Some 12,000 people are said to have attended the first public performance of his orchestral piece Music for the Royal Fireworks.

Handel's oratorios are often performed in sacred buildings, such as this performance in the Hofkirche, Dresden, Germany.

PEOPLE & PLACES	DOCUMENTS, ART, & ARTIFACTS	WORSHIP & DOCTRINE

EUROPE

1759 Voltaire writes *Candide*, a major work in developing Enlightenment philosophy.

1760 William Boyce, forced to halt composing by deafness, begins collecting English church music, including works by composers such as William Byrd and Henry Purcell; the collection is still used in Anglican services today.

1763 The King of Prussia grants Jewish scholar Moses Mendelssohn the status of "protected Jew," meaning that he can live unmolested in Berlin.

1765 Three years after being executed for murder, largely as a result of religious persecution, French Protestant Jean Calas is found not guilty thanks in part to a campaign led by the philosopher Voltaire.

1756 Swedish scientist Emanuel Swedenborg begins writing a series of mystical texts.

1757 Jacques-Germain Soufflot builds the neoclassical Church of St. Geneviève, patron saint of Paris; during the Revolution, the saint's remains are publicly burned and the church is renamed the Panthéon.

1758 Swiss poet Salomon Gessner writes *The Death of Abel*, an epic that spearheads a rococo movement in Europe.

1762 Jean-Jacques Rousseau writes *Émile*, which is the greatest expression of sentimental Deism.

1764 Pope Clement XIV says of a statue of St. Bruno, sculpted by Jean-Antoine Houdon, "He would speak were it not that the rules of his order impose silence."

1759 The Jesuits are expelled from Portugal.

1760 Cosmas of Aetolia leaves Mount Athos on his first missionary trip through northern and western Greece, where he founds more than 100 schools to encourage the learning of Greek as "the language of the church."

1765 After the expulsion of the Jesuits from France, the Commission des Réguliers is founded to reform the existing monastic orders.

1766 Catherine the Great grants religious freedom in Russia.

THE AMERICAS

1758 In New Jersey Samuel Davies, president of what later becomes Princeton University, preaches a recruiting sermon against "French papists" in the Americas so successful that the army has to turn away volunteers.

1760 Richard Allen, later founder of the African Methodist Episcopal Church, is born to slaves in Virginia.

1768 Father Junipero Serra leads 14 missionaries into Lower California.

1762 Quaker John Woolman publishes the second part of *Some Considerations on the Keeping of Negroes*.

1759 Jesuits are expelled from Brazil because of their support for Indian rights.

1763 Touro synagogue, in Newport, Rhode Island, becomes the first major Jewish center to open in North America.

1764 Penoboscot Native Americans petition the governor of Massachusetts to send them a priest.

1764 Brown University is the first college in the Americas to accept students of any religious affiliation.

1767 The Spaniards expel the Jesuits from New Spain.

1768 The first Methodist center in North America, Wesley Chapel, opens in New York.

ASIA & OCEANIA

1761 The Muslim Hyder Ali captures the throne of Mysore in southwestern India.

1762 The Mogul ruler of Bengal goes to war against the increasing activity of the British East India Company (📄 page 241).

1767 Hyder Ali begins the First Mysore War against British forces in southern India.

Built in 1763, the Touro synagogue in Newport, Rhode Island, is the oldest surviving Synagogue in the United States.

AFRICA & THE MIDDLE EAST

1762 The Hamadj dynasty become rulers of the Sultanate of Funj in northern Sudan.

1765 Abd al-Aziz becomes emir after the death of his father, Muhammad Ibn Saud, and extends Saudi rule in the Arabian peninsula.

1755 New British laws are passed to allow Jews to become naturalized citizens.

1755 A huge earthquake destroys the Portuguese capital, Lisbon, killing up to 40,000 people and toppling virtually every church in the city; the disaster has a profound impact on European theologians, who struggle to explain why an apparently just God should inflict such suffering on a people renowned for their devoutness.

1762 The Jesuits are expelled from France.

1767 The Jesuits are expelled from Spain and the Kingdom of the Two Sicilies.

1758 At the Yearly Meeting in Philadelphia, Quakers vote to exclude slave traders and appoint a committee to lead an abolition campaign.

1759 After the British conquer Quebec, they guarantee the free exercise of religion to Canada's Catholics.

1765 John Adams calls upon New England Episcopalians to reject the authority of English bishops.

1765 In response to the Stamp Act, a further tax imposed by the British, Jonathan Mayhew in Boston preaches an inflammatory sermon on the Bible verse "Ye have been called unto liberty."

1756 The Seven Years' War begins, putting Prussia and Britain in opposition to Austria, France, Sweden, Russia, and other states.

1759 Austrian and Russian troops inflict a heavy defeat on Prussia at the Battle of Kunersdorf in Poland.

1762 War breaks out between Britain and Spain.

1762 After Peter III ends hostilities with Prussia on disadvantageous terms, angry Russian nobles replace him with his wife, Catherine II, "the Great."

1763 The Treaty of Paris ends the Seven Years' War.

1768 Russia invades Ottoman-held Bulgaria.

1755 In a harbinger of the Seven Years' War, the French and Indian War breaks out between British and French settlers in North America and their respective native allies.

1759 The British defeat the French at Quebec, securing supremacy over Canada.

1763 The Treaty of Paris ends the Seven Years' War with most French territories in North America being ceded to Britain.

1765 The British impose the unpopular Stamp Act; colonial Americans form the Sons of Liberty movement in response.

1769 A Spanish expedition leaves Baja California to establish missions farther north in California (box, right).

CALIFORNIA'S MISSIONS

In 1769 Spanish Franciscan monks built the first mission in California, the Mission of San Diego de Alcala. Over the next 50 years they built another 20 missions to extend their influence in the region, each positioned within about a day's ride of the last along a coast road known as El Camino Real (The Royal Highway).

The missions, which varied from simple shelters to substantial adobe structures, functioned as both religious and military outposts. They were central to controlling Spain's growing territory in the Americas. Not only could missionaries convert the native peoples; the missions also brought Native Americans into the colonial economy. They provided a focus for trade (many missions attracted settlers and grew into major urban centers) and allowed indigenous peoples to be taxed to raise revenues for the Spanish crown. However, the missions never became self-sufficient and with the Mexican War of Independence in 1810, Spain could no longer afford to fund them.

John Woolman

There were always individuals who disapproved of slavery. Until the middle of the 18th century, however, there was no organized opposition to the practice. The campaign for abolition began in the 1760s when John Woolman, a Quaker preacher from New Jersey, began to address Quaker meetings across the 13 Colonies. Woolman's sermons and his antislavery tracts gained many supporters. In 1772 Woolman traveled to the Quaker Yearly Meeting in London to persuade the assembled leaders that they had a moral duty to oppose slavery. Quakers went on to form the backbone of the British and American abolitionist movements.

The Mission San Francisco de Asis gave its name to the city that grew up around it.

THE GLORIES OF ESFAHAN

THE CITY OF ESFAHAN (ISFAHAN) WAS THE capital of Persia from 1598 to 1722, and remains one of the great cultural treasures of Shiite Islam. The 2,000-year-old city, located on a fertile plain in the middle of present-day Iran, was chosen as the capital by the Safavid king, Shah Abbas the Great, because the city lay far from the troubled border with the Ottoman Empire to the west. It also stood on the important trade routes between East Asia and the Mediterranean known as the Silk Road, which attracted many foreign merchants who brought their languages, religions, and customs to the city. Under Abbas, architecture, science, decorative arts, calligraphy, and miniature painting all flourished.

Shah Abbas built his city around a huge *maidan*, or public space, the Naghsh-e Jahan Square. A two-story arcade housing two hundred shops surrounded the four sides, behind which stood four of the city's most important and beautiful buildings, decorated with colored tiles, marble, plaster, and painted wood.

On the south side of the maidan is the Imam Mosque, the heart of religious life in 17th-century Esfahan. The mosque took 26 years to build, and remains one of the most stunning buildings in Iran. The Sheikh Lotfollah Mosque, Shah Abbas' private place of worship, is located on the east side of the square.

The A'li Qapu Palace, home to the Safavid rulers, is on the west side of the square. Set in magnificent gardens, the Palace was made up of many separate pavilions, which served as audience chambers, banqueting halls, and residential apartments for the royal family. On the north side of the square lies the enormous Bazaar Qaisarieh, or Great Bazaar. The bazaar held shops that sold almost every imaginable item, as well as mosques, tea-houses, and banks.

The rest of the city spread out around the maidan, and included religious schools, workshops, inns, shops, public baths, mosques, merchants' mansions, and artisans' dwellings. It is connected to the suburbs of the city by beautiful bridges over the Zayandeh River.

The Sheikh Lotfollah Mosque in Esfahan, Iran, is one of the finest examples of Safavid Iranian architecture. It was built in the early 1600s as a private royal mosque, and a tunnel constructed under the public square allowed private access from the palace.

PEOPLE & PLACES	DOCUMENTS, ART, & ARTIFACTS	WORSHIP & DOCTRINE

EUROPE

1770 British evangelist George Whitefield dies; he is best known for his missionary work in North America, where he is said to have inspired the creation of more than 50 colleges and universities.

1774 English natural philosopher Joseph Priestley is an early supporter of Unitarianism.

1775 After a conclave lasting five months, Cardinal Gianangelo Braschi is elected as Pope Pius VI.

1778 Rousseau and Voltaire, the two leading deists of the age, die within a year of one another.

1783 Mozart writes his celebrated *Mass in C Minor*.

1782 The *Philokalia* is published for the first time in Venice; a collection of spiritual texts written by monks in the Eastern Orthodox tradition over the previous thousand years, the book is profoundly influential in the Orthodox Church.

1783 In Germany, Moses Mendelssohn writes *Jerusalem*, calling for civil rights for Jews in Europe.

1771 John William Fletcher writes *Five Checks to Antimonianism*, a counter to the popular theory that followers of a faith need not obey its rules because salvation is gained by predestination alone.

1773 Pope Clement XIV suppresses the Jesuit Order.

1777 German philosopher Gotthold Lessing formulates the problem of Lessing's Ditch: how can miracles be used as a base of a faith when we have no proof of miracles? "That is the ugly great ditch which I cannot cross, no matter how earnestly I have tried to make that leap."

THE AMERICAS

1770 Father Junipero Serra reaches Monterey and begins to preach to native Californians (📄facing page).

1772 Episcopalian Devereux Jarratt begins to preach; his "circuit" covers some 600 miles in Virginia.

1773 In Bogotá, Colombia, botanist Mutis is charged with heresy for lecturing on Copernican theory.

1774 Mother Ann Lee moves to North America, where she founds the Shaker movement.

1781 Mother Ann Lee leads Shaker missionaries in Massachusetts and Connecticut.

La Parroquia, in San Miguel de Allende, Mexico, is an outstanding example of a Spanish colonial church.

1780 *History of Ancient Mexico* is written by Jesuit Francisco Clavigero, exiled in Italy after the expulsion of the Jesuits from New Spain.

1773 The First Methodist Conference is held in North America.

1776 In New California, Franciscan missionaries make many converts after Spanish pioneers enter the region.

1784 The American Methodist Church formally separates from the Anglican Church.

ASIA & OCEANIA

1772 Hyder Ali, the Muslim leader of Mysore, India, is defeated by a Hindu army.

1778 Hyder Ali takes advantage of fighting between British and French forces in India to attack both the East India Company and his Hindu neighbors.

1782 Hyder Ali dies and is succeeded by his son Tipu Sultan, the "Tiger of Mysore."

1773 In China, the Qianlong emperor orders the compilation of existing books into a vast encyclopedia covering the whole of Chinese knowledge; the 36,381 volumes of the *Siku quanshu* take nine years to compile and include classics of Chinese philosophy such as the *Analects of Confucius*. However, books judged to be hostile to the Manchu dynasty are destroyed, and their owners frequently murdered.

FAITH AND LIFE

Mother Ann Lee

Ann Lee, founder of the Shakers, was born in Manchester in 1736. After an unhappy marriage—all four of her children died in infancy—she began to preach a form of Christianity defined by gender equality and the rejection of marriage and sex. Ann Lee migrated to America in 1774, where her followers became known as the Shakers for their energetic style of prayer. She remained the "mother" of the community until her death in 1784. At their height, there were several thousand Shakers; no doubt as a result of the policy of celibacy, the movement is now extinct.

AFRICA & THE MIDDLE EAST

1772 In Morocco, the ruler Sidi Muhammad II gives Jews senior positions in his diplomatic service.

RELIGION IN THE WORLD	WORLD EVENTS
1772 The Roman Catholic Inquisition is abolished in France. **1781** With the Patent of Tolerations, Emperor Joseph II grants religious freedoms to non-Catholic Christians living in the Habsburg Empire; however, while the patent extends the rights of Jews in the empire, it also takes away much of their autonomy.	**1774** War between the Russians and the Ottoman Empire ends in the Treaty of Kuchuk-Kainarji; territory in the Caucasus and Black Sea region passes to Russian control. **1774** Louis XVI becomes king of France on the death of his grandfather, Louis XV. **1783** The Montgolfier brothers demonstrate their invention of a hot-air balloon to King Louis XVI at Versailles; the first manned balloon flight takes place over Paris later that year.
1774 Isaac Backus protests to the Continental Congress in Philadelphia about tax laws imposed specifically on Baptists. **1776** Presbyterian John Witherspoon, president of Princeton, preaches openly in favor of severing ties with Britain. **1779** In response to moves to make Christianity the established faith in Virgina, Thomas Jefferson proposes a bill in favor of religious freedom and against tax support for churches. **1781** Franciscan monks settle in what is now Los Angeles. **1784** Thomas Coke becomes Methodist superintendent of America, the foundation of the Methodist Episcopal Church.	**1770** British troops shoot five people dead during a riot in Boston. **1775** The Battle of Lexington sees the first exchange of fire in the American Revolutionary War. **1776** The Declaration of Independence is signed by representatives of the 13 colonies on July 4. **1781** British forces in North America Surrender at Yorktown, bringing the fighting in the American Revolutionary War to an end. **1782** Spanish settlers found Los Angeles. **1783** U.S. independence is confirmed by the Treaty of Versailles.
ca 1780 Delhi is captured from the Mogul emperor by the Hindu Mahadji Sindhia (📄 page 241). **1781** The Qing rulers of China put down a Muslim rebellion in Gansu province. **1784** Tipu Sultan imprisons up to 60,000 Christians from Mangalore in southwestern India, mainly for supporting his British enemies, and destroys many Christian churches.	**1770** Explorer James Cook discovers the east coast of Australia and claims it for Britain. **1775** Persia's Shah Karim Khan Zand captures the port of Basra from the Ottomans. **1779** On his third Pacific expedition James Cook is killed in a sudden violent dispute with a group of Islanders in Hawaii.
1777 In Morocco, the enslavement of Christians is abolished.	**1772** The Mamluk sultan of Egypt, Ali Bey, is defeated by the Ottomans.

MISSIONARIES IN NORTH AMERICA

Christian missionaries arrived in the New World from the middle of the 16th century onward. The earliest arrivals were Spanish Franciscan friars, but they were soon joined by Dominicans and Jesuits from across Europe. From 1718 French Catholic missionaries began traveling to Louisiana and Canada.

The Protestant Church started to send missionaries at the end of the 16th century, mainly to the East Coast. As American society became more established on the East Coast throughout the eighteenth century, missionaries headed west to seek converts among Native Americans. Often they met with violence. The Iroquois destroyed Huronia, a Jesuit-built settlement, in 1650 and with it the Jesuit dream of making the Huron Indians the focal point of their evangelism. Other native groups became Christian, however, and actively petitioned church authorities to send them missionaries and priests.

Spanish missionaries preach to Native Americans in California in this contemporary illustration.

The French enlightenment thinker Voltaire was an outspoken opponent of organized religion and superstition. He was forced into exile on several occasions after his remarks angered the political and religious elite.

RELIGION AND THE ENLIGHTENMENT

THE ENLIGHTENMENT WAS A PHILOSOPHICAL MOVE-ment that influenced many aspects of European society and culture in the 18th century, during an era also known as the Age of Reason. Basing their ideas on the principles of rational enquiry into the world, its proponents believed that humankind could follow a path of steady material and spiritual progress that would gradually raise it toward perfection.

Horrified by the widespread violence that religious strife had caused in the 16th and 17th centuries, many scholars sought alternative ways for people to bring meaning and order to their lives. In *An Essay Concerning Human Understanding*, published in 1690, the English philosopher John Locke stated a key principle of the new thinking: he argued that people are not naturally evil and irrational but can be made so by their circumstances. Even when thinkers did not reject religion outright, they claimed for humankind a more personal, natural relationship with God than traditionally allowed by orthodox faiths, with their dogma and hierarchies. In place of miracles and divine revelation, this "deist" view proposed a benign but distant God who had given humans the capacity for reason and empowered them to control their own fate.

The rise of the natural sciences in the 17th century had discredited traditional explanations of the universe. Instead, Enlightenment thinkers put their trust in close observation of natural phenomena and in experiment (a method known as empiricism) to reveal the workings of nature. The English scientist Isaac Newton epitomized the new approach, while personally retaining a deeply religious view of the world.

Along with the challenge to established religion came a demand for social change. French philosophers such as Montesquieu, Voltaire, and Rousseau took the lead in advocating civil liberties, including equality before the law, free speech, and government that obeyed the general will as the basis of a "social contract" between the ruler and the ruled. Modern notions of religious pluralism and racial tolerance also first found a voice; in Germany, for example, the Jewish Enlightenment movement, or Haskalah, called for political emancipation and a strong Hebrew culture.

Toward the end of the 18th century the American and French revolutions adopted many key Enlightenment tenets; yet in France the optimism of the Age of Reason quickly gave way to horrors of the Reign of Terror, plunging Europe into a new cycle of bloodshed and turmoil.

Credulity, Superstition, and Fanaticism, *an engraving by the English artist William Hogarth, is representative of the opinion many Enlightenment thinkers had of religion. It shows a preacher using demons and witches to scare a congregation more interested in more worldly pursuits.*

| | PEOPLE & PLACES | DOCUMENTS, ART, & ARTIFACTS | WORSHIP & DOCTRINE |

EUROPE

1785 British MP William Wilberforce undergoes a conversion experience and becomes an evangelical Christian.

1788 English composer Charles Wesley dies after writing thousands of hymns and carols, including "Hark the Herald Angels Sing."

1791 John Wesley, founder of Methodism, dies.

1794 The French revolutionary Maximilien Robespierre introduces the Cult of the Supreme Being as a state religion based on rational devotion to a deity; the new faith perishes on the guillotine with its creator.

1794 In *The Age of Reason*, English-born Enlightenment writer Tom Paine asserts "My mind is my own church."

1789 Freed slave Olaudah Equiano, living in Europe, publishes an autobiography that details both his past as a slave and his spiritual conversion to Methodist Christianity, influenced by preacher George Whitefield.

1793 The *Philokalia*, a compilation of spiritual texts from the Eastern Orthodox Church, is translated into Slavonic.

1799 German theologian Fredrich Daniel Ernst Schleiermacher, called "the father of modern Protestantism," writes in *Addresses on Religion*: "Religion is the outcome neither of the fear of death, nor of the fear of God. It answers a deep need in man. It is neither a metaphysic, nor a morality, but above all and essentially an intuition and a feeling."

Wolfgang Amadeus Mozart died in 1791 at age 35. Mozart's last work, the Requiem, *was first performed at his memorial service at St. Michael's Church in Vienna a few weeks after his death.*

THE AMERICAS

1786 Isaac Backus estimates that some 40,000 Baptists have deserted to join the Separatist Church.

1786 Canada becomes home to Mennonites moving from central Europe.

1789 President George Washington receives an appeal from Baptists to prevent taxes being used to support other churches.

1790 John Carroll of Baltimore is the first Roman Catholic bishop to be consecrated in North America.

1790s In Mexico, the Virgin of Guadalupe is transformed from an icon of the Catholic Church to a symbol of Creole nationalism.

1785 James Madison writes the *Memorial and Remonstrance against Religious Assessments*.

1798 Politician Thomas Jefferson conceives of a new kind of Bible, which removes its supernatural elements and treats its message as a philosophical system.

ASIA & OCEANIA

1785 The Emerald Buddha Chapel is built in Bangkok, Thailand.

1794 The eunuch Agha Muhammad Qajar establishes his authority over Persia in place of the Zand dynasty.

1785 Korean authorities ban Catholicism.

1797 The first Christian missionaries arrive in the Pacific islands of Tahiti and Tonga.

1799 After the British kill Tipu Sultan, the Christians of Mangalore are freed from their 15-year captivity at Seringapatam in India; of the 60,000 captives, only about one-third remain Christians: many have been forced to convert to Islam.

AFRICA & THE MIDDLE EAST

1786 Ottoman sultan Abdulhamid I strengthens his control in Egypt.

1790 Jews are persecuted in Morocco, mainly as a reaction to their privileged status under the previous ruler, Sidi Muhammad II.

Images of the Virgin of Guadalupe are common features on churches in Mexico.

THE AGE OF REASON

RELIGION IN THE WORLD	WORLD EVENTS

1787 Protestant marriages are legalized in France.

1789 The Estates-General proposes selling off church property in France.

1790 The National Assembly—the revolutionary government of France—forbids the taking of monastic vows.

1791 Half of the French clergy reject the Civil Constitution of the Clergy, which subordinates the church to the revolutionary government and abolishes all religious orders.

1793 During the Reign of Terror in France, revolutionaries implement de-Christianization by eliminating the Roman Catholic Church in favor of a Cult of Reason; many bishops, priests, nuns, and monks are murdered.

1788 The British Parliament regulates the slave trade.

1789 On July 14 the citizens of Paris storm the fortress-prison of the Bastille, regarded as the opening event of the French Revolution (📄 box, right).

1792 France becomes a republic; the French Revolutionary War opens with victories at Valmy (against the Prussians) and Jemappes (against the Austrians).

1793 Louis XVI, deposed king of France, is guillotined by revolutionaries in Paris

1796 An English doctor, Edward Jenner, develops a vaccination against smallpox.

1787 Meeting in Philadelphia, the Constitutional Convention adopts the U.S. Constitution, which is later ratified by all 13 states.

1789 George Washington is elected first U.S. president.

1791 Inspired by the ideals of the French revolution, François Toussaint, a former slave, leads a successful uprising of slaves in Haiti.

This illustration shows missionaries explaining a solar eclipse to a native audience in Thailand.

1789 The French missionary Pigneau de Behaine organizes political and military support to enable Nguyen Anh to establish the Nguyen dynasty in Vietnam.

1796 The White Lotus Rebellion breaks out against the Qing dynasty in China, inspired by the White Lotus secret religious society, which predicts the imminent return of Buddha.

1798 A Sikh kingdom is founded in India by Ranjit Singh, known as the Lion of the Punjab.

1788 The First Fleet of British settlers, including more than 700 convicts, lands at Botany Bay in Australia.

1793 The Wahhabi conquer Riyadh in Arabia, where clerics fill judicial and teaching posts.

1787 The U.S. government pays Morocco $10,000 to stop attacks on its shipping by pirates.

1798 A French force under Napoleon occupies Egypt but is defeated by the British at the Battle of the Nile.

RELIGION AND REVOLUTION

The French Revolution of 1789 brought a profound change to the position of the Catholic Church in France. The original reaction against the *ancien régime* attracted many parish priests who resented the dominant position of the nobility among the senior hierarchy of the church. Advancement for the lower orders was virtually impossible. In addition, many among the clergy had been influenced by some of the anticlerical ideas of the Enlightenment.

Following the Revolution, however, the revolutionaries embarked on a transformation of French society that largely rejected the institution of the church, which was considered to be too closely associated with the landowners of the French aristocracy. In December 1789 the church's vast land holdings were confiscated. By 1790 religious orders had been dissolved, with monasteries and convents closed and monks and nuns encouraged to return to private life. Previously powerful religious institutions, like the abbey at Cluny, were dissolved and their buildings demolished. The 1790 Civil Constitution of Clergy Act made the remaining clergy state employees with set rates of pay and an election system for parish priests and bishops.

A final split between the Revolution and the church came when the National Assembly required bishops and priests to take an oath of allegiance to the Civil Constitution. Many priests—known as non-jurors—refused; they were forbidden from preaching. Those clerics who took the oath, meanwhile, often angered their congregations, who remained conservative in faith. The victims of Reign of Terror between 1793 and 1794 included priests who were massacred and imprisoned as the de-Christianization of France entered its final phase.

In 1800, Napoleon and the Church signed an agreement to restore the Catholic religion. Their rules for the coexistence of the Catholic Church and French state would last until 1905.

RELIGIONS OF AUSTRALIA AND THE PACIFIC

THE NATIVE PEOPLES OF AUSTRALIA, NEW ZEALAND, AND the Pacific Islands were not exposed to foreign cultural influences until the late 18th century, when the first explorers ventured into the Pacific. In this isolation, the indigenous peoples of the vast region developed their own religious beliefs and practices. Reflecting ancient contacts between peoples, however, these religions shared some common characteristics—most importantly the belief that Earth is a sacred place that must be respected.

The Aboriginal peoples of Australia believed that the land was home to invisible spiritual forces and covered in sacred paths of energy known as Songlines. This sacred landscape appeared during a period in the distant past known as Dreamtime, when fantastic half-human, half-animal creatures lived on Earth and shaped the landscape. Dance, song, and ritual were integral to daily life, as were bark paintings that traced the origins of the world. When European settlers colonized Aboriginal ancestral land in the 18th century, forcing the Aborigines into reservations and cities, they precipitated a spiritual crisis.

The myths of Oceania (Polynesia, Micronesia, and Melanesia) reflected island life, with the sea and fishing featuring prominently. In New Zealand, the Maori shared similar beliefs. The Maori trickster god, Maui, was the most important god of the region.

In the Hawaiian Islands, which have the world's highest levels of volcanic activity, the most important deity was Pele, the goddess of volcanoes. The Hawaiians performed daily rituals to try and keep the goddess happy. They believed volcanic activity was a sign of her anger.

Polynesian gods were all responsible for different aspects of daily life. The priests were responsible for mediating with the gods on behalf of the islanders. The priests were also responsible for maintaining the oral tradition of retelling the creation myths and stories of the gods. Such high responsibilities meant that priests occupied an important position in Polynesian society.

Uluru, also known as Ayers Rock, is a holy site for the Aboriginal peoples of Australia, for whom its location at the heart of the continent makes it a central location for the Songlines.

Idols, such as this Polynesian fertility idol, played an important role in the practice of many Pacific Island religions.

PEOPLE & PLACES	DOCUMENTS, ART, & ARTIFACTS	WORSHIP & DOCTRINE

EUROPE

1800 Cardinal Barnaba Chiaramonti is elected Pope Pius VII.

1803 Working in London, U.S. artist Benjamin West paints *Christ Healing the Sick.* commissioned for the first hospital in the United States, in Pennsylvania; it is so successful that British authorities force West to sell it to them to hang in the new National Gallery. West later paints a new version for the hospital.

1809 In "Essay on the Generative Principle of Political Constitutions and Other Institutions," French philosopher Joseph de Maistre argues that constitutions are not created by humankind but come from God.

1804 The British and Foreign Bible Society is founded; the nondenominational charity, which aims to make the Bible available worldwide, is formed in response to the lack of availability of Welsh Bibles in Wales, where a girl reports having to walk 20 miles to buy one.

1806 Napoleon Bonaparte creates the Assembly of Jewish Notables, a consistory to organize Jewish congregations in France.

THE AMERICAS

1800 Elihu Palmer, a former Presbyterian preacher struck blind by yellow fever in 1793, founds *The Temple of Reason*, a newspaper that reflects his deist views.

1805 Joseph Smith, the founder of the Mormons, is born in Vermont.

1807 Northern Irish Presbyterian Thomas Campbell arrives in America to preach religious reform on the Frontier.

1808 Henry Ware becomes professor of divinity at Harvard; he is controversial because of his unitarian beliefs.

Outdoor gatherings, such as this Methodist camp meeting, were a common occurrence during the period known as the Second Great Awakening.

ASIA & OCEANIA

FAITH AND LIFE

William Wilberforce

In 1784 William Wilberforce, a British politician, underwent an evangelical conversion. He renounced his previously dissolute lifestyle and devoted his life to the promotion of moral causes. The newly converted Wilberforce soon became a key figure in the abolitionist movement, lending his political influence—as well as his talents as a public speaker—to the cause. By 1807 Wilberforce had successfully lobbied for a ban on the slave trade, and he was involved in the campaign to made slavery illegal within the British Empire until his death in 1833. The Slavery Abolition Act was passed a year later.

1801 The first major persecution begins of Roman Catholics in Korea.

1807 Robert Morrison becomes the first Protestant missionary in China, although it is still illegal to spread Christianity there.

AFRICA & THE MIDDLE EAST

1802 German philologist Georg Grotefend deciphers Babylonian cuneiform script, allowing scholars to gain a deeper understanding of ancient religions.

1803 With their occupation of the Hejaz in Arabia, the Wahhabi sect take control of the Muslim holy cities of Mecca and Medina (📄 facing page).

1804 In western Sudan, the Fulani religious leader Usman dan Fodio is proclaimed commander of the faithful; he declares jihad—holy war—against neighboring kingdoms where Islam coexists with traditional religions.

RELIGION IN THE WORLD	WORLD EVENTS
1801 Napoleon Bonaparte, First Consul of France, makes a concordat with Pope Pius VII that reestablishes the Roman Catholic Church in France; the "restoration of the altars" reflects Napoleon's belief that religion will add stability to postrevolutionary France.	**1800** Italian scientist Alessandro Volta invents the voltaic pile, the first chemical battery capable of storing electricity.
1804 The Christian Serbs rebel against their Muslim Ottoman rulers.	**1801** Paul I, Tsar of Russia, is murdered by army officers trying to force him to abdicate.
1807 The British Parliament makes the slave trade illegal after lobbying led by evangelical Christian William Wilberforce.	**1804** The English inventor Richard Trevithick designs the first self-propelled steam engine.
1808 Napoleon abolishes the Inquisition in Spain and Italy.	**1805** A British fleet under the command of Admiral Horatio Nelson defeats a combined French and Spanish fleet at the Battle of Trafalgar; Nelson himself is shot and killed.
	1807 Serfdom is abolished in Prussia.

1801 The Second Great Awakening begins in Kentucky; it draws scattered rural worshipers together at long revivalist "camp meetings."	**1803** Through the Louisiana Purchase the United States acquires from France an area including present-day Louisiana, Arkansas, Kansas, Iowa, Nebraska, and parts of Montana and Wyoming.
1801 U.S. Congregationalists and Presbyterians agree on a "plan of union"; the union is dissolved in 1837.	**1804** Jean-Jacques Dessalines makes himself emperor of Haiti; he is assassinated two years later.
1804 A new age of missionary activity in North America begins when Lewis and Clark's journey opens the route to the West.	**1804** Meriwether Lewis and William Clark lead an overland expedition from the great Continental Divide to the Pacific Ocean and back.
1806 Five students at Williams College, Massachusetts, gather at the Haystack Prayer Meeting to discuss missionary work; two years later, one of them, Samuel Mills, forms the first American missionary society.	
1808 Baltimore becomes the first Roman Catholic see in the United States.	

This painting depicts U.S. missionary Robert Morrison and his assistants translating the Bible into Chinese.

1806 Indian soldiers in the British Army at Vellore mutiny against rules that forbid Hindus from wearing religious marks on their foreheads and force Muslims to shave their beards.

1805 In Egypt, Ottoman army officer Muhammad Ali proclaims himself viceroy and begins a long rule marked by reform.

1806 The British capture the Dutch colony at the Cape of Good Hope (South Africa).

THE WAHHABIS OF ARABIA

Wahhabis is the name given to members of a Muslim movement that strictly follows the teachings of the Koran and the example of the life of Muhammad. It was founded by Muhammad ibn 'Abd al-Wahhab (1703–1787) in the 18th century as a puritan movement in Najd, central Arabia (now Saudi Arabia).

Ibn 'Abd al-Wahhab believed that Islam had become corrupted by generations of foreign influence and human weakness. He argued that Muslims should return to a pure form of Islam as it had been practiced by the first few generations after the death of Muhammad. He prohibited the veneration of any Muslim leader, including Muhammad himself, because he saw it as a type of polytheism. He also encouraged the destruction of tombs, shrines, and buildings associated with the early history of Islam in order to prevent them becoming sites of worship in the future. Al-Wahhab also rejected all aspects of contemporary Islamic law derived from analytical or logical reasoning, because such techniques were developed from Greek philosophy. His followers lived austere lifestyles and consulted the scripture for guidance on every aspect of their everyday lives. They called themselves *al-Muwahhidun* (Unitarians) to emphasize their strict monotheism.

Wahhabism has always been linked with the Saudi dynastic family. Following their military victories in Arabia, by the end of the 18th century they controlled all of Najd, as well as occupying Mecca and Medina, two of Islam's holiest cities, in western Arabia. In 1818, the Ottoman sultan ended the first Wahhabi Empire but the faith revived under the Saudi ruler Faisal I. The Rashidiyah of northern Arabia destroyed it for a second time at the end of the 19th century. When Ibn Saud took control of the region and created the Kingdom of Saudi Arabia in 1932, the Wahhabis' religious and political domination was secure.

PEOPLE & PLACES	DOCUMENTS, ART, & ARTIFACTS	WORSHIP & DOCTRINE

EUROPE

1814 Pope Pius VII is freed from virtual captivity after the fall of Napoleon I; he returns to Rome, reinstitutes the Inquisition and the Index of Prohibited Books, brings back the Jesuits, and condemns Protestant missionary activity.

1817 Pius VII commissions the building of the Bracci Nuova ("New Wing") of the Vatican Museum, which now holds antiquities collected by popes for over 300 years.

1810 German artists living in an abandoned monastery in Rome form the Nazarene movement, which encourages a revival of the spirit of medieval religious art as a reaction against neoclassicism.

1817 Former secretary of the Inquisition Juan Llorente publishes *History of the Inquisition in Spain*.

1818 Austrian schoolteacher Franz Xaver Huber writes music to accompany words written by the young curate Joseph Mohr; their song, *Silent Night*, becomes the most famous of all Christmas carols.

1819 Danish sculptor Bertel Thorvaldsen carves *Christ and Twelve Apostles* for Copenhagen Cathedral.

1810 In Geneva, Switzerland, Protestant revivalists found the Société des Amis.

1811 In the "Great Schism," two-thirds of Welsh Protestants leave the Anglican church.

1812 The Hardenberg Reforms emancipate Jews in Prussia.

1815 The Basel Missionary Society is founded in Switzerland.

1817 Lutherans and Calvinists form a unified church in Prussia and other German states.

THE AMERICAS

1816 Circuit rider and joint superintendent of the Methodist Church Francis Ashbury dies, having traveled over 300,000 miles on horseback to preach.

Richard Allen became the first African-American bishop when he was ordained in 1816.

1816 The American Bible Society is founded with the aim to make the Bible available to all people in all languages.

1811 Frontier preacher Thomas Campbell and his colleagues found the Disciples of Christ, which they intend to unite all Christian churches.

1815 Unitarianism—a liberal theology that teaches the oneness of God, rather than the threefold nature of the Trinity—emerges from Congregationalism in the United States.

1816 Richard Allen founds the African Methodist Episcopal church (AME).

1819 The first provincial council of U.S. Catholic bishops is held at Baltimore.

ASIA & OCEANIA

1812 Pomare II, King of Tahiti, becomes a Christian.

1814 Thomas Fanshawe Middleton becomes bishop of Calcutta, the first Anglican bishop anywhere in Asia.

1814 Samuel Marsden, senior Anglican minister in New South Wales, Australia, begins a mission to introduce Christianity to the Maori of New Zealand (pages 254–255).

A missionary preaches to natives in Hawaii in 1823; the Christian churches saw the islands as a highly promising location for missionary activity.

AFRICA & THE MIDDLE EAST

1810 Radama I becomes king of Merina in the highlands of Madagascar; he encourages the spread of mission schools.

1817 The Scottish Congregationalist Robert Moffat arrives in South Africa at the start of over 50 years' missionary work in Africa.

1818 The Christian emperor Tewodros II begins a 50-year rule in Ethiopia; he will later pull a gun on a European missionary who describes him in a book as barbaric, cruel, and unstable.

RELIGION IN THE WORLD	WORLD EVENTS

Will you defend your religion and your rights as true patriots? Long live our Lady of Guadalupe! Death to bad government! Death to the gachupines!

MIGUEL HIDALGO DE COSTILLA, GRITO DE DOLORES

1811 Britain's King George III is declared insane; his son becomes prince regent, marking the start of the Regency period.

1812 Napoleon's army invades Russia and occupies Moscow, but the severe winter weather forces it to retreat; only 10 percent of Napoleon's army survive the journey back to France.

1814 The Dutch outlaw the slave trade.

1814 Napoleon is exiled to the Mediterranean island of Elba. He escapes a year later, but is decisively defeated at the Battle of Waterloo.

THE CHURCH AND MEXICAN INDEPENDENCE

Miguel Hidalgo was a Mexican creole priest who fell foul of the ruling Spanish colonial government because of his interest in the ideas of the Enlightenment. In 1810, Hidalgo joined a group of revolutionaries plotting against the government; when the plot was uncovered, he hastily called for a nationalist uprising. This was the Grito de Dolores (the Cry of Dolores) uttered on September 16, 1810, now celebrated as Mexico's Day of Independence.

Hidalgo's protest did not condemn the monarchy nor the social order of Mexico; instead it criticized the failure of the government in Madrid. In Spain, meanwhile, political conditions had shifted dramatically as Napoleon Bonaparte's army swept away the Iberian rulers.

Hidalgo led a brief uprising but was captured and executed in July 1811. His place was taken by another Roman Catholic priest, José María Morelos, who led a military campaign that set up a short-lived National Constituent Congress; Morelos was himself executed for treason in 1815.

The Grito, Hidalgo's call for self-government, is still acknowledged as the start of the fight for Mexican independence, finally achieved in 1821.

1810 The Grito de Dolores: Mexican priest Miguel Hidalgo de Costilla declares Mexican independence (September 16); he is defeated and executed the following year (📄 box, right).

1810 Nationalist rebels in Mexico use the Virgin of Guadalupe as their standard, proclaiming her the patron saint of the oppressed.

1812 Samuel Mills and his colleagues form the American Board of Commissioners for Foreign Missions, the first U.S. missionary society.

1812 The Second Great Awakening gains impetus from the spiritual upheaval that accompanies the War of 1812 against the British.

1812 The United States declares war on Britain (the War of 1812), citing as the cause the continued blockading of its ports and attacks on its commerce; U.S. forces invade Canada.

1814 British troops burn Washington, D.C., during the War of 1812, which is ended by the Treaty of Ghent, signed in December.

1816 Argentina declares its independence from Spain.

1819 Simón Bolivar frees Colombia from Spanish control.

1813 The renewed charter of the British East India Company makes it easier for missionaries to enter India.

1819 Sikh forces led by Ranjit Singh capture Kashmir from Muslim rule.

1819 British soldiers rediscover second-century Buddhist caves at Ajanta, India, decorated with remarkable carvings and paintings (📄 pages 260–261).

1815 Mount Tambora, a volcano in Indonesia, erupts, killing more than 92,000 people; the explosion throws so much ash into the atmosphere that 1816 will be known as "the year without a summer."

1817 Australia is officially named; earlier the island had been known as New Holland.

1819 A British trading station is founded on the southern tip of the Malay Peninsula; it will develop into the present-day state of Singapore.

1811 The Ottoman emperor sends Muhammad Ali of Egypt to confront the Saud dynasty in the Arabian peninsula.

1814 The Muslim Omanis strengthen their control over the Swahili coast of East Africa.

1817 Usman dan Fodio establishes the Sokoto Caliphate in the Hausa lands.

1818 Shehu Ahmad Lobbo founds an Islamic state in Masina (present-day Mali), with its capital at Hamdallahi.

1816 Shaka becomes king of the Zulus and begins to expand Zulu power in southern Africa.

Father Miguel Hidalgo, a Catholic priest, was one of the key figures in the Mexican independence movement.

REDISCOVERING THE BUDDHIST PAST

FOR A THOUSAND YEARS FROM THE FIRST CENTURY B.C. Buddhism inspired the construction of remarkable monuments throughout South and Southeast Asia. By the time that Westerners reached the region, however, many of these structures had been forgotten by all but local inhabitants. Even they had no knowledge of who had constructed the monuments.

As Europeans spread around the world, these monuments were gradually revealed. In 1819 near the village of Ajanta in southern India, for example, British soldiers hunting tigers discovered caves decorated with Buddhist statues and frescoes. The caves traced the evolution of Buddhist art over eight centuries. Soon artists' re-creations were printed in newspapers and magazines around the world.

On the Indonesian island of Java, meanwhile, another Buddhist monument had come to light. Built between 778 and 850, Borobudur was the largest Buddhist monument in the world. Abandoned when local dynasties turned to Hinduism, the vast stone mountain had been buried under volcanic ash and largely forgotten. Rediscovered in 1814, the monument was cleared through the rest of the century, mainly by Dutch archaeologists. Reconstruction continued until the 1970s, by which time Borobudur had again become a major regional pilgrimage center.

In Cambodia the enormous temple city built by the Khmer at Angkor had never been entirely forgotten, but the site was only popularized by the French explorer Henri Mouhot in the 1860s. Originally constructed as a Hindu monument, Angkor eventually grew to include the Buddhist temple of Bayon, which was decorated with over two hundred delicately carved faces, the Buddhist university Preah Khan, and the temple of Ta Prohm. By the 16th century, following its sacking by the Thais in 1431, Angkor had been largely abandoned to the encroaching jungle. The romance of the jungle-hidden city, with walls covered in massive tree roots, greatly appealed to Western readers.

Detailed carvings such as this one decorate almost every available surface at the magnificent temple complex of Angkor Wat.

Originally Hindu, the main temple complex at Angkor is one of the largest Buddhist monuments in the world. Although it is often described as a "forgotten" holy site, it was well known within the region prior to its rediscovery by the French explorer Henri Mahout in 1860.

PEOPLE & PLACES	DOCUMENTS, ART, & ARTIFACTS	WORSHIP & DOCTRINE

EUROPE

1823 Pius VII dies and is replaced by Annibale de la Genga, reigning as Pope Leo XII.

1827 John Darby founds the Plymouth Brethren, a nondenominational, evangelical Christian group, in Dublin, Ireland.

1829 Composer Felix Mendelssohn rediscovers and revives the *St. Matthew Passion* by Johann Sebastian Bach, exactly 100 years after its first performance.

1820 English poet and artist William Blake completes his illustrations for the Book of Job.

1821 Jean-François Champollion uses the Rosetta Stone to decipher hieroglyphics, opening the way to increased understanding of ancient Egyptian religion.

1823 Ludwig van Beethoven completes his *Missa Solemnis*, one of the most celebrated of all mass settings.

1825 Nazarene artist Johann Overbeck paints *Christ's Entry into Jerusalem*.

1827 Churchman John Keble publishes *The Christian Year*, a volume of devotional poetry that becomes a popular bestseller in Britain.

1820 The Jesuits are expelled from Rome.

1820 Scottish aristocrat and theologian Thomas Erskine tries to reform Calvinism to create a doctrine closer to Calvin's intentions.

ca 1820s In Germany and England the Romantic movement in art and literature seeks spiritual nourishment from heightened feelings in the individual and an admiration of the "sublime" in nature, often with regard to wild, lonely, and mountainous landscapes.

THE AMERICAS

1820 Calvinist Charles Hodge begins a 58-year tenure as president of Princeton Theological Seminary, during which, he boasts, "not one idea entered or left the institution."

1823 Joseph Smith has his first vision of the angel Moroni, the messenger of God who will guide him to found the Church of the Latter Day Saints (Mormons) (📄facing page).

1823 African-American missionary Betsey Jackson begins preaching in the Sandwich Islands.

1829 Ralph Waldo Emerson is ordained at Second Church in Boston.

Indian religious and social reformer Raja Ram Mohan Roy led an influential campaign against the Hindu caste system and traditional practices that discriminated against women.

1820 Christian missionaries arrive in Hawaii and Tonga.

1824 The Sunday School Union is founded in the United States.

1826 Among the newly independent states of Latin America, religious orders are widely suppressed, in part as a reaction to the Roman Catholic Church's support for the Spanish monarchy against nationalist movements; liberals in many countries develop a wider distrust of official religion.

ASIA & OCEANIA

1825 The queen of Tonga, Kaahumanu, is a notable convert to Christianity.

1826 The ruler of Bareli in northern India calls on Indian Muslims to launch a jihad, or holy war, against the Sikhs.

1827 The intrepid Cynthia Farrar leaves Boston to become a missionary in India.

1821 Joshua Marshman publishes the first Chinese translation of the Bible after 15 years' work.

1828 David Collie, a missionary at Malacca, Indonesia, translates the Four Books of classical Chinese philosophy into English.

1825 As Sandwich Islanders are baptized, a U.S. missionary proclaims "It is Millennium"; others speculate that the new reign of Christ might begin in the Pacific Islands.

1828 The British in India forbid the Hindu practice of *suttee*, the forced cremation of a living widow with her husband's body.

AFRICA & THE MIDDLE EAST

1820 Scots Congregationalist minister John Philip arrives in South Africa, where he becomes one of the most celebrated missionaries of the age.

1821 Patriarch Gregory V of Constantinople is hanged by the Ottoman Turks for his failure to prevent a violent Greek uprising against Ottoman rule.

We are well satisfied to stay where wisdom abounds and the gospel is free.

RICHARD ALLEN

1820 American Protestants arrive in Lebanon to seek converts, but they face strong resistance from the Maronite Christians, members of the Eastern Orthodox Church, who already live there.

RELIGION IN THE WORLD RELIGION IN THE WORLD	WORLD EVENTS

1821 The Vatican makes a concordat with Prussia for the reform of Catholicism in the state.

1825 Under French law, sacrilege becomes a capital offense.

1829 In Britain the Catholic Relief Act completes the process of Roman Catholic emancipation: Catholics can now become members of Parliament (although they cannot become monarchs).

1821 The Greeks begin a war of independence against Ottoman rule: they gain full independence in 1832.

1825 The world's first railroad, the Stockton and Darlington Railway, opens in northern England; regular passenger service begins five years later.

1829 The Ottoman Empire recognizes the Greeks' right to rule themselves (although full independence is not granted until 1832).

1822 Inspired by the 1791 revolution in Haiti and angered that authorities have closed his branch of the African Methodist Episcopal Church, Denmark Vesey plans a slave revolt in South Carolina; the plan leaks and Vesey and others are hanged.

1825 Welsh philanthropist Roger Owen buys land in Indiana to found New Harmony, a community in which he hopes an ideal environment will promote sound morality.

1827 Methodist Richard Allen objects to the work of the colonization movement, which seeks to resettle freed slaves in Africa, mainly in the new colony of Liberia, purchased for the purpose.

1829 Catholics begin to found parochial schools throughout the American West.

1821 Mexico wins independence from Spain.

1822 Brazil gains its independence from Portugal.

1823 U.S. President James Monroe recognizes the newly independent states of Latin America and warns against further European interference in the Americas (the Monroe Doctrine).

1820 When Minh Manh becomes emperor of Vietnam, he revives Confucianism: one consequence is a wave of persecutions against Christians.

1825 Muslims in Java, Indonesia, revolt against Dutch rule; the uprising lasts until 1830.

1828 The Brahmo Samaj, a reformist Hindu group dedicated to the worship of Brahma, holds its first meetings in Kolkata, India.

1828 Mahmud II introduces Western dress in an attempt to modernize the Ottoman Empire.

THE COMING OF THE MORMONS

In the early 19th century a new Christian movement emerged in the United States. The Latter Day Saints, more commonly known as Mormons, followed the teachings of Joseph Smith, Jr. (1805–1844), who was revered as a prophet.

Smith told how, in 1823, an angel named Moroni revealed to him the existence of a set of golden plates. These plates held the history of the ancient peoples of America. Four years later, the angel translated them while Smith wrote down the translation. In 1830, he published the translation as the Book of Mormon. He then founded the Church of Christ in New York.

Smith drew many of his beliefs from the Hebrew Bible and his followers believed he was a prophet to whom God gave direct instructions. In 1835, he published the first 65 revelations in the Book of Commandments.

With his converts, Smith relocated to Kirtland, Ohio, before moving west and settling in Illinois in 1839. There he founded Nauvoo, which soon became the second largest city in the state after Chicago. When a local newspaper attacked his ideas, such as polygamy, Smith ordered its destruction. He was arrested for promoting a riot and was killed by a mob in 1844 while awaiting trial.

This painting shows Joseph receiving the golden tablets from the Angel Moroni in the woods near his home in Manchester, New York.

O great one, I salute you

O great one, I salute you

O great one, I salute Elegua Eshu on the road.

SANTERÍA PRAYER

AFRICAN RELIGIONS IN THE AMERICAS

THE AFRICANS FORCIBLY REMOVED FROM THEIR CONTINENT and sold into slavery in the New World were usually forced to convert to the Christian religions of their masters. Often, however, the slaves continued to follow the religions with which they were familiar from home, even if they had to practice in secret, perhaps late at night. Eventually elements from both traditions were brought together to form new faiths, a process known as syncretism. The syncretic faiths still attract devotees in the Americas today.

In Brazil and Cuba, two somewhat different religions emerged from the faith of the Yoruba of West Africa. In Brazil, Candomblé emerged at the start of the 19th century, mixing African beliefs in spirits and ancestor worship with Catholic beliefs. It was also known as Sango, the name of the Yoruba god of thunder. In Cuba, the Afro-Cuban syncretic religion known as Santería has one supreme being and hundreds of lesser gods or orisas. Followers believe that the spirits (orisas) have the power to mediate with god on people's behalf. Yoruba gods are identified with Christian saints: Sango is paired with Saint Barbara, while Obatala is Our Lady of Mercy. Elegua Eshu is at one and the same time a personification of death, the god who grants people good or ill fortune, and the god of travelers and roads, particularly crossroads.

Possibly the most famous of the syncretized religions is Haiti's voodoo, which again included Yoruba traditions but now combined with influences from two other African peoples: the Fon of what is now Benin and the Kongo of what are now Zaire and Angola. The influence of Catholicism is reflected in voodoo's emphasis on ritual and image rather than in its theology. Voodoo is notorious for its supposed belief that the dead can be raised as zombies. While this is a minor aspect of worship, respect for the dead and ancestors does have a crucial role in voodoo, as does a belief in the supernatural.

A house in Havana, Cuba, is decorated with motifs associated with Santería. The syncretic religions of the Americas often use abstract symbols as elements in their worship.

PEOPLE & PLACES	DOCUMENTS, ART, & ARTIFACTS	WORSHIP & DOCTRINE

EUROPE

1832 German philosopher Karl Krause dies as his philosophy of panentheism is beginning to attract attention: it proposes that God is in everything in the Universe but also contains the Universe—a combination of theism and pantheism.

1833 Churchman Edward Bouverie Pusey associates himself with the leaders of the so-called Oxford Movement.

1834 German historian Leopold von Ranke writes *The Roman Popes* (as a Protestant, he is barred from the Vatican archives). Catholics condemn his colorful portrayal of the Counter-Reformation as biased; his fellow Protestants complain that it is too neutral.

1835 German theologian David Strauss causes controversy with his *Life of Jesus*, which portrays Christ as a historical rather than divine figure; one critic calls it "the most pestilential book ever vomited out of the jaws of Hell."

1832 The Serbian Orthodox Church becomes autonomous.

1833 The Oxford Movement in Britain begins to introduce reforms to the Anglican Church (📄 facing page).

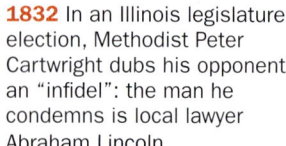

Presbyterian minister Lyman Beecher found himself at the center of a theological controversy after he refused to allow African Americans to study at his seminary.

THE AMERICAS

1832 In an Illinois legislature election, Methodist Peter Cartwright dubs his opponent an "infidel": the man he condemns is local lawyer Abraham Lincoln.

1834 Theological student John Humphrey Noyes declares himself free of sin and begins to preach a doctrine of Perfectionism.

1837 Mary Lyon founds the Mount Holyoke Female Seminary in Massachusetts.

1838 Francis Norbert Blanchet arrives in Oregon Territory and becomes the first Catholic archbishop of what is now Portland.

1836 Angelina Grimké writes *Appeal to the Christian Women of the United States*, against slavery.

1836 Orestes Brownson publishes *New Views of Christianity, Society, and the Church*.

1836 Ralph Waldo Emerson writes *Nature*, the founding document of the Transcendentalists (📄 pages 270–271).

1838 Ralph Waldo Emerson gives a notorious lecture at Harvard in which he criticizes the "exaggeration" of Jesus' role in Christianity.

1830 Joseph Smith and his supporters form the Church of Jesus Christ of Latter-day Saints (Mormons) (📄 page 263).

1830 The magazine *Protestant* is founded to lead a Nativist crusade against Catholics.

1832 The Disciples of Christ preach a return to a primitive form of Christianity.

1834 Methodist brothers Jason and Daniel Lee join a wagon train to preach to the Flathead in Oregon.

1836 New England intellectuals found the Transcendental Club in Massachusetts.

1837 Presbyterians split into New School and Old School factions, based partly on opposing views of slavery.

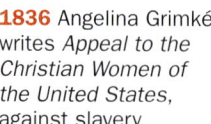

ASIA & OCEANIA

1831 The king of Tonga, George Tupou I, is baptized as a Christian.

1834 Sikhs in northern India capture the city of Peshawar on the Northwest Frontier from the Afghans.

1836 Ramakrishna, later a Hindu saint, is born in India.

If the stars should appear one night in a thousand years, how would men believe and adore, and preserve for many generations the remembrance of the city of God which had been shown!

RALPH WALDO EMERSON, *NATURE*

AFRICA & THE MIDDLE EAST

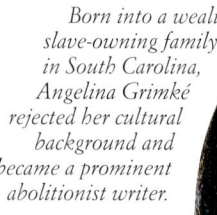

Born into a wealthy slave-owning family in South Carolina, Angelina Grimké rejected her cultural background and became a prominent abolitionist writer.

1834 The Egyptian governor of Syria, Ibrahim Pasha, provokes a Muslim revolt when he extends conscription into the army, previously limited to poorer sections of society.

1835 Ibrahim Pasha orders the rebuilding of synagogues in Jerusalem.

1838 Thousands of enslaved Africans, most of whom are Muslims, are emancipated in Sierra Leone.

RELIGION IN THE WORLD	WORLD EVENTS
1839 Pope Gregory XVI issues a bull condemning slavery.	**1834** Slavery is abolished throughout the British Empire. **1834** A five-year civil war erupts in Spain between Carlists (followers of Don Carlos) and the supporters of Isabella II over the disputed succession to the throne. **1837** Victoria becomes queen of Great Britain, beginning a reign that will last 64 years.
1833 Congregationalism loses its status as an official religion in Massachusetts, the last U.S. church to be disestablished. **1834** Nativist rioters burn down a Catholic (Ursuline) convent in Charlestown, Boston. **1834** Students quit Lane Theological Seminary over Lyman Beecher's refusal to admit African Americans. **1837** Samuel Morse sends the first telegraph message from Washington, D.C., to Baltimore, Maryland: "What hath God wrought!" **1839** As a result of requests from local Native Americans to Washington, Catholic priest Pierre Jean de Smet is sent to preach in Oregon Territory.	**1831** Nat Turner leads a slave revolt in Virginia that leaves around 60 white Americans dead. In the aftermath 56 slaves associated with the rebellion are executed and many more are killed by vigilante mobs. **1836** Texas wins independence from Mexico in a war that ends at the Battle of San Jacinto; at the Alamo mission 188 defenders hold out against a Mexican army for 11 days before being overwhelmed. **1837** Two separate revolts break out against British rule in Canada, led by Louis Papineau in Lower Canada and William McKenzie in Upper Canada; both are put down.
1836 The first bishops arrive in Australia, representing the Roman Catholic and Anglican churches.	**1838** British forces invade Afghanistan and capture the emir, Dost Muhammad.

The Alamo Mission in San Antonio, Texas, was the site of a famous siege of Texan patriots by the Mexican army.

THE OXFORD MOVEMENT

The most influential force in 19th-century Anglicanism took its name from the University of Oxford, where its leaders were also leading clergy. The Oxford Movement aimed to revive aspects of Roman Catholic practice and ritual within the Anglican Church, which they believed had become too secularized and bland. They saw the Anglican Church as being one of three branches of the one true church, along with the Roman Catholic and Eastern Orthodox churches.

The emergence of the Oxford Movement was prompted by a change in British law that allowed Roman Catholics to hold high office previously barred to them. The passing of these new laws between 1828 and 1832 seemed to threaten the primacy of Anglicanism; the possibility of disestablishing the Church of England temporarily seemed very real.

To affirm the legitimacy of the Church of England, a small group of theologians set out to show that it could trace its roots back to Jesus' apostles. Their main ideas were recorded in *Tracts for the Times* (1833–1841), written by the deacon of Christ Church College, John Henry Newman. (Newman later became a high-profile convert to Roman Catholicism.) The people who supported the ideas outlined by Newman became known as the Tractarians. They emphasized the teachings of the early church before it split into Catholicism and Anglicanism during the Reformation of the 16th century.

The Oxford Movement's influence was felt across the Church of England. It prompted the inclusion of more ceremonial and ritual elements in church services, the establishment of monasteries for men and women, and the provision of more theological education for the clergy.

PEOPLE & PLACES	DOCUMENTS, ART, & ARTIFACTS	WORSHIP & DOCTRINE

EUROPE

1841 Henry Venn becomes secretary of the Church Missionary Society: he is largely responsible for the idea that missionaries are temporary visitors whose aim should be to create "indigenous churches."

1843 John Henry Newman preaches his last sermon as an Anglican, "On the Parting of Friends"; two years later he is received into the Roman Catholic Church.

1844 German political philosopher Karl Marx observes, "Religion is the opium of the people."

1840 The first Mormon missionaries arrive in England.

1843 In the "Scottish Disruption," a decade of controversy within the established Church of Scotland over relations with the state ends with the creation of the Free Church of Scotland by some 450 dissident ministers.

1846 The Evangelical Alliance is founded in London as a charitable organization to support the activities of evangelical Christians in Britain.

THE AMERICAS

1843 Joseph Smith announces that God has instructed him to practice polygamy.

1844 Joseph Smith is killed by a mob in Illinois.

1845 Henry David Thoreau moves to Walden Pond, where he practices simple living and yoga, and reads the *Bhagavad Gita* and Chinese and Persian scriptures (📖 pages 270–271).

1847 Henry Ward Beecher becomes minister at Plymouth Church, Brooklyn, where he earns a national reputation for his successful attempts to make religion more "everyday."

Rebels besiege a town in China during the Taiping Rebellion, which broke out late in 1850; the civil war's origins lay in the 1840s, particularly in China's humiliating defeat at the hands of the British in the First Opium War.

1843 "The Great Disappointment": when the Second Coming predicted by Adventist William Miller fails to occur, he revises his prediction to 1844 … again unsuccessfully.

1845 Both Baptists and Methodists in the U.S. South split from their northern churches, in part over attitudes toward slavery.

1846 The Methodist mission in Oregon ends, having cost $250,000 without making a single recorded convert.

1846 Bohemian rabbi Isaac Mayer Wise arrives in the United States, where he becomes a leader of Reform Judaism.

1849 The Disciples of Christ hold their first national convention.

ASIA & OCEANIA

1842 George Augustus Selwyn becomes the first Anglican bishop of New Zealand.

1843 The emirs of Sind and Punjab are defeated by Charles Napier of the British East India Company.

MONUMENTS OF FAITH

Joshua Trees

In the deserts of the Southwest Joshua trees grow scattered across thousands of square miles of forbidding landscape. For Mormons heading west in the mid-19th century, the tree's contorted branches recalled the Israelite leader Joshua stretching his arms out to heaven during prayer. The imagery was comforting to them. Forced from several settlements by local hostility, the Mormons drifted constantly westward, reminded by their leaders that their predicament was comparable with the struggles of the Israelite tribes in the Bible.

AFRICA & THE MIDDLE EAST

1840 Scot David Livingstone arrives in Africa in the footsteps of his father-in-law, missionary Robert Moffat.

1840 Judah Alkalai, a rabbi in Bosnia, first suggests the idea of a Jewish homeland, beginning the modern idea of Zionism.

1849 David Livingstone sends his family to the United Kingdom as he plans to travel deeper into the African interior on his mission.

1844 Nationalist Ilija Garasanin formulates a plan to increase Serb influence in the Balkans by encouraging dissatisfaction among Christians in the Ottoman Empire.

1847 In Switzerland the Sonderbund War breaks out between conservative and liberal cantons in response to liberal moves to reduce the power of the Catholic Church.

1848 During a liberal revolution in Rome, Pope Pius IX flees briefly to Genoa; revolutionaries declare a Roman republic.

1845 A potato blight causes a famine in Ireland that will claim the lives of around a million people and drive many more into exile over the next decade.

1848 Slavery is abolished in France and all of its territories.

1848 Liberal uprisings take place in many countries across Europe, including Italy, France, Germany, Austria, and Hungary. In France, King Louis Philippe hands over power to the Second Republic.

1842 The American Protestant Movement is founded to promote Nativist politics that exclude non-Protestant immigrants.

1842 Nativists in Philadelphia riot for three days to protest Catholics being given the right to translate their own Bible.

1846 Hoping to escape persecution, Brigham Young leads the Mormons westward.

1846 The Mexican War encourages fears of a worldwide Catholic conspiracy.

1848 The headquarters of the Mormon church is established in Salt Lake City, Utah.

1848 Spiritualism enjoys a popular vogue in the United States.

1845 The United States annexes Texas.

1846 Hostilities break out when the United States and Mexico fail to reach agreement on the purchase of New Mexico; Mexican forces are routed at the battles of Palo Alto and Resaca.

1848 The Mexican War ends with the United States gaining all lands north of the Rio Grande—California, Arizona, and New Mexico.

1849 Harriet Tubman escapes from slavery; she later returns to the South a number of times to lead more than 300 slaves to freedom on the so-called Underground Railroad, a secret route to freedom in the North.

1844 An imperial edict allows the Catholic Church to start operating again in China.

1845 The First Anglo-Sikh War breaks out when Sikh forces invade British territory in northern India; the conflict ends in 1846.

1849 At the end of the Second Anglo-Sikh War, the British capture Sind and Punjab.

1840 Britain and China fight the First Opium War after Chinese authorities order the destruction of a large consignment of the drug. The war ends two years later with Britain seizing the city of Hong Kong.

1842 At the end of the First Afghan War, the British withdraw from Kabul after a native revolt: of the original 60,000 invaders, only 121 survive the retreat.

1840 Western missionaries, including the renowned German Johann Ludwig Krapf, are expelled from Abyssinia (Ethiopia).

1841 The Africa Civilization Society begins a mission along the Niger River.

1847 The Catholic archbishopric of Abyssinia is created.

1847 Liberia in western Africa, founded as a colony for freed slaves from the United States, becomes independent.

1840s Non-Muslims under Ottoman rule get more rights as part of the reform process known as Tanzimat, an attempt to modernize and strengthen the empire.

EXISTENTIALISM

The Danish philosopher and theologian Søren Kierkegaard (1813–1855), a nonpracticing ordained minister, believed that the Christian Church in Denmark was the root of many of his society's ills.

Kierkegaard believed that it was an individual's responsibility to give their life meaning. His writings dealt with the reality of living over abstract thinking. Kierkegaard's belief in the absurdity of life, discussed in *Begrebet Angst*, underpins the concept of existentialism. Although the philosopher never used the term existentialism, Kierkegaard is regarded as the father of the movement.

Broadly defined, existentialism has at its root a belief in the absurdity of life. Unlike Christianity, it argues that life has no meaning and that moral authority comes from the individual, not from God. Kierkegaard's writings inspired many other philosophers and writers, including Friedrich Nietzsche, Albert Camus, and Jean Paul Sartre.

THE TRANSCENDENTAL MOVEMENT

TRANSCENDENTALISM IS THE NAME GIVEN TO A MOVEMENT that originated in New England in the middle of the 19th century. Both religious and literary in its influence, the movement is often said to have been the creation of the U.S. essayist, philosopher, and poet Ralph Waldo Emerson, who believed that everything was closely connected with God and that therefore everything was divine.

In 1836, Emerson published anonymously the essay *Nature*, in which he spelled out the philosophy of transcendentalism and laid out a new approach that was dubbed America's "intellectual Declaration of Independence." The essay championed individual experience of the natural world as the primary means of achieving spiritual communion with God. Emerson drew some of his ideas from the German philosopher Immanuel Kant, who had described "all knowledge transcendental which is concerned not with objects but with our mode of knowing objects." In addition to turning to German idealism, Emerson also looked to the ancient Sanskrit texts—the Vedas—and English Romanticism. The new philosophy gained a formal shape when Emerson and his followers founded the Transcendental Club.

The movement was a protest against the state of U.S. society, with its emphasis on intellectualism and Unitarianism and the values of their elders. Instead it was based on intuition and looked beyond the Christian Bible to Hindu and Buddhist scripts. Its core belief was that someone should live in an ideal spiritual state that "transcends" any physical and empirical state. Rather than living by the doctrines of established religion, individuals should use their intuition to guide them. To Emerson, God did not need to reveal the truth: it came from nature and daily life. As he said, "What is popularly called Transcendentalism among us, is Idealism; Idealism as it appears in 1842."

Emerson later refined transcendentalism to argue that a spark of divinity exists within every person. The individual soul is identical to the world soul, so that everything in the world is a microcosm of existence. In 1840 Emerson, along with Margaret Fuller, started the Transcendentalists' own journal, *The Dial*. Following Fuller's death in a shipwreck in 1850, however, Emerson lost faith in transcendentalism and believed the movement was dying out.

Walden Pond was the idyllic rural location where Emerson's follower Henry David Thoreau lived for several years. It was his simple life here that informed many of his ideas about nature and philosophy.

DOES RELIGION HAVE A PLACE IN AN INDUSTRIAL WORLD WHERE CROWDED cities, mechanical labor, and mass production have replaced the intimate, personal, and sensitive? Is it the job of faith to interfere in areas that are usually the preserve of politics to try to ameliorate the suffering of the poor? Such debates were central to faith in the United States and Europe in the late 19th and early 20th century. The Social Gospel movement preached that it was the church's responsibility to tackle the worst excesses of a society that showered riches on the few and poverty and misery on the many. The Salvation Army was one among many faith-based organizations that emerged to combine charitable works with moral improvement.

The U.S. experience was complicated in many ways. First was the split between Northern and Southern churches, which widened largely over their respective attitudes toward slavery but were deepened by the Civil War and the aftermath of Reconstruction. The split continued into the 20th century over race. Second was the rich mix of religions in the country, which was increased by immigration from the largely Catholic countries of southern and southeastern Europe, while Asian immigrants began to practice Buddhism, Hinduism, and other faiths on a smaller scale. But the pattern for U.S. religion had been settled: a mainly Protestant country with a sizable, largely urban Catholic minority supplemented by emigration from southern Europe and from Mexico.

The frontier of the "Wild West" was declared closed in 1893 and the United States fully settled; in 1908 the Vatican declared that Catholicism in the United States would no longer be administered by the church department responsible for missionary activity. Followers of the traditional religions of Native Americans, meanwhile, were converted or driven from their ancestral lands and holy places. The last stand of native faiths was the Ghost Dance, a movement that combined spiritual religion with political desperation as native prophets preached a future in which the burden of dispossession would be lifted from the peoples of North America. The Ghost Dance perished with the killing of a Sioux band by U.S. troops at Wounded Knee in 1890.

Everywhere Islam was in occlusion: in Africa and Asia the religion was often associated with the victims of Europe's rampant imperialism. The high points of Muslim culture belonged to the past. The Ottoman Empire of Turkey was in a terminal decline that ended in defeat in World War I. In India, the Raj brought together the majority Hindus and the minority Muslims and Sikhs under British rule. The period began with religious tensions contributing in 1857 to the outbreak of the Indian Mutiny by native soldiers of the British Army; it ended in 1947 with the partition of South Asia into

The 31st Ohio Volunteers listen to a sermon from their chaplain at a camp in Kentucky during the Civil War in 1861.

Gandhi (right) clasps the shoulder of Muhammad Ali Jinnah, leader of the All India Muslim League at a meeting about India's future in September 1944.

two independent states: mainly Hindu India and mainly Muslim Pakistan (which itself later split again into Pakistan and Bangladesh). India's struggle for independence was led by one of the most remarkable individuals of the 20th century. A lawyer by training, Mohandas Gandhi became the spiritual leader of Indian independence through his philosophy of nonviolence. Gandhi envisioned Hindus and Muslims living together, but Muslims wary of their weak position in a Hindu country insisted on the creation of Pakistan. The actual partition was achieved only with great violence and the deaths of up to a million victims—among them Mahatma ("Great Soul") Gandhi himself, assassinated by a fanatical Hindu in 1948.

As ever, there were those who sought spiritual consolation in smaller branches of faith, including historically questionable throwbacks to the ancient religions of the druids and others. The large-scale casualties of World War I sparked a rise of interest in spiritualism, inspired by people's desperation to contact dead loved ones. In the United States, meanwhile, variations on Christianity appeared, including the Christian Scientists and what would later become the Jehovah's Witnesses; Americans were also attracted for the first time to the intensely personal spiritual messages of Buddhist and Hindu philosophy, as encapsulated by the renowned U.S. monk Thomas Merton, whose spiritual journey led him to Trappist isolation.

Previous pages Pilgrims gather at the holy city of Varanasi to bathe in the waters of the Ganges, which is sacred to Hindus, who venerate the river in the form of a goddess. Bathing in the river is believed to help Hindus to break the endless cycle of regeneration to ascend to heaven.

A statue of Buddha gazes serenely over Borobudur on Java, Indonesia. Having been rediscovered by Dutch colonial officials in 1814, the great monument remained relatively obscure until the middle of the 19th century, when it was surveyed and became the subject of a first monograph.

	1850	1860	1870	1880	1890
EUROPE	**1850** The Roman Catholic hierarchy is reestablished in England and Wales. **1854** Pope Pius IX establishes the Immaculate Conception of the Virgin Mary as an article of the Catholic faith. **1859** Charles Darwin writes the influential *On the Origin of Species*, proposing a theory of evolution by adaptation.	**1864** Pope Pius IX causes controversy with his deeply conservative encyclical *Quanta Cura* and its attached "Syllabus of Errors": the document condemns democracy, socialism, the separation of church and state, and freedom of conscience.	**1870** The First Vatican Council promulgates the decree of papal infallibility. **1878** Former Methodist minister William Booth founds the Salvation Army. **1878** German politician Heinrich von Treitschke becomes an outspoken antisemitic critic of Jewish influence in Germany's history.	**1881** Jews are persecuted in Russia. **1881** The Vatican archives are opened to scholars researching church history. **1883** In his novel *Thus Spake Zarathustra*, German writer Freidrich Nietzsche describes what he terms "the death of God."	**1891** The Russian government forces thousands of Jews from Moscow to live in ghettos. **1894** Jewish army captain Alfred Dreyfus is found guilty of treason by a French court-martial in a trial that exposes antisemitic prejudice throughout the French establishment; he is eventually pardoned in 1906 after a long campaign.
THE AMERICAS	**1852** Harriet Beecher Stowe publishes *Uncle Tom's Cabin*. **1857** The Utah War breaks out between Mormons and federal forces when the U.S. government attempts to limit Mormon governance and the practice of polygamy.	**1863** Ellen Gould White founds the Seventh-Day Adventists. **1864** The motto "In God We Trust" first appears on U.S. coins. **1868** Isaac Leeser founds Maimonides College in Philadelphia, the first Jewish seminary in the Americas.	**ca 1870** The Paiute prophet Wodziwob develops the first, brief-lived Ghost Dance. **1876** T. H. Huxley makes a lecture tour of the United States promoting his doctrine of agnosticism. **1879** Mary Baker Eddy founds the Church of Christ, Scientist. **1879** Crawford H. Toy is forced to resign from the Southern Baptist Convention for his support of Darwinism as a "truth revealed by God."	**ca 1880** The African Methodist Episcoplian Church has about 400,000 members. **1885** American Judaism formally splits into Reform and Counter-Reform branches. **1889** The Paiute seer Wovoka has a vision in which he sees all Whites driven from America; the vision will become the basis of the Ghost Dance movement.	**1890** In their efforts to gain statehood for Utah, Mormons formally abolish polygamy. **1890** The Sioux convert to the Ghost Dance; the Bureau of Indian Affairs makes its first efforts to limit the movement. **1895** Pope Leo XIII advocates the union of church and state in the United States: non-Catholics already distrust his alleged attempts to gain control of the public schools.
ASIA & OCEANIA	**1851** State support of religion is ended in South Australia. **1857** The Indian Mutiny breaks out when native soldiers in Britain's Indian Army refuse to use new rifle cartridges said to be covered with pig and cattle grease, taboo to Muslims and Hindus, respectively.	**1864** After China's Taiping Rebellion, Buddhism has been destroyed to such an extent that the faith has to be reintroduced to China from Japan. **1865** The China Inland Mission is founded.	**1871** The Fifth Buddhist Council meets in Mandalay, Myanmar. **1873** Diplomatic pressure from Western countries ends open persecution of Christians in Japan.	**ca 1880** Acharya Rajendrasuri begins a reform movement within Jainism. **1884** The first permanent Protestant missionary arrives in Korea. **1886** The Indian mystic Ramakrishna dies after establishing a following for his individual form of Hinduism.	**1896** Nepalese archaeologists rediscover the great stone pillar of Asoka at Lumbini. **1898** The first Protestant missionaries arrive in the Philippines. **1899** Anglicans form the first "Bush Brotherhood," to preach to settlers in the Australian Outback.
AFRICA & THE MIDDLE EAST	**1852** In Jerusalem the Church of the Holy Sepulcher is permanently divided among six Christian churches, each with strictly demarcated and jealously guarded areas inside (the key to the main door has been looked after by two Muslim families since 1192).	**1860** The Russian Orthodox Church founds a monastery in Jerusalem. **1861** Abdul Aziz becomes Ottoman sultan and opens the empire to Western influences. **1865** The Bible is published in an Arabic language translation.	**1873** Johannes IV comes to the throne of Ethiopia and continues to try to reconstruct the Christian empire there. **1878** In Buganda—part of modern-day Uganda—King Mutesa encourages infighting among Catholic, Protestant, and Islamic missionaries.	**1882** The "First Aliyah," a wave of Jewish settlement, begins in Ottoman Palestine: some 30,000 European and Yemeni Jews arrive in the next 20 years. **1886** The Muslim visionary Jamal ad-Din al-Afghani is invited by the Persian shah to participate in government, but the alliance is shortlived.	**1891** Muslim visionary Jalal ad-Din al-Afghani is expelled from Persia for constant criticism of the Shah. **1895** The Ottomans begin a series of massacres of Christian Armenians living in Turkey; about 200,000 people will die. **1896** A follower of Jamal ad-Din al-Afghani murders Persian shah Nasr al-Din.

1900	1910	1920	1930	1940–1949
1903 Anti-Jewish pogroms take place in Russia. **1904** Historian Max Weber defines the "Protestant work ethic" as being instrumental to the growth of the European economy in the early modern world. **1907** Pope Pius X issues the encyclical *Pascendi*, which condemns all aspects of "Modernism," including secularism and modern philosophy.	**1917** The British government indicates in the Balfour Declaration its support for the future creation of a Jewish homeland in Palestine. **1918** The new revolutionary Soviet government in Russia issues a decree separating church and state; it soon becomes clear that the church is to be subjugated by the state.	**1920** The first ecumenical council brings together European, American, and Eastern churches. **1928** In the encyclical *Mortalium Animos*, Pope Pius XI argues that Christian churches cannot form a broad federation, but that all other churches should rejoin the Roman Catholic Church.	**1933** The Nazis in Germany create a new "national" church, the German Evangelical Church, which will draw the church and state together. **1938** On *Kristallnacht*, the Night of Broken Glass, Nazis attack Jewish homes, synagogues, and businesses.	**1940** In Warsaw, 350,000 Polish Jews are forced into a ghetto. **1942** Nazi leader Reinhard Heydrich reveals his plan to exterminate 11 million Jews in the "final solution." **1943** German pastor Dietrich Bonhoeffer, a founder of the Confessing Church, is arrested for his part in the plot to assassinate Adolf Hitler; he is hanged in 1945.
1900 The Catholic Church in the United States claims about 12 million members. **1900** An estimated 97 percent of Lutheran congregations in the Midwest use German or other non-English languages for prayer. **1905** Soyen Shaku becomes the first Zen Buddhist teacher in the United States when he spends a year in San Francisco.	**1915** U.S. Secretary of State William J. Bryan resigns, saying that president Wilson's warlike stance toward World War I "does not befit the greatest Christian nation." **1919** The Eighteenth Amendment introduces Prohibition in the United States; William J. Bryan remarks, "Let the world rejoice. The greatest moral reform of the generation has been accomplished."	**1922** Harvard faculty reject a proposal from the president and students to limit the number of Jewish students in the university. **1928** In the face of rising antisemitism, U.S. Christians and Jews form the National Conference of Christians and Jews. **1929** A Methodist periodical—*The Christian Advocate*—argues that enforcing Prohibition is the single most pressing requirement in the United States.	**1932** William Joseph McGlothlin, president of the Southern Baptist Convention, refuses to accept an honor from the black moderator of a Baptist association in Rochester, New York. **1938** Radio preacher Charles Coughlin defends the Nazi treatment of the Jews and calls for the creation of a Christian Front to protect the United States from Jewish influences.	**1941** Thomas Merton, who has converted to Catholicism in 1938, enters the Our Lady of Gethsemani monastery in Kentucky. **1945** After the first successful test of an atomic bomb in New Mexico, the physicist in charge of the atomic program, J. Robert Oppenheimer, recalls a quotation from the Hindu *Bhagavad Gita*: "Now I am become Death, the destroyer of worlds."
1900 In China, the Righteous Harmony Society Movement—the Boxers—rebel against Western influence, killing hundreds of missionaries and local Christians. **1900** Shintoism is reinstated in Japan to try to limit Buddhist influence.	**1912** Bengali poet Rabindranath Tagore publishes *Gitanjali*, a collection of devotional poems. **1919** At Amritsar, British soldiers open fire on unarmed Indian demonstrators, killing 379 Hindus, Muslims, and Sikhs, and wounding some 1,100 more.	**1927** In Madras, India, a landmark high court decision recognizes Jainism as a distinct religion rather than a strand of Hinduism. **1927** Indian Catholic priest Varghese Palakkappillil founds the Congregation of the Sisters of the Destitute in Kerala.	**1932** In India the Poona Pact gives voting rights to the lowest caste of society, the Untouchables. **1938** Mohandas (Mahatma) Gandhi and Muhammad Ali Jinnah, leader of the Muslim League, meet to resolve differences between Hindus and Muslims in India, but fail.	**1945** Defeat in World War II ends government attempts to control Shinto and other religions in Japan. **1947** Indian and Pakistan are partitioned to create largely Hindu and Muslim states, respectively. **1948** Mohandas (Mahatma) Gandhi is assassinated by a Hindu fanatic.
1901 Zionist Theodor Herzl meets Ottoman sultan Abdülhamid II to request land in Palestine to form a Jewish state. **1903** Russian Jews escaping pogroms arrive in Palestine. **1908** Frank Weston becomes the Anglican bishop of Zanzibar in East Africa.	**1914** In Ghana and Ivory Coast, Prophet Wade Harris enjoins some 120,000 followers to give up traditional religions, become baptized, and await the arrival of white missionaries to teach them the Bible. **1915** In Nigeria the prophet Garrick Braid stirs an upsurge in religious fervor.	**1921** In the Belgian Congo, the prophet Simon Kimbangu begins a brief ministry of preaching and healing before he is arrested by Belgian colonial authorities; he dies in captivity. **1928** Hasan al-Banna, an Egyptian revivalist Muslim, founds the Muslim Brotherhood.	**1932** After the creation of the Kingdom of Iraq and an Assyrian uprising against the rule of King Faisal, Iraqis massacre some 3,000 Assyrian Christians. **1936** British authorities limit Jewish immigration to Palestine as clashes with Arabs grow more violent.	**1946** Jewish militants blow up the King David Hotel in Jerusalem, killing 91 people. **1947** The United Nations agrees on a plan to divide Palestine into Jewish and Arab states. **1948** The Jewish state of Israel is created; it immediately has to defend itself against its Arab neighbors in the Arab-Israeli War.

PEOPLE & PLACES	DOCUMENTS, ART, & ARTIFACTS	WORSHIP & DOCTRINE

EUROPE

1858 French miller's daughter Bernadette Soubirous has 18 visions of "a small young lady" at Lourdes in the foothills of the Pyrenees; the Roman Catholic Church later confirms the apparition to be genuine, starting pilgrimages to the shrine of Our Lady of Lourdes, which gains a reputation for miracles of healing.

1858 Lionel de Rothschild becomes the first Jewish member of the British Parliament.

1854 Pre-Raphaelite artist William Holman Hunt paints *The Light of the World*, an allegorical portrait of Jesus Christ.

1859 Charles Darwin writes the influential *On the Origin of Species*, proposing a theory of evolution by adaptation (📄 pages 284–285).

1850 The Roman Catholic hierarchy is established in England and Wales.

1854 Pope Pius IX establishes the Immaculate Conception of the Virgin Mary as an article of the Catholic faith.

WORDS OF DEVOTION

Uncle Tom's Cabin

Few books have had as much impact on the world as the novel written by Harriet Beecher Stowe, a preacher at Hartford Female Academy in Connecticut. Stowe's tale told of the Christian slave Uncle Tom, his sufferings, his faith, and his eventual martyrdom (illustrated here). Sustained by visions of Jesus, the dying slave forgives the men who beat him to death, who then both convert to Christianity. Stowe's novel revealed a glimpse of slave life that became a powerful tool in the campaign for abolition. It is said that when the author met Abraham Lincoln during the Civil War, the president commented "So you are the little woman who wrote the book that started this great war!"

THE AMERICAS

1853 Congregationalist Antoinette Louisa Brown becomes the first woman to be ordained in the United States.

1855 When shoe salesman Dwight L. Moody is "born again" and called to preach, a deacon advises that his grammar is so poor that he should serve the Lord in other ways: Moody goes on to become the most celebrated preacher of the age.

1855 Reverend Sylvester Graham promotes dietary reform, arguing that healthy bodies go together with healthy souls.

1852 Harriet Beecher Stowe publishes *Uncle Tom's Cabin*.

1854 Henry David Thoreau writes *Walden, or Life in the Woods* (📄 pages 270–271).

1855 Isaac Meyer Wise calls the Cleveland Conference to rally behind "an American Judaism, free, progressive, enlightened, united, and respected."

ASIA & OCEANIA

1850 The Bab, an Islamic mystic, is executed for heresy in Persia, and his followers are expelled (📄 facing page).

Both Hindus and Muslims rebelled against the British in the Indian Mutiny, but despite great bloodshed on both sides, the Raj survived for nearly another century.

1851 State support of religion is ended in South Australia (it will end in the other Australian territories by 1895).

1851 In Thailand, the reign of King Mongkut sees the growing influence of a Buddhist reform sect, Thammayutika Nikaya.

AFRICA & THE MIDDLE EAST

1854 Scottish missionary David Livingstone begins a two-year journey across Africa from the west to the east coast.

1859 Constantin Tischendorf discovers the Codex Sinaiticus, a fourth-century Greek manuscript of the Bible, in a monastery on Mount Sinai; he later claims it had been set aside to be burned as trash.

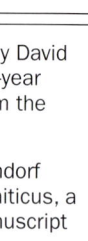

1852 Baha Ulla, successor to the Bab, preaches the Baha'i faith in Turkey and later in Israel (📄 facing page).

1857 The Universities' Mission to Central Africa is founded.

RELIGION IN THE WORLD	WORLD EVENTS
1850 Edgardo Mortara, a young Jewish boy, is seized by the authorities of the Papal States following his secret baptism by a domestic servant. The case is used by Italian revolutionaries as an example of the Papal States' intolerance.	**1851** The Crystal Palace in London is the scene of the Great Exhibition, a world's fair celebrating industry and manufacture. **1852** Louis Napoleon is crowned Louis III of France, ending the French Republic. **1853** In Paris, Baron Haussmann imposes order on the city center with a series of sweeping boulevards, said to be so wide as to prevent them being barricaded by future demonstrators. **1854** The Crimean War begins when France and Britain come to the aid of Turkey against Russia; it ends in 1856 in Russian defeat. **1859** After experiencing the Battle of Solferino, Swiss businessman Henri Dunant founds the International Red Cross.
1855 Having lost its lands to the state, the Catholic Church in Oregon is bankrupt. **1856** In Mexico, the Ley Lerdo redistributes uncultivated church land to farmers. **1857** The Utah War breaks out between Mormons and federal forces when the U.S. government attempts to limit Mormon governance and the practice of polygamy. **1858** In the Mountain Meadows Massacre, Mormon militia in southwestern Utah murder 120 immigrants heading for California, including unarmed women and children; the massacre is blamed on hysteria caused by the conflict with the U.S. government.	**1850** The Fugitive Slave Act causes outrage among abolitionists by obliging Northern states to return escaped slaves to their owners. **1855** Benito Juárez comes to power as president of Mexico, beginning a period of liberal reform. **1857** U.S. courts overturn the Missouri Compromise on slavery in the Dred Scott case, heightening tension between North and South. **1858** As part of his campaign for the U.S. Senate, Abraham Lincoln attracts national attention in his debates with opponent Stephen Douglas; regarding slavery, Lincoln comments "A house divided against itself cannot stand."
1857 The Indian Mutiny breaks out when native soldiers in Britain's Indian Army refuse to use new rifle cartridges said to be covered with pig and cattle grease, taboo to Muslims and Hindus, respectively. **1858** The Treaty of Tianjin imposed on China by Western powers allows free access for Christian missionaries to the Chinese interior.	**1850** Claiming to be the younger brother of Jesus Christ and inspired by a combination of Christian beliefs and utopianism, Hong Xiuquan leads the Taiping Rebellion (Taiping means "Heavenly Kingdom of Great Peace") against China's Qing dynasty; in 14 years of civil war, some 20 million people die. **1856** The Second Opium War breaks out between China and Britain.
1852 In Jerusalem the Church of the Holy Sepulcher is permanently divided among six Christian churches, each with strictly demarcated and jealously guarded areas inside (the key to the main door has been looked after by two Muslim families since 1192). **1855** Emperor Theodorus of Ethiopia begins to reconstruct its former Christian empire.	**1851** The discovery of gold in southern Africa begins a rush of settlers to the continent. **1857** A rail line opens between Cairo and Alexandria in Egypt. **1857** The Ottomans ban the African slave trade throughout their empire.

BAHA'I

The world's youngest independent religion, Baha'i was created in Iran in the mid-19th century on the principle that humanity is one race that must concentrate on breaking down prejudices.

Baha'i believes that all religions are unified and that its founder Baha Ullah (Arabic for "glory of god") is one in a line of messengers from God that include Muhammad, Buddha, and Jesus Christ. Baha Ullah and his predecessor, known as the Bab, preached that a new messenger of God would come and overturn old religious practices. Baha'i grew out of the Babi faith, which in turn grew out of Shiite Islam.

After Baha Ullah joined the Babis, he was arrested in 1852 and jailed. Exiled to Baghdad and then to Constantinople, Baha Ullah declared he was the messenger of God predicted by Bab. Before his death in 1892, Baha Ullah appointed his son as the new leader of the movement. Abdul Baha was responsible for spreading Baha'i across the globe.

During the 1960s, Baha'i grew rapidly. By the end of the 20th century it had more than 150 spiritual assemblies across the world, although it was persecuted in its homeland following the 1979 Islamic Revolution in Iran. The country's 300,000 Baha'is were persecuted by the fundamentalist regime.

The religion is notable for having no priesthood or ritual forms of worship. Every Baha'i between the ages of 15 and 70 is expected to fast for 19 days a year.

Built in 1986, the New Delhi headquarters of Baha'i in India is known as the Lotus Temple for its flowerlike shape. It can hold up to 2,500 worshipers.

T. H. HUXLEY AND AGNOSTICISM

AGNOSTICISM IS THE VIEW THAT THE EXISTENCE OF GOD can not be proved nor disproved. The term was coined by British biologist Thomas Henry Huxley (1825–1895) to describe his own views on religion. Although the term was new, the attitude was not; philosophers and scientists throughout history have expressed agnostic views.

Huxley's agnosticism had its origins in his empiricism—he approached all ideas, whether new or widely accepted, with a skeptical attitude. Huxley had received almost no formal schooling—financial difficulties forced him to leave school at age 10—and as a result acquired his knowledge through personal study and experiment. As a young man, while training to be a surgeon, he pursued a strenuous private curriculum that included philosophy, theology, foreign languages, and science.

In the 1850s the biologist Charles Darwin showed Huxley an early draft of his work on evolution. Huxley had published scathing opinions of earlier, similar ideas, such as Jean-Baptiste Lamarck's "transmutation of species," but after many weeks of discussion he became a supporter of Darwin's theory. Over the next 10 years, Huxley became known as "Darwin's bulldog" for his fierce defense of Darwin's ideas in public debates with clergymen. His frequent clashes with religious figures led him to question the fundamental assumption (the existence of God) from which they derived their authority.

Huxley was not opposed to religion in principle, and he believed that religious beliefs could be socially and morally useful, but he could find no proof of God's existence. He began to describe himself as an agnostic, a term he derived from the Greek word meaning "unknowable." Agnosticism can also be understood as the difference between unquestioning belief and skeptical knowledge, as much as a rejection of traditional religious belief, in this sense it is tentatively permitted by some churches, including the Roman Catholic church. People from many different religious traditions consider themselves agnostic. For some people it is a fixed philosophical position, while for others it is a way of expressing their uncertainty about the existence of God. In 2008, a survey of religious attitudes in the United States reported that 35 million people described themselves as having "no religion," of which 2 million specifically identified as agnostic.

U.S. lawyer Robert G. Ingersoll was a prominent agnostic who delivered a series of popular lectures on the topic to audiences in the 1870s and 1880s. A forceful orator, it is said that he could speak for three hours—from memory—without his audience once feeling restless.

This cartoon of Thomas H. Huxley appeared in a British magazine to accompany a feature on "Men of the Day," reflecting the preeminence Huxley had gained.

PEOPLE & PLACES	DOCUMENTS, ART, & ARTIFACTS	WORSHIP & DOCTRINE

EUROPE

1865 A pawnbroker from Nottingham, William Booth, moves to London to found the Christian Revival Association (later the Salvation Army) (📄 pages 288–289).

1867 Celebrated U.S. evangelical preacher Dwight L. Moody tours England.

1868 Johannes Brahms writes *A German Requiem*.

1864 Pope Pius IX causes controversy with his deeply conservative encyclical *Quanta Cura* and its attached "Syllabus of Errors": the document condemns modern fallacies, including democracy, socialism, the separation of church and state, and freedom of conscience.

1867 The First Lambeth Conference of the Bishops of the Anglican Communion attracts 76 bishops.

THE AMERICAS

1863 Ellen Gould White cures her two sons of diphtheria through prayer; she has a vision of God's great vision—"pure, soft water."

1866 After falling on ice, Mary Baker Eddy cures herself through positive thought, laying the foundation for her later development of Christian Science ((📄 page 291).

1868 Crawford H. Toy joins the faculty of the Southern Baptist Seminary.

A souvenir postcard shows Pope Pius IX opening the First Vatican Council, which met in June 1868.

1869 Warren Evans publishes *The Mental Cure*, which uses the ideas of Emanuel Swedenborg and Phineas P. Quimby to promote a theory of physical healing through spiritual strength.

1863 Ellen Gould White founds the Seventh-Day Adventists.

1868 Isaac Leeser founds Maimonides College in Philadelphia, the first Jewish seminary in the Americas.

ASIA & OCEANIA

The will of God prevails. In great contests each party claims to act in accordance with the will of God. Both may be and one must be wrong. God cannot be for and against the same thing at the same time.

ABRAHAM LINCOLN

AFRICA & THE MIDDLE EAST

1866 Protestant missionaries in Beirut, Lebanon, found the American University, which helps inspire an Arabic literary revival among Christians in Syria.

1866 Scots explorer David Livingstone begins his final journey to Africa.

1865 The Bible is published in an Arabic language translation.

David Livingstone studies the Bible in camp. The explorer noted, "All that I am I owe to Jesus Christ, revealed in his divine book."

1860 The Russian Orthodox Church founds a monastery in Jerusalem.

RELIGION IN THE WORLD

1865 Pius IX forbids Catholics from joining Masonic associations.

1860 The conservative Gabriel García Moreno begins a presidency in Ecuador marked by strong Roman Catholicism—one of the most staunchly religious administrations in Latin American history.

1864 The motto "In God We Trust" first appears on U.S. coins.

1865 A church-state clash begins in Brazil when Emperor Pedro II forbids the promulgation of the papal decree barring Catholics from freemasonry.

1867 After the execution in Mexico of the short-lived emperor Maximilian, Benito Juárez implements anticlerical laws originally passed in the 1850s.

ca 1860 After a long period of persecution by foreign powers, growing nationalism inspires a major revival of lay and monastic Buddhism in Ceylon (Sri Lanka).

1864 After China's Taiping Rebellion, Buddhism has been destroyed to such an extent that the faith has to be reintroduced to China from Japan.

1865 The China Inland Mission is founded.

1861 Abdul Aziz becomes Ottoman sultan and opens the empire to Western influences.

1863 Anglican bishop John Colenso of Natal is deposed by his fellow bishops in Africa; they object to his suggestion that parts of the Old Testament should not be read literally—and to his outspoken support for African peoples.

1865 In Turkey, the Young Ottoman Society promotes Islamic modernism.

WORLD EVENTS

1860 Italian patriot Giuseppe Garibaldi leads his famous Red Shirts in a rebellion in southern Italy that leads in 1861 to the unification of the country.

1861 In Russia, Tsar Alexander II emancipates the serfs.

1862 Otto von Bismarck becomes prime minister of Prussia and begins to strengthen links among German states.

1867 With the creation of the Dual Monarchy, Habsburg emperor Francis Joseph I becomes ruler of Austria-Hungary.

1867 The German communist philosopher Karl Marx publishes the first part of his analysis of capitalism, *Das Kapital*.

1861 The Civil War begins in the United States (📄 box, right).

1862 The French establish a short-lived puppet empire in Mexico.

1863 Abraham Lincoln issues the Emancipation Proclamation, freeing slaves in Confederate territory.

1864 Paraguay begins the six-year War of the Triple Alliance, fighting Argentina, Brazil, and Uruguay.

1865 The Civil War ends with the surrender of the Confederacy; Abraham Lincoln is assassinated by a supporter of slavery.

1868 The Fourteenth Amendment grants U.S. citizenship to freed slaves.

Men of the 9th Massachusetts Infantry gather with their chaplain before a church service at a camp in Virginia in 1861.

THE CIVIL WAR

In the 1850s Americans were divided over slavery—as were their churches. Presbyterians, Baptists, Episcopalians, and Methodists split over the issue. Most of the soldiers who went to war in 1861 believed in a Supreme Being, and the majority were Protestant Christians.

Church services were rare, and soldiers routinely engaged in gambling and drinking—sins according to many Protestant churches. Nevertheless, a religious revival took place. Troops on both sides coped with danger by accepting that divine Providence would either keep them safe or take them to heaven.

Religious services were held by army chaplains, who occupied a unique place: As volunteers, they received no uniforms and, for much of the war, were issued only a private's rations. Some chaplains entered the ministry to avoid soldiering (although some of them fought alongside the troops); some were not even ordained ministers. A number worked with several regiments at the same time.

Religious support also came from missionaries who visited camps and hospitals. The U.S. Christian Commission, founded by the Young Men's Christian Association in 1861, had 5,000 volunteers who distributed literature and stationery, and provided food, humanitarian aid, and comfort for the wounded.

DARWIN AND EVOLUTION

FAITH AND SCIENCE HAD CLASHED BEFORE, BUT THE THEORY of evolution put forward by English naturalist Charles Darwin (1809–1882) in 1859 presented the most significant challenge yet to the biblical account of history. Darwin was not the first person to suggest that life forms had changed over time, or that the age of the Earth was far greater than could be explained by the Bible (in 1650, Anglican bishop James Ussher had used the Bible to calculate that the world was created during the night preceding October 23, 4004 B.C.). But his work *On the Origin of Species by Means of Natural Selection* became seen as the leading expression of such views. Not only did Darwin's theory challenge the story of creation given in the Book of Genesis. Its implication that humans were descended from other primates and therefore related to the apes, which Darwin further explained in his book *The Descent of Man*, also called into question the Bible's insistence that man was created "in God's image."

Darwin based his ideas on observations he had made on a long voyage on HMS *Beagle* that took him to Africa, South America, and New Zealand. Everywhere Darwin observed and collected rocks, plants, and animals. Back in England, Darwin studied the ideas of geologist Charles Lyell, who argued that the world was in a constant state of change, and economist Thomas Malthus, who described a "struggle for existence." Darwin recognized a similar state among animal species—only the fittest animals survive. A process of "natural selection" was the mechanism that made some more fit than others.

Darwin's theory was that evolution takes place in stages by chance mutations. Favorable mutations are inherited and passed on to offspring, so producing a gradual change in a whole species. Eventually new, fitter species come into existence and old, less fit ones become extinct (a process Darwin could not explain but which is now accounted for by genetics).

Darwin delayed publishing his theory for some 20 years because he feared the controversy that would follow. It duly arrived, with a public outcry and cartoons that portrayed Darwin as a monkey. For some Christians, the debate continues: evolution is a theory, and is therefore no more deserving of acceptance than creationism, a belief in the literal truth of the Bible. Most scientists, however, agreed with Darwin's own argument that, while natural selection is indeed only a theory to explain evolution, evolution itself is an observable fact.

Darwin, here in an 1872 caricature, said: "I cannot persuade myself that a beneficent and omnipotent God would have designedly created parasitic wasps with the express intention of their feeding within the living bodies of caterpillars."

In the Galápagos Islands, Darwin noted how isolated species of finches had evolved different shaped beaks depending on their diet of fruits, insects, or nuts, confirming his belief in the importance of species' adaptation.

PEOPLE & PLACES	DOCUMENTS, ART, & ARTIFACTS	WORSHIP & DOCTRINE

EUROPE

1873 Helena Blavatsky leaves Russia to emigrate to the United States, where she will found the Theosophical Society to promote the study of spiritualism.

1878 Former Methodist minister William Booth founds the Salvation Army (📄 pages 288–289).

1878 German politician Heinrich von Treitschke becomes an outspoken antisemitic critic of Jewish influence in Germany history.

1874 Giuseppe Verdi writes *Requiem Mass* in honor of the Italian patriotic writer Alessandro Manzoni.

Henry Morton Stanley greets David Livingstone on the shores of Lake Tanganyika in 1871 with the words "Dr. Livingstone, I presume."

1870 The First Vatican Council promulgates the decree of papal infallibility.

1871 The mainly Germanic-speaking Old Catholic Church splits from the Catholic Church over papal infallibility.

1871 The Anglican Church is disestablished in Ireland.

1872 The patriarch of Constantinople condemns the Bulgarian Church's unilateral decision to become independent.

1875 The World Alliance of Reformed and Presbyterian Churches is formed in Geneva, Switzerland.

1879 The Serbian Orthodox Church becomes self-governing.

THE AMERICAS

ca 1870 The Paiute prophet Wodziwob develops the Ghost Dance, reintroduced in 1889 (📄 pages 292–293).

1872 Scientist John Tyndall promotes Darwinism in the United States as an alternative to religious teachings.

1875 Future president Woodrow Wilson undergoes a conversion experience that shapes the rest of his life.

1876 T. H. Huxley makes a lecture tour of the United States promoting his doctrine of agnosticism (📄 pages 280–281).

1879 Crawford H. Toy is forced to resign from the Southern Baptist Convention for his support of Darwinism as a "truth revealed by God."

1875 Mary Baker Eddy publishes *Science and Health with Key to the Scriptures*, which becomes "the textbook of Christian Science."

1870 The predominantly black Christian Methodist Episcopal church is founded in the U.S. South.

1873 The Union of American Hebrew Congregations is founded.

1878 The Niagara Creed, formulated at the annual Protestant Bible conference, asserts a millennarian belief in Christ's return to Earth.

1879 Mary Baker Eddy founds the Church of Christ, Scientist (📄 page 291).

ASIA & OCEANIA

1873 Southern Baptist Charlotte Digges "Lottie" Moon begins a 40-year mission to China for the Foreign Mission Board.

1879 King Mindon Min of Burma oversees a new edition of the Buddhist Pali canon; he has the new texts engraved on 729 stone stelae and erected in a major Buddhist monastery.

1871 The Fifth Buddhist Council meets in Mandalay, Burma.

1879 Australian Methodists begin missions to the Solomon Islands.

AFRICA & THE MIDDLE EAST

1873 Johannes IV comes to the throne of Ethiopia and continues to try to reconstruct the Christian empire there.

1873 In Morocco, the reforms of Sultan Moulay al-Hassan are resisted by conservative clerics.

1878 In Buganda—part of modern-day Uganda—King Mutesa encourages infighting among Catholic, Protestant, and Islamic missionaries.

Reform rabbi Isaac Meyer Wise worked through the 1870s to achieve a union of American Jews, but met resistance from more conservative Jews.

1870 France grants French nationality to Jews in Algeria.

RELIGION IN THE WORLD	WORLD EVENTS

1872 Jesuits are expelled from Germany.

1875 All religious orders are abolished in Prussia.

1879 In France, reformer Jules Ferry promotes lay education rather than the traditional system of Catholic schools.

1870 In the Franco–Prussian War, Prussians besiege Paris and capture Emperor Napoléon III, marking the end of the Second Empire.

1870 Italy annexes the Papal States: now only the Vatican remains outside the unified country.

1871 Germany is unified when Otto von Bismarck creates the Second Reich, ruled by Emperor William I of Prussia.

1874 In France, a group of artists hold an unofficial exhibition; critics name them the Impressionists.

1875 In Spain a new constitution restores the monarchy.

1877 Russia supports Slavs rising against Ottoman rule in the Balkans.

Don't get angry today.

Don't worry today.

Be grateful today.

Work hard today.

Be kind to others today.

MEIJI EMPEROR, ADMONITION

1871 The Great Fire of Chicago leaves about 100,000 people homeless.

1876 At the Battle of the Little Bighorn in Montana, Sioux warriors led by Sitting Bull wipe out U.S. forces commanded by General George Custer.

1876 Authorities in Pennsylvania execute leaders of the Molly Maguires, a violent labor movement.

1877 Reconstruction in the Southern states ends as part of a compromise over the disputed presidential election in 1876.

1879 Frank W. Woolworth opens his first "5 and 10 cent" store in Utica, New York—after an initial "5 cent" store fails within weeks.

1870 In China suspicion of Christian missionaries—who are alleged to kidnap children for their orphanages—leads to the Tianjin massacre, in which some 50 to 60 local and foreign Christians are killed.

1871 Japan's Ministry of Divinities is formed to implement State Shinto (📄 box, right).

1873 Diplomatic pressure from Western countries ends open persecution of Christians in Japan.

STATE SHINTO IN JAPAN

Shinto had long been the main religion of Japan before the Meiji Restoration in 1868. To help unify Japan's various states during a period of rapid modernization, the new emperor made Shinto the sole religion and "purified" it by removing its Buddhist and Confucian ideals. In 1871, a Ministry of Divinities was formed to implement this new Kokka Shinto. The Japanese state now oversaw the clergy and the moral education of the people.

State Shinto became the foundation of Japanese life. Every Japanese had to pledge allegiance to the faith (although they were then free to follow their own beliefs). Over time, Shinto became ever more closely linked to allegiance to the state and the emperor. It sought to promote a sense of nationhood through patriotism and shrine worship—particularly of the Ise Shrine, dedicated to the imperial family.

During the Showa period, Shinto became aligned with an increasing militarism. With defeat in World War II in 1945, however, State Shinto came to an abrupt end as the Japanese sought to understand the failures of the war.

Shinto monks pray at the Meiji Shrine in Japan. Built in 1915, the shrine was intended to hold the spirits of the Meiji Emperor and his wife. Until State Shinto was abolished in 1946, the shrine occupied the highest rank of government-supported holy sites.

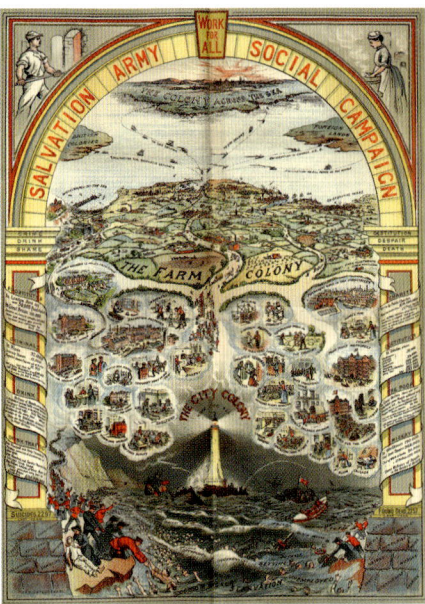

This illustration from William Booth's 1890 book In Darkest England and the Way Out *envisages the Salvation Army's social campaign as a lighthouse guiding people to a better life in the city, in the country, and in "the colony across the sea"—the United States.*

THE SALVATION ARMY

THE SALVATION ARMY, INSTANTLY RECOGNIZABLE BY ITS distinctive red badge, is a worldwide evangelical Christian movement that started in the East End of London, England. Its founder was a former Methodist minister, William Booth (1829–1912), who preached his Christian message on street corners rather than in churches, but initially had little success among the 500 other Christian charities working in the London slums.

That changed in 1878, after Booth renamed his movement the Salvation Army to suggest the idea of a war against sin. People started to join, attracted by the mixture of evangelical activity and charitable work. Booth believed that if the poor, homeless, and hungry first had their physical needs met, he could then cater for their spiritual needs. He aimed to provide the three "s's": soup, soap, and salvation.

Booth established the Army along military lines, with himself as general for life. Members wore uniforms to show they belonged to an army and to make them instantly recognizable. Women members were always equal to men. Once a recruit joined, he or she could not drink, gamble, take drugs, or smoke. The Army was divided into corps led by officers with ranks from lieutenant to brigadier; corps were arranged into divisions and divisions into national territories (the United States was split into four territories because of its size).

To further distinguish the movement, musicians became an essential part of a Salvation Army gathering. Originally a band worked with Army preachers as "bodyguards," playing music to distract potential hecklers. The Salvation Army became noted for the high quality of its brass bands and choirs.

The first meeting of the Salvation Army in the United States was held in Philadelphia in 1879 by 17-year-old Lieutenant Eliza Shirley, an English immigrant. When Booth heard of the popularity of her meetings, he sent reinforcements from England who arrived in 1880. Despite little initial success, within three years the Salvation Army was operating in many U.S. states. Salvationists were welcomed to the White House by President Grover Cleveland in 1886.

The Army's popularity grew in the United States after it helped with the 1906 San Francisco Earthquake. Charitable works continue to be a vital part of the Army's existence. Their thrift stores continue to be a strong presence in towns and cities across the country, while in many cities the sight of Salvation Army musicians singing Christmas carols is a sign that the holiday period has arrived.

Renowned photographer Dorothea Lange took this image at a Salvation Army rally in San Francisco in 1939. The Great Depression put great strain on "Sallys," the missions that provided food and shelter for the homeless. Costs rose by more than 500 percent before federal relief was provided in 1933.

PEOPLE & PLACES	DOCUMENTS, ART, & ARTIFACTS	WORSHIP & DOCTRINE

EUROPE

1880 Cologne Cathedral in Germany is completed some 632 years after it was begun in 1248.

1885 In *My Religion*, Russian author Leo Tolstoy outlines a simple Christian morality based mainly on the Sermon of the Mount.

1887 Sir Thomas More, a Catholic cardinal executed during the English Reformation, is beatified by Pope Leo XIII (he is canonized in 1935).

1887 Austrian composer Anton Bruckner writes his *Te Deum*, a setting of an early Christian work; on his copy of the score, Gustav Mahler replaces the words "for chorus, soloists, and orchestra" with "for the tongues of angels, heaven-blest, chastened hearts, and souls purified in the fire!"

1881 Westcott and Hort publish a new Greek-language edition of the New Testament.

1889 T. H. Huxley publishes *Agnosticism* (📄 pages 280–281).

Jews pray at the Western Wall in Jerusalem, the only part that still remains of the Second Temple built by Herod in about 19 B.C.

1882 Russian anarchist Mikhail Bakunin rejects in *God and the State* a view in which the primacy of God reduces humans to a lowly status.

1883 In his novel *Thus Spake Zarathustra*, German writer Friedrich Nietzsche describes what he terms "the death of God."

1885 Edward Benson, archbishop of Canterbury, establishes contact with Assyrian Christians in what is now Iraq.

1885 The Romanian Orthodox Church is created from the Wallachian, Moldavian, and Transylvanian churches.

THE AMERICAS

1880 The African American Henry McNeal Turner becomes a bishop in the African Methodist Episcopal Church.

1884 Archbishop James Gibbons of Baltimore attempts to draw together the various strands among American Catholics.

1886 Archbishop Gibbons becomes a cardinal.

1889 Charles and Myrtle Fillmore found the Unity School of Christianity, an eclectic faith that draws on the teachings of various esoteric faiths. Charles asserts "We have borrowed the best from all religions, that is the reason we are called Unity."

1880 In *American Nervousness*, U.S. neurologist George Beard analyzes the human spiritual condition in terms of a stressful background of industrialization and urbanization.

1883 Publication begins of the *Christian Science Monitor* (📄 facing page).

ca 1880 The African Methodist Episcoplian Church has about 400,000 members.

1882 Isaac Meyer Wise argues that Zionism has no place in Reform Judaism.

1883 At the Niagara Bible Conference, evangelical Protestants split between conservatives (often millennarians and dispensationalists) and progressives.

1885 American Judaism formally splits into Reform and Counter-Reform branches.

1889 The Central Conference of American Rabbis is founded in Detroit.

ASIA & OCEANIA

ca 1880 Acharya Rajendrasuri begins a reform movement within Jainism.

1886 The Indian mystic Ramakrishna dies after establishing a following for his individual form of Hinduism.

1889 In Chennai, India—then the headquarters of the Theosophical Society—Helena Blavatsky remarks that the society's real purpose is to prepare humanity for the return of the "World Teacher."

1882 Two jade statues of Buddha, imported from Burma, inspire the founding of the Jade Buddha Temple in Shanghai, China.

1884 The first permanent Protestant missionary arrives in Korea.

1886 The Roman Catholic hierarchy is established in India.

AFRICA & THE MIDDLE EAST

1881 The Mahdi, an Islamic religious leader, launches a Sudanese rebellion against Egypt.

ca 1885 Simon Kimbangu is born in the Congo Free State, now a personal possession of Leopold II of Belgium; he will gain a reputation as a prophet and a Congolese national leader.

1886 The Muslim visionary Jamal ad-Din al-Afghani is invited by the Persian shah to participate in government, but the alliance is shortlived.

In 1883 Mary Baker Eddy began publishing the Christian Science Monitor; today it remains a well-respected periodical renowned for high editorial standards.

RELIGION IN THE WORLD	WORLD EVENTS

1881 Jews are persecuted in Russia.

1881 The Vatican archives are opened to scholars researching church history.

1889 Monks at the abbey of Solesmes in France revive the original form of Gregorian chant after years of study.

The First Church of Christ, Scientist, the mother church of the Christian Scientists, was built in Boston in 1894.

1881 In Russia, the reformist Tsar Alexander II is assassinated by anarchists; his son Alexander III is far more reactionary.

1882 Irish nationalists assassinate British politicians in Dublin.

1883 Germany, Austria, and Italy form the Triple Alliance.

1884 Divorce again becomes legal in France, having been abolished in 1816.

1885 Prussia expels all ethnic Poles and Jews who do not hold German citizenship.

1889 The Paiute seer Wovoka has a vision in which he sees all Whites driven from America; the vision will become the basis of the Ghost Dance movement (pages 292–293).

1889 Brazilians overthrow Emperor Pedro II and proclaim a republic that separates church and state.

1881 U.S. president James Garfield is assassinated after less than a year in office.

1881 Clara Barton founds the American Red Cross.

1883 A series of legislation that will effectively end U.S. immigration from East Asia begins with the Chinese Exclusion Act.

1883 After four years, Chile wins the War of the Pacific and annexes territory from Peru and Bolivia.

1886 The French people donate the Statue of Liberty to the United States.

1889 Brazil becomes a republic after Emperor Pedro II is overthrown by a military coup.

1885 The Indian National Congress is founded; later known as the Congress Party, it represents the interests of India's majority Hindus.

1882 Lord Ripon, governor of India, establishes a commission to extend education oportunities to Indian children.

1889 In Japan, the New Constitution establishes a parliament but ensures that real power remains with the emperor.

1889 New Zealand holds a general election based on universal (male) suffrage.

1882 The Tembu National Church is founded in South Africa.

1882 The "First Aliyah," a wave of Jewish settlement, begins in Ottoman Palestine: some 30,000 European and Yemeni Jews arrive in the next 20 years.

1885 Mwanga, new ruler of Buganda, assassinates a visiting bishop and begins a persecution of Christians that leaves hundreds dead—but the number of Christian converts rises steadily.

1881 Britain is defeated in the First Boer War in southern Africa.

1884 The Mahdi—the Muslim messiah— leads a siege of British troops commanded by General Charles Gordon in Khartoum, Sudan.

1884 At the Berlin Conference, European governments divide Africa into spheres of influence.

1889 Cecil Rhodes founds the colony of Rhodesia in southern Africa.

CHRISTIAN SCIENCE

Christian Science was founded in the United States by Mary Baker Eddy based on accounts of Jesus' healing miracles in the New Testament. Plagued by ill health, Eddy met a charismatic healer named Phineas Parkhurst Quimby, who influenced her belief in the role of the mind in disease. In 1866, when she unexpectedly survived mortal illness, she attributed her recovery to the power of her mind and the study of Christian texts.

In 1870, Eddy taught her first Christian Science class. She continued to write and revise the Christian Science manual for the next 35 years. In 1879, she and her followers founded the Church of Christ, Scientist in order to rediscover the lost healing element of Christianity.

In the late 19th and early 20th centuries, the movement grew thanks largely to healing work performed by Eddy's students. She reorganized the church again in 1892 with the Mother Church in Boston and branches around the world.

Christian Scientists deviate from traditional Christianity in their belief that Jesus belonged to all men and women as their divine son. They stress his healing works and believe in the cure of disease through prayer.

THE GHOST DANCE

THE GHOST DANCE CULT ORIGINATED AMONG THE PAIUTE of the Great Basin between the Rockies and the Sierra Nevada in the late 19th century during a time of great upheaval as European Americans threatened the very survival of Native American culture. The Paiute and other peoples turned to the power of the spirit world for protection.

The roots of the Ghost Dance lay in a vision experienced by a shaman named Wodziwob in 1869; he described a journey to the spirit world and a promise from the spirits of the dead to help the living. The message was echoed 20 years later by another Paiute shaman, Wovoka, the son of one of Wodziwob's companions. On New Year's Day 1889 a solar eclipse plunged the Great Basin into darkness; at the same time, Wovoka claimed, he entered the spirit world and learned of a new world for all Native Americans that would be brought about by a ritual called the Ghost Dance. The message borrowed heavily from Christian beliefs, including the ending of the existing world and its replacement by a new one.

Wovoka foretold that if Native Americans fasted and performed the Ghost Dance, the very ground would rise up and bury the white people. As this catastrophic event was happening, all Native Americans would float safely above the Earth before returning. At the same time, the ghosts of their ancestors would be restored to life, the buffalo would return to the plains, and all would be as it once was.

The Ghost Dance cult opened the privileged spiritual world of the shaman to all Native Americans who chose to follow it. Before, only shamans had performed ritual dances and chanted incantations to exert their power. Now every individual could participate in the Ghost Dance: anyone who took part would be able to enter the spirit world and contact the souls of the dead. The Ghost Dance itself was a remarkable ceremony. The dancing would last at least a whole night, and sometimes it went on for several days, with only brief pauses to rest. Some dancers would pass out; when revived, they would describe their brief stays in the spirit world and what they saw there.

The Ghost Dance cult spread rapidly among western tribes in 1890. The U.S. government feared that it would lead to a pantribal uprising, despite Wovoka's pacifist message. That same year, along a creek in South Dakota called Wounded Knee, U.S. troops massacred 350 Sioux who were wearing Ghost Dance shirts they believed would protect them from the soldiers' bullets. The massacre marked the end of the Ghost Dance—and effectively of the independence of the Native Americans.

Ogallala Sioux take part in a Ghost Dance in an illustration from 1891.
Communal dancing featured in the rituals of many native peoples, encouraging
the spread of the Ghost Dance movement into California and Oklahoma.

PEOPLE & PLACES	DOCUMENTS, ART, & ARTIFACTS	WORSHIP & DOCTRINE

EUROPE

1892 French Impressionist painter Claude Monet begins a renowned series of paintings of the West Front of Rouen Cathedral in various light conditions.

1893 British journalist William T. Stead writes *If Christ Came to Chicago*, based on his visit to the World's Fair.

1895 In London, the foundation stone is laid of Westminster Cathedral.

1896 Austro-Hungarian journalist Theodor Herzl writes *The Jewish State* to express his belief that the Jews cannot assimilate in Europe and propose the creation of a Jewish homeland in Palestine.

Journalist Theodor Herzl rejected the idea that Jews could assimilate in European society.

1891 In the papal bull *Rerum Novarum* (*Of New Things*), subtitled "On Capital and Labor," Pope Leo XIII describes the ills of industrial society and condemns both unrestricted free markets and socialism.

1895 The World Student Christian Federation, the first international student organization, is founded in Sweden by student leaders from ten countries.

1896 Rome declares Anglican religious orders "null and void."

THE AMERICAS

1893 Protestant cleric Josiah Strong, a founder of the Social Gospel movement, declares: "Surely, to be a Christian and an Anglo-Saxon and an American in this generation is to stand on the mountain-top of privilege."

1895 Methodist John Mott begins a lifelong global mission on behalf of the Student Volunteer Movement.

1896 A miracle-working religious fanatic known as the "Counselor" leads a millenarian movement in Brazil that ends when its followers are slaughtered by federal troops.

1899 Death of Dwight L. Moody, the best-known evangelist of his day.

1892 Walter Rauschenbusch writes in the charter of his Brotherhood of the Kingdom, "The Spirit of God is moving men in our generation toward a better understanding of the idea of the Kingdom of God on Earth."

1895 The Jefferson Bible, compiled at the start of the century by Thomas Jefferson, is finally published.

1898 Elizabeth Cady Stanton publishes *The Women's Bible*.

1890 As a response to mass immigration, Catholic bishops appeal to Rome to provide bishops who share the same nationality as their congregations.

1890 In their efforts to gain statehood for Utah, Mormons formally abolish polygamy.

1895 African Americans found the National Baptist Convention of the U.S.A.

1899 In a papal letter, Pope Leo XIII condemns "Americanism" to discourage support among U.S. bishops for liberalism, individualism, freedom of speech, and the separation of church and state.

ASIA & OCEANIA

1893 Buddhist monks Anagarika Dharmapala and Soyen Shaku attend the World Parliament of Religions in Chicago, along with the Jain Virachand Gandhi.

1899 Gordon Douglas is the first Westerner to be ordained in the Theravada Buddhist tradition.

1896 Nepalese archaeologists rediscover the great stone pillar of Asoka at Lumbini.

1894 The Roman Catholic Church in Australia lends its support to the Australian Labour Party.

1898 The first Protestant missionaries arrive in the Philippines.

1899 Anglicans form the first "Bush Brotherhood," to preach to settlers in the Australian Outback.

AFRICA & THE MIDDLE EAST

1891 Muslim visionary Jalal ad-Din al-Afghani is expelled from Persia for constant criticism of the Shah.

1897 Theodor Herzl organizes a Zionist Congress to begin Zionist immigration to the Holy Land.

1892 The Ethiopian Church—later the Order of Ethiopia, part of the Anglican Church—is founded in South Africa by Mangena Mokoni.

Soldiers stand by while a Jew is attacked by a mob in Kiev in 1881. Persecution of Jews was well established in Russia by the 1890s.

RELIGION IN THE WORLD

1890 In France the "Raillement"—an appeal to national rejuvenation—draws Catholic support for the Republican government, with the encouragement of Pope Leo XIII, despite the Republic's perceived hostility to the church.

1891 The Russian government forces thousands of Jews from Moscow to live in ghettos.

1894 Jewish army captain Alfred Dreyfus is found guilty of treason by a French court martial in a trial that exposes antisemitic prejudice throughout the French establishment; he is eventually pardoned in 1906 after a long campaign.

1890 The Sioux convert to the Ghost Dance; the Bureau of Indian Affairs makes its first efforts to limit the movement (📄 pages 292–293).

1893 The World Parliament of Religions, held as part of the Chicago World's Fair, marks the first attempted global dialogue of faiths.

1895 Pope Leo XIII advocates the union of church and state in the United States; non-Catholics already distrust his alleged attempts to gain control of the public schools.

WORDS OF DEVOTION

A Hindu Speaks

The appearance of Swami Vivekananda at the World Parliament of Religions in Chicago in 1893 marked the beginning of U.S. interest in Hinduism. Vivekananda's speech was met with a three-minute ovation. He observed, "Sectarianism, bigotry, and its horrible descendant, fanaticism, have long possessed this beautiful earth. They have filled the earth with violence, drenched it often and often with human blood, destroyed civilization, and sent whole nations to despair."

1895 The Ottomans begin a series of massacres of Christian Armenians living in Turkey; about 200,000 people will die—the Turkish government still maintains that the genocide did not take place.

1896 A follower of Jamal ad-Din al-Afghani murders Persian shah Nasr al-Din.

WORLD EVENTS

1890 German emperor William II fires Chancellor Otto von Bismarck.

1894 On the death of Alexander III, Nicholas II becomes tsar of Russia.

1896 The first modern Olympic Games are held in Athens, Greece.

1896 Swedish industrialist Alfred Nobel—inventor of dynamite—leaves funds in his will to establish annual prizes for literature, science, and peace.

1898 Representatives of 26 countries meet in the Hague in the Netherlands for the first International Peace Conference.

1893 A crash on Wall Street begins a four-year depression in the United States.

1898 After victory in the Spanish-American War, the United States takes effective control of Cuba, Puerto Rico, and the Philippines, all largely Catholic countries.

1898 The United States annexes Hawaii.

The onion domes of the Holy Virgin Cathedral in San Francisco are covered in gold leaf. The church was built in the 1970s as the center of the Russian Orthodox Church in the Western United States.

1893 The border between British India and Afghanistan is established by the Durand Line.

1893 New Zealand is the first country to give women the vote.

1894 Japan and China go to war after Japan invades Korea.

1898 Russian forces seize Port Arthur in China.

1896 Italy recognizes Ethiopian independence after defeat at the Battle of Adowa, the first time Africans have defeated a modern European army.

1898 Inspired by black leader James Milton Turner, 198 African Americans emigrate from Savannah, Georgia, to Liberia; unable to support themselves, they depend on charity from the local Africans.

1899 In South Africa, Boers and the British clash in the Second Boer War.

IMMIGRANT FAITHS IN NORTH AMERICA

The waves of immigration to the United States in the decades around 1900 drastically altered the religious balance. Migrants from south and southeast Europe were predominantly Catholic. That is true again today, when immigrants from Central and South America (61 percent of all immigrants in the first decade of the 21st century) are largely Catholic.

Other immigrant Christian faiths that first became visible at the end of the 19th century included the Orthodox Greek and Russian Churches (now 0.6 percent of U.S. Christians). Some Buddhists arrived from China before Asian immigration was halted; Buddhism later revived, thanks in part to its popularity among native-born Americans. Later in the century immigrants from North Africa, the Middle East, and East Asia included large numbers of Muslims and Jews. Migrants from South Asia were predominantly Hindu (55 percent).

The U.S. religious demographic remains highly fluid. At the end of the first decade of the 21st century, the country was on the verge of becoming a minority Protestant country, with barely 51 percent Protestants.

PEOPLE & PLACES	DOCUMENTS, ART, & ARTIFACTS	WORSHIP & DOCTRINE

EUROPE

1902 Austrian visionary Rudolf Steiner becomes secretary of the Theosophical Society in Germany; he later splits from the society over its leaning toward Eastern mysticism.

1900 Edward Elgar composes the oratorio *The Dream of Gerontius*, setting a religious poem by Cardinal Henry Newman.

1903 Building work begins on Liverpool Cathedral in England.

1906 Albert Schweitzer writes *The Quest of the Historical Jesus*, suggesting that Christ's ethics are no longer relevant.

1907 The Russian monk Illarion publishes *On the Caucasus Mountains*, asserting that "The name of God is God Himself and can produce miracles"; particularly popular among some Russian monks on Mount Athos in Greece, the book encourages "onomatolatry"—the worship of words—that is rejected by the majority of monks, stirring controversy.

1904 Historian Max Weber defines the "Protestant work ethic" as being instrumental to the growth of the European economy in the early modern world.

1905 British druids celebrate the Summer solstice at Stonehenge, despite the owner's decision to charge an admission fee to cover the damage caused by the annual festival (facing page).

1907 Pope Pius X issues the encyclical *Pascendi*, which condemns all aspects of "modernism," including secularism and modern philosophy; Catholic clergy have to take an oath rejecting modernism until 1967.

1907 The United Methodist Church is established in Britain.

THE AMERICAS

1901 Solomon Schechter—an English rabbi originally from Romania—arrives in the United States to lead Counter-Reform Judaism.

1903 Pronouncing himself the seventh angel of the Book of Revelations, Benjamin Purnell founds the House of David in Benton Harbor, Michigan, to gather the tribes of Israel to prepare for Christ's Second Coming.

1905 Soyen Shaku becomes the first Zen Buddhist teacher in the United States when he spends a year in San Francisco.

1906 Only four years before her death, Mary Baker Eddy publishes the final revision of *Science and Health*, the textbook of Christian Science; she has constantly revised it over the previous 30 years (page 291).

1900 In the influential essay "Ariel," Uruguayan author José Enrique Rodó urges Latin Americans to reject materialism and follow humanistic values.

1902 U.S. philosopher Wiliam James publishes *The Varieties of Religious Experience*; he argues that "personal religious experience has its root and centre in mystical states of consciousness."

1903 The sermons of Charles Taze Russell, founder of the Watch Tower Society (later the Jehovah's Witnesses), are syndicated in some 4,000 newspapers worldwide.

1907 Walter Rauschenbusch writes *Christianity and the Social Crisis*, which argues using Christian values to solve the problems of an industrialized, urban world.

1900 The Catholic Church in the United States claims about 12 million members.

1900 An estimated 97 percent of Lutheran congregations in the Midwest use German or other non-English languages for prayer.

1908 After 416 years, the pope removes administration of the Catholic Church in the United States from the Congregation de Propaganda Fide, meaning that the church no longer sees it as a target for missionary activity.

1908 The Methodist Church produces a "social creed."

1908 The larger evangelist Protestant churches of the United States form the Federal Council of the Churches of Christ in America.

ASIA & OCEANIA

1904 Thubten Gyatso, the 13th Dalai Lama, flees Lhasa after British forces arrive in Tibet.

1904 A Jain temple is built at the Louisiana Purchase Exposition at St. Louis, Missouri.

A sacred cow rests in India. The early years of the 20th century saw a growing interest in Hindu rights in India, matched by concern for the rights of Indian Muslims, a minority—but over 10 percent of the population and the world's third-largest Muslim population.

1900 Shintoism is reinstated in Japan to try to limit Buddhist influence (page 287).

1902 The Iglesia Filipina Independiente splits from the Roman Catholic Church.

1905 The Japan Congregational Church becomes independent from missionary control.

1908 Presbyterians, Congregationalists, and Dutch Reformed churches combine to form the South India United Church.

AFRICA & THE MIDDLE EAST

1900 Sir Arthur Evans discovers the Minoan culture on Crete, with evidence that the Minoans worshiped bulls.

1903 East Africa is proposed as a possible homeland for the Jews.

1908 Frank Weston becomes the Anglican bishop of Zanzibar in East Africa.

RELIGION IN THE WORLD	WORLD EVENTS

RELIGION IN THE WORLD

1901 The Fifth Zionist Congress founds the Jewish National Fund to raise money to purchase land in Palestine.

1902 The Pilgrims Association is founded in Britain and America to encourage visits to holy sites.

1903 Anti-Jewish pogroms take place in Russia.

1906 The church and state are separated in France, with the state taking church property.

Abdülhamid II became the Ottoman emperor in 1876 but was deposed by the Young Turks in 1909; his reign marked the death throes of the greatest Muslim empire of the time.

WORLD EVENTS

1900 The socialist Labour Party is founded in Britain.

1901 The death of Queen Victoria marks the end of the Victorian age.

1901 Guglielmo Marconi sends the first radio message across the Atlantic.

1903 In Russia, the Social Democratic Party splits into Mensheviks and Bolsheviks.

1905 In the face of mounting unrest, Tsar Nicholas II introduces reforms in Russia.

1908 Bulgaria and Crete declare independence from the Ottoman Empire.

1901 U.S. President William McKinley is assassinated by an anarchist.

1902 In Colombia the end of the War of a Thousand Days leaves some 100,000 dead.

1906 San Francisco is devastated by an earthquake that is followed by a huge fire.

1908 U.S. engineer Henry Ford produces the first Model T Ford.

1909 U.S. African-American leader W.E.B. Dubois founds the National Association for the Advancement of Colored People (NAACP); it still exists today.

1900 In China, the Righteous Harmony Society Movement—the Boxers—rebel against Western influence, killing hundreds of missionaries and local Christians.

1905 British viceroy George Curzon divides Bengal in India into mainly Hindu Western Bengal and mainly Muslim Eastern Bengal.

1906 The Simla Deputation calls for improved rights for Muslims in India; they are supported by the newly created All India Muslim League.

1901 Zionist Theodor Herzl meets Ottoman sultan Abdülhamid II to request land in Palestine to form a Jewish state.

1903 Russian Jews escaping pogroms arrive in Palestine.

New Age druids celebrate the summer solstice at Stonehenge in 2003; according to critics, the connections between Celtic druids and the monument, and between neopagans and ancient practices, are tenuous at best and bogus at worst.

THE NEW PAGANS

No-one knows when druids first came to the great stone circle at Stonehenge in southern England. Sometime during the 19th century, the white-robed priests began meeting there to mark sunrise on the summer solstice. They believed that the monument had been used for the same purpose by their forebears, the druids of the ancient Celts (in fact, we now know that Stonehenge predated the Celts by some 2,000 years).

The druids were just one group of neopagans (new pagans) who emerged in the 19th century. Strongly influenced by the romantic movement, they reacted to an industrial and urban world by turning to what they perceived as "purer" forms of spirituality. These shared a belief in the divine aspect of nature, often manifested in worship of different nature deities and ritualistic marking of the changing seasons. Believers worship outdoors to be close to nature.

Along with druids, neopagan groups include wiccans, shamans, sacred ecologists, odinists, and heathens. Neopaganism flourishes in the United States, the United Kingdom, and Scandinavia. The largest pagan movement is the Church of All Worlds, based on worship of the earth-mother goddess.

PEOPLE & PLACES	DOCUMENTS, ART, & ARTIFACTS	WORSHIP & DOCTRINE

EUROPE

1912 Rudolf Steiner founds the Anthroposophical Society, an esoteric movement that sets out to explore spirituality through inner development.

1913 Albert Schweitzer abandons his theological career and opens a hospital at Lambaréné in French Congo, Africa.

1919 Swiss theologian Karl Barth publishes a commentary on The Epistle to the Romans, which is acknowleged as one of the most important theological works of the 20th century.

The Bengali poet Rabindranath Tagore wrote in a devotional style that was well established in Hindu religious tradition.

1910 The World Conference of Protestant Missionaries is held in Edinburgh, Scotland, presided over by U.S. missionary John Mott.

1914 An act is passed for the disestablishment of the Anglican Church in Wales (it is enacted in 1920, after the end of the war).

1917 Christians begin making pilgrimages to Fatima in Portugal, where children have reported seeing visions of the Virgin Mary.

1917 The patriarchate is reestablished in Georgia.

1918 The Council of the Russian Orthodox Church reestablishes the Moscow patriarchate.

THE AMERICAS

1910 Mary Baker Eddy dies leaving a note that reads "God is my life."

1915 On the death of founder Ellen Gould White, the Seventh-Day Adventists claim 136,000 followers.

1915 Asa Griggs Chandler, founder of the Coca-Cola company and devout Methodist, makes a $1-million donation to allow Emory College become a Methodist university.

1918 Cardinal James Gibbons of Baltimore claims of World War I, "We have conquered because we believe that righteousness exalteth a nation" (📄 pages 300–301).

1910 *The Fundamentals*, a tract, promotes temperance.

1912 Walter Rauschenbusch publishes *Christianizing the Social Order*.

1917 Rauschenbusch writes *A Theory for the Social Gospel*.

A Seventh-Day Adventist preacher surveys his congregation. Today the church has some 16 million followers worldwide.

1913 Southern Baptist James B. Gambrell argues in favor of Christian unity—as long as all other Christians become Baptists.

1917 Although they are just 1 in 6 of the population, Catholics form a quarter of the U.S. Army and a half of the U.S. Navy.

1919 The Eighteenth Amendment introduces Prohibition in the United States; William J. Bryan remarks, "Let the world rejoice. The greatest moral reform of the generation has been accomplished."

ASIA & OCEANIA

1912 Bengali poet Rabindranath Tagore publishes *Gitanjali*, a collection of devotional poems.

AFRICA & THE MIDDLE EAST

1913 In Nyasaland (Malawi), Baptist prophet John Chilembwe leads a nationalist uprising.

1914 In Ghana and Ivory Coast, Prophet Wade Harris enjoins some 120,000 followers to give up traditional religions, become baptized, and await the arrival of white missionaries to teach them the Bible.

1915 In Nigeria the prophet Garrick Braid stirs an upsurge in religious fervor.

RELIGION IN THE WORLD	WORLD EVENTS

1913 Condemned for "onomatolatry"—the worship of words—Russian monks are deported at gunpoint from the St. Panteleimon Monastery on Mount Athos, Greece, by a naval forces sent from Russia.

1916 Irish Catholics lead the Easter Rebellion in Dublin against British rule.

1917 The British government indicates in the Balfour Declaration its support for the future creation of a Jewish homeland in Palestine.

1918 The new revolutionary Soviet government in Russia issues a decree separating church and state; it soon becomes clear that the church is to be subjugated by the state (📄 page 321).

1914 World War I breaks out after the assassination of the heir to the Austrian throne by a Serbian nationalist; a complex system of alliances draws the major European powers into the conflict.

1915 Albert Einstein suggests his General Theory of Relativity.

1917 Revolutions in Russia overthrow Tsar Nicholas II; eventually the Bolsheviks of Vladimir Lenin come to power.

1918 World War I ends with an armistice signed between Germany and the Allies.

1919 The Versailles Peace Treaty redraws the shape of the peacetime world.

1919 Italian journalist Benito Mussolini founds the Fascist party.

1914 Woodrow Wilson and William J. Bryan, president and secretary of state of the United States, are both pacifist Presbyterians.

1915 William J. Bryan resigns, saying that Wilson's warlike stance toward World War I "does not befit the greatest Christian nation."

1917 After the United States joins the war, U.S. pacifists come under pressure to support the conflict (📄 pages 300–301).

1917 Wilson recommends his Fourteen Points to the Senate as "the single supreme plan of peace, the revelation of our Lord and Saviour."

1918 The American Jewish Committee gives only tepid support to the idea of a Jewish homeland in Palestine.

1911 Revolutionaries led by Pancho Villa and Emiliano Zapata overthrow the government in Mexico.

1912 U.S. forces invade Nicaragua, which they will occupy for 20 years.

1915 A second Ku Klux Klan is created to campaign against Catholics, Jews, and Blacks.

1916 The first birth control clinic in the United States is opened by Margaret Sanger in Brooklyn.

1917 The United States declares war on Germany; it sends some two million soldiers to fight in Europe.

1910 At the request of Hindus in India, the new British governor annuls the partition of Bengal.

1912 The Presbyterian Church in Australia founds the Australian Inland Mission to spread God's word and hospital facilities to people "beyond the farthest fence."

1919 At Amritsar, British soldiers open fire on unarmed demonstrators, killing 379 Hindus, Muslims, and Sikhs, and wounding some 1,100 more.

1910 Japan annexes Korea.

1911 Sun Yat-Sen leads a nationalist revolution in China.

1915 Japan issues "21 Demands," which threaten Chinese sovereignty.

1919 In French Indochina, Ho Chi Minh founds the Indochinese Communist Party, which will eventually lead Vietnam's campaign for independence.

1913 British missionaries meet at Kikuyu in British East Africa to plan a federation of Christians in the protectorate; Bishop Frank Weston of Zanzibar attacks the scheme for attempting to create a church for Africa without the involvement of a single African.

1916 Catholic hermit Charles de Foucauld is murdered at the fort he has built for the protection of the Tuareg among whom he lives in Algeria; his death encourages the creation of communities of Little Brothers of Jesus to follow his teaching.

THE ROSICRUCIANS

Often treated with suspicion, Rosicrucians share a belief system drawn from hermeticism, Jewish mysticism, and Christian gnosticism. The movement blends religious beliefs with the occult and takes its name from its symbol of a rose on a cross. Rosicrucians are united by their belief that they possess secret knowledge that has been handed down from generation to generation from ancient times.

The original ideas come from three books by 16th-century author Johann Valentin Andreae, a Lutheran theologian. One book described how Christian Rosenkreuz, the movement's founder (now thought to be fictional), traveled to the Middle East and North Africa seeking secret wisdom before establishing the Rosicrucian order on his return to Germany. He allegedly erected a tomb in 1409 in which he was buried in 1484. The tomb's discovery 120 years later marked the public revelation of the order's existence.

The movement's mixture of alchemy and mysticism attracted many followers, but it declined during the 18th century as the ideas of the Enlightenment took over. The movement revived during the 19th and 20th centuries during a general occult revival in the West.

Conspiracy theorists have long seen the unfinished pyramid and the all-seeing eye that appear on the dollar bill as secret symbols of the Rosicrucians (or other groups such as the Freemasons or the Illuminati). There is not a shred of evidence to support such theories.

God heard the embattled nations sing and shout;

"God strafe England" and "God save the King,"

God this, God that, and God the other thing;

"Good God," said God, "I've got my work cut out."

JOHN C. SQUIRE (ATTRIBUTED)

FAITH IN WARTIME

Like all conflicts, the Great War stirred a flowering of spiritual feeling. It took various forms, from soldiers' emphasis on superstition and fate—a feeling that a bullet might have one's "number" on it—to an upsurge on the home front of an interest in spiritualism, mediums, and seances as means to contact the recently dead.

People sought solace in traditional faiths, but the churches faced a dilemma. Many were established churches, closely tied to the state. Although Christian teaching promoted pacifism and love, the churches were obliged by patriotic duty to support their own side. In a particularly extreme sermon, Arthur Winnington-Ingram, bishop of London, preached: "Everything that loves freedom and honor, everyone that puts principle above ease, and life itself beyond mere living, are banded in a great crusade—we cannot deny it—to kill Germans: to kill them not for the sake of killing, but to save the world…." The Catholic Church, meanwhile, had followers on both sides. It announced its neutrality, much to the fury of French Catholics after France was invaded. When Pope Benedict XV made peace overtures in 1917, the church position was so weak that they were rejected out of hand.

At the front, army chaplains ministered spiritual support. At the start of the war neither the French nor the U.S. armies had any chaplains, France to avoid possible clerical opposition to the republic and the United States because of the consitutional separation of church and state. That soon changed, while the British increased the number of nonconformist chaplains represented in the army. In Russia, the tsar encouraged mystical religious fervor at the front, where officers displayed religious icons to men before battle.

Stories proliferated of miraculous events, such as statues that survived unharmed the destruction of the churches around them or the Angels of Mons, said to have appeared in the sky to protect retreating British soldiers in Belgium in August 1914.

An army chaplain delivers a sermon from the cockpit of a bomber at an army base in Britain in 1918.

PEOPLE & PLACES	DOCUMENTS, ART, & ARTIFACTS	WORSHIP & DOCTRINE

EUROPE

1920 Pope Benedict XV canonizes French national heroine Joan of Arc.

1922 Veniamin, the Metropolitan of St. Petrograd, is accused by the Soviet government of resisting the confiscation of sacred artifacts needed to raise money to alleviate famine; after a show trial during which he displays remarkable dignity, he and four codefendants are executed.

1926 In Germany, Catholic mystic Therese Neumann manifests the stigmata—the wounds of Christ—with blood pouring from her head, eyes, hands, and feet; she claims to survive until her death in 1962 by eating only one communion wafer a day and drinking nothing.

1923 English artist Stanley Spencer paints *The Resurrection*, showing the dead leaving their graves in an English parish churchyard.

1928 German Jewish scholars begin to publish a huge *Encyclopedia Judaica*; they reach volume 10 before Nazi persecution halts the project in 1934.

1928 In the encyclical *Mortalium Animos*, Pope Pius XI argues that Christian churches cannot form a broad federation, but that all other churches should rejoin the Roman Catholic Church.

1920 The Serbian patriarchate is reestablished.

1920 The first ecumenical council brings together European, American, and Eastern churches.

1920 The Lambeth Conference of Anglican bishops calls for Christian unity.

1924 The Finnish and Polish Orthodox churches become independent.

1927 The Faith and Order Movement is founded to work toward "visible unity" among Christian churches.

THE AMERICAS

1924 On his death, President Woodrow Wilson is interred in a new episcopal National Cathedral.

1925 Methodist tobacco magnate James B. Duke makes a $40 million grant to Trinity College, North Carolina, which changes its name to Duke University.

1926 Father Charles Coughlin, a Catholic priest from Michigan, broadcasts on radio station WJR; in the 1930s he becomes an extreme right-wing critic of Roosevelt.

1927 After legal action, industrialist Henry Ford apologizes for asserting the authenticity of the *Protocols of the Elders of Zion*, an antisemitic hoax purporting to contain a Jewish plan for world domination.

FBI agents pour away illegal alcohol after a raid during Prohibition.

1925 Bruce Barton writes *The Man Nobody Knows*, a bestseller that portrays Jesus as an executive.

1927 James Weldon Johnson writes *God's Trombones: Seven Negro Sermons in Verse*, a celebration of African-American "folk sermons" from his youth.

1920 *The Baptist* regrets the passing of the Social Gospel movement, noting that Christians are "going back to the old ideas that made a hell of the world."

1928 In the face of rising antisemitism, U.S. Christians and Jews form the National Conference of Christians and Jews.

1929 A Methodist periodical—*The Christian Advocate*—argues that enforcing Prohibition is the single most pressing requirement in the United States.

ASIA & OCEANIA

1927 In Madras, India, a landmark high court decision recognizes Jainism as a distinct religion rather than a strand of Hinduism.

1927 Indian Catholic priest Varghese Palakkappillil founds the Congregation of the Sisters of the Destitute in Kerala.

The first official mass was celebrated at the Sanctuary of Our Lady of Fatima, in Portugal, in 1924, seven years after the visions that inspired its creation.

AFRICA & THE MIDDLE EAST

1925 Josiah Olunowo Oshitelu, a first-generation Nigerian Christian, experiences a vision and forms the Church of the Lord (Aladura) as an independent African church (it still exists today).

1928 Hasan al-Banna, an Egyptian revivalist Muslim, founds the Muslim Brotherhood (pages 332–333).

RELIGION IN THE WORLD	WORLD EVENTS

1922 A change in French law allows the monks of Solesmes—famous for reviving Gregorian chant—to return to their abbey after 21 years of exile.

1927 Metropolitan Sergii Stragorodski leads an attempt by the remaining handful of Russian bishops to make an agreement with the Communist government; the Soviet antireligious campaign continues and the position of Christians in the Soviet Union remains weak and potentially dangerous (🔖 page 321).

1929 The Lateran Treaty between the Kingdom of Italy and the Holy See establishes the sovereignty of the Vatican City within Italy and regulates the influence of the Roman Catholic Church in Italian life.

1922 The Union of Soviet Socialist Republics (U.S.S.R.) is created by Lenin.

1922 Benito Mussolini becomes prime minister of Italy.

1923 Hyperinflation destroys the German economy.

1927 After a power struggle following the death of Lenin, Joseph Stalin emerges as the leader of the Soviet Union.

Haile Selassie ruled Ethiopia from 1930 to 1974. Selassie himself was head of the Orthodox Ethiopian Church; according to reports, he neither accepted nor denied the Rastafarians' claims of his divinity.

1921 The *Presbyterian Continent* argues that control of immigration would violate the brotherhood of man.

1922 Harvard faculty reject a proposal from the president and students to limit the number of Jewish students in the university.

1925 John T. Scopes is found guilty of teaching evolution in the "Scopes Monkey Trial" (🔖 pages 304–305).

1928 Democrat Alfred E. Smith becomes the first Catholic to run for the U.S. presidency as a major-party candidate.

1920 American women get the vote in the Nineteenth Amendment.

1924 The Ku Klux Klan reaches a postwar peak of 5 million followers.

1924 The Exclusion Act severely restricts immigration into the United States.

1924 Native Americans are given full U.S. citizenship.

1928 Brazil suffers an economic crash after overproduction of coffee floods the market.

1929 U.S. shares lose billions in the Wall Street Crash, which contributes to the beginning of the Great Depression in 1930.

Josiah Oshitelu

The founder of the Aladura Church was typical of African charismatics who attracted followers through prophecy or healing. Schooled by missionaries and baptized in 1914, Josiah Oshitelu spent three years in spiritual seclusion, where he had a vision of holy words with miraculous power. Taking the title "Primate," he began a ministry of healing through holy water, prayer, and fasting. His adoption of Islamic dietary laws helped the church spread into even Muslim parts of Nigeria.

1920 Central Asia is divided into a series of autonomous Soviet Socialist Republics.

1924 Mohandas (Mahatma) Gandhi, who has emerged as a leader of India's independence movement, fasts for 21 days as a protest against fighting between India's Hindus and Muslims.

1926 Hirohito becomes emperor of Japan.

1929 The All-India Congress claims independence, but without effect.

1921 In the Belgian Congo, the prophet Simon Kimbangu begins a brief ministry of preaching and healing before he is arrested by Belgian colonial authorities; he dies in captivity.

1922 The discovery of the tomb of Tutankhamun offers new insights into the civilization of Ancient Egypt.

1924 The Ottoman state and caliphate are dissolved following defeat in World War I.

1924 Saudi forces conquer the holy city of Mecca and, in 1925, all of Arabia.

1929 Fighting between Jews and Arabs kills about 250 people in Palestine.

RASTAFARIANISM

Rastafarianism is a young religion. It emerged in Jamaica in the 1930s after the coronation of Haile Selassie I as king of Ethiopia in 1930. Its followers saw Haile Selassie as a god who would return one day to save Africans dispersed from their homeland by colonization and the slave trade. It is what is known as an exocentric religion: Haile Selassie is not actually part of the faith. The faith also draws on the ideas of the black U.S. activist Marcus Garvey.

In 1935 Jamaican Leonard P. Howell began the Rastafarian religion by preaching the gospel of Haile Selassie: one day black people would gain superiority over the white population.

Rastafarians do not have any religious buildings: they meet in community halls or private homes where they hold "reasoning sessions" during which they sing, chant, pray, and discuss local business. Their rituals also involve playing music and smoking marijuana. Jamaican reggae singer Bob Marley is widely credited with spreading the popularity of Rastafarianism during the 1970s.

Rastafarians are easily recognizable because they do not cut their hair, which they wear as dreadlocks, and wear only four colors: red, black, gold and green. They also adhere to strict dietary rules.

EVOLUTION ON TRIAL

A TINY COURTROOM IN A SMALL TOWN in Tennessee was for two weeks in 1925 the scene of a trial that preoccupied the world's press. In the dock was young Dayton schoolteacher John T. Scopes, charged with teaching high-school students the principles of Charles Darwin's theory of evolution. The "Monkey Trial" highlighted a debate that still continues in the United States today.

The trial was provoked by the American Civil Liberties Union—with the agreement of Scopes and the town of Dayton—to challenge a Tennessee law against the teaching of evolution. The law stipulated that "It shall be unlawful for any teacher … to teach any theory that denies the story of the divine creation of man as taught in the Bible, and to teach instead that man has descended from a lower order of animals."

In July 1925 Dayton became the center of the first full-blown media circus in U.S. history thanks to the heavyweights involved in the trial. The defense was led by Clarence Darrow, one of the most famous trial lawyers in the country. The prosecution, meanwhile, was led by William Jennings Bryan. A former populist politician and secretary of state, Bryan was a Presbyterian and a staunch anti-evolutionist. Although he rejected the literal interpretation of the book of Genesis, he also rejected evolution. "Darwinian theory," he said, "represents man as reaching his present perfection by the operation of the law of hate—the merciless law by which the strong crowd kill off the weak."

For six days the court listened to the defense argument that evolution was true, and that the Tennessee law was ill-conceived. Bryan warned that "If evolution wins, Christianity goes." On the seventh day Darrow called Bryan as a witness. In a brilliant cross-examination, he forced the other man to admit that the Bible should not always be taken literally. In order to deny Bryan the chance to make a summing up, Darrow asked the judge to find his client guilty: the teacher was fined $100 (the verdict was later overturned on a technicality).

Although the ACLU had not overturned the Tennessee law, it was clear that anti-evolutionary teaching had been damaged. Later attempts by states to pass laws enforcing the teaching of creationism were rejected in the U.S. Supreme Court in 1987 because they sought to promote "the religious belief that a supernatural being created humankind," in violation of the constitutional ban against the establishment of religion.

This anti-evolution bookstore was set up in Dayton during the trial. The elders of the town agreed to stage the trial to help raise Dayton's profile: they were dismayed to be characterized in national newspapers as rural hicks.

The presence of national figures Clarence Darrow (left) and William Jennings Bryan (right) made the trial a media sensation; only a week after his hollow "victory," Bryan collapsed and died.

PEOPLE & PLACES	DOCUMENTS, ART, & ARTIFACTS	WORSHIP & DOCTRINE

EUROPE

1933 Despite being rejected by leaders of the German Protestant Federation, the committed Nazi Ludwig Müller is elevated to the position of *Reichsbischof* of the German Evangelical Church thanks to the maneuvering of his supporter, Adolf Hitler.

1933 German theologian Paul Tillich, dismissed from his academic position by Adolf Hitler, moves to the United States at the invitation of U.S. theologian Reinhold Niebuhr.

1938 German pastor Martin Niemoeller is imprisoned in Sachsenhausen concentration camp by the Nazis, but widespread publicity reportedly prevents his planned execution.

1934 Swiss philosopher Max Picard writes in *The Flight from God* that society has become so secular that people no longer need to make a conscious decision to turn their backs on religious belief.

1931 The Oxford Group is founded by Frank Buchanan to encourage missionary work among the wealthy elites of Europe and the United State.

1933 The Nazis in Germany get the Protestant Federation to agree to the creation of a new "national" church, the German Evangelical Church, which will draw the church and state together.

1934 German Protestants form the Confessing Church in opposition to the Nazi-sponsored German Evangelical Church.

1937 The Albanian Orthodox Church becomes self-governing.

THE AMERICAS

Jehovah's Witnesses perform a total immersion baptism in a public swimming pool in 1950.

1932 William Joseph McGlothlin, president of the Southern Baptist Convention, refuses to accept an honor from the black moderator of a Baptist association in Rochester, New York.

1933 George Barker, better known as Father Divine, sets up the headquarters of his black cult movement in Harlem, New York.

1933 The Hindu monk Bramachari influences young American Thomas Merton when he represents his monastery at the Chicago World's Fair; Merton later becomes a famous Trappist monk.

1934 *Judaism as a Civilization*, by Mordecai Kaplan, aims to make secular Jews comfortable with their cultural history.

1937 Psychologist Henry C. Link publishes *The Return to Religion*, explaining his decision to rejoin the church after 25 years.

1931 The Zion's Watch Tower Tract Society founded by Charles Taze Russell is renamed the Jehovah's Witnesses.

1934 Radio priest Father Charles E. Coughlin founds the National Union for Social Justice; the movement is nationalistic and antisemitic.

1934 Philosopher John Dewey outlines a case for a common Christian faith in the United States.

1937 There are some 3,700 Jewish congregations in the United States, an increase of 600 from ten years previously.

1939 The Methodist churches unite, forming the largest Protestant church in the United States.

ASIA & OCEANIA

1938 Mahatma Gandhi and Muhammad Ali Jinnah, leader of the Muslim League, meet to resolve differences between Hindus and Muslims in India, but fail.

1930 The Soka Gakkai cult, based on Nichiren Buddhism, is founded in Japan by Tsunesaburo Makiguchi to encourage a humanistic approach to finding value in human life: despite angering the militaristic government, Soka Gakkai survives—today it includes some 10 percent of Japanese.

1936 The Office of the Propaganda Fide in the Vatican declares that Japanese Shinto rites are compatible with Catholicism as they are patriotic rather than religious.

AFRICA & THE MIDDLE EAST

Untouchables—the lowest level of the Hindu castes—protest in 1931 against the caste system that prohibited their social mobility in India.

1932 After the creation of the Kingdom of Iraq and an Assyrian uprising against the rule of King Faisal, Iraqis massacre some 3,000 Assyrian Christians.

1936 British authorities limit Jewish immigration to Palestine as clashes with Arabs grow more violent.

1939 The French deny Algerian Muslims citizenship.

RELIGION IN THE WORLD	WORLD EVENTS
1933 Books by Jewish authors are burned in Germany, Jewish businesses are boycotted, and the first concentration camps are built.	**1931** The Spanish declare a republic; the king goes into exile.
1935 In Germany, the Nuremberg Laws restrict Jewish rights.	**1932** Stalin's attempt to control agriculture in Ukraine leads to famine that causes millions of deaths.
1937 Having made a concordat with Hitler in 1933, Pope Pius XI now publishes an encyclical condemning Nazi racism and totalitarianism and Nazi breaches of the concordat.	**1933** Adolf Hitler is elected chancellor of Germany; he outlaws all opposition and rules as a dictator.
1938 On *Kristallnacht*, the Night of Broken Glass, Nazis attack Jewish homes, synagogues, and businesses.	**1934** Stalin purges his enemies in a series of show trials and executions.
	1936 Right-wing nationalists and left-wing republicans begin the Spanish Civil War, won by Franco's nationalists in 1939.
	1939 World War II begins as a result of Hitler's invasion of Poland, part of a program of German expansion in Europe.
1932 Franklin D. Roosevelt invites Father Charles Coughlin to the Democratic National Convention; shortly afterward Coughlin turns against Roosevelt's New Deal.	**1930** In Brazil, Getúlio Vargas begins to govern as a dictator.
1934 With the Nazis in power in Germany, *The Christian Century* claims that 20 million Protestants are against any war that might occur in the future.	**1932** Bolivia and Paraguay begin the three-year Chaco War, which Paraguay eventually wins.
1938 Charles Coughlin defends the Nazi treatment of the Jews and calls for the creation of a Christian Front to protect the United States from Jewish influences.	**1933** At the height of the Great Depression, Prohibition ends in the United States; President F. D. Roosevelt says "I think this would be a good time for beer."
	1934 Drought turns much of the U.S. Midwest into a Dust Bowl.
	1939 The outbreak of war in Europe and the demand for materiel from the Allies helps move the U.S. economy out of depression.
1932 In India the Poona Pact gives voting rights to the lowest caste of society, the Untouchables.	**1934** Mao Zedong leads China's communists on the "Long March" to a remote part of the country.

FAITH AND LIFE

The Nazis and the Jews

Antisemitism had a long history before Adolf Hitler came to power in Germany in 1933, but the Nazi regime made it a systematic policy. Hitler blamed the Jews for Germany's economic woes after World War I and portrayed them as less than human. In power, he used laws to limit Jewish rights and used the SS to harrass Jews and Jewish businesses (left). *Kristallnacht*, when thugs destroyed Jewish property and synagogues, provoked public sympathy for the victims, so Hitler carried on his campaign more secretly. Eventually it would lead to the concentration camps and gas chambers of the Holocaust.

NATION OF ISLAM

In summer 1930 a former American peddler of obscure origins named Wallace D. Fard began preaching Islam among African-American families in Detroit, Michigan. As his following grew, Fard announced the formation of the Temple of Islam, which later became Temple No. 1 of the Nation of Islam (NOI).

Fard's teachings argued that Islam was the only true religion. He claimed that a crazy black scientist named Yakub had created white people 6,000 years ago as a curse and a test for the more advanced black races. Fard said that he had been sent by Allah to reclaim his people, the tribe of Shabazz, who had been kidnapped and sent to America in chains. Nation of Islam theology states: "We believe that Allah (God) appeared in the person of Master W. Fard Muhammad, July 1930; the long awaited 'Messiah' of the Christians and the 'Mahdi' of the Muslims."

Fard disappeared without a trace in Chicago in 1934. His place as leader was taken by Elijah Muhammad, whom Fard had named supreme minister of Islam. Elijah Muhammad drew on the African nationalist philosophy of the black thinker Marcus Garvey (1887–1940) to call the bluff of white segregationists. Rather than call for civil rights, like other African Americans, he argued that the separation of the races had not gone far enough. The NOI advocated the creation of an independent black state and economic and cultural self-sufficiency for African Americans. Islam had little history in North America; the NOI set out to make it as visible as possible (including by the later adoption of uniform suits and sunglasses).

Elijah Muhammad and the young organizer Malcolm X toured the country, setting up temples in various cities. Although orthodox Muslims rejected NOI theology and its elements of black supremacism, the faith met with considerable success among African-American communities. In later decades, however, it clashed with the church-based civil rights movement and spawned numerous offshoots of its own.

PEOPLE & PLACES	DOCUMENTS, ART, & ARTIFACTS	WORSHIP & DOCTRINE

EUROPE

1940 Swiss monk Roger Schutz founds the Taizé Community in France near Cluny, home of Western monasticism.

1942 Nazi leader Reinhard Heydrich reveals his plan to exterminate 11 million Jews in the "final solution."

1943 German pastor Dietrich Bonhoeffer, a founder of the Confessing Church, is arrested for his part in the plot to assassinate Adolf Hitler; he is hanged in 1945.

1949 Hungarian cardinal Jósef Mindszenty, an outspoken opponent of communism and persecution, is sentenced to life imprisonment after a show trial finds him guilty of "high treason."

1942 British composer Benjamin Britten writes his *Sinfonia Requiem*.

1943 British sculptor Henry Moore carves a characteristically rounded *Madonna and Child*.

British soldiers attend a prayer meeting on board a warship in World War II.

1945 With postwar Germany divided between East and West, Protestant churches form the Evangelical Church in Germany (the communist authorities force East German churches to quit in 1969).

1946 In the Soviet Union the Uniate Catholic Church is abolished.

1946 Pope Pius XII creates 32 new cardinals.

1948 The World Jewish Congress meets in Montreux, Switzerland.

1948 The World Council of Churches is formed in Amsterdam.

THE AMERICAS

1941 Thomas Merton, who has converted to Catholicism in 1938, enters the Our Lady of Gethsemani monastery in Kentucky, three days after the Japanese attack on Pearl Harbor.

1945 William L. Sperry writes *Religion in America*.

1946 Nun and missionary Francis Xavier Cabrini (1850–1917) becomes a saint, the first U.S. citizen to be canonized by the Catholic Church.

1946 Methodist layman John Mott, a leading world missionary, wins the Nobel Peace prize.

1947 Thomas Merton seeks permission from his abbot to live in solitude.

1941 Christian fundamentalists form the "militantly pro-Gospel and antimodernist" American Council of Christian Churches; milder fundamentalists form the Moody Bible Institute in Chicago.

1949 John Courtney Murray, editor of the Jesuit journal *Theological Studies*, argues that the old divisions between Protestants and Catholics in the United States are lesser threats to the country than the rise of secularism.

1949 Evangelist Billy Graham begins his "crusades" when he preaches in a huge tent—a "canvas cathedral"—in Los Angeles (pages 318–319).

ASIA & OCEANIA

1948 Mahatma Gandhi is assassinated by a Hindu fanatic.

1949 After centuries of foreign and Hindu administration, Buddhists regain some control over the Mahabodhi Temple in Bodh Gaya, marking the site of Buddha's Enlightenment.

AFRICA & THE MIDDLE EAST

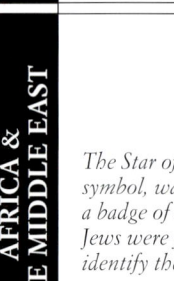

The Star of David, a sacred Jewish symbol, was turned by the Nazis into a badge of discrimination: German Jews were forced to wear yellow stars to identify themselves.

O Lord, remember not only the men and women of good will, but also those of ill will. But do not remember all the suffering they have inflicted on us, remember the fruits we have bought, because of this suffering—our comradeship, our loyalty, our humility, our courage, our generosity, the greatness of heart that has grown out of all of this, and when they come to judgment, let all the fruits we have borne be their forgiveness.

RAVENSBRUCK PRAYER, FOUND IN THE CLOTHES OF A CONCENTRATION CAMP VICTIM

RELIGION IN THE WORLD	WORLD EVENTS
1940 In Warsaw, 350,000 Polish Jews are forced into a ghetto.	**1941** In Operation Barbarossa, Germany invades the Soviet Union.
1943 The Russian Orthodox Church makes a concordat with Stalin; needing church support to bolster the "Great Patriotic Struggle," Stalin allows Sergii Stragorodskii to be installed as patriarch and allows churches to be reopened (📄 page 321).	**1942** The Nazis begin the "final solution," seeking to exterminate Europe's Jews.
	1944 On D-Day, Allied troops land in northern France and begin a campaign to liberate Europe.
1943 In Britain, George Bell, bishop of Chichester, condemns the bombing of German cities.	**1945** Germany is defeated; Hitler commits suicide in Berlin.
	1949 Germany is divided into the democratic Federal Republic of Germany and the communist People's Republic of Germany.
	1949 To counter Soviet aggression, European and North American nations set up the North Atlantic Treaty Organization (NATO).
1943 The U.S. Supreme Court rules in a case brought by Jehovah's Witnesses that children need not salute flags in school if it is against their religion.	**1941** The United States joins World War II after the Japanese bomb the Pacific naval base at Pearl Harbor on Hawaii.
1944 A British visitor to the United States calls the public school system "the formally unestablished national church."	**1945** Franklin D. Roosevelt is elected president for a fourth term, but dies in office shortly after.
1945 After the first successful test of an atomic bomb in New Mexico, the physicist in charge of the atomic program, J. Robert Oppenheimer, recalls a quotation from the Hindu *Bhagavad Gita*: "Now I am become Death, the destroyer of worlds."	**1946** Argentines elect Juan Perón as president.
	1947 The House Un-American Activities Committee investigates communist influence in the United States.
1949 Newspaper owner William Randolph Hearst wires his editors the instruction, "Puff Graham."	**1948** The Organization of American States is formed to promote regional peace and security.
1945 Defeat in World War II ends government attempts to control Shinto and other religions in Japan; Shintoism is banned in Japan.	
1945 Communists in North Korea impose new restrictions on religion.	
1947 Indian and Pakistan are partitioned— divided—to create largely Hindu and largely Muslim states, respectively (📄 box, right).	
1949 The Communist revolution in China effectively ends Christian missionary activity in the new People's Republic.	
1946 Jewish militants blow up the King David Hotel in Jerusalem, killing 91 people.	
1947 The United Nations agrees on a plan to divide Palestine into Jewish and Arab states.	
1948 The Jewish state of Israel is created; it immediately has to defend itself against its Arab neighbors in the Arab-Israeli War. More than 1 million Palestinians leave Israel, while some 250,000 Holocaust survivors arrive from Europe.	

THE PARTITION OF INDIA

One of the great religious tragedies of history unfolded when India achieved independence from Great Britain on August 14, 1947. At the same time, the country was partitioned to create two new countries: the Dominion of Pakistan (later the Islamic Republic of Pakistan and the People's Republic of Bangladesh) and the Union of India (later the Republic of India). The split was made purely on religious grounds.

For almost 190 years the British rulers had fostered divisions between the Hindu majority and Muslim minority. When independence came, India's political leaders could see no future for a united nation.

At midnight on August 14, the states of Punjab and Bengal were split. In Punjab, Muslims moved west, into Pakistan, while Hindus and Sikhs moved to East Punjab, which remained in India (more than 99 percent of Sikhs chose to live in India). In Bengal, Hindus moved west while Muslims moved to East Bengal (later Bangladesh).

Families were divided and split up as millions moved by train, foot, or bullock cart. Rape, looting, and widespread violence marked partition. The number of dead remains disputed but some sources claim it was as high as 500,000.

Bodies lie in a Muslim area of Calcutta in 1946 following a riot that reflected growing religious tensions in the run-up to Partition.

On the banks of the Ganges at Hardiwar in India Hindus celebrate a night puja. At the start of the 21st century there were an estimated 900 million Hindus in India—over 80 percent of the population.

Previous pages *Martin Luther King waves to the crowd during the March on Washington in August 1983. The march was the occasion of King's famous "I have a dream" speech: "Let freedom ring. And when this happens, and when we allow freedom to ring—when we let it ring from every village and every hamlet, from every state and every city, we will be able to speed up that day when all of God's children—black men and white men, Jews and Gentiles, Protestants and Catholics—will be able to join hands and sing in the words of the old Negro spiritual: 'Free at last! Free at last! Thank God Almighty, we are free at last!'"*

RELIGION HAS BECOME EVER MORE INEXTRICABLY LINKED WITH POLITICS— if indeed they were ever truly separate. The second half of the 20th century was a period of increasing globalization, when events on one side of the world could influence those on the other. For much of the period the globe was split by the Cold War into two ideologically opposed camps: the West, led by the United States and its NATO allies, which supported a capitalist, free-market economy; and the Soviet Union and its allies, who propounded a communist philosophy in which the state regulated economic activity and individual freedom. Religion was frowned upon in communist societies such as the Soviet Union and China—communism's founder, Karl Marx, had condemned it as "the opium of the people"—and worship was discouraged. The Chinese invasion of Tibet in 1950—seen by the Chinese as asserting their right to a traditional part of China—eventually drove thousands of Buddhists into exile, including the 14th Dalai Lama. Buddhist monks were also persecuted by governments in Laos and Vietnam, by Pol Pot's Khmer Rouge regime in Cambodia, and by the military junta in Burma (Myanmar). One reason governments are so highly suspicious is the monks' reputation for selflessness and the respect in which they are held by ordinary people.

Religion has endured, even in the face of personal danger. When the Cold War ended in 1989 with the collapse of the Soviet Empire, congregations of worshipers of all faiths again began practicing openly. Without restrictive state control, however, religion has the potential to become a source of tension among different societies living side by side, as was seen in the continuing attacks on Russian targets carried out by Islamist separatists from the Caucasus.

The end of the European empires in the decades following World War II transformed religion in Asia and Africa. The colonial masters had often introduced Christianity, but with their withdrawal it seemed that other faiths—primarily Islam but also Buddhism and Hinduism—became a rallying point for nationalist identity. The world's largest Muslim country is Indonesia, far from the faith's origins in Arabia; in the third largest, India, the 160 million or so Muslims are nevertheless vastly outnumbered by the Hindu majority, with resulting conflicts.

Within Islam, more fundamentalist forms of the faith emerged. Iran fell to an Islamic revolution in 1979 that passed power to a theocratic council determined to sweep away Western elements in Iranian society. In Afghanistan, the Taliban ("Students") took advantage of the political chaos left by the withdrawal of the Soviet occupation in 1989 to set up a theocratic government so extreme that the traditional sport of kite flying was banned, along with recorded music, and women were forbidden from paid employment. Under Taliban government, Afghanistan became a safe haven for Islamists who had originally arrived in the region to help the *mujahidin* fight the Russians in a conflict seen by Muslims as an attack on Islam. Among the newcomers was the wealthy Saudi Osama bin Laden, who was disaffected with mainstream Islam by its accommodation with the West, particularly over the Persian Gulf War of 1990–1991. Bin Laden's al Qaeda group became notorious for its terrorist activities, most notably the 9/11 attacks on the United States in 2001. For the vast majority of Muslims, the Islamists' use of their faith as an excuse for violence is entirely unjustified, but has caused a great deal of soul-searching about the nature of the faith and how it interacts with the rest of the world.

A similar debate continues within Christianity about the interaction of faith and the world. In the United States in particular the political character of religion seems to have changed. Churches were a socially transformative force in the civil rights movement of the 1960s; by the 1990s they had ostensibly become a highly conservative force, as manifested in the rise of the religious right as a political power. Touchstone issues have emerged, such as abortion, prayer in public schools, or the controversy about displaying Christian symbols in public buildings. Despite controversy, however, the faith thrives: the United States can claim more Christians than any other nation (just under half of Americans are Protestants and just over a quarter are Catholics). The presence of flourishing congregations from non-Christian faiths, too, confirms the enduring importance of religion in the world's most modern society.

A young U.S. woman prepares to take part in the annual Muslim Day Parade on Sixth Avenue in New York in 2005. Muslims inside the United States—a total of some 5 to 8 million people—faced collective suspicion and discrimination after the attacks of 9/11 that persisted for much of the decade.

	1950	1955	1960	1965	1970
EUROPE	**1950** Pope Pius XII proclaims the Assumption of Mary—that the mother of Jesus was taken up to heaven—to be a dogma of the Catholic faith. **1952** Franco-German theologian Albert Schweitzer wins the Nobel Peace Prize for his philosophy of "reverence for life": "Good consists in maintaining, assisting, and enhancing life, and to destroy, to harm, or to hinder life is evil."	**1958** In the Soviet Union premier Nikita Khrushchev begins a six-year anti-religious campaign. **1958** The Italian Cardinal Roncalli becomes Pope John XXII. **1959** The Vatican forbids Italians from voting for the Communist Party.	**1962** *War Requiem* by British composer Benjamin Britten is premiered in the new Coventry Cathedral in England. **1963** The Second Vatican Council convenes; it will be responsible for numerous changes, including ending the use of Latin as the language of the liturgy.	**1965** Pope Paul VI absolves the Jews of blame for their part in the crucifixion of Jesus Christ. **1966** The Catholic and Anglican churches hold their first official meeting for 400 years. **1968** The encyclical *Humanae Vitae* (*Of Human Life*) reaffirms Catholic opposition to abortion and all artifical forms of contraception, disappointing many liberal Catholics.	**1972** At the Munich Olympic Games in Germany, Arab terrorists murder 11 Israeli athletes. **1972** In Northern Ireland, British soldiers kill 14 unarmed Catholics during demonstrations on what becomes known as Bloody Sunday. **1972** Proposals for a constitutional union between the Anglican and Methodist churches collapse.
THE AMERICAS	**1950** The National Council of Churches is formed, bringing together mainstream Protestant, Orthodox, African-American, and Evangelical churches. **1953** Church membership in the United States reaches a record high of 59.5 percent. **1953** L. Ron Hubbard founds the Church of Scientology in Camden, New Jersey.	**1955** Black church leaders, including Martin Luther King, lead a 381-day boycott of buses in Montgomery, Alabama, after Rosa Parks is arrested for refusing to give up her seat to a white passenger. **1957** U.S. Buddhist convert Alan Watts writes *The Way of Zen*, helping promote Zen's guide to "ultimate Oneness."	**1962** The U.S. Supreme Court rules that compulsory prayer in public schools is unconstitutional. **1963** Martin Luther King writes his "Letter from Birmingham Jail." **1964** Malcolm X, outspoken former leader of the Nation of Islam, converts to Sunni Islam; he is assassinated by members of NOI a year later.	**1967** The Living Room, a storefront mission in San Francisco, is a focus for the creation of the evangelistic Jesus Movement, which thrives among the hippie counterculture into the 1970s. **1968** Martin Luther King is assassinated. **1968** Mexican American labor leader Cesár Chávez undertakes a fast as penance for violence encouraged by his fellow labor leaders.	**1970** Blue Lake in New Mexico is preserved as a sacred site of the Taos. **1971** Reverend Sun Myung Moon, founder of the Unification Church, moves from his native Korea to the United States. **1971** Peruvian priest Gustavo Gutiérrez writes *A Theology of Liberation*, which argues that priests have a duty to fight poverty.
ASIA & OCEANIA	**1952** In Calcutta, India, Albanian nun Mother Teresa opens the Immaculate Heart Home for Dying Destitutes. **1954** In South Korea, the Reverend Sun Myung Moon founds the Unification Church, today followers are known as the Moonies.	**1956** Pakistan becomes an Islamic republic. **1959** A Tibetan rebellion against Chinese rule is crushed by Chinese troops; the 14th Dalai Lama flees into exile with some 100,000 Tibetans.	**1963** Catholic president Ngo Dinh Diem of South Vietnam is assassinated in a coup. **1963** Buddhist monk Thich Quang Durc burns himself to death in Vietnam to protest government oppression of Buddhism.	**1965** In Burma, the government arrests more than 500 Buddhist monks for refusing to accept government rule. **1966** At the start of the Cultural Revolution in China, Red Guards close all Christian churches.	**1970** Pope Paul VI survives an assassination attempt in the Philippines. **1972** Christian churches lead protests against martial law in South Korea.
AFRICA & THE MIDDLE EAST	**1950** Israel grants automatic citizenship to any immigrant Jews in a new "law of return." **1950** The Arab League begins an economic boycott of Israel. **1953** The founder of Saudi Arabia, Ibn Saud, dies having established the Wahhabi sect of Islam as the state's centralized government.	**1956** In Egypt, President Gamal Abdel Nasser becomes a figurehead of pan-Arabism after retaining control of the Suez Canal in the second Arab-Israeli war. **1959** Palestinian Yasser Arafat founds the militant Arab group al-Fatah in Kuwait; its aim is the destruction of Israel and the establishment of a Palestinian state.	**1962** Former Gestapo chief Adolf Eichmann is hanged in Israel. **1963** Ayatollah Ruhollah Khomeini is exiled from Iran for his criticism of the shah's dictatorship. **1964** Yasser Arafat founds the Palestine Liberation Organization (PLO), with himself as leader.	**1965** Israel establishes formal diplomatic relations with Germany. **1966** In Egypt, an international effort dismantles and relocates the ancient temples of Abu Simbel to save them from rising waters caused by the new Aswan High Dam.	**ca 1970** Islam begins to replace secular pan-Arabism as the political rallying cry in the Arab world. **1973** The oil-producing Islamic countries embargo oil exports to Europe in response to Western support for Israel.

1975	1980	1985	1990	2000–2010
ca 1975 Turkey's secular constitution is pressured by a revival of Islamism. **1977** The Vatican reaffirms its ban on female priests in the Catholic Church. **1978** Pope John Paul I dies after only 33 days in office; the Polish cardinal Karol Wojtyla is elected as John Paul II, the first non-Italian pope for over 450 years.	**1980** The Vatican rules that married Episcopal priests can join the Roman Catholic Church. **1984** The Vatican declares that the Inquisition was in error when it convicted Galileo for heresy in 1632 for supporting the Copernican view of the universe. **1984** In France more than a million marchers protest government moves to limit the independence of faith schools.	**1989** In Romania, Hungarian parishioners protect the home of pastor Lásízó Tokes from state authorities; Romanians join an uprising, which grows to overthrow the dictatorship of President Ceausescu. **1989** In an unprecedented meeting, John Paul II meets Soviet leader Mikhail Gorbachev.	**1992** Civil war breaks out in Bosnia, in the former Yugoslavia, as Serbia, which is largely Christian, tries to oust Bosnian Muslims and Croats. **1998** The encyclical *Fides et Ratio* argues that faith and reason depend upon one another. **1999** Catholics and Lutherans agree in the Augsburg Accord over the role of faith in justification, a sticking point for nearly 500 years.	**2003** The Vatican launches a worldwide campaign against homosexuality. **2004** Islamist bombers kill 191 people in rush-hour attacks on Madrid, Spain. **2005** Islamist suicide bombers kill 56 people on London's mass transit system. **2007** Pope Benedict reasserts the universal primacy of the Catholic Church and urges all other churches to join it.
1975 Boxer and follower of the Nation of Islam Muhammad Ali converts to Sunni Islam. **1978** A new revelation granted to Mormon elders allows the appointment of black elders. **1979** The Marxist Sandanistas come to power in Nicaragua; many priests support their "Church of the People," even though it has no official position in the church.	**1980** The New Christian Right, a faith and political grouping, plays an influential role in the election of President Ronald Reagan. **1980** In El Salvador, gunmen assassinate Archbishop Oscar Romero, an outspoken supporter of social justice. **1984** The Southern Baptist Convention rejects the ordination of women.	**1987** Evangelist Pat Robertson founds the Christian Coalition as an advocacy group. **1988** The Evangelical Lutheran Church is founded by smaller churches; it becomes the largest Lutheran church in the United States. **1988** Barbara C. Harris is elected the first female Episcopalian archbishop. **1988** Popular U.S. televangelist Jim Bakker is convicted of fraud.	**1993** True Love Waits is set up to encourage sexual abstinence among young Americans. **1993** The Supreme Court overturns a ban on animal sacrifice in Hialeah, Florida, in a case brought by a Santería church. **1997** The Heaven's Gate cult commit suicide when Comet Hale-Bopp is at its brightest; thirty-nine people die.	**2001** Four planes are hijacked by Islamist terrorists in the United States: two are flown into the World Trade Center in New York, another into the Pentagon; the fourth plane is brought down by passengers in Pennsylvania. **2003** In New England, Gene Robinson becomes the first openly gay cleric to be nominated as a bishop, causing a split in the global Anglican Church.
1976 As tension grows between Buddhist monks and the government in Burma, officials claim that leading monk Ba La is a murderer and a cannibal. **1979** Albanian Catholic nun Mother Teresa wins the Nobel Peace Prize for her 50 years' work among the poor of Calcutta, India.	**ca 1980** After the 1979 Soviet invasion of Afghanistan, Islamists from around the world join Afghan *mujahidin* to fight a guerrilla campaign against the invaders. **1984** After Indian Army troops storm the Sikh Golden Temple at Amritsar, prime minister Indira Gandhi is assassinated by her Sikh bodyguards.	**1985** After 30 years' imprisonment, the Chinese release the former Roman Catholic bishop of Shanghai and reopen the Catholic cathedral in Beijing. **1986** In the Philippines Catholics and other Christians lead the peaceful revolt that ends the presidency of Ferdinand Marcos.	**1995** Shoko Asahara, founder of Japan's Aum Shinrikyo, an apocalyptic cult, is sentenced to death for organizing poison gas attacks on the Tokyo subway system. **1996** Expelled from Sudan, Saudi-born Osama bin Laden relocates his al Qaeda organization to Afghanistan.	**2001** The Taliban destroys two huge statues of Buddha built into the cliff in Bayman, Afghanistan, in the sixth century A.D., on the grounds that they encourage idolatry. **2001** The Kumbh Mela festival in Allahbad, India, is the largest religious gathering in world history.
1975 In Lebanon, Imam Musa al-Sadr founds the Amal (Hope) Party to defend the rights of Shiite Muslims, by violence if necessary. **1979** Ayatollah Khomeini becomes head of state in Iran after an Islam-inspired revolution overthrows the Shah.	**1981** Islamic militants assassinate Egyptian president Anwar Sadat for making peace with Israel. **1982** The militant Islamic organization Hezbollah (Party of God) is founded in Lebanon to oppose the Israeli occupation of the south of the country; its main funding comes from Iran.	**1989** Ayatollah Khomeini of Iran calls for the death of the Indian-born British author Salman Rushdie for blasphemy in his novel *The Satanic Verses*; Muslims around the world burn the book, while Rushdie begins nearly 10 years in hiding. **1989** Shiite Muslims bomb the U.S. Embassy in Beirut, killing more than 200 Marines.	**1993** Yitzhak Rabin and Shimon Peres of Israel negotiate the Oslo Accords with PLO leader Yasser Arafat. **1995** Yitzhak Rabin is assassinated by a Jewish extremist for ceding land to the Palestinians at Oslo. **1996** Yasser Arafat is elected president of the Palestine National Authority.	**2001** Right-winger Ariel Sharon is elected president of Israel in the face of mounting violence between Israelis and Palestinians. **2007** Ethiopian troops invade Somalia and shut down Islamic courts in Mogadishu.

PEOPLE & PLACES	DOCUMENTS, ART, & ARTIFACTS	WORSHIP & DOCTRINE

EUROPE

1952 Franco-German theologian and humanitarian Albert Schweitzer wins the Nobel Peace prize for his philosophy of "reverence for life," which he sums up: "Good consists in maintaining, assisting, and enhancing life, and to destroy, to harm, or to hinder life is evil."

1956 Cardinal József Mindszenty, sentenced to life imprisonment for treason in Hungary in 1949, is freed in the Hungarian Revolution; when Soviet troops invade to restore communism, he claims political asylum in the U.S. Embassy in Budapest—he will be confined there for 15 years.

1958 The Italian Cardinal Roncalli becomes Pope John XXII.

1950 Pope Pius XII proclaims the Assumption of Mary—that the mother of Jesus was taken up to heaven—to be a dogma of the Catholic faith.

The Unification Church, founded in 1954 by the Reverend Sun Myung Moon, is well known for conducting mass wedding ceremonies.

THE AMERICAS

1950 After visiting President Harry S. Truman, Billy Graham gives details of the conversation to the press and is photographed praying on the White House lawn; when Truman does not speak to him for years, Graham learns to keep private details of his relations with all of the presidents since (📄 pages 318–319).

1951 California dairy farmer Demos Shakarian founds the Full Gospel Business Men's Fellowship in a cafe in San Francisco.

1953 L. Ron Hubbard founds the Church of Scientology in Camden, New Jersey (📄 page 331).

1955 The Republican National Committee calls President Dwight D. Eisenhower "not only the political leader, but the spiritual leader of our times."

1952 Reinhold Niebuhr publishes *The Irony of American History*; it begins to formulate his philosophy of Christian Realism, which rejects liberalism and draws on faith, politics, and pragmatism to create a way to approach the problems of the 20th century.

1955 In *Protestant–Catholic–Jew*, Will Herberg examines the connection between immigration, ethnicity, and faith in the United States. He later argues that modern U.S. religions are a form of "cut-flower culture": they are attractive but cannot survive while they are separated from their roots in the Judeo-Christian tradition.

1957 U.S. Buddhist convert Alan Watts writes *The Way of Zen*, helping promote Zen's guide to "ultimate Oneness" (📄 pages 136–137).

1953 Church membership in the United States reaches a record high of 59.5 percent.

ASIA & OCEANIA

1952 In Calcutta, India, Albanian nun Mother Teresa opens the Immaculate Heart Home for Dying Destitutes.

1954 In South Korea, the Reverend Sun Myung Moon founds the Unification Church; today followers are called Moonies.

1956 B. R. Ambedkar, a leader of India's Untouchables, converts to Buddhism with some 350,000 followers, creating the Neo-Buddhist movement.

MONUMENTS OF FAITH

Coventry Cathedral

Work began in 1955 on a new cathedral in Coventry, England, intended to echo the spiritual ambition of the great monuments of the Middle Ages. The city's 14th-century cathedral had been destroyed in one of the most destructive air raids of World War II—its ruins were now left as a site for remembrance and reconciliation. Nearby arose the new modernist structure by architect Basil Spence which, on its completion in 1963, became a symbol of Britain's postwar reconstruction. The interior is decorated with celebrated artworks, such as John Piper's massive "Sun" stained-glass window. The altar cross is made from fragments retrieved from the old cathedral's roof.

AFRICA & THE MIDDLE EAST

1953 Ibn Saud dies having established the Wahhabi sect of Islam as the basis of Saudi Arabia's government (📄 page 257).

1956 In Egypt, President Gamal Abdel Nasser becomes a figurehead of pan-Arabism after retaining control of the Suez Canal in the second Arab-Iraeli war.

1959 Palestinian Yasser Arafat founds the militant Arab group al-Fatah in Kuwait; its aim is the destruction of Israel and the establishment of a Palestinian state.

RELIGION IN THE WORLD	WORLD EVENTS
1952 Germany agrees on financial compensation with Israel for damages done to Jews by the Nazis.	**1952** Elizabeth II becomes queen of Great Britain.
1958 In the Soviet Union premier Nikita Khrushchev begins a six-year antireligious campaign.	**1953** DNA—the genetic mechanism of heredity—is revealed as a double helix by British physicist Francis Crick and U.S. biologist James Watson.
1959 The Vatican forbids Italians from voting for Communist Party candidates in elections.	**1955** The Soviet Union organizes its allies to form the Warsaw Pact, a power bloc that rivals NATO.
	1956 Soviet troops invade Hungary to prevent it withdrawing from the Warsaw Pact.
	1958 The Soviet Union intensifies the space race when it puts the Sputnik satellite into orbit.
	1958 The European Economic Community, or Common Market, is created.

1950 The National Council of Churches is formed, bringing together mainstream Protestant, Orthodox, African-American, and Evangelical churches.	**1950** Senator Joseph McCarthy begins investigations to root out communists he believes are prominent in U.S. life.
1955 Black church leaders, including Martin Luther King, lead a 381-day boycott of buses in Montgomery, Alabama, after Rosa Parks is arrested for refusing to give up her seat to a white passenger (📄 page 322–333).	**1952** U.S. medical researcher Jonas Salk discovers the polio vaccine.
1958 U.S. theologian Reinhold Niebuhr affirms God's covenant with the Jews and urges U.S. evangelists to abandon their mission to win Jewish converts.	**1954** In *Brown* v. *Board of Education*, the U.S. Supreme Court rules that segregation of schools is unconstitutional.
1959 Fidel Castro comes to power in Cuba, marking a serious limitation on religious freedom.	**1954** The CIA helps organize a coup that overthrows the government in Guatemala.
	1955 President Juan Peron flees Argentina when the military seize power.
	1958 Fidel Castro begins a revolution in Cuba.

1956 Pakistan becomes an Islamic republic.	
1957 Roman Catholics in Australia support the breakaway of the Democratic Labour Party from the Australian Labour Party.	
1958 In China, the government approves and consecrates Catholic bishops, despite opposition from the Vatican.	
1959 A Tibetan rebellion is crushed by Chinese troops; the 14th Dalai Lama flees into exile with some 100,000 Tibetans (📄 box, right).	

Tenzin Gyatso, the 14th Dalai Lama, has declared that the 15th Dalai Lama will be discovered in exile rather than in Tibet.

1950 Israel grants automatic citizenship to any immigrant Jews in a new "law of return."	
1950 Jews from Iraq migrate en masse to Israel.	
1950 The Arab League begins an economic boycott of Israel.	
1953 Jews from North Africa begin emigrating in large numbers to Israel.	
1955 Civil war breaks out in Sudan between Muslims and non-Muslims.	

THE DALAI LAMA IN EXILE

His Holiness the Dalai Lama is one of the most recognizable religious figures in the modern world. Tenzin Gyatso is the 14th reincarnation of the spiritual leader of the Tibetan Buddhists—but the first to become a global figure. Previous Dalai Lamas had lived largely in isolation in the Potala Palace in Lhasa, but following the Chinese invasion of Tibet in 1950, persecution of Buddhists made the presence of the Dalai Lama increasingly untenable.

In 1959, when Chinese troops put down a Tibetan rebellion, the current Dalai Lama fled into exile in Dharamsala, India, where he established a government-in-exile. Thousands of Tibetans followed him, settling in India.

The Dalai Lama started to travel the world in the 1970s, visiting Europe for the first time in 1973 and the United States in 1979. He has two stated aims: to raise awareness of the problems Tibet has faced since the Chinese invasion and to spread Buddhism.

His travels have made the Dalai Lama an international celebrity and the most visible lama in the history of Buddhism. This has brought him into conflict with the Chinese government, which has attempted to discredit him.

BILLY GRAHAM

CHRISTIAN EVANGELIST BILLY GRAHAM WAS ONE OF THE first religious leaders to realize the potential of the mass media, particularly radio and television, as a tool for spreading a religious message. In a career that has spanned more than 70 years, Billy Graham has met with every U.S. president since Harry S. Truman (1945–1952) and preached to millions of people across the world.

Billy Graham was born on November 7, 1918, in Charlotte, North Carolina, and raised as a Presbyterian. After meeting a traveling preacher at age 16, Graham underwent a religious conversion and became a Baptist. He attended the Bob Jones College in Cleveland, Tennessee, and then the Florida Bible Institute (now Trinity College) in Tampa. In 1939 he was ordained as a minister in the Southern Baptist Church. Four years later he completed a bachelor's degree in anthropology at Wheaton College, Illinois. Graham was pastor of the First Baptist Church in Western Springs, Illinois, from 1943 to 1945, before becoming a traveling preacher.

During the late 1940s Graham developed a reputation as an inspirational orator. His massive revival meetings—known as "missions" or "crusades"—attracted audiences of thousands to huge tents or sports stadiums to hear Graham's rousing sermons calling for repentance and moral renewal. His first large-scale crusade was held in Los Angeles in 1949; when its nightly meetings ran for more than eight weeks, Graham came to the attention of the U.S. media and became a national celebrity. In 1950 he began recording a radio program, the *Hour of Decision*, which is still broadcast across the United States every Sunday. Graham's broadcasts and sermons avoided divisive sectarian topics, so they appealed to Christians from many different denominations. In addition to featuring on radio and TV, Graham also wrote books. *Peace with God*, published in 1953, sold over two million copies. Since 1952 Graham has authored a nationally syndicated newspaper column entitled "My Answer."

Billy Graham has been active in several political campaigns, although he has generally avoided party politics. During the 1950s and 1960s he was a prominent, if cautious, supporter of the civil rights movement. At a time when Southern churches divided black and white congregations, he refused to segregate the audiences at his revivals. Graham met with Martin Luther King on several occasions, and urged white ministers and politicians not to oppose desegregation when it was enforced in the mid-1960s.

Billy Graham retired from public appearances in 2005 due to poor health, but he continued to write and record his radio show. His close connection to the presidency also continued; in April 2010, Graham met with president Barack Obama at his home in North Carolina.

A mural decorates the wall of Billy Graham's birthplace in Palatka, Florida. Graham grew up to preach directly to more people than any other individual in history; his global audience is well over 2 billion.

PEOPLE & PLACES	DOCUMENTS, ART, & ARTIFACTS	WORSHIP & DOCTRINE

EUROPE

1963 Pope John XXII grants an audience to U.S. President John F. Kennedy.

1968 Paul VI becomes the first pope to visit Latin America when he arrives in Colombia.

1962 *War Requiem* by British composer Benjamin Britten is premiered in the new Coventry Cathedral in England.

1963 In Germany, a play about World War II indicts Pope Pius XII for complicity with the Nazis, outraging many Catholics.

1969 Pope Paul VI contributes a "goodwill message" left on the surface of the moon by Apollo 11. It features Psalms 8 ("O Lord Our Lord, how excellent is thy name in all the earth!") with the message "To the Glory of the name of God who gives such power to men, we ardently pray for this wonderful beginning."

1961 The encyclical *Mater et Magistra* reaffirms the Catholic Church's stance on social conditions, arguing in favor of labor association and against both free-market capitalism and communism.

1963 The Second Vatican Council convenes; it will be responsible for numerous reforms, including ending the use of Latin as the language of the liturgy.

1966 The Catholic and Anglican churches hold their first official meeting for 400 years.

1968 The encyclical *Humanae Vitae* (*Of Human Life*) reaffirms Catholic opposition to abortion and all artifical forms of contraception, disappointing many liberal Catholics.

THE AMERICAS

1964 Malcolm X, former leader of the Nation of Islam, converts to orthodox Islam; he is assassinated by members of NOI a year later.

1964 Martin Luther King wins the Nobel Peace prize for his civil rights campaigns (📄 pages 322–323).

1968 Martin Luther King is killed.

1968 Mexican-American labor leader Cesár Chávez undertakes a fast as penance for violence encouraged by his fellow labor leaders.

1968 After two years' teaching meditation, Maharishi Mahesh Yogi returns to India disappointed at his lack of results in the United States.

1960 Jesuit priest John Courtney Murray makes the cover of *Time* magazine with the publication of *We Hold These Truths*, which argues that the Catholic Church must recognize that a new moral truth has emerged outside the church.

1963 Arrested for his part in civil rights demonstrations, Martin Luther King writes his "Letter from Birmingham Jail."

1963 At the March on Washington, Martin Luther King tells around 250,000 civil rights protestors "I have a dream."

1962 The U.S. Supreme Court rules that compulsory prayer in public schools is unconstitutional.

1965 A.C. Bhaktivedanta founds Krishna Conciousness in New York; it spreads when he moves to San Francisco.

1966 Worshipers at Duquesne University claim to be "baptized in the spirit" and speak in tongues, heralding the emergence of a new pentecostalism.

1967 The Living Room, a storefront mission in San Francisco, is a focus for the creation of the evangelistic Jesus Movement, which thrives among the hippie counterculture into the 1970s.

ASIA & OCEANIA

1963 Catholic president Ngo Dinh Diem of South Vietnam is assassinated in a coup.

1963 Buddhist monk Thich Quang Durc burns himself to death in Vietnam to protest government oppression of Buddhism.

1966 Korean minister Reverend Sun Myung Moon writes *The Divine Principle*.

1966 The World Buddhist Sangha Council meets in Sri Lanka to try to bring greater unity between Mahayana and Theravada Buddhism.

AFRICA & THE MIDDLE EAST

1962 Former Gestapo chief Adolf Eichmann is hanged in Israel.

1966 In Egypt, an international effort dismantles and relocates the ancient temples of Abu Simbel to save them from rising waters caused by the new Aswan High Dam.

This mural in the West Bank depicts Palestinian leader Yasser Arafat, who founded the Palestinian Liberation Organization (PLO) in 1964.

RELIGION IN THE WORLD	WORLD EVENTS

1965 Pope Paul VI absolves the Jews of blame for their part in the crucifixion of Jesus Christ.

1966 Roman Catholic priests are given the right to leave the clergy to marry.

1960 The mainly Catholic Irish Republican Army (IRA) begins a guerrilla campaign against British rule in Protestant-majority Northern Ireland.

1968 Student riots in France lead to changes in the education system.

1968 Soviet troops invade Czechoslovakia when the USSR suspects the Czech government of weakening its commitment to communism.

1969 The Soviet Union and the United States respond to fears of global nuclear war by beginning talks to limit strategic arms.

The Second Vatican Council, convened by Pope Paul VI in 1963, was responsible for many important changes to Catholic practice, ritual, and doctrine.

1960 The first Catholic president is elected, John F. Kennedy.

1962 The pope excommunicates Cuban revolutionary leader Fidel Castro.

1963 John F. Kennedy is assassinated in Dallas, Texas.

1965 The Civil Rights Act grants equality to African Americans.

1968 After the assassination of Robert Kennedy during the election campaign, Richard Nixon is elected U.S. president.

1964 In Japan, the Clean Government Party is founded by the Soka Gakkai religious movement.

1965 In Burma, the government arrrests more than 500 Buddhist monks for refusing to accept government rule.

1966 At the start of the Cultural Revolution in China, Red Guards close all Christian churches.

1964 U.S. troop numbers in Vietnam rise after North Vietnamese patrol boats are alleged to attack U.S. destroyers in Vietnamese waters.

1968 The North Vietnamese launch the Tet Offensive against U.S. and South Vietnamese forces.

1969 The United States begins to hand more duties in the Vietnam War to its Vietnamese allies.

1963 Ayatollah Ruhollah Khomeini is exiled from Iran for his criticism of the shah's dictatorship (📄 page 325).

1964 Yasser Arafat founds the Palestine Liberation Organization (PLO), with himself as leader.

1965 Israel establishes formal diplomatic relations with Germany.

1967 Israeli forces win a decisive victory over their neighbors in the Six Day War.

1967 The PLO reacts to the loss of the West Bank in the Six Day War by developing as a guerrilla army.

1969 In Libya Muammar Qaddafi comes to power proclaiming a doctrine of Islamic socialism.

BEHIND THE IRON CURTAIN

Karl Marx famously dismissed religion as "the opium of the people," meaning that it was a form of capitalist social control and thus anathema to communism. After the Russian Revolution of 1917, the Communist Party banned religious organizations from teaching or collecting money, effectively depriving priests of their means of support. All church property was nationalized; works of religious art were destroyed and churches were converted into schools, cinemas, or even granaries. Schools promoted atheism, while people who held on to their religious beliefs were associated with counter-revolutionaries. Books on religious subjects were banned, unless they were strongly critical of religion.

In place of religion, the Communist Party encouraged a kind of veneration of Soviet icons. For example, in 1931 the Cathedral of Christ the Savior was demolished to make way for the "Palace of the Soviets," which was to house huge statues of Marx, Friedrich Engels, and Lenin. Work was interrupted by World War II, when Stalin found the popularity of the Orthodox Church useful in rallying Russians to the nationalist patriotic cause. Under Stalin, the Soviet Union changed from an atheist state to a secular state from 1945, allowing the church to recover its position somewhat. Government hostility to religion remained, however, until the 1970s, when some religious buildings were restored as historical monuments. Restrictions on worship remained in place until the dissolution of the Soviet Union in 1991.

Despite the restrictions, faith endured throughout the Soviet Empire, even though congregations had to worship in secret. Within Russia, membership of the Russian Orthodox Church actually rose. In other parts of the empire, Jewish congregations, Buddhist monasteries, and Islamic mosques survived to flourish again after the fall of the communist regime in the late 1980s.

*F*ree at last! Free at last!

Thank God Almighty, we are free at last!

GOSPEL SONG QUOTED BY MARTIN LUTHER KING, MARCH ON WASHINGTON

MARTIN LUTHER KING, JR.

MARTIN LUTHER KING, JR. WAS THE OUTSTANDING LEADER of the civil rights movement, drawing on the long tradition of African-American religious oratory to protest discrimination and inspire social change. His philosophy of nonviolent protest was based closely on that of the 20th-century Indian nationalist and spiritual leader Mahatma Gandhi.

Born to a minister and a teacher in Atlanta, Georgia, in 1929, King was raised in an environment of public service: both his father and his grandfather were prominent members of the National Association for the Advancement of Colored People (NAACP). At age 24 King was inspired to follow his father's example and join the church. His involvement with the civil rights movement began soon after he became a Baptist minister in Montgomery, Alabama. When Rosa Parks, a local member of the NAACP, was arrested for refusing to give up her seat to a white passenger on a bus in 1956, King emerged as the leader of a boycott of Montgomery public buses. After more than a year of the boycott, during which King and his church were attacked, the bus company was forced to desegregate its buses.

After this initial success brought him to national prominence, King quickly became established as one of the leading voices in the civil rights movement, thanks at least in part to his eloquent oratory. To him, the fight for equal rights was a spiritual as well as a social necessity. In many of his sermons he described the civil rights struggle as one between good and evil, a fight to restore the moral conscience of the United States and save it from damnation. It was this religious fervor that underpinned his most famous utterances, such as the famous "I Have a Dream" speech, which was delivered to an audience of 250,000 at the March on Washington in 1963. Even after he had become a nationally celebrated figure with tremendous social and political influence, King still considered himself primarily as a preacher.

King's prominence made him a controversial figure among conservative Americans. In his later career he campaigned against the Vietnam War and launched the Poor People's Campaign for economic justice. As his successes grew, so too did his enemies. King's friends and family became increasingly worried about his safety. Their fears were proved right when King was shot dead on April 4, 1968, in Memphis, Tennessee.

Martin Luther King (front, second from left) leads antisegregation protesters in the March on Washington on August 28, 1963.

This statue of Martin Luther King was placed above the entrance to Westminster Abbey, London, in 1998 as part of a memorial to 20th-century Christian martyrs.

PEOPLE & PLACES	DOCUMENTS, ART, & ARTIFACTS	WORSHIP & DOCTRINE

EUROPE

1971 Hungarian Cardinal Mindszenty ends 15 years refuge in the U.S. embassy in Budapest when he flies to the United States.

1975 Pope Paul VI canonizes the first saint born in the United States, Elizabeth Ann Bayley Seton, who founded religious houses in Maryland in the early 1800s.

1978 Pope John Paul I dies after only 33 days in office; the Polish cardinal Karol Wojtyla is elected as John Paul II, the first non-Italian pope for over 450 years.

Albanian nun Mother Teresa became a religious inspiration for her work among the destitute in India.

1970 The World Alliance of Reformed Churches is created from the Congregational and Presbyterian churches.

1972 In England, the United Reformed Church is formed.

1972 Proposals for a consitutional union between the Anglican and Methodist churches collapse.

1977 The Vatican reaffirms its ban on female priests in the Catholic Church.

THE AMERICAS

1970 Blue Lake in New Mexico is preserved as a sacred site of the Taos.

1971 Reverend Sun Myung Moon, founder of the Unification Church, moves from his native Korea to the United States.

1975 Boxer and follower of the Nation of Islam Muhammad Ali converts to Sunni Islam.

1976 "Born-again" Southern Baptist Jimmy Carter is elected U.S. president, putting evangelism in the mainstream.

1978 Jim Jones leads more than 900 followers of his People's Temple in mass suicide in Guyana (📄 page 331).

1970 In *New Religions*, Jacob Needleman chronicles the proliferation of churches and cults in California.

1971 Peruvian priest Gustavo Gutiérrez writes *A Theology of Liberation*, which argues that priests have a duty to fight poverty (📄 page 327).

1973 *The Late, Great Planet Earth* by Hal Lindsey is the first bestseller to paint an image of the "End Times."

1973 In *God is Red*, Vine Deloria Jr. argues that Native American religion is more suited to the needs of the modern world than many mainstream faiths.

1971 The Religious News Writers Association designates the Jesus Movement as the most important event in contemporary faith.

1975 Maharishi Mahesh Yogi introduces a new form of Transcendental Meditation, TM-Sidhi, which includes the practice of "yogic flying."

1976 The Episcopalian Church votes to ordain women.

1978 A new revelation granted to Mormon elders allows for the first time the appointment of black elders.

1979 Speaking in Puebla, Mexico, Pope John Paul II condemns what he calls the excesses of liberation theology, which links Christianity with class struggle (📄 page 327).

ASIA & OCEANIA

1970 Pope Paul VI survives an assassination attempt in the Philippines.

1976 As tension grows between Buddhist monks and the government in Burma, officials claim that leading monk Ba La is a murderer and a cannibal.

1979 Albanian Catholic nun Mother Teresa wins the Nobel Peace Prize for her 50 years' work among the poor of Calcutta, India.

1975 Communists led by Pol Pot try to wipe out Buddhism in Cambodia: in the next three years they destroy virtually every Buddhist temple and library, murdering monks or driving them into exile.

1972 Christian churches lead protests against martial law in South Korea.

1975 In Laos, the communist government urges monks to work rather than beg for alms; many monks return to lay life.

1979 Churches in China reopen for public worship.

AFRICA & THE MIDDLE EAST

1975 In Lebanon, Imam Musa al-Sadr founds the Amal (Hope) Party to defend the rights of Shiite Muslims, by violence if necessary.

1978 Alice Lenshina, an evangelical prophet in Zambia, dies under house arrest.

1979 Ayatollah Khomeini becomes head of state in Iran after an Islam-inspired revolution overthrows the Shah and establishes an Islamic republic (📄 facing page).

In 1979, Barbara Harris was one of the first women to be ordained in the Episcopal Church; a decade later she became the first female Episcopalian bishop.

RELIGION IN THE WORLD

1972 At the Munich Olympic Games in Germany, Arab terrorists murder 11 Israeli athletes.

1972 In Northern Ireland, British soldiers kill 14 unarmed Catholics during demonstrations on what becomes known as Bloody Sunday.

ca 1975 Turkey's secular constitution is pressured by a revival of Islamism.

1977 Italy ends the position of Roman Catholicism as the state religion.

1979 Pope John Paul II visits President Jimmy Carter in the White House.

1974 Reverend Moon takes out newspaper advertisements supporting President Richard Nixon over the Watergate scandal.

1976 *Newsweek* magazine hails "The Year of the Evangelicals."

1978 Evangelical TV networks bring a new generation of "televangelists" to public consciousness.

1979 The Marxist Sandanistas come to power in Nicaragua; many priests support their "Church of the People," even though it has no position in the official church.

WORDS OF DEVOTION

Liberation Theology

During the 1970s many Roman Catholic priests in Latin America became involved in radical left-wing politics. They were inspired by liberation theology, a movement founded in the early 1970s by Peruvian priest Gustavo Gutiérrez. In his book *A Theology of Liberation*, Gutiérrez argued that the teachings of Jesus Christ were a call to liberate people from economic, social, or political oppression. He asserted that priests had a duty to oppose the institutions and political systems that kept people living in poverty.

ca 1970 Islam begins to replace secular pan-Arabism as the political rallying cry in the Arab world (📄 pages 332–333).

1973 The oil-producing Islamic countries embargo oil exports to Europe in response to Western support for Israel.

WORLD EVENTS

1975 The death of General Franco ends Spain's dictatorship; King Juan Carlos I becomes king.

1978 British scientists create the first "test-tube" baby, conceived outside the mother's body.

1979 Conservative Margaret Thatcher becomes Britain's first female prime minister and begins privatizing state institutions.

1973 In *Roe* v *Wade*, the U.S. Supreme Court rules abortion legal during the first six months of pregnancy.

1974 President Richard M. Nixon resigns after being implicated in a cover-up over the Watergate scandal.

1974 In Chile, Augusto Pinochet introduces a free-market economy.

1972 After a civil war in Pakistan, East Pakistan becomes independent as Bangladesh.

1975 Led by Pol Pot, the communist Khmer Rouge takes over Cambodia in a coup that will leave two million Cambodians dead in the so-called Killing Fields.

1976 After the surrender of South Vietnam the previous year, Vietnam is reunited after 22 years of civil war.

1971 Iran celebrates 2,500 years of continuous monarchy.

1973 In the Yom Kippur War, Egypt launches a surprise attack on Israel but fails to win back its lost territory.

1975 Lebanon is riven by civil war between the Christian government and Muslim rebels.

1978 The U.S.-brokered Camp David Accords mark a historic peace treaty between Israel and Egypt.

IRAN'S ISLAMIC REVOLUTION

For most of the 20th century Iran was ruled by the autocratic shahs. From the 1960s and 1970s Islam became a focus for groups criticizing the shahs' decadence and closeness to the West, and calling for reform. Opposition rallied particularly around the religious leader Ayatollah Ruhollah Khomeini, who had been exiled in 1963 for criticizing the regime.

Ayatollah Khomeini (center, with white beard) returns from exile to establish the Islamic republic in Iran.

In January 1979, while the shah was out of the country, he was overthrown by a popular revolution. Khomeini returned from exile and declared Iran an Islamic republic. The move was widely welcomed by Iranians seeking a return to core Islamic moral values, but few foresaw the repressive clampdown that followed. The clergy took control of the government, excluding their former leftwing, nationalist, and intellectual allies. Islamic codes of dress and behavior were introduced, and a revolutionary guard was created to enforce them. One result was a mass exodus of the Iranian middle classes; another was Iran's isolation in world affairs, thanks in part to its hostility to what it perceived as the decadence of the West.

PEOPLE & PLACES	DOCUMENTS, ART, & ARTIFACTS	WORSHIP & DOCTRINE

EUROPE

1981 Pope John Paul II survives being shot in an assassination attempt.

1989 Traditionalist Catholic archbishop Marcel Lefebvre, founder of the Society of St. Pius X, is excommunicated by the pope for consecrating four bishops without authority.

1989 In Romania, Hungarian parishioners protect the home of pastor Láslzó Tokes from state authorities; Romanians join their uprising, which grows to overthrow the dictatorship of President Nicolae Ceausescu.

1988 Radio-carbon dating methods suggest that the fabric of the Turin Shroud was woven between about 1260–1390 and that therefore the artifact cannot be the burial shroud in which Jesus' body was wrapped; many believers reject the finding.

1983 The Pope declares an Extraordinary Holy Year to mark the 1,950th anniversary of the death and resurrection of Christ.

1983 The Catholic Church recognizes annulment of marriage in certain circumstances.

1985 Pope John Paul II preaches to a congregation of more than a million people in Venezuela.

Flags of the militant group Hezbollah wave at a rally in southern Lebanon.

THE AMERICAS

1980 Jerry Falwell founds the "Moral Majority."

1981 Louis Farrakhan announces the reconstitution of the Nation of Islam (📄 page 307).

1982 Reverend Sun Myung Moon marries 2,075 couples in Madison Square Garden.

1987 Evangelist Oral Roberts claims to have raised people from the dead.

1988 Barbara C. Harris is elected the first female Episcopalian bishop.

1988 Televangelist Jim Swaggart tearfully confesses to adultery during a live broadcast.

1988 Televangelist Jim Bakker is convicted of fraud.

1983 U.S. Catholic bishops issue the pastoral letter *The Challenge of Peace*, reaffirming that war can be "just" but urging the reduction of nuclear arms.

1988 Director Martin Scorsese makes the controversial movie *The Last Temptation of Christ*.

1984 The Southern Baptist Convention rejects the ordination of women.

1988 The Evangelical Lutheran Church is founded by smaller churches; it becomes the largest Lutheran church in the United States.

ASIA & OCEANIA

Desmond Tutu, Archbishop of Cape Town, is a globally respected human rights campaigner.

1980 The Burmese military assert authority over the Buddhist monkhood, or *sangha*, beginning a decade of violent oppression.

1983 In Sri Lanka, ethnic minority Tamils begin fighting the government to create a non-Buddhist state.

1985 After 30 years' imprisonment, the Chinese release the former Roman Catholic bishop of Shanghai and reopen the Catholic cathedral in Beijing.

AFRICA & THE MIDDLE EAST

1989 Ayatollah Khomeini of Iran declares a *fatwa* (death sentence) on the Indian-born British author Salman Rushdie for blasphemy in his novel *The Satanic Verses*; Muslims around the world burn the book, while Rushdie begins nearly 10 years in hiding.

ca 1980 Islamist organizations take over the provision of private medical care and social services throughout the Middle East as government welfare services end (📄 pages 332–333).

1984 Bishop Desmond Tutu, general secretary of the South African Council of Churches, wins the Nobel Peace Prize.

1987 Palestinians launch an *intifada*, or uprising, against Israeli occupation of the West Bank and Gaza.

RELIGION IN THE WORLD	WORLD EVENTS
1980 The Vatican rules that married Episcopal priests can join the Roman Catholic Church.	**1980** In Poland, shipyard worker Lech Walesa becomes chairman of the Solidarity labor union, which demands political reform.
1984 The Vatican declares that the Inquisition was wrong to convict Galileo in 1632 for supporting the Copernican view of the universe (📄 page 213).	**1986** An accident at the Chernobyl Power Station in Ukraine causes nuclear fallout over large parts of Europe.
1984 More than a million marchers—the largest demonstration in French history—protest government moves to limit the independence of faith schools.	**1987** In the Soviet Union, Secretary General Mikhail Gorbachev promotes a process of *perestroika* (reconstruction) together with a new policy of *glasnost* (openness).
1988 The millennium of Christianity in Russia leads to optimism that the Soviet government will be more tolerant of religion (📄 page 321).	**1988** Libyan-backed terrorists are blamed for blowing up a Pan Am 747 over Lockerbie, in Scotland.
1989 Pope John Paul II meets Soviet leader Mikhail Gorbachev.	**1989** The Berlin Wall is demolished after the communist government of East Germany resigns.

1980 The New Christian Right, a faith and political grouping, plays an influential role in the election of President Ronald Reagan.	**1981** The space shuttle makes its maiden flight.
1980 Leading evangelicals found Washington for Jesus, to influence national politics.	**1981** Aquired immune deficiency syndrome (AIDS) is identified for the first time.
1980 In El Salvador, gunmen assassinate Archbishop Oscar Romero, an outspoken supporter of social justice.	**1981** MTV broadcasts for the first time.
1983 Evangelical Jerry Falwell refers to AIDS as a "gay plague."	**1981** U.S. software company Microsoft releases the Disk Operating System (MS-DOS) for the IBM personal computer.
1987 Pat Robertson founds the Christian Coalition as an advocacy group.	**1982** Argentina seizes the British Falkland Islands but its occupation is defeated by a British task force.
1989 In a Mississippi court case, the Salvation Army is told that it is not allowed to dismiss an employee for her pagan beliefs.	**1986** The U.S. government is implicated in a secret plan to sell arms to Iran to fund the antigovernment Contras in Nicaragua.

ca 1980 After the 1979 Soviet invasion of Afghanistan, Islamists from around the world join Afghan *mujahidin* to fight a guerrilla campaign against the invaders.	
1984 After Indian Army troops storm the Sikh Golden Temple at Amritsar, Indian Prime Pinister Indira Gandhi is assassinated by her Sikh bodyguards.	
1986 In the Philippines Catholics and other Christians lead the peaceful revolt that ends the presidency of Ferdinand Marcos.	

1981 Islamic militants assassinate Egyptian president Anwar Sadat in retaliation for his making peace with Israel.	
1982 The militant Islamic organization Hezbollah (Party of God) is founded in Lebanon to oppose the Israeli occupation of the south of the country; its main funding comes from Iran.	
1989 Shiite Muslims bomb the U.S. Embassy in Beirut, killing more than 200 Marines; U.S. forces withdraw from Lebanon.	

Quiche Maya listen to a pentecostalist in a church at Santiago Atitlan, Guatemala; small, informal congregations are gathering members throughout Latin America.

EVANGELISM IN LATIN AMERICA

Since eager Spanish and Portuguese missionaries arrived with the military in the 16th century and began proselytizing, Latin America has been predominantly Roman Catholic. During the later 19th century, however, evangelist churches began to appear across the region as Protestant missionaries arrived from the United States, Great Britain, and Germany.

While most evangelist churches have remained relatively small, there has been a rapid growth in the number of pentecostal members in the last part of the 20th century in Brazil, Chile, Guatemala, and Mexico. By 2000, it was estimated that some 60 million Latin Americans were evangelical Protestants. Today, pentecostalism is the second largest religion in Latin America after Roman Catholicism.

Pentecostalism differs from Roman Catholicism in its emphasis on spiritual redemption and spiritual gifts, and its belief in the second coming of Jesus Christ. There also tends to be a far closer bond between ministers and their congregations than in the Catholic Church. This closeness might help explain pentecostalism's rapidly growing popularity among ordinary people who feel alienated by the sometimes austere traditions of the Catholic Church.

SECULAR HUMANISM

SECULAR HUMANISM HAS ITS ORIGINS IN THE RATIONALISM of the 18th-century Enlightenment and the free-thinking movement of the 19th century. Humanism refutes the existence of any kind of supreme being. Humanists believe that people should live moral lives and perform good deeds out of respect for human life, rather than because they are hoping for any divine reward. Humanist philosophy stresses the importance of individual morality and active engagement with social problems.

Although humanism as it exists today is a relatively modern invention, many of the ethical and social ideas that humanists promote have existed since ancient times. It might be argued, for example, that some forms of Buddhism—with their emphasis on good deeds and minimal references to the idea of a heavenly reward—constitute an early humanist philosophy. Similarly many principles of humanist ethics are present in the writings of 18th-century deists such as Thomas Jefferson, who argued that, although God exists, he neither requires worship nor has any interest in human affairs.

British Humanist Christopher Hitchens stirred up controversy in 2007 with his book God is Not Great, *which argued that religion causes more social and political problems than it solves.*

Modern humanist beliefs developed rapidly during the 19th century as scientific understanding of the universe increased. Many phenomena which previously could only be explained by supernatural intervention were found to be the result of natural processes. Discoveries in geology, biology, and astronomy challenged the biblical account of the creation, leading many people to reevaluate their faith. During the 20th century, Western culture as a whole became less religious; many people stopped following any organized religion.

Some of those who abandoned religious faith but who still felt the need of an organized system of values turned to secular humanism. Influential thinkers such as British philosopher Bertrand Russell and the U.S. scientist Carl Sagan developed and refined humanist philosophy and challenged established ideas about the social utility of religion.

The cultural and social influence of secular humanism grew throughout the 20th century, with a growing number of individuals identifying themselves as humanists. Groups such as the American Humanist Association, founded in 1941, have promoted humanist ideas and count many influential writers, scientists, and philosophers among their members. Contemporary advocates of humanism include a group of writers nicknamed the "Four Horsemen," which includes evolutionary biologist Richard Dawkins, journalist and writer Christopher Hitchens, philosopher Daniel Dennett, and neuroscientist Sam Harris, all of whom have written bestselling books on the subject of religion. The group has deliberately challenged the rise of religious fundamentalism and those who believe in the literal truth of the Bible and other religious texts.

Humanist Association members George Porter and Lawrence Bragg, photographed at the Royal Institution in London in 1964, were typical of a generation of scientists who became vocal supporters of secular humanism.

PEOPLE & PLACES	DOCUMENTS, ART, & ARTIFACTS	WORSHIP & DOCTRINE

EUROPE

1992 Galileo Galilei is rehabilitated by the Roman Catholic Church (📄 page 213).

1997 The funeral of Diana, princess of Wales, is watched by some two billion people worldwide after her death in a car accident.

1997 An earthquake badly damages the Basilica of San Francis in Assisi, killing four people and destroying a Cimabue fresco.

1990 The Vatican excommunicates the African-American Catholic Congregation founded by George Augustus Stallings.

1991 John Paul II issues the encyclical *Centesimus Annus* to mark the centenary of *Rerum Novarum*, reaffirming Catholic commitment to a fairer distribution of wealth among nations and within societies.

1998 The encyclical *Fides et Ratio* argues that faith and reason depend upon one another.

1999 Catholics and Lutherans agree the Augsburg Accord over the role of faith in justification, a sticking point for nearly 500 years.

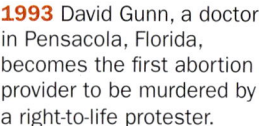

The funeral of Ayatollah Khomeini in 1989 was attended by thousands of mourners from across Iran.

THE AMERICAS

1993 David Gunn, a doctor in Pensacola, Florida, becomes the first abortion provider to be murdered by a right-to-life protester.

1996 Louis Farrakhan, leader of the Nation of Islam, wins the Al-Qaddafi International Prize for Human Rights, awarded by the Libyan leader for whom it is named.

1999 Evangelical Christians condemn Tinky Winky, a character in children's TV series *Teletubbies*, whom they suspect of being gay.

1995 *Left Behind*, a novel describing the End Times predicted in Christian Dispensationalism, is the first of 16 books in a best-selling series.

1993 True Love Waits is set up to encourage sexual abstinence among young Americans.

1994 The Southern Baptist Convention issues a formal apology to black Americans for their treatment in the past.

1995 The Nation of Islam organizes the Million Man March on Washington, D.C. to change images of black men; some 400,000 to 800,000 marchers attend (📄 page 307).

1996 The Southern Baptist Convention boycotts Disney when the organization grants rights to gay employees.

ASIA & OCEANIA

1995 Shoko Asahara, founder of Japan's apocalyptic Aum Shinrikyo cult, is sentenced to death for organizing poison gas attacks on the Tokyo subway system.

1996 Expelled from Sudan, Saudi-born Osama bin Laden relocates his al Qaeda terrorist organization to Afghanistan, which has been taken over by the Islamic fundamentalist Taliban (📄 pages 332–333).

1997 Mother Teresa receives a state funeral in Calcutta, India.

1992 A 60-foot-tall statue of Buddha is built on an island in Hussain Sagar Lake, Hyderabad, India.

1991 Chinese Protestants form the Three-Self Patriotic Movement to make the church free of foreign involvement; most missionaries leave China or are imprisoned.

AFRICA & THE MIDDLE EAST

1990 Shiite Hashemi Rafsanjani brings a moderate approach to Iran's government after the 1989 death of Ayatollah Khomeini (📄 page 325).

1993 Yitzhak Rabin and Shimon Peres of Israel negotiate the Oslo Accords with PLO leader Yasser Arafat.

1995 Rabin is assassinated by a Jewish extremist for ceding land to the Palestinians.

1996 Yasser Arafat is elected president of the Palestine National Authority.

FAITH AND LIFE

Louis Farrakhan

Louis Farrakhan, born Louis Walcott in 1933, is the leader of the Nation of Islam, a U.S. religious group that was founded in Detroit, Michigan, in the 1930s. Farrakhan joined the movement in 1955 and soon became a close disciple of then-leader Elijah Muhammad. In 1978, unhappy with the group's movement away from its original teachings toward those of orthodox Sunni Islam, Farrakhan established his own breakaway group, which took the name Nation of Islam after the original organization was disbanded. Through his leadership of the NOI Farrakhan has become an influential, although often controversial, figure in African American politics.

RELIGION IN THE WORLD	WORLD EVENTS
1992 Civil War breaks out in Bosnia, in the former Yugoslavia, as Serbia, which is largely Christian, trys to oust Bosnian Muslims and Croats.	**1990** East and West Germany are reunited into one country.
1994 The Vatican establishes full diplomatic relations with Israel.	**1990** Former labor leader Lech Walesa becomes president of an independent Poland.
1995 The Vatican creates its first—very basic—website.	**1991** Breakthroughs by British scientist Tim Berners-Lee make the World Wide Web a practical way to link computers on the Internet.
1997 The Vatican apologizes to France for the Roman Catholic Church's failure to object to the deportation of French Jews to Nazi Germany in World War II.	**1991** The Soviet Union fragments after various republics declare independence.
1998 Germany institutes a pension fund to pay compensation to Holocaust survivors in Central and Eastern Europe.	**1991** Boris Yeltsin is elected president of the Russian Federation.
	1999 NATO launches airstrikes against Yugoslavia to force its withdrawal from the province of Kosovo.

1992 The Christian Coalition distributes guides advising churchgoers who to vote for.	**1992** The Nobel Peace Prize is awarded to Mayan Rigoberta Menchu for her campaign to hold the Guatemalan Army accountable for human rights abuses.
1993 The Supreme Court overturns a ban on animal sacrifice in Hialeah, Florida, in a case brought by a Santería church.	**1993** Islamist terrorists explode a bomb inside the World Trade Center in New York City.
1993 Seventy-six members of the Branch Davidians, led by David Koresh, die in an FBI siege of the sect's compound in Waco, Texas.	**1994** The United States, Canada, and Mexico sign the North American Free Trade Agreement (NAFTA).
1997 The Heaven's Gate cult commit suicide when Comet Hale-Bopp is at its brightest; thirty-nine people die (box, right).	**1995** Right-wing terrorists bomb a federal office in Oklahoma City.

The Million Man March was organized by Louis Farrakhan, leader of the Nation of Islam, to promote a positive value system for African-American men.

1990 U.S. troops lead a coalition based in Saudi Arabia to overturn Iraq's occupation of Kuwait.

1994 Jordan and Israel sign a peace agreement.

NEW RELIGIOUS MOVEMENTS

The 1960s and 1970s saw a boom in new religious movements (NRMs) or cults in the United States, many of which came from California. The cults were varied but shared common aspects as a response to a wider background of distrust of authority, youthful rebellion, and social upheaval. Their leaders tended to be charismatic; recruits were typically young, isolated, and perhaps alienated from their immediate family.

One characteristic of the new cults was the provision of an alternative to limitations of mainstream Christianity. Some drew on spiritual Eastern religions such as Buddhism and Hinduism, which had grown in California thanks to rising Asian immigration after 1945. In the 1960s, a number of flamboyant Hindu spiritual leaders such as the Maharishi Mahesh Yogi became popular among celebrities such as the actress Mia Farrow and the world's most famous pop group, the Beatles.

Apocalyptic cults preached that their members alone would be saved when Judgment Day arrived. Jim Jones was an ordained Methodist minister who set up his People's Temple in northern California before moving it to Guyana, where in 1978 he led hundreds of his followers to mass suicide. Jones had become increasingly authoritarian, which is a common trait of cult leaders; the pattern was repeated later by David Koresh, who set up the Branch Davidians as an offshoot of the Seventh-Day Adventists. Koresh and his followers died when federal agents stormed their compound in Waco, Texas, in 1993.

Other NRMs included the science-based Heaven's Gate, which was set up by Marshall Applewhite in the mid-1970s in California. Applewhite and his followers committed suicide in 1997. Some observers argue that, despite its longevity, the Church of Scientology founded by science fiction writer L. Ron Hubbard in 1953 also shares characteristics of the NRMs.

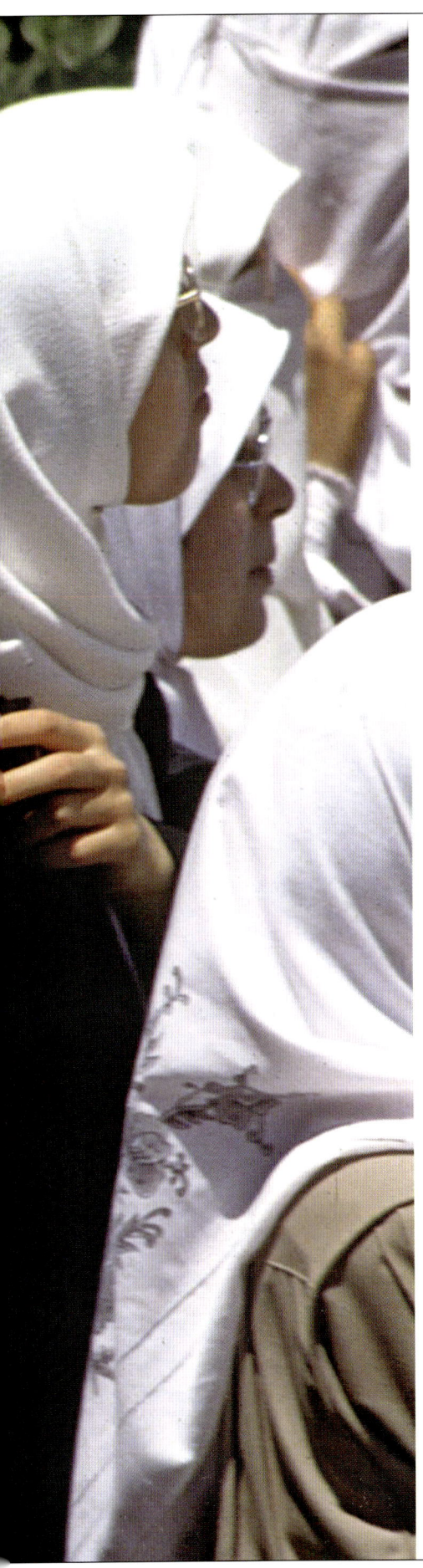

THE GROWTH OF ISLAMISM

ISLAMISM IS THE NAME GIVEN TO THE POLITICAL IDEOLOGY derived from an uncompromising interpretation of Islamic scripture. The central aim of Islamism is the creation of a pan-Islamic political body, or caliphate, that transcends national boundaries. This expansive Muslim world would require the elimination of the non-Muslim world (the West) and would be ruled by sharia, or Islamic law. Although Islamism is today closely associated in the minds of many non-Muslims with terrorist activity, it is not necessarily a militant ideology; many Islamists are entirely nonviolent, while some Muslim terrorist groups do not align themselves with Islamist ideology.

The origins of Islamism can be traced back to the Muslim Brotherhood founded by Hassan al Banna in Egypt in 1928. Al Banna and other theorists, such as Sayyid Kutb, called on Muslims to renounce the influence of Western secularism and create a society closely modeled on Islamic teachings. The movement rapidly spread across the region, peaking in the 1940s with around half a million followers. An armed wing emerged early in the decade and carried out bombings and killings, including the assassination of the Egyptian prime minister in 1948. The movement was forced underground in the 1950s following its failure to assassinate the president, Gamal Abdel Nasser. Although it remains officially banned, the Muslim Brotherhood is still active in Egyptian politics as an unoffficial party.

The Arab world's continuing stance against Israel, and the United States' continued support for Israel, have helped to strengthen Islamism. The rapid defeat of Arab troops by Israel during the Six Day War in 1967 profoundly shocked those who believed in the need for a unified Muslim World. During the 1970s and 1980s Islamists helped to fight the Soviet Union in Afghanistan and took part in the Lebanese civil war. To them, the collapse of the Soviet Union shortly after its withdrawal from Afghanistan in 1989 represented the destruction of a superpower by the power of Islam.

Islamists were further convinced of the need to return to establish a caliphate after U.S. and other non-Muslim troops were based in Saudi Arabia during the First Gulf War (1990–1991). The Saudi request for military assistance from the United States precipitated a backlash within Saudi Arabia of those who, including Osama bin Laden, claimed it was a puppet of the West. After the war the Islamist opposition within Saudi Arabia—mainly highly educated academics and Islamic preachers—grew stronger. The difficulty for the Saudi ruling family was that their power base relied on their Islamist views, which their critics argued they had betrayed.

Jordanian women take part in an anti-U.S. demonstration in Amman during the Gulf War in 1990 to protest Western interference in the Middle East.

PEOPLE & PLACES	DOCUMENTS, ART, & ARTIFACTS	WORSHIP & DOCTRINE

EUROPE

2003 Dr. Rowan Williams is enthroned as archibishop of Canterbury, head of the Anglican Church.

2004 The film *The Passion of the Christ*, presents a dramatic portrayal of the last days of Jesus Christ's life. It is filmed in Italy with input from several prominent Catholic scholars.

2000 The World Youth Festial attracts more than two million young people to the Vatican for what is termed a "Catholic Woodstock."

2003 The Vatican launches a worldwide campaign against homosexuality.

This memorial at Ground Zero—the site of the World Trade Center—was created from girders pulled from the destroyed building.

THE AMERICAS

2003 In Alabama, the Supreme Court orders the removal of a carving of the Ten Commandments from a courtroom on the grounds that it violates the separation of church and state.

2003 U.S. author Dan Brown writes worldwide bestseller *The Da Vinci Code*, a mystery based on various conspiracy theories about the history of the church, and particularly about the role of Mary, the mother of Jesus, in the Bible story.

I categorically go against a committed Muslim's embarking on such attacks. Islam never allows a Muslim to kill the innocent and the helpless.

YUSUF AL-QARADAWI, 2001

ASIA & OCEANIA

2001 Osama bin Laden, who orchestrated the September 11 terrorist attacks in the United States, evades capture when a U.S.-led coalition invades Afghanistan and overthrows the Taliban government (📄 facing page).

2003 Mother Teresa is beatified.

2001 The Taliban destroys two huge statues of Buddha built into the cliff in Bayman, Afghanistan, in the sixth century A.D., on the grounds that they encourage idolatry.

2001 The Kumbh Mela festival takes place in Allahabad, India; with up to 60 million visitors, it is the largest religious gathering in world history.

AFRICA & THE MIDDLE EAST

2001 Right-winger Ariel Sharon is elected president of Israel in the face of mounting violence between Israelis and Palestinians.

2003 Iranian human rights lawyer Shirin Ebadi becomes the first Muslim woman to win the Nobel Peace Prize.

2004 After the death of Yasser Arafat, Mahmoud Abbas becomes president of the Palestinian Authority.

George W. Bush prays at a meeting of America's Promise—The Alliance for Youth in 1997. On becoming president in 2000, Bush held regular prayer breakfasts in the White House.

RELIGION IN THE WORLD	WORLD EVENTS
2000 Pope John Paul II visits Israel, where he calls for improved rights for Palestinians.	**2000** Serbia's president Slobodan Milosevic is ousted in a popular uprising; he will later be indicted for war crimes and put on trial by an international court.
2002 John Paul II calls for an end to violence in the Holy Land.	**2000** Vladimir Putin is elected president of Russia.
2004 Scandal has been engulfing the Catholic Church with years of allegations that child abuse by priests has been covered up by their superiors; there are now some 11,000 allegations of child molestation worldwide.	**2002** The euro becomes the official currency for most of the countries in the European Union.
2004 Islamist bombers kill 191 people in rush-hour attacks on Madrid, Spain.	**2004** A group of Chechen separatists take several hundred children and adults hostage at a school in Beslan, North Ossetia. More than 330 people die when the Russian army attempts to storm the building.
2001 Four planes are hijacked by Islamist terrorists in the United States: two are flown into the World Trade Center in New York, another into the Pentagon; the fourth plane is brought down by passengers in Pennsylvania.	**2000** Republican George W. Bush emerges as the winner of the U.S. presidential election. He is reelected in 2004.
2002 Pat Robertson condemns the Prophet Muhammad as a "wild-eyed fanatic."	**2003** Energy company Enron declares bankruptcy amid allegations of financial irregularities. It is the largest bankruptcy case in U.S. history.
2003 The National Association of Evangelicals condemns churchmen for making anti-Islamic statements.	
2003 In New England, Gene Robinson becomes the first openly gay cleric to be nominated as a bishop, causing a split in the Anglican Church.	
2003 In Massachusetts, the Supreme Court allows gay marriage.	

During the early 21st century many European countries and several states in the U.S. passed laws to allow same-sex couples to legally marry.

THE WAR ON TERROR

Following the terrorist attacks of September 11, 2001, U.S. president George W. Bush announced a "war on terror" to fight international terror groups, particularly al Qaeda. The campaign initially garnered global support for Operation Enduring Freedom, the U.S.-led invasion of Afghanistan. Operation Enduring Freedom toppled the Taliban, but al Qaeda became highly active in Pakistan and India, while its leader, Osama bin Laden, escaped.

Some observers judged that the real targets of the campaign were not terrorists but all Muslims; they believed grounds for their misgivings came five days after the 9/11 attacks, when Bush referred to the war on terror as a "crusade," echoing the language of the medieval conflicts between Christians and Muslims. Critics also saw domestic legislation introduced in the United States and elsewhere to allow government agencies to monitor individuals perceived to be a threat to national security as discriminatory against Muslims.

The most controversial episode in the war on terror came in 2003, when the U.S. and its allies invaded Iraq, alleging both that it had weapons of mass destruction and that it was linked to al Qaeda. The impression among Muslims that the invasion was simply another example of Western interference in the Muslim world was subsequently reinforced by reports of prisoner abuse by U.S. forces in Iraq, by the detention of Muslims without trial in Guantanamo Bay, and by the use of torture by U.S. intelligence agencies.

The war on terror did have some positive results. It brought security and a measure of democracy to both Afghanistan and Iraq, although neither was entirely peaceful. In 2009, however, the new administration of Barack Obama followed the lead of European governments which had already abandoned the use of the phrase "war on terror" as inflammatory toward Muslims.

	PEOPLE & PLACES	DOCUMENTS, ART, & ARTIFACTS	WORSHIP & DOCTRINE
EUROPE	**2005** John Paul II dies; the German Benedict XVI is elected pope. **2007** Former British prime minister Tony Blair converts from the Anglican Church to the Roman Catholic faith of his wife, Cherie.	**2005** A Danish newspaper publishes controversial cartoons of the Prophet Muhammad, sparking Muslim protests around the world. **2006** British biologist Richard Dawkins writes *The God Delusion*, an argument against the existence of a supreme deity which establishes him as a leader of the secular humanist movement. **2007** U.S.-based British author Christopher Hitchens writes *God Is Not Great*, another vigorous celebration of atheism.	**2005** The Vatican rules that men with "transitory" homosexual feelings may be ordained after a period of abstinence and prayer, but that those with "deep-seated" homosexual feelings may not. **2007** The Russian Orthodox Church is reunited after an 80-year schism. **2007** Pope Benedict reasserts the universal primacy of the Catholic Church and urges all other churches to become reattached to it. **2009** The Catholic Church relaxes its rules to make it easier for disaffected Anglicans to convert.
THE AMERICAS	**2007** The 14th Dalai Lama meets publicly with President George W. Bush and is presented by the U.S. Congress with the Congressional Gold Medal. **2009** Barack Obama, the son of a Kenyan Muslim, is inaugurated as the 44th president of the United States. **2009** St. Damien of Molokai is canonized for his work caring for lepers in Hawaii in the late 19th century.	 **2007** The Creation Museum opens in Kentucky with displays that support the Genesis account of Creation, which the museum dates in around 4000 B.C.	*Pope Benedect XVI has met with many world leaders, such as the Russian prime minister Dimitri Medvedev.* **2007** In California, conservatives form the breakaway Diocese of San Joaquin in protest at the Anglican Church's acceptance of gay clergy and the ordination of women. **2009** Some 150 leaders of the Evangelical, Catholic, and Orthodox churches sign the *Manhattan Declaration*, which asserts the right to life, the importance of traditional marriage, and freedom of religion. **2009** The Rosicrucian Fellowship celebrates its centenary at its California headquarters.
ASIA & OCEANIA	**2006** Muhammad Yunus wins the Nobel Peace Prize for his pioneering microcredit schemes in Bangladesh. **2007** Former Pakistani prime minister Benazir Bhutto, the first woman to lead a Muslim country, is assassinated at an election rally, probably by Islamist terrorists. **2009** In Iran, conservative Mahmoud Ahmadinejad is reelected president to widespread opposition demonstrations.		**2006** The First World Buddhist Forum is held in the Peope's Republic of China. **2006** India's Supreme Court rules that "Jain religion is indisputably not a part of the Hindu relgion." **2007** Buddhist monks and nuns lead protests against the military regime in Burma which are met with violence and arrests. **2008** In Tibet, monks in Lhasa are the focus for protests against Chinese rule; Chinese troops put down the revolt with violence.
AFRICA & THE MIDDLE EAST		**2006** The *Gospel of Judas*, discovered in the 1970s in the Egyptian desert, is translated into English; in this gnostic account, Jesus asks Judas to betray him to the Romans in order to fulfill his destiny.	**2006** A vision of Mary is reported at Assiut in Egypt, already the location of a similar vision in 2000. **2007** Ethiopian troops invade Somalia and shut down Islamic courts in Mogadishu.

RELIGION IN THE WORLD	WORLD EVENTS
2005 Islamist suicide bombers kill 56 people on London's mass transit system. **2006** Pope Benedict offends many Muslims when he seems to assert that Islam is a religion of violence; he apologizes and later becomes the first pope to visit a Muslim-majority country, Turkey. **2009** For the first time, financial pressure forces the Vatican radio station to accept advertising.	**2007** Gordon Brown replaces Tony Blair as prime minister of Great Britain. **2008** Dmitry Medvedev becomes president of Russia.
2005 U.S. churches rally to send aid to New Orleans after Hurricane Katrina. **2006** Two Buddhists are elected for the first time to the U.S. Congress. **2009** Suspected Islamist terrorists are arrested in the United States. **2010** Pat Robertson blames the Haiti earthquake on Haitians' historical "pact with the devil."	**2005** Hurricane Katrina hits the Gulf Coast of the United States, flooding the city of New Orleans. It is one of the worst natural disasters in U.S. history. **2010** A massive earthquake strikes near the city of Port-au-Prince, Haiti. More than 200,000 people are thought to have died, and millions are made homeless.

Young people attend a True Love Waits meeting; despite such campaigns, the U.S. has a high rate of teenage pregnancies—in 2007 the rate was reported to have risen 3 percent above the previous year.

2007 More than 20,000 extra troops are deployed to Iraq as part of a "surge" strategy intended to weaken Iraqi terrorist groups.

2008 Robert Mugabe is relected as president of Zimbabwe in disputed elections.

THE FUTURE OF RELIGION

Falling church numbers, the greater ability of science to explain the universe, and the materialism and commercialization that displace spiritual concerns from everyday life all seem to threaten the survival of religion. And yet faith endures. In churches from the Guatemalan highlands to the tundra of Siberia, in mosques from Boston to Beijing, in synagogues from Scandinavia to Australia, in temples throughout South and East Asia, and in homes around the world billions of adherents perform their own rituals of devotion. The appeal of the divine and the purpose, discipline, and fulfillment it gives to individuals is as potent as ever in the modern age.

Faith itself continues to evolve, with major religions giving rise to a multiplicity of smaller branches. While some adherents take refuge in more fundamental, less tolerant forms of worship, others crave a return to more spiritual, less worldly forms of faith. Others look to faiths they see as being inherently spiritual, such as the beliefs of Native Americans or druids—albeit sometimes an imperfectly reconstructed version of such beliefs. There are those, too, for whom faith is inextricably knitted with politics or nationalism. Israel, India, Pakistan, China, and Somalia have all seen religion inspire ongoing strife.

The multiplicity of faiths and the geographical mixing that has resulted from human migration present rewards in the richness of religious experience but also problems in the form of tensions between different traditions. The costs of multiculturalism are the subject of debate in Europe, for example, where some employees have been refused the right to wear either a veil or a crucifix as a sign of religious commitment. Such questions are likely to remain real: yet for billions of people around the world, faith continues to be a beacon that lights the way to tolerance, brotherhood, and what the Dalai Lama has called "a good heart and a positive mind."

BUDDHISM

The key form of Buddhist scripture is the sutra, a passage that deliberates a point of doctrine. The Tipitaka, the complete canon of Theravada Buddhism, includes sutras and discourses attributed to Buddha himself (Tipitaka, or Three Baskets, refers to the containers in which monks kept their scrolls when Buddha's teachings were written down in the first century B.C.). The more inclusive Mahayana form of Buddhism also uses the Tipitaka, but includes sutras about the bodhisattvas, who have delayed their own entry to nirvana to help others.

This monk of wisdom here, devoid of desire and passion,
attains to deathlessness, peace, the unchanging state
* of nirvana…*
The steadfast go out like this lamp…
Where no-thing is the Isle of No-Beyond.
Nirvana do I call it—the utter extinction of aging
* and dying.*
TIPITAKA

What I have attained in total Enlightenment is the same as what
all others have attained. It is undifferentiated, regarded neither
as a high state, nor a low state. It is wholly independent of any
definite or arbitrary conceptions of an individual self, other selves,
living beings, or a universal self.
DIAMOND SUTRA, CHAPTER 23

CHRISTIANITY

At the heart of Christianity is the Bible, and particularly the New Testament gospels that record the life and teachings of Jesus, whom Christians believe was the son of God. The Old Testament, which includes ancient Jewish scripture, describes the acts of the prophets who paved the way for Jesus' arrival.

And God said, Let us make man in our image, after our likeness:
and let them have dominion over the fish of the sea, and over the
fowl of the air, and over the cattle, and over all the earth, and over
every creeping thing that creepeth upon the earth.
So God created man in his own image, in the image of God created
he him; male and female created he them.
And God blessed them, and God said unto them, Be fruitful,
and multiply, and replenish the earth, and subdue it: and have
dominion over the fish of the sea, and over the fowl of the air, and
over every living thing that moveth upon the earth.
GENESIS 1:26–28

Blessed are the poor in spirit, for theirs is the kingdom of heaven.
Blessed are those who mourn, for they shall be comforted.
Blessed are the meek, for they shall inherit the earth.
Blessed are those who hunger and thirst for righteousness, for
* they shall be satisfied.*
Blessed are the merciful, for they shall obtain Mercy.
Blessed are the pure in heart, for they shall see God.
Blessed are the peacemakers, for they shall be called Sons
* of God.*
Blessed are those who are persecuted for righteousness' sake, for
* theirs is the kingdom of heaven.*
Blessed are you when men revile you and persecute you and utter
* all kinds of evil against you falsely on my account.*
Rejoice and be glad, for your reward is great in heaven, for so men
* persecuted the prophets who were before you.*
MATTHEW 5:3–12, SERMON ON THE MOUNT

CONFUCIANISM

Confucius' followers wrote down their teacher's sayings in a collection known as the *Analects*. They were published sometime between the fifth and second centuries B.C.

The Master said, "To rule a country of a thousand chariots, there must be reverent attention to business, and sincerity; economy in expenditure, and love for men; and the employment of the people at the proper seasons."

The Master said, "A youth, when at home, should be filial, and, abroad, respectful to his elders. He should be earnest and truthful. He should overflow in love to all, and cultivate the friendship of the good. When he has time and opportunity, after the performance of these things, he should employ them in polite studies."
ANALECTS

The Master said, "At fifteen, I had my mind bent on learning.
"At thirty, I stood firm.
"At forty, I had no doubts.
"At fifty, I knew the decrees of Heaven.
"At sixty, my ear was an obedient organ for the reception of truth.
"At seventy, I could follow what my heart desired, without transgressing what was right."
ANALECTS

HINDUISM

Hindu scripture is based on the Vedas, or sacrificial hymns, a collection of texts that reveal truths about how people should lead their lives, and the Upanishads, which included codes of behavior for Hindus. The Bhagavad Gita, or Gita, is part of the Mahabharata, a Sanskrit epic poem about the Hindu gods.

You have control over doing your respective duty only, but no control or claim over the results. The fruits of work should not be your motive, and you should never be inactive.

Do your duty to the best of your ability, O Arjuna, with your mind attached to the Lord, abandoning worry and selfish attachment to the results, and remaining calm in both success and failure. The selfless service is a yogic practice that brings peace and equanimity of mind.

A Karma-yogi or the selfless person becomes free from both vice and virtue in this life itself. Therefore, strive for selfless service. Working to the best of one's abilities without becoming selfishly attached to the fruits of work is called Karma-yoga or Seva.

Karma-yogis are freed from the bondage of rebirth due to renouncing the selfish attachment to the fruits of all work, and attain blissful divine state of salvation or nirvana.
BHAGAVAD GITA, 2:51

Now, whether they perform a cremation for such a person or not, people like him pass into the flame,
from the flame into the day.,
from the day into the fortnight of the waxing moon,
from the fortnight of the waxing moon into the six months when the sun moves north,
from these months into the year, from the year into the sun,
from the sun into the moon, and from the moon into the lightning.

Then a person who is not human—he leads them to Brahman.
This is the path to the gods, the path to Brahman.
Those who proceed along this path do not return to this human condition.
CHANDOGYA UPANISHAD 4: 15.5

ISLAM

Muslims see the 114 chapters of the Koran as the Word of God as revealed to the Prophet Muhammad. The sacred scripture is infallible in its guidelines to what Muslims should believe and how they should behave. The Koran is supplemented by Hadith, collections of narratives about the sayings and actions of Muhammad which are an important reference for Sharia, or Islamic law.

In the name of Allah, the Beneficent, the Merciful.
Praise be to Allah, Lord of the Worlds:
The Beneficent, the Merciful: Owner of the Day of Judgment.
Thee alone we worship; Thee alone we ask for help.
Show us the straight path: The path of those whom Thou
*   hast favored;*
Not the path of those who earn Thine anger nor of those who
*   go astray.*
AL-FATIHA (THE OPENING), KORAN 1:1–6

For Muslim men and women, For believing men and women,
For devout men and women, For true men and women,
For men and women who are patient and constant,
For men and women who humble themselves,
For men and women who give in charity,
For men and women who fast (and deny themselves),
For men and women who guard their chastity,
And for men and women who engage much in Allah's praise,
For them Allah has prepared forgiveness and great reward.
THE CLANS, KORAN 33:35

JAINISM

The primary scriptures of the Jains are the Agams, sutras that contain the story and teachings of Mahavira, the founder of the religion. Different sects recognize different sutras as authentic, up to a total of 45. All the sutras teach strict vegetarianism and reference for all life.

Neglecting his body, the Venerable Ascetic Mahavira meditated on his Self, in blameless lodgings, in blameless wandering, in restraint, kindness, avoidance of sinful influence, living chastely, in patience, freedom from passion, contentment; control, circumspectness, practicing religious postures and acts; walking the path of nirvana and liberation, which is the fruit of good conduct. Living thus he with equanimity bore, endured, sustained, and suffered all calamities arising from divine powers, men, and animals with undisturbed and unafflicted mind, careful of body, speech, and mind.
AKARANGA SUTRA, BOOK 2, PART 3: 24

JUDAISM

Judaism's sacred writ is based on the Torah and the Talmud. The Torah—also known as the Pentateuch—is God's law as made up of the first five books of the Old Testament of the Bible: Genesis, Exodus, Leviticus, Numbers, and Deuteronomy. The Talmud is Jewish oral law that was originally created in Palestine and Babylon.

Hear, O Israel: The Lord is our God, the Lord alone.
You shall love the Lord your God with all your heart,
*   and with all your soul, and with all your might.*
Keep these words that I am commanding you today in
*   your heart.*
Recite them to your children and talk about them when you
*   are at home and when you are away,*
when you lie down and when you rise.
Bind them as a sign on your hand,
fix them as an emblem on your forehead,
and write them on the door posts of your house and on
*   your gates.*
SHEMA, DEUTERONOMY 6:4–9.

The Lord is my strength and my might,
and he has become my salvation; this is my God,
and I will praise him, my father's God,
and I will exalt him. The Lord is a warrior;
the Lord is his name. Pharaoh's chariots and his army be cast
    into the sea....
Who is like you, O Lord, among the gods?
Who is like you, majestic in holiness, awesome in splendor,
    doing wonders?

In your steadfast love you led the people whom you redeemed;
    you guided them by your strength to your holy abode.
You brought them in and planted them on the mountain of your
    own possession, the place, O Lord, that you made your abode,
    the sanctuary, O Lord, that your hands have established.
The Lord will reign forever and ever.
MOSES' SONG OF PRAISE, EXODUS 15:2–18

SIKHISM

Since 1708, Sikhs have honored their scripture, the Adi Granth, as a teacher and the final arbiter on doctrine, giving it the title Guru Granth Sahib and placing it in the tradition of their ten gurus in human form. Every copy of the book has an identical format: 1,430 pages divided into 39 chapters. The work was compiled by the Fifth Guru, Arjan Dev, from the scattered hymns and prayers of the founder of Sikhism, Guru Nanak, and other early teachers.

The Names of the Lord are Countless and Unfathomable.
My Sovereign Lord is Unfathomable and Incomprehensible.
The virtuous and the spiritual teachers have given it great thought,
but they have not found even an iota of His Value.
    They sing the Glorious Praises of the Lord, the Lord of the
Universe forever. They sing the Glorious Praises of the Lord

of the Universe, but they do not find His limits. You are
Immeasurable, Unweighable, and Infinite, O Lord and Master;
no matter how much one may meditate on You, Your Depth cannot
be fathomed.
ADI GRANTH, RAAG KALYAAN, FOURTH MEHL, 1319:5–7

ZOROASTRIANISM

Most Zoroastrian scripture was destroyed in fourth century B.C. by the troops of Alexander the Great. Our main knowledge of the religion comes from the Avesta, which contains the Gathas, said to have been composed by Zoroaster himself. The Gathas recount parts of Zoroaster's life and a philosophy based on dualism, or opposites such as good and bad.

Hear with your ears the best things; look upon them with clear-
seeing thought, for decision between the two Beliefs, each man for
himself before the Great consummation, bethinking you that it be
accomplished to our pleasure.

Now the two primal Spirits, who reveal themselves in vision
as Twins, are the Better and the Bad, in thought and word and
action. And between these two the wise ones chose aright, the
foolish not so.

And when these twain Spirits came together in the
beginning, they created Life and Not-Life, and that at the last
Worst Existence shall be to the followers of the Lie, but the Best
Existence to him that follows Right.

Of these twain Spirits he that followed the Lie chose doing the
worst things; the holiest Spirit chose Right, he that clothes him
with the massy heavens as a garment. So likewise they that are
fain to please Ahura Mazda by dutiful actions.
AHUNAVAITI GATHA (AVESTA, YASNA, 30:2–5)

ILLUSTRATIONS CREDITS

Special thanks to Topfoto for their spectacular images.

Cover: All images Shutterstock

Pages 2–3 Topfoto: The Image Works

Chapter 1: The Origins of Religion Prehistory–0
8, Topfoto/J. D. Dallet/Spainpix; 12–13, Shutterstock/Timo Kohlbacher; 14, istockphoto; 15, Thinkstock/istockphoto; 18, Artmedia/HIP; 19, Hal Beral & V&W; 20, Thinkstock/Photos.com; 21, Shutterstock Ajay Bhaskar; 22, Topfoto/ Topham Picturepoint ; 23b, Shutterstock/Jozef Sedmak; 23t, Shutterstock/Sergey Khachatryan; 24, Thinkstock/istockphto; 25, Jupiter; 26, istockphoto; 27b, Shutterstock/jocrebbin; 27t, Thinkstock/Photos.com; 28-29, Topfoto/; Elmar R. Gruber; 30b, Topfoto/alinari; 30t, Topfoto; 31, Topfoto/Ullsteinbild; 32, Shutterstock/Jarno Gonzalez; 33t, Topfoto/ Elmar R. Gruber; 33b, Shutterstock/Zvonimir Atletic; 34,Topfoto/World History Archive; 35, Topfoto/RIA Novosti; 36, Thinkstock/Photos.com; 37, Thinkstock/Photos.com; 38–39, Topfoto/Polfoto; 40, Topfoto/RIA Novosti; 41, Topfoto/Fiore; 42, Shutterstock/ Buchan; 43, Werner Forman Archive.

Chapter 2: Dawn of the Christian Era 0–550
44-45, Topfoto/Ullstein; 46, Topfoto/Topham Picturepoint; 47, Thinkstock/Photos. com; 50, Shutterstock/Catmando; 51, Thinkstock/Photos.com; 52, Shutterstock/ Jarno Gonzalez; 53b, Thinkstock/Photos.com; 53t, Topfoto/Topham Picturepoint; 54, Topfoto/The Granger Collection; 55, Topfoto/Museum of London/HIP; 56, Thinkstock/ Photos.com; 57, Topfoto/The Granger Collection; 58, Thinkstock/Photos.com; 59, Topfoto/The British Library/HIP; 60, Topfoto/The Granger Collection; 61, Topfoto/The Granger Collection; 62, Topfoto/The Granger Collection; 63, Topfoto/Ullsteinbild; 64, Topfoto; 65, Thinkstock/Photos.com; 66t, Topfoto/Ullsteinbild; 65b, Public Domain/ Ministry of Land, Infrastructure and Transport Government of Japan & moja; 67, Thinkstock/Photos.com; 68–69, Topfoto/The Granger Collection; 70, Topfoto/The Granger Collection; 71, Topfoto/Roger-Viollet; 72, Shutterstock/Melikstyan Marianna; 73, Topfoto/alinari; 74. Thinkstock/Photos.com; 75, Werner Forman Archive; 76, Topfoto/The Granger Collection; 77, Topfoto/The Granger Collection; 78, Thinkstock/ Photo Objects.net; 79, Topfoto/The Granger Collection; 80, Topfoto/The Granger Collection; 81b, Topfoto/RIA Novosti; 81t, Topfoto/E&E Images/HIP.

Chapter 3: A New Faith 550–1000
82-83, Thinkstock/istockphoto; 84, Shutterstock/ayazad; 85, Takaoshi Nakajima; 88, Topfoto/The Granger Collection; 89, Topfoto/The Granger Collection; 90, Topfoto/Luisa Ricciarini; 91, Topfoto/Luisa Ricciarini; 93tl, Shuterstock/Factora Singular fotogafia; 93tr, Shutterstock/Zvonimir Atetic; 94, Topfoto/Image Works; 95, Topfoto/RIA Novosti; 96, Shutterstock/Nicholas Peter Gavin Davies; 97, Shutterstock/RJ Lerich; 98, Shutterstock/Aleksandar Todovovic; 99 Topfoto/Topham Picturepoint; 100, Werner Forman Archive; 101, Topfoto/The Granger Collection; 102, Topfoto/The Granger Collection; 103, Werner Forman Archive; 104, Shutterstock/Dmitry Kalinovsky; 105, Shutterstock/Mountainpix; 106, Topfoto/The Granger Collection; 107, Shutterstock/ Serg Zastavkin; 108, Thinkstock/Photos.com; 109, Shutterstock/Tiberiu San; 110t, Shutterstock/Colman Lerner Gerardo; 110b, Topfoto/The Granger Collection; 111, Shutterstock/Olly; 112t, Shutterstock/Dmitry Chernobrov; 112b, Shutterstock/Sergey Kamshylin; 114, Werner Forman Archive; 115, Topfoto/The Granger Collection.

Chapter 4: Age of Gods and Kings 1000–1350
116-117, Shutterstock/Luciano Mortula; 118, Topfoto/The Granger Collection; 119, Shutterstock/St. Nick; 122, Shutterstock/Bzzuspajk; 123, Jupiter; 124, Shutterstock/ Paul Cowan; 125, Shutterstock/Mikhail Zahranichny; 126, Shutterstock/Steffen Foerster Photography; 127, Thinkstock/Photos.com; 128-129, Shutterstock/Gavin Taylor; 130,Thinkstock/Photos.com; 131, Thinkstock/Photos.com; 132-133, Topfoto/ Artmedia/HIP; 134, Topfoto/The British Library/HIP; 135, istockphoto; 136-137, Thinkstock/ablestock; 138l, Thinkstock/Photos.com; 138r, Jupiter; 139, Shutterstock/ Mehmetcan; 140, Topfoto/The Granger Collection; 141, Topfoto/Charles Walker; 142b, Topfoto/The Granger Collection; 142t, Thinkstock/Photos.com; 143, Thinkstock/ Photos.com; 144, Shutterstock; Herbert Eisengruber; 145, Topfoto/The Granger Collection; 146, Shutterstock/ Hailin Chen; 147t, Thinkstock/Photos.com; 147b, Topfoto/Artmedia/HIP; 148, Shutterstock/S Borisov; 149, istockphoto; 150, Topfoto/ Topham Picturepoint; 151, Topfoto/The Granger Collection.

Chapter 5: Renaissance and Reformation 1350–1575
152-153, Shutterstock/david; 154b, istockphoto; 154t, Shutterstock/Shipov Oleg; 155, The Granger Collection; 158, Jupiter; 159, Shutterstock/Andrew Buckin; 160, Jupiter; 161, istockphoto; 162, Topfoto/Elmar R. Gurber; 163, Jupiter; 164b, Jupiter; 164t, Shutterstock/Timur Kulyain; 165, Jupiter; 166-167, istockphoto; 168b, Shutterstock/PhotoBarmaley; 168t, Thinkstock/Photos.com; 169, Shutterstock/ Arteki; 170, Shutterstock/piotr; 171, Jupiter; 172b, Shutterstock/Asier Villafranca; 172t, Topfoto/The Granger Collection; 173, Topfoto/Print Collector/HIP; 174, Topfoto/ The Granger Collection; 175t, istockphoto; 175b, Topfoto/The Granger Collection; 176, Shutterstock/Caitlin Mirra; 177, Topfoto; 178, Shutterstock/Mark Higgins; 179, istockphoto; 180b, Topfoto/Luisa Ricciarini; 180t, Topfoto/The Granger Collection; 181,

Shutterstock/Uwe Bumann; 182, Topfoto/The Granger Collection; 183, Shutterstock/ Richard Melichar; 184, Topfoto/The Granger Collection; 185l, Jupiter; 185r, Jupiter; 186, Shutterstock/Evok; 187, Topfoto/Rose Deakin; 188, Shutterstock/dundanim; 189, Jupiter; 190, Jupiter; 191 Topfoto/Lisa Ricciarini; 192-193, Shutterstock/Aron Brand.

Chapter 6: New Worlds, New Faiths 1575–1725
194-195, istockphoto; 196, Topfoto/The Granger Collection; 197, Shutterstock/ Aleksandar Todorovic; 200, Topfoto/The Granger Collection; 201, Shutterstock/Luciano Mortula; 202b, Shutterstock/Tomasz Parys; 202t, Topfoto/Charles Walker; 203, Thinkstock/Photos.com; 204-205, Shutterstock/Serdar Duzgider; 206b, Topfoto/ Topham Picturepoint; 206r, Jupiter; 207, Jupiter; 208-209 Topfoto/The Granger Collection; 210b, Thinkstock/Photos.com; 210t, Topfoto/The Granger Collection; 211, Thinkstock/Photos.com; 212b, Thinkstock/Photos.com; 212r, Jupiter; 213, Shutterstock/Pichugin Dmiry; 214, Shutterstock/Sam D. Cruz; 215, Jupiter; 216b, Shutterstock/Lichtmeisster; 216t, Thinkstock/Photos.com; 217, Topfoto/RIA Novosti; 218-219, Topfoto/Topham Picturepoint; 220, Topfoto/The Granger Collection; 221, Topfoto/Ken Welsh/VWPICS; 222, Thinkstock/Photos.com; 222-223, istockphoto; 224, Topfoto/The Granger Collection; 225, Topfoto/The Granger Collection; 226, Topfoto; 227b, Topfoto/The Granger Collection; 227t, Topfoto/Charles Walker; 228, Thinkstock/Photos.com; 229, Topfoto/The Granger Collection; 230, istockphoto; 231, Thinkstock/Photo Objects.net.

Chapter 7: The Age of Reason 1725–1850
232-233, Shutterstock/Worldoctopus; 234, Thinkstock/istockphoto; 235t, Topfoto/ Ullstein; 235b, Thinkstock/istockphoto; 238, Topfoto/The Granger Collection; 239, Topfoto/The Granger Collection; 240b, Shutterstock/Doug Stacey; 240t, Topfoto/The Granger Collection; 241, Thinkstock/ablestock; 242, Topfoto/The Granger Collection; 243, Topfoto/ArenaPal; 244, Topfoto/The Granger Collection; 245, Shutterstock/ Mariusz S. Shutterstock/Jurgielewicz; 246-247, istockphoto; 248, Shutterstock/Bryan Busovicki; 249, Topfoto/The Granger Collection; 250, Topfoto/The Granger Collection; 251,Topfoto/Roger-Viollet; 252b, Shutterstock/Bryan Busovicki; 252t, Thinkstock/ Photos.com; 253, Thinkstock/Photos.com; 254, Topfoto/EE Images/HIP; 255, Shutterstock/Fedor Selivanov; 256, Topfoto/The Granger Collection; 257, Topfoto/ The Granger Collection; 258t, Topfoto/The Granger Collection; 258b, Topfoto/The Granger Collection; 259, Topfoto/The Granger Collection; 260, Shutterstock/Luciano Mortula; 261, Jupiter; 262, Topfoto/The British Library/HIP; 263, Topfoto/The Granger Collection; 264-265, Topfoto/The Image Works; 266b, Toptoo/The Granger Collection; 266t, Thinkstock/Photos.com; 267, Thinkstock/Photos.com; 268b, Thinkstock/ ablestock; 268t, Topfoto/The Granger Collection; 269, Topfoto/The Granger Collection; 270-271, Topfoto/The Granger Collection;

Chapter 8: Industry, Empire, and Religion 1850–1950
272-273, Topfoto/The Image Works; 274b, Topfoto/Ullstein; 274t, Topfoto/The Granger Collection; 275, Thinkstock/istockphoto; 278b, Thinkstock/Photos.com; 278t, Thinkstock/Photos.com; 279, Thinkstock/istockphoto; 280 Thinkstock/Photos.com; 281, Topfoto/The Granger Collection; 282t,Thinkstock/Photos.com; 282b, Topfoto/ Stapleton/HIP; 283, LOC; 284, Topfoto/The Granger Collection; 285, Topfot/Topham Picturepoint; 286t, Topfoto/The Granger Collection; 286b, Topfoto/The Granger Collectcion; 287, Topfoto/Ullstein; 288, Topfoto/Topham Picturepoint; 289, Topfoto/The Granger Collection; 290t, Topfoto/Roger-Viollet; 290b, Topfoto/The Granger Collection; 291, Shutterstock/Chee-Onn Leong; 292-293, Topfoto/The Granger Collection; 294t, Thinkstock/Photos.com; 294b, Topfoto/The Granger Collection; 295, Jupiter; 296, istockphoto; 297t, Thinkstock/Photos.com; 297b, Topfoto/The Image Works; 298t, Thinkstock/Photos.com; 298b, Topfoto/The Image Works; 299, Shutterstock/Paul Paladin; 300, Robert Hunt Library; 301, Topfoto/Topham Picture point; 302b, Jupiter; 302t, LOC; 303, Topfoto/Topham Picturepoint; 304, Topfoto/Topham Picturepoint; 305, Topfoto/Topham Picturepoint; 306t, Topfoto; 306b, Topfoto/The Granger Collection; 307, Robert Hunt Library; 308t, Robert Hunt Library; 308b, Shutterstock/Howard Sandler; 309, Topfoto;

Chapter 9: Faith in the Modern World 1950–2010
310-311, Robert Hunt Library; 312, Shutterstock/De Visu; 313, Topfoto/The Image Works; 316t, Topfoto/The Image Works; 316b, Topfoto/Woodmansterne; 317, Shutterstock;318-319, Topfoto/The Image Works; 320, Shutterstock/Ryan Rodrick Beiler; 321, Topfoto/Spectrum/HIP; 322, Topfoto/Roger-Viollet; 323, Jupiter; 324t, Topfoto/Brian Little; 324b, Topfoto/The Image Works; 325, Topfoto/Keystone Archives/HIP; 326b, Topfoto/AP; 326t, istockphoto; 327, Topfoto/The Image Works; 328, Topfoto/The Image Works; 329, Topfoto/John Hedgecoe; 330, Topfoto/AP; 331, Topfoto/AP; 332-333, Topfoto/Roger-Viollet; 334t, istockphoto; 334b, Topfoto/The Image Works; 335, Topfoto/Aaron Fineman; 336, Topfoto/RIA Novosti; 337, Topfoto/ The Image Works

Brown Reference Group has made every attempt to contact copyright holders. If anyone has any information, please contact info@brownreference.com

Anabaptists Christians who broke from the Roman Catholic Church who emphasize baptism as the key ritual of Christianity

Bodhisattva A Buddhist who has achieved enlightenment who helps others achieve the same

Cabalah A mystical tradition of Judaism

Caliph A successor to Muhammad as Islam's spiritual authority

Calvinist A follower of John Calvin's branch of reform Christianity

Caste A Hindu class system

Conservative Judaism An American movement of non-Orthodox religious practice

Coptic Church Christian church in Egypt and Ethiopia

Dharma The collective name for the Buddha's teachings

Eastern Orthodox Church A federation of Eastern churches which follow Byzantine rites and acknowledge the authority of the Patriarch of Constantinople

Enlightenment In Buddhism, the liberation from the cycle of death and rebirth

Episcopalian A member of the Anglican Church in the United States

Gnosticism A branch of Christianity that included elements from Babylonian astrology and Greek philosophy

Hadith A collection of sayings of Muhammad, used as a sacred book of Islam

Hajj A Muslim's pilgrimage to Mecca

Hegira Muhammad's escape from Mecca to Medina in 622, the first year of the Islamic calendar

Icons Physical images of Jesus, Mary, and holy saints displayed in some Christian churches

Imam In Islam, a cleric who leads prayers

Karma In Buddhism, the consequences of an action in this or a future life

Liturgy Formal religious services

Mishnah A collection of Jewish oral law

Nicene Creed A canon of Christian faith stating belief in the Holy Trinity

Nirvana In Buddhism, the state of release from the cycle of death and rebirth

Orthodox Church The Christian church that follows Constantine's original canons of faith

Orthodox Judaism Jews who are faithful to the literal interpretation of the Torah

Pentecostalism A branch of Christianity that emphasizes the individual's experience of grace, including speaking in tongues, faith healing, and highly expressive forms of worship

Presbyterianism A usually Calvinistic form of Christianity administered by local ministers and elders

Puja A Hindu act of daily worship

Puritan A follower of a particularly strict version of Anglican Christianity

Quaker A pacifist and antimaterialist Christian sect

Reform Judaism A non-Orthodox Jewish movement

Sangha The community of Buddhist believers

Stupa A Buddhist shrine, also known as a pagoda

Talmud A compilation of Jewish holy scripture, including the Torah and the Mishnah

Tipitaka The collective name for Buddhist doctrine, based on accounts from Buddha's life

Torah In Judaism, God's law as revealed in the first five books of the Old Testament

Zionism A movement for the creation of a Jewish state

General Reference

Confucius, (Raymond Dawson, ed.) *The Analects*. New York: Oxford University Press, 2008.

Doniger, Wendy, ed. *The Rig Veda*. London: Penguin, 2005.

Eknath Easwaran, ed. *The Bhagavad Gita*. Tomales, CA : Nilgiri Press, 2007.

Fieser, James, John Powers, eds. *Scriptures of the World's Religions*. Boston: McGraw-Hill, 2008.

Fisher, Mary Pat. *Living Religions*. Upper Saddle River, NJ: Pearson Prentice-Hall, 2008.

Kaur Singh, Nikky-Guninder. *Sikhism: An Introduction*. New York: I. B. Tauris, 2010.

Lao Tzu. *Tao Te Ching*. New York : Penguin, 2008.

Long, Jeffrey D. *Jainism: An Introduction*. New York: I. B. Tauris, 2009.

Lopez, Donald, ed. *Buddhist Scriptures*. London: Penguin, 2004.

Mariner, Rodney, ed. *The Torah*. New York: Henry Holt and Co., 1997.

Matthews, Warren. *World Religions*. Belmont, CA: Wadsworth, 2008.

Molloy, Michael. *Experiencing the World's Religions*. Boston: McGraw Hill Higher Education, 2008.

Narayan, R. K. *The Ramayana: A Shortened Modern Prose Version*. London: Penguin, 2006.

Nigosian, Solomon. *World Religions: A Historical Approach*. Boston: St. Martin's, 2008.

Oxtoby, Willard, and Alan F. Segal, eds. *A Concise Introduction to World Religions*. New York: Oxford University Press, 2007.

Rose, Jenny. *Zoroastrianism: An Introduction*. New York: I. B. Tauris, 2009.

Smith, John D., ed. *The Mahabharata*. London: Penguin, 2009.

Solomon, Norman, ed. *The Talmud: A Selection*. London: Penguin, 2009.

van Voorst, Robert E, ed. *Anthology of World Scriptures*. Belmont, CA: Wadsworth, 2010.

Wright, Robert. *The Evolution of God*. New York: Little, Brown, 2009.

Chapter 1: The Origins of Religion 5000 B.C.–0

Armstrong, Karen. *The Great Transformation: The Beginning of Our Religious Traditions*. New York: Knopf, 2006.

Berlin, Andrea M. and J. Andrew Overman. *The First Jewish Revolt: Archaeology, History, and Ideology*. New York: Routledge, 2002.

Burl, Aubrey. *A Brief History of Stonehenge*. New York : Carroll & Graf Publishers, 2007.

Coogan, Michael, ed. *The Oxford History of the Biblical World*. New York: Oxford University Press, 1998.

Homer. *The Iliad*. London: Penguin, 2003.

Kriwaczek, Paul. *In Search of Zarathrustra*. New York: Knopf, 2003.

Lopez, Donald. *The story of Buddhism: A Concise Guide To Its History and Teachings*. San Francisco: Harper, 2001.

Maringer, Johannes. *The Gods of Prehistoric Man*. London: Phoenix Press, 2002.

Pinch, Geraldine. *Egyptian Mythology: A Guide to the Gods, Goddesses, and Traditions of Ancient Egypt*. New York: Oxford University Press, 2004.

Sjoestedt, Marie-Louise. *Celtic Gods and Heroes*. New York: Dover Publications, 2000.

Skilton, Andrew. *A Concise History of Buddhism*. Cambridge: Windhorse Publications, 2004.

Chapter 2: Dawn of the Christian Era 0–550

Augustine of Hippo. *Augustine in his Own Words*. Washington, D.C.: Catholic University of America Press, 2010.

Belby, James K. and Paul R. Eddy, eds. *The Historical Jesus: Five Views*. Downers Grove, IL: IVP Academic, 2009.

Breen, John. *A New History of Shinto*. London: Blackwell, 2010.

Butcher, Carmen Acevedo. *Man of Blessing: A Life of St. Benedict*. Brewster, MA: Paraclete Press, 2006.

Crossan, John Dominic. *In Search of Paul*. San Francisco: Harper, 2004.

Ehrman, Bart D. *Lost Christianities: The Battles for Scripture and the Faiths We Never Knew*. New York: Oxford University Press, 2005.

Gabra, Gawdat. *Historical Dictionary of the Coptic Church*. Lanham, MD: Scarecrow Press, 2008.

Lynch, Joseph H. *Early Christianity: A Brief History*. New York: Oxford University Press, 2009.

Odahl, Charles. *Constantine and the Christian Empire*. New York: Routledge, 2006.

Pagels, Elaine. *The Gnostic Gospels*. New York: Random House, 2004.

Sanders, E. P. *The Historical Figure of Jesus*. New York: Penguin, 1996.

Chapter 3: A New Faith 550–1000

Armstrong, Karen. *Muhammad: A Prophet for Our Time*. New York: HarperOne, 2007.

De Hamel, Christopher. *The Book: A History of the Bible*. New York: Phaidon, 2001.

Esposito, John. *The Oxford History of Islam*. New York: Oxford University Press, 2000.

Hawting, G.R. *The First Dynasty of Islam: The Umayyad Caliphate*. New York: Routledge, 2000.

Herrin, Judith. *Byzantium: The Suprising Life of a Medieval Empire*. Princeton, NJ: Princeton University Press, 2009.

Kennedy, Hugh. *When Baghdad Ruled the Muslim World: The Rise and Fall of Islam's Greatest Dynasty*. Cambridge, MA: Da Capo Press, 2005.

Kennedy, Hugh. *The Great Arab Conquests: How the Spread of Islam Changed the World We Live In*. Cambridge, MA: Da Capo Press, 2008.

Lindow, John. *Norse Mythology: A Guide to Gods, Heroes, Rituals, and Beliefs*. New York: Oxford University Press, 2002.

Robinson, Francis. *Islam and Muslim History in South Asia*. New York: Oxford University Press, 2004.

Chapter 4: Age of Gods and Kings 1000–1350

Burton, Keith Augustus. *The Blessing of Africa: The Bible and African Christianity*. Downers Grove, IL: IVP Academic, 2007.

Clendenin, Daniel. *Eastern Orthodox Christianity: A Western Perspective*. Grand Rapids, MI: Baker Academic, 2003.

Harmless, Wiliam. *Desert Christians: An Introduction to the Literature of Early Monasticism*. New York: Oxford University Press, 2004.

Lawrence, C. H. *Medieval Monasticism: Forms of Religious Life in Western Europe in the Middle Ages*. New York: Longman, 2001.

Maloof, Amin. *The Crusades Through Arab Eyes*. New York: Schocken Books, 1985.

Payton, James R. *Light from the Christian East: An Introduction to the Orthodox Tradition*. Downers Grove, IL: IVP Academic, 2007.

Phillips, Jonathan. *Holy Warriors: A Modern History of the Crusades*. New York: Random House, 2010.

Rumi, Jelaluddin. *Selected Poems*. New York: Penguin, 2005.

Schutz, Bernhard, and Henri Gaud. *Great Monasteries of Europe*. New York: Abbeville Press, 2004.

Wilson, Christopher. *The Gothic Cathedral: The Architecture of the Great Church*. New York: Thames and Hudson, 2005.

Chapter 5: Renaissance and Reformation 1350–1575

Bireley, Robert. *The Refashioning of Catholicism, 1450–1700: A Reassessment of the Counter Reformation*. Washington, DC: Catholic University of America Press, 1999.

Gill, Sam. *Native American Religions: An Introduction*. Belmont, CA: Wadsworth Thomson, 2005.

Green, Toby. *Inquisition: The Reign of Fear*. New York: Thomas Books, 2009

MacCulloch, Diamaid. *The Reformation*. New York: Penguin, 2005.

Nicholls, Stephen. *The Reformation: How a Monk and a Mallet Changed the World*. Crossway Books, 2007.

Norman, Alexander. *Secret Lives of the Dalai Lama: The Untold Story of the Holy Men Who Shaped Tibet, from Pre-history to the Present Day*. New York: Doubleday, 2010.

Robinson, David. *Muslim Societies in African History*. Cambridge: Cambridge University Press, 2004.

Welch, Evelyn. *Art in Renaissance Italy: 1350–1500*. New York: Oxford Unversity Press, 2001.

Wright, Jonathan. *God's Soldiers: Adventure, Politics, Intrigue, and Power—A History of the Jesuits*. New York: Doubleday, 2004.

Chapter 6: New Worlds, New Faiths 1575–1725

Brockey, Liam Matthew. *Journey to the East: The Jesuit Mission to China, 1579–1724*. Cambridge, MA: Belknap Press, 2007.

Bremer, Francis J. *The Puritan Experiment: New England Society from Bradford to Edwards*. Hanover: University Press of New England, 1995.

Bunyan, John. *The Pilgrim's Progress*. New York: Penguin, 2009.

Eraly, Abraham. *The Mughal Throne: The Saga of India's Great Emperors*. London: Weidenfeld & Nicolson, 2003.

Hill, Frances. *A Delusion of Satan: The Full Story of the Salem Witch Trials*. New York: Da Capo Press, 1997.

Philbrick, Nathaniel. *Mayflower: A Story of Courage, Community, and War*. New York: Viking, 2006.

Silverman, Kenneth. *The Life and Times of Cotton Mather*. New York: Welcome Rain Publishers, 2001.

Chapter 7: The Age of Reason 1725–1849

Aston, Nigel. *Religion and Revolution in France*, 1780–1804. Washington, DC: Catholic University of America Press, 2000.

Byrne, James. *Religion and the Enlightenment*. Louisville, KY: Westminster John Knox Press, 1997.

Commins, David Dean. *The Wahhabi Mission and Saudi Arabia*. New York: I.B. Tauris, 2006.

de la Torre, Miguel. *Santeria: The Beliefs and Rituals of a Growing Religion in America*. Grand Rapids, MI: William B. Eerdmans Publishing, 2004.

Francis, Richard. *Ann the Word: The Story of Ann Lee, Female Messiah, Mother of the Shakers*. New York: Arcade, 2001.

Greer, Allan. *The Jesuit Relations: Natives and Missionaries in Seventeenth-Century North America*. Boston: St. Martin's, 2000.

Gura, Philip F. *American Transcendentalism: A History*. New York: Hill and Wang, 2008.

Kidd, Thomas. *The Great Awakening: The Roots of Evangelical Christianity in Colonial America*. New Haven, CT: Yale University Press, 2007

Chapter 8: Industry, Empire, and Religion 1850–1949

Bowers, Kenneth. *God Speaks Again: An Introduction to the Baha'i Faith*. Wilmette, IL: Bahá'í Publications, 2004.

Friedlander, Saul. *The Years of Persecution: Nazi Germany and the Jews 1933–1939*. New York: HarperCollins, 2006.

Friedlander, Saul. *The Years Of Extermination: Nazi Germany And The Jews 1939–1945*. New York: HarperCollins, 2007.

Gariepy, Henry. *Christianity in Action: The History of the International Salvation Army*. Grand Rapids, MI: William B. Eerdmans Publishing, 2009.

Hittman, Michael. *Wovoka and the Ghost Dance*. Lincoln: University of Nebraska Press, 1997.

Larson, Edward J. *Summer for the Gods: The Scopes Trial and America's Continuing Debate Over Science and Religion*. New York: BasicBooks, 1997.

Lyons, Sherrie L. *Thomas Henry Huxley: The Evolution of a Scientist*. Amherst, NY: Prometheus Books, 1999.

Miller, Randall. *Religion and the American Civil War*. New York: Oxford University Press, 1998.

Stowe, Harriet Beecher. *Uncle Tom's Cabin: Or, Life Among the Lowly*. New York: Literary Classics of the United States, 2010.

Chapter 9: Faith in the Modern World 1950–2010

Dawkins, Richard. *The God Delusion*. Boston: Houghton Mifflin Co., 2008.

Dawson, Lorne L. *Comprehending Cults: The Sociology of New Religious Movements*. New York : Oxford University Press, 2006.

Dawson, Lorne L. *Cults and New Religious Movements: A Reader*. Malden, MA: Blackwell, 2003.

Epstein, Greg. *Good Without God: What a Billion Nonreligious People Do Believe*. New York : William Morrow, 2009.

Gibbs, Nancy. *The Preacher and the Presidents: Billy Graham in the White House*. New York: Center Street, 2007.

Hitchens, Christopher. *God Is Not Great: How Religion Poisons Everything*. New York: Twelve, 2007.

Keddie, Nikki R. *Modern Iran: Roots and Results of Revolution*. New Haven, CT: Yale University Press, 2006.

Rowland, Christopher. *The Cambridge Companion to Liberation Theology*. New York: Cambridge University Press, 2007.

Stenger, Victor J. *The New Atheism: Taking a Stand for Science and Reason*. Amherst, NY: Prometheus Books, 2009.

Sweeney, Douglas A. *The American Evangelical Story: A History of the Movement*. Grand Rapids, MI: Baker Academic, 2005.

Tsoukalas, Steven. *The Nation of Islam: Understanding the Black Muslims*. Phillipsburg, NJ: P & R, 2001.

INDEX

CONCISE HISTORY OF WORLD RELIGIONS

PREPARED BY THE BOOK DIVISION

Barbara Brownell Grogan *Vice President and Editor in Chief*
Marianne R. Koszorus *Director of Design*
Susan Hitchcock *Senior Editor*
Carl Mehler *Director of Maps*
R. Gary Colbert *Production Director*
Jennifer A. Thornton *Managing Editor*
Meredith C. Wilcox *Administrative Director, Illustrations*

STAFF FOR THIS BOOK

Susan Straight *Editor*
Rebecca Barns *Copy Editor*
Samantha Foster, Andy Tybout *Interns*
Erin Stone *Production Manager*

THE BROWN REFERENCE GROUP LTD

Jeremy Black *Consultants on original material*
Frederic L. Cheyette
Stephen A. McKnight
Ben Hollingum *Text Editor*
Anita Croy *Additional Text*
David Poole *Design Manager*
Geoff Ward *Designers*
Kim Browne
Supriya Sahai
Theresa Maynard
Sophie Mortimer *Picture Manager*
Lindsey Lowe *Editorial Director*
Alastair Gourlay *Production Director*
Richard Berry *DTP Design*
Christie Michaud *Indexer*
Tim Cooke *Managing Editor*

MANUFACTURING AND QUALITY MANAGEMENT

Christopher A. Liedel *Chief Financial Officer*
Phillip L. Schlosser *Vice President*
Chris Brown *Technical Director*
Nicole Elliott *Manager*
Rachel Faulise *Manager*

Since 1888, the National Geographic Society has funded more than 13,000 research, exploration, and preservation projects around the world. National Geographic Partners distributes a portion of the funds it receives from your purchase to National Geographic Society to support programs including the conservation of animals and their habitats.

National Geographic Partners
1145 17th Street NW
Washington, DC 20036-4688 USA

Get closer to National Geographic explorers and photographers, and connect with our global community. Join us today at nationalgeographic.com/join

For information about special discounts for bulk purchases, please contact National Geographic Books Special Sales: specialsales@natgeo.com

For rights or permissions inquiries, please contact National Geographic Books Subsidiary Rights: bookrights@natgeo.com

ISBN 978-1-4262-0698-6
ISBN 978-1-4262-0699-3 (deluxe)
ISBN 978-1-4262-2105-7 (special sales ed.)

Printed in Hong Kong

19/PPHK/1